Social Science and Human Behavior

Social Science and Human Behavior

Edited by
Chayma Hamdani

Willford Press
www.willfordpress.com

Published by Willford Press,
118-35 Queens Blvd., Suite 400,
Forest Hills, NY 11375, USA

ISBN: 978-1-68285-513-3

Cataloging-in-Publication Data

Social science and human behavior / edited by Chayma Hamdani.
p. cm.
Includes bibliographical references and index.
ISBN 978-1-68285-513-3
1. Social Sciences. 2. Human behavior. 3. Social psychology. I. Hamdani, Chayma.
H61 .S63 2018
300.1--dc23

For information on all Willford Press publications
visit our website at www.willfordpress.com

WILLFORD PRESS

Printed in China.

Contents

Preface

Human behavior is a complex field of study. Social science is a widely studied academic discipline which aims to study the society in a holistic manner. This involves an in-depth study of the behavior of individuals, their relationship with each other and the factors affecting that behavior. This book provides significant information of this discipline to help develop a good understanding of social science and related fields. As this field is emerging at a rapid pace, the concepts of this book will help the readers understand the modern concepts and applications of the subject.

The researches compiled throughout the book are authentic and of high quality, combining several disciplines and from very diverse regions from around the world. Drawing on the contributions of many researchers from diverse countries, the book's objective is to provide the readers with the latest achievements in the area of research. This book will surely be a source of knowledge to all interested and researching the field.

In the end, I would like to express my deep sense of gratitude to all the authors for meeting the set deadlines in completing and submitting their research chapters. I would also like to thank the publisher for the support offered to us throughout the course of the book. Finally, I extend my sincere thanks to my family for being a constant source of inspiration and encouragement.

Editor

Wholistic and Ethical: Social Inclusion with Indigenous Peoples

Kathleen E. Absolon

Faculty of Social Work, Wilfrid Laurier University, Waterloo, ON N2L 3C5, Canada; E-Mail: kabsolon@wlu.ca

Abstract

This paper begins with a poem and is inclusive of my voice as Anishinaabekwe (Ojibway woman) and is authored from my spirit, heart, mind and body. The idea of social inclusion and Indigenous peoples leave more to the imagination and vision than what is the reality and actuality in Canada. This article begins with my location followed with skepticism and hope. Skepticism deals with the exclusion of Indigenous peoples since colonial contact and the subsequent challenges and impacts. Hope begins to affirm the possibilities, strengths and Indigenous knowledge that guides wholistic cultural frameworks and ethics of social inclusion. A wholistic cultural framework is presented; guided by seven sacred teachings and from each element thoughts for consideration are guided by Indigenous values and principles. From each element this paper presents a wholistic and ethical perspective in approaching social inclusion and Indigenous peoples.

Keywords

Anishinaabe; colonization; ethical; exclusion; inclusion; Indigenous; Indigenous knowledge; oppression; racism; reconciliation; restoration; resurgence; wholistic

Issue

This article is part of the issue "Social Inclusion and Indigenous Peoples", edited by Pat Dudgeon (University of Western Australia, Australia), Waikaremoana Waitoki (University of Waikato, New Zealand), Rose LeMay (Wharerātā Group, Canada) and Linda Waimarie Nikora (University of Waikato, New Zealand).

---

1. Introduction

Crunch crunch crunch crunch.
Whispy biting wind swipes my checks like sandpaper and salt.
It tingles in a refreshing way. I like it—but not too much.
Crunchy crispy snow sends vibrations of my walk across creation.
There is no hiding or sneaking up on anything in this crispy cold snow.
I like that sound. It's alive and I am here. I am included.
I stop, breath and take in what I am often too busy to see and experience.
Looking, feeling, listening and sensing. Thoughts go quiet.
Attention to sounds and sights.
It's often the little things that we exclude, that we don't look at or feel.
Vast blueness covers the sky and it's chillingly deceiving—it looks summery.
Blue skies and cold airs flow in an invisible icy veil.
The wind bites my face and the snow would turn my toes black if exposed.
Rays of sunshine line my face and send warmth that allows forgiveness of the biting cold.
Beautifully powerful and powerfully deadly.
Dualities exist all around us.
Spirit is here. I feel Creation. I know I am part of Creator's web.
Creation will teach and guide for life's inclusion—we must listen.

When I was invited to submit an article for this special edition I initially thought maybe they invited the wrong person. Who me? I realized this initial response is an impact of being excluded and feeling alienated throughout my life. With caution I proceeded and accepted the invitation. Now what? Inclusion begins with voice in Creation experiencing and being. I know I belong. Inclusion simply begins with an invitation. Come on in! I acknowledge the journal for making the invitation. In this article, I include my whole self and locate who I am. I use whole with a "w" to denote wholeness as in complete, circular and full. Canada is my context. The settler colonial history directly impacts my experiences and the place from which I write.

I am an Anishinaabekwe (Ojibwe woman). My Anishinaabe name is Minogiizhigokwe which means Shining Day Woman. I am a member of Flying Post First Nation which is in Northern Ontario, Canada. In Canada, Indigenous territories have been eroded to "lands reserved for Indians" under the assimilative Federal legislation of the Indian Act 1876.[1] I have never lived on my reserve lands; exclusion not inclusion is the reason; Indian Act legislation outlawed and excluded us from ourselves at every level of our existence. When my Ojibwe mother married my British father and under the patriarchal and sexist Indian Act legislation, her Treaty rights and Indian Status were revoked. In 1985, the Indian Act was amended with Bill C 31 as a result of Indigenous women's activism. She then had her Indian status reinstated along with all her offspring. Aggressive policies of assimilation were Federally legislated in Canada and from the ages of 5 to 15 my mother was sent to the Chapleau Indian Residential School in Northern Ontario. Despite the assimilators efforts to eradicate our culture, we were raised close to the land and my family kept us closely connected to Creation. My blend includes many layers comprised of my connection to the land, cultural identity, impacts of colonial socialization and internalization, decolonizing and Indigenizing while reclaiming, relearning and recovering my whole self. My voice, spirit, heart, mind and body guide my writing. How I locate in my writing will shift and change as I shift and grow.

Within this paper, I include as a key reference my Ojibwe/Anishinaabe teaching and learning as Indigenous researcher, educator, knowledge carrier and community helper. I also acknowledge the duality of exclusion and inclusion in the Indigenous and Canadian peoples' contexts. It may not speak to readers who require Eurowestern literature to substantiate Indigenous knowledge. My approach contributes to the collective by including my Indigenous lens. Change is imperative. I participate in change by challenging the dominance of Eurowestern theories and beliefs and put forth a wholistic perspective rooted in Anishinaabe teachings relative to social inclusion and Indigenous peoples. These teachings come from oral narratives, teachings and written work. Practices rooted in local contexts and traditions inform this paper and I strive to incorporate and recover my Indigenous traditions into thought and models of social inclusion in an authentic manner whereby, "the local culture is used as a primary source for knowledge and practice development" (Gray, Coates, & Yellow Bird, 2008, p. 5). Rooted in my Anishinaabe tradition my writing has goals of generating space for re-storing Indigenous knowledge and perspectives. As Dumbrill and Green (2008) note, this assertion is necessary and needed for the disruption of ongoing dominance of Eurowestern worldviews. My challenge is to recognize that values and ideas of inclusion from and within a colonized environment still contain western values that I have internalized. I need to use Anishinaabe wholistic frameworks to keep me in check and to ensure my perspective is inclusive and whole. Authors Mel Gray, John Coates and Michael Yellow Bird (2008) believe that "good and effective social work practice demands that we make culture explicit in thinking and practice. This [was] a substantial conclusion that emerged in our workshops, which brought together scholars from around the world to discuss the most significant global trends related to Indigenous and cross cultural social work" (p. 6). My challenge is to present an Anishinaabe wholistic worldview that is inclusive, yet not pan-Indian, that also presents a universal circular philosophy, yet recognizes our unique locations. It's not easy. However, I too believe that practice that is driven by cultural values is relevant and good practice. I proceed knowing that I will make mistakes inclusively.

An Ojibwe worldview is a wholistic circular worldview inclusive of all directions and could be described to be a 360 degree lens (Dumont, 1976). The resurgence of Indigenous pedagogies and knowledge are relevant in making contributions to insightful models toward change (Cajete, 1994; Simpson, 2011). Today, many Indigenous authors are promoting this stance where "Nishnaabeg thinkers believe we are in the period of the Seventh Fire. It is the responsibility of the new people, the Oshkimaadiziig, to pick up the pieces of our lifeways, collectivize them and build a political and cultural renaissance and resurgence" (Simpson, 2011, p. 66). Citing pioneering authors' work demonstrates this journey. The journey continues toward asserting our existence and being included.

This article is presented and organized firstly with a gaze of skepticism by illuminating the challenge of social inclusion in the contexts where exclusion dominates. Following this awakening is a glance into the spaces where hope resides and change is resident. Wholistic and ethical change is then presented within a medicine wheel circle to facilitate inclusivity and balance where each direction of spirit, heart/relationship, mind/knowledge and physical/presence are explored. Historically, concepts of the Medicine Wheel were derived from central North America and contribute in the resurgence of wholistic Indigenous approaches (Linklater, 2014). Following, each direction are guiding questions to reflect upon and perhaps act upon. Finally, each direction of the whole is guided by principles of humility, love, truth, honesty, respect, wisdom and

[1] To learn more about the Indian Act, University of British Columbia has a critically informed website: http://indigenousfoundations.arts.ubc.ca/home/government-policy/the-indian-act.html

bravery: the seven sacred teachings (Simpson, 2011). These principles ground each direction in terms of values and ethics of practice. Concluding thoughts bring closure to this article. I skeptically begin.

2. Skepticism and Hope: The Duality in Ex/Inclusion

My skepticism emerges in a critical gaze at how colonialism in Canadian policy and practice has aggressively been driven to exclude, erode, erase and oppress Indigenous peoples in our homeland. Imperialism, colonialism, racism and oppression are all culprits eventually leading to the Canadian Federal Government instituting policies of aggressive assimilation such as Church run Indian Residential Schools (Dickason & Newbigging, 2015; Graveline, 2010). These policies severely impacted my family and community; they systematically dismembered many of our families from one another at spiritual, emotional, mental and physical levels. Socially driven legislation and policies have been created to 'rid the Indian from the child' through the Indian Act, Residential School Act, Child Welfare, land dispossessions and so much more (Dickason & Newbigging, 2015). All efforts were made to sever Indigenous peoples connection from our life source, our Mother Earth to pursue capitalism and global market power. Since contact on North America, invading colonizers have attacked Indigenous sovereignty, land rights and title in pursuit of the land and her natural resources to accumulate wealth and power. While there were many dehumanizing and very unsocial exclusionary mechanisms in colonial agendas for domination, they are not the focus of this paper. With that being said, recognizing that the intent of all subsequent and consequent institutional and structural acts and actions of social exclusion has been to actualize the colonizer's power and control over Indigenous peoples in order to have a reigning hand on the land and her resources. There are many layers and mechanisms of exclusion of Indigenous peoples in Canada. Consequently, as in many other colonized countries, Indigenous peoples' inclusion is often superficial and token.

Will is a key factor. Is there political will to begin becoming socially inclusive? For example, when commissions or inquiries are undertaken, such as the Royal Commission on Aboriginal Peoples[2] from 1992 to 1996, the Manitoba Justice Inquiry,[3] and the more recent Truth and Reconciliation Commission (TRC)[4] from 2000 to 2015, comprehensive recommendations solidly based in individual, community testimonies and ethical research are made in final reports. These recommendations need to be taken seriously by Governments by placing them on strategic agendas and action plans with accompanying resources. In my experience, at many municipal and community levels, Indigenous people are not consulted and if it is a 'consultation,' it is constructed to seem like one, but is not authentically driven. Social inclusion in social policy, welfare, child welfare, social services and health is yet to be actualized. Indigenous people continue to represent the highest social statistics, yet are not included in solution finding and funding to remedy high mortality rates, homicide rates, suicide rates (an ultimate manifestation of exclusion), incarceration, violence, abuse, addictions, homelessness and poverty. This goes without saying, but it seems we need to keep saying that Indigenous peoples need to be included in discussions and decision-making processes to create solutions that are relevant and meaningful.

Indigenous peoples are leading the roads to change within our own communities which are as diverse as communities can be. With that being said, the road to social inclusion is clogged with political and social control agents, social ignorance, lack of political will, institutional racism, colonized structures and internalized colonialism and oppression. The idea of social inclusion and Indigenous people leaves more to the imagination and vision than current reality and actuality in Canada.

The whole picture is further complicated by the internalized contexts of Indigenous peoples. Indigenous peoples have many layers of internalized colonialism, racism and oppression to unravel while decolonizing, healing and restoring. Understanding the layers of historicity, impacts of genocide, colonization and subsequent intergenerational unresolved traumas that continue to plague and wreak havoc is foundational to having constructive conversations to redress exclusion in social movements. Inclusion in problem identification, problem solutions, and in all areas of restoration and reconciliation is necessary.

Are we ready? Ready for what? We don't know what we don't know. Susan Dion, a leading Lenape-Potawatami educator and scholar, accurately describes amnesia as a powerful tool breeding ignorance and inaction. Key variables and obstacles that impact any capacity to address social inclusion are ignorance, cultural and colonial amnesia, power, privilege and greed (Dion, 2009). Ignorance is a result of a society that doesn't know what it doesn't know until exposed to information, knowledge and experiences. Cultural and colonial amnesia is endemic and a lack of accurate knowledge in education creates a society that forgets, avoids, denies and negates the connections between personal and political, present, past and future. Through a gross omission, education is one of the main culprits in propagating social ignorance and colonial amnesia about Indigenous peoples and colonization in Canada. Let's not negate or ignore the underlying culprits and government's role in creating and maintaining colonial illit-

---

[2] See http://www.aadnc-aandc.gc.ca/eng/1307458586498/1307458751962

[3] See www.ajic.mb.ca/volume.html

[4] See www.trc.ca

eracy and inaction, ultimately leaving social injustice and inequity under the social radar and without social accountability by society. The connection becomes clearer in identifying who benefits when Canadians at large are socialized into a norm of ignorance and amnesia.

In Canada, ignorance prevails about the history and ongoing colonizing tactics against Indigenous peoples, thereby fuelling ignorance and amnesia at gross levels. People don't know what they don't know. Though this is changing with a new Federal leadership and recent media coverage of the Truth and Reconciliation book launch and a national inquiry into Murdered and Missing Aboriginal women, there is much work to do. Amidst this, Indigenous peoples want to grow and thrive as Indigenous peoples, not colonized Indigenous peoples. Many people unknowingly participate in colonial mechanisms because they just don't know or understand how to step into becoming a part of positive change so they either defer to Indigenous peoples (pass the buck) or freeze (and do nothing). I believe Indigenous peoples' history in Canada must be included to inform and address the illiteracy and ignorance. Undoubtedly, power is a major player in the operation of exclusion and power is never easily or voluntarily relinquished (Pinderhuges, 1998). The roots of exclusion must continue to be unveiled with a goal to depersonalize blaming the victims of a culture that perpetuates amnesia. Critical North American Indigenous scholars such as Howard Adams, Harold Cardinal, Sheila Cote-Meek, Vine Deloria Jr., Lauri Gilchrist, Eber Hampton, Emma LaRoque, Patricia Monture-Angus, Raven Sinclair, Fyre Jean Graveline (to name a few) and many others have published to restore accurate accounts and impacts of colonization for this very reason. Paulo Freire (1996) from Central America was an educator and alley who wrote about educating for change by teaching oppressed people to read and develop a critical consciousness about their conditions. The principles of critical education resonate within the Canadian context where people have been kept ignorant about oppression and colonization. As a critical Indigenous educator, I have witnessed that when learners grow in their political and social consciousness through knowledge based on the accurate and truthful accounts of colonization, they are in fact decolonizing, critically reflecting and connecting this knowledge to themselves and ultimately their social consciousness. Authentic action follows. Education ought to be created to foster socially conscience people and truth telling that emancipates peoples' minds, hearts, bodies and spirits is a part of that. Canada is a society that is in a treaty relationship with Indigenous peoples, the original Nations of this land (Dickason & Newbigging, 2015). Only when the Canadian populous understand their treaty obligations in this relationship can we begin to understand the principle of inclusion.

Despite the skeptical picture, I confess my spirit carries hope and faith that we must never surrender or give up on taking our place in society and Creation. Decolonizing has begun and while Indigenous knowledge systems contain ethics, values and principles from which to build inclusion, we are continually confronted with the impacts of colonial trauma and must continue to do our work to restore ourselves individually and collectively. We must problematize archaic notions of paternalism and recognize the necessity of including those impacted by legislation, policies, practices and services in the development, planning and delivery at all phases and stages. This article crafts a culturally based framework and lens from which inclusion can be considered, operationalized and authentically acted upon.

3. Hope: Culturally-Based Frameworks for Inclusion

Indigenous peoples' resistance and resilience have always been strong and our spirit of survival even stronger because we know we belong, we stand up for Creation—she is our life source. Through my daughters Amanda and Healy, I have heard a slogan for inclusion, 'nothing about us without us' and while it has its roots in the Apartheid and HIV movements, it seems marginalized communities who are fighting for inclusion have adopted it. This term also resonates and echoes with what we in the Indigenous community are saying. 'Nothing about us without us' is clear in meaning and intent toward inclusion. Agendas that are rooted in equality, social justice and respect for diversity will create fertile ground for social inclusion in addressing matters of spiritual, emotional, mental and social wellness at individual, community, national and allied levels.

Leroy Little Bear (2000, 2012), a Blackfoot scholar, along with Vine Deloria Jr. (1973) and many other leading Indigenous knowledge keepers have lead the arduous journey of asserting Aboriginal knowledge, philosophy and foundations in guiding policy, education, research, science, law and justice. Little Bear (2000) affirms the cyclical, wholistic and paying attention to process in the whole:

> "The idea of all things being in constant motion or flux leads to a holistic and cyclical view of the world. If everything is constantly moving and changing, the cosmic cycles are in constant motion, but they have regular patterns that result in recurrences such as the seasons of the year, the migration of the animals, renewal ceremonies, songs, and stories. Constant motion, as manifested in cyclical or repetitive patterns, emphasizes process as opposed to product." (p. 79).

Wholistic frameworks are important lenses to ensure and ground inclusivity in engagements with Indigenous peoples (Twigg & Hengen, 2009). Indigenous worldviews and philosophies are guided by natural cycles and natural law with cyclical and circular frameworks representing the layers and interconnections of relationships within Creation and life (Little Bear, 2000, 2012). Indigenous peoples are the knowledge keepers of this land and within our knowledge are cultural frameworks and teachings (Graveline, 1998; Verniest, 2006; Nabigon & Wenger-Nabigon, 2012). Indigenous Elders tell us our original teachers are in Creation and it is important to observe and regard the natural world for guidance in contemplating issues and approaches wholistically. In this article, I am integrating a Medicine Wheel framework and Seven Sacred Teachings to help write about wholistic and ethical social inclusion. Other Indigenous scholars, like myself, have derived meaning and guidance from the natural world and Creation to inform how we contemplate and present wholistic approaches (Aboriginal Field of Study, 2015; Absolon, 2010, 2011; Cote-Meek, Dokis-Ranney, Lavallee, & Wemigwans, 2012; Deloria Jr., 1973; Freeman & Lee, 2007; Green, 2009; Little Bear, 2000; Nabigon & Nabigon-Wenger, 2012). Culturally informed responses and culturally based programs to individual and social issues are having positive results in healing and wellness movements; that is a fact (Wesley-Esquimaux & Smolewski, 2004). Like many Indigenous knowledge keepers, I too believe wholistic frameworks will create lenses to facilitate wholistic thinking in development, planning and action toward comprehensive responses for complex and multifaceted issues and problems. Medicine Wheel frameworks, the Oolichan fishing, whole petal flowers, whole trees, stitching and sewing and other countless examples can facilitate balance and considerations of all aspects within the spiritual, emotional, mental and physical elements; and all those elements in relationship with and to the whole environment, past, present and future (Graveline, 1998; Green, 2009; Hart, 2002; Jackson, Coleman, Strikes With A Gun & Sweet Grass, 2015). Additionally, wholistic frameworks based on the hand drum and sacred circle teachings with all its' elemental directions have guided a lens for considerations and movement toward inclusion (Goudreau, Cote-Meek, Madill, & Wilson, 2008; Hart, 1996, 2002; Nabigon, 2006).

Figure 1 presents an illustration of a wholistic framework drawn from the Four Directions of Medicine Wheel and Seven Sacred Teachings (Benton-Benai, 1988; Nabigon, 2006). This wholistic framework is comprised of four interconnected and interrelated directions: spirit and vision; emotional and relationship; mental and knowledge; and physical and presence. Social inclusion of Indigenous peoples ought to be wholistic in perspective, approach and application. I begin with spirit and move around the circle following the direction of the sun. All directions are interdependent and interconnected and create a whole. Each must be attended. Balance is achieved by being mindful of all directions together to create a wholistic and ethical approach. Further, each element in this framework is guided by the Seven Sacred Teachings[5] of humility, love, truth, honesty, respect, wisdom and bravery.

[5] Also commonly known as Seven Grandfather teachings. See the *Mishomis Book* (Benton-Banai, 1988) to understand the traditional story (*aadizookaan*) where the Seven Grandfathers presented a little child with each principle now known as the Seven Grandfather teachings. In this article I prefer seven sacred teachings to not exclude the notion of grandmothers.

Figure 1. Wholistic and ethical social inclusion.

These seven sacred teachings are guiding ethics governed by traditional knowledge intended to maintain and restore balance and harmony in Creation. The following illustration provides a visual of this culturally-based wholistic and a lens. This framework is a beginning and others will see what I have not and I invite others to build on this in a manner that promotes *mino bimaadsiwin* (a good life) for all. I begin with Spirit and move clockwise to include all directions; individually they are unbalanced, together they are whole.

4. Spirit

Spirit is ethically guided by the sacred teachings of *humility* and *love*. Inclusion has to be guided by unconditional love: love for the people, the project, humanity, healing and reconciliation. To know peace is to know the beauty and power of love. Humility is present when you know yourself as a sacred part of creation and that includes the spirit world. An Anishinaabe Elder, Pathfinder-bah, who I had worked with and learned from (now in the spirit world), shared that we are spiritual beings having a human experience. How humble is that! We are dependent on the air, water, sun and earth plus her inhabitants and plants for survival. Human beings are in humble position with respect to Creation. Indigenous teachings are simple and humble and walking with humility is a value enacted in learning to listen with presence and respect. New born babies encompass new life and renewal and are the closest to Spirit and they bring pure love into this earth lodge. I believe love is a spiritual virtue from Creator and because our Creator purely loves us unconditionally, we have been given everything we need to live a good life. Everything we need is in Creation unconditionally present. Life is offered and medicines to help us are offered in Creation. Attending to spirit is attending to that sacred relationship to Creator and Creation with love and humility. We are spiritual people whose worldview and philosophies are enacted acknowledging that we live in relationship with a Great Spirit, spirits in Creation and ancestral spirits. There is a fine line between this earthly realm and the spirit realm. Our[6] ceremonies, feasts, dances, and gatherings all recognize and include Spirit. We are aware of the presence of spirit and nurturing our spiritual connection is one element of our whole human experience and an important determinant of social wellbeing. Further, it goes without saying that including Indigenous people in anything means attending to Spirit.

Colonial forces have attacked and attempted to annihilate our spirituality and connection to our Mother the Earth in an effort to sever this sacred connection in pursuit of land, mineral and resource exploitation. Because Indigenous spirituality and ways of life are intrinsically linked to Creation, the earth and all her resources, severing this connection was one key colonial agenda. However, words alone cannot describe the sacred and profoundly deep connection much like an umbilical cord between the people of Creation and our Mother the earth. The love is unconditional. She is the one who bestows life, food and medicine to Creation. She is the one who gives life to those who inhabit her. From Spirit, we consider affirming spirit along with a process of rebirth and new life. In any day we can try again and each new day is a new opportunity. Attending to the spirit is about affirming Indigenous peoples' spirit, culture, and language with humility and love toward rebirth and regeneration of social inclusion.

Some questions to guide in determining whether the spirit of Indigenous peoples is included are:

- Is spirit being attended to?
- What does cultural humility look like here?
- Are Indigenous peoples invited?
- Are spiritual leaders invited to guide spiritual inclusion?
- Are cultural protocols informing how people are invited and related to? If you don't know the cultural protocols identify who can help.
- Are Indigenous spiritual practices present and evident?
- Is there space for Indigenous peoples' medicine and ceremony?
- Who can provide leadership in creating space for spiritual practices?
- Are we including land based spiritual practices?
- Have we secured natural spaces for spirit and land based ceremony?
- What languages should be included?
- Others...?

Land and spirit are intrinsically connected. Being on the land is being in relationship with spirit. Indigenous people generally love being on the land. I encourage large land holders to share land space and places by invitation. Work with Indigenous peoples toward restoration of relationships with the original stewards of the land and Creation. On a purely idealistic level, I believe land must be returned to Indigenous peoples in order for the inclusion of Indigenous ceremonial practices to occur without permission or apology. Our ceremonies require a land base. The land is where the medicines, animals, helpers exist: this is where our life source is. We know the land will be our salvation for life and spaces and places are essential. Indigenous knowledge and learning doesn't happen in classrooms or inside buildings; it happens on the land and in Creation. Creation is comprised of our relatives and in order to enact spiritual practices, the Spirit of the land is central.

[6] When I say "our" my reference is intended to include Indigenous peoples' ceremonies.

5. Emotional: Rebuilding Relationships

The Emotional direction is guided by the sacred teachings of *truth* and *honesty*. Honesty is an important Indigenous ethic and when enacted brings strength to sharing ideas, experiences and knowledges. When people need strength and courage to speak their truth, they will often hold onto an eagle feather and it is believed that the spirit of that feather will bring the truth forward. Sometimes people speak their truth while holding onto the feather without having contemplated sharing it. Being truthful with self is the beginning and then being truthful and mindful with others fuels authentic relationship building. It takes courage to be truthful and honest about our place and challenges in any dynamics of oppression/oppressor, colonizer/colonized, settler/Indigenous, and decolonizing/indigenizing. Through conversations genuine humanity can be restored. Truth and honesty require humility and love and all these values will teach us how to be real in healing and restoring wounded relationships within self and others.

Feeling included and invited are important emotional experiences on the pathway to social inclusion, restoration and reconciliation. Being invited is a positive experience and says 'we want you here'. We want you here indicates that your presence matters and what you have to offer will make a difference. Building relationship begins with an invitation. Through invitations and encounters possibilities exist to gain understanding, knowledge, connection, compassion and so much more. Relationships require contact and connections. With regard to relationship building, Leroy Little Bear (2000) again sums up how essential it is to meet, share, and exchange experiences, stories, truths and ideas. There are many truths and ideas of how, where, when, and what to do to bring social health and wellness to creation. He states:

> "In a context of jagged worldviews, I cannot take for granted that you see and know the same things that I see and know. The only things I know for sure are the things I experience, see, feel, and so on. The rest of it is presumption and persuasion....That is why we engage in conversation, so I can share my experiences with you and make you understand what I am feeling. When you respond, you are doing the same thing with me." (p. 85)

The above quote echoes a strong need for dialogue because we (Indigenous and non-Indigenous and everyone in between) have so much to sort out in restoring and rebuilding relationships based on respect. Relationship are key says Shawn Wilson when considering and engaging in ethical and inclusive Indigenous research (2008). Restoring healthy relationships was a primary recommendation for youth work in resiliency and recovery from substance abuse (Haring, Freeman, Guiffrida & Dennis, 2012). Sharing, talking, healing, learning and teaching circles carry the means for creating respectful spaces for listening and sharing (Gaveline, 1998). Throughout this article, our diverse make-up has been established. Values of kindness in learning and sharing are leading pathways to building and restoring wounded relationships within ourselves and amongst each other. We have to tell our stories about who we are, where we come from and what all that means to us. We all could practice acceptance and respect for diversity in the truth that we all have diverse histories and social stories. We all have commonalities and bridge building is possible. Creating space to begin or to continue listening and learning is a start in any relationship. I believe that most people can attest to the fact that healthy relationships require time, space, energy and honesty. There are many other factors that contribute to relationship building; however, the main point here is that for inclusion to become an experience, relationship building needs to be attended to with truth, honesty and respect. What a respectful relationship to experience when we are accepted for who we are, not by how others think we should be. I would definitely want to nurture and engage in those kinds of relationships. That means, as Leroy Little Bear as stated, our conversations of learning and sharing need to be less about verifying our presumptions and assumptions and more about learning, acceptance and respect.

Some of the following questions may guide the lens of attending to relationship building with truth and honesty:

- How will we create an inclusive and relationship building process?
- Who will coordinate a planning session to begin?
- Are Indigenous people who are relevant to the topic invited?
- Who will you invite? Inviting people who have interests indicates an investment in a meaningful and purposeful process.
- Is there a space that generates respect in the sharing of ideas? Creating spaces that allow people space to share, engage & be on land is helpful.
- What mechanisms are in place to ensure Indigenous people are listened to?
- How will respect be enacted?
- What truths need to be shared?
- What Indigenous process can be integrated to foster respectful sharing and listening: relationship building? Ask about the circle process.
- What activities and events can be planned that build respectful and inclusive relationships with Indigenous peoples?

- Other suggestions...?

Attending to relationships with truth and honesty is not only restorative; interwoven in these values are integrity and respect. Settler–Indigenous relations have been riddled with the presence of puzzled and jagged worldviews colliding crashing, clashing and smashing (Little Bear, 2000). Sorting out the puzzle is not easy, but in the spirit of renewal, truth telling and truth listening will foster the sorts of relationships that people want to be involved in. I think people are tired of contrived attempts (rightly so) and are thirsty for real conversations about real life experiences, issues, challenges, journeys toward truth building and truthful problem solving.

6. Mental: Knowledge and Understanding

The mental direction calls attention to knowledge building and critical reflection and are guided by the sacred teachings of *respect* and *wisdom*. Herb Nabigon (2006) explains respect as having the capacity to look twice at things. Herb, an Anishinaabe Elder, was one of my first cultural teachers many years ago. He taught me that by learning to look twice at what we are observing or thinking about, we learn about respect. We can learn to not react, but to become reflective and retrospective in thought. Showing respect is to take time to take a second look and let the first re-action go, to reflect and look again. What this means in acts of inclusion is to not make quick judgements at who belongs and who doesn't, but to reflect and invest in thoughtfulness before acting or reacting. Knowledge can emerge when time and space are created and from this knowledge, developments, planning and movements that are respectful can emerge. There is wisdom in Indigenous knowledge, traditions, ceremonies and teachings. As this article is promoting, show respect for Indigenous knowledge and wisdom through authentic inclusion. What I mean by authentic inclusion is inclusion that Indigenous people feel and experience as real, genuine and meaningful.

Readiness is always a factor that enables or disables any process from moving forward in a productive manner. Education and training become important to preparing and fostering a climate of readiness. For example, if a group wants to include Indigenous peoples in a movement, the group must understand that Indigenous peoples in Canada have both a rich cultural history and deep colonial history. Both of these histories are real and have significant implications for truth and reconciliation in Canada. Both of these histories have led to excluding or including. The rich cultural traditions of Indigenous peoples which this article promotes, will lead toward pathways that foster inclusion. Mechanisms of colonization, assimilation, annihilation and genocide have led to the exclusion of Indigenous peoples. The pathway is clear for those that are invested in working toward inclusion of Indigenous peoples.

When considering the mental or knowledge portal of a wholistic and ethical action toward social inclusion and Indigenous peoples, as I stated earlier, the importance of understanding who Indigenous peoples are in terms of our cultural histories, territories, languages and our colonial histories cannot be emphasized enough. For example, when considering Indigenous peoples' cultural histories and locations, Canada is a composite of diverse and vast Indigenous territories comprised of over six hundred First Nation communities on reserve; urban Indigenous communities and rural Indigenous communities (Dickason & Newbigging, 2015). Research states that there are up to seventy Indigenous languages which are linguistically grouped into twelve groups (Official Languages and Bilinguialism Institute, n.d.). The geographical, land and territorial diversity of Indigenous peoples in Canada is large. Any individual or group wanting to include and engage with Indigenous peoples needs to learn about, understand and educate themself on who they are engaging with, thus avoiding a pan-Indian response. There are similarities and commonalities, the challenge is to be able to discern what these are.

Similar to other colonized countries, Canada has a history of cultural genocide against Indigenous peoples (TRC, 2015). The Federal Government funded Church run schools to assimilate Aboriginal children with an attempt to kill the culture in them. This resulted in an unforgettable era and legacy of residential schooling which left thousands of Indigenous children and following generations with deep-seeded trauma and wounds steeped in the spiritual, emotional, mental and physical abuses the children and their families incurred. This history was largely ignored and in 2007 the Canadian Federal Court Approved an Indian Residential Schools Settlement Agreement in Canada which led the pathway to a process called the Indian Residential School Truth and Reconciliation Commission[7] from 2010 to 2015. From the TRC website I include the following:

> **What is the TRC?**
> The TRC is a component of the Indian Residential Schools Settlement Agreement.
> Its mandate is to inform all Canadians about what happened in Indian Residential Schools (IRS). The Commission will document the truth of survivors, families, communities and anyone personally affected by the IRS experience.
> This includes First Nations, Inuit and Métis former Indian Residential School students, their families, communities, the Churches, former school employees, Government and other Canadians.

[7] Go to www.trc.ca for more information, resources and to see the 94 recommendations in the final report.

> The Commission has a five-year mandate and is supported by a TRC Secretariat, which is a federal government department.
> **What does the TRC hope to achieve?**
> The TRC hopes to guide and inspire Aboriginal peoples and Canadians in a process of reconciliation and renewed relationships that are based on mutual understanding and respect. (TRC, 2015)

In June, 2015, my partner and I attended the final events of the TRC in Ottawa, Ontario where Justice Murray Sinclair presented the final summary and subsequent 94 recommendation report compiled from 5 years of statement gathering and research. The recommendations directly address issues of inclusion in all areas of child welfare, health, justice, education, language and culture, youth, churches, museums, buried children and national monuments, a national centre for reconciliation, the Royal Proclamation and a covenant for reconciliation, and United Nations declaration for Indigenous peoples. The recommendations themselves indicate that inclusion across the board is necessary. A call for action is the foundation of the recommendations—calls for action by the Federal Government in all areas of funding, legislation, institutional development, education and policy to redress and begin to move forward toward reconciliation.

At the closing event on May 31, 2015, my husband and I walked alongside seven thousand other people through the streets of Ottawa with a call to action to the Government and many other witnesses to support the truths of Indian residential school survivors and their families. On that particular day, thousands of people united and there was a felt inclusion for the support and intentions of the TRC. The march, like many, created a visible presence of support with a hope that the millions of witnesses watching from the sidelines of the streets, media and social media would care and step forward to move the Federal Government to respond to this call to action. Later, I made a statement on the impact of the Indian residential school on my uncles, aunts, grandparents and parents and the intergenerational impacts on myself, siblings, cousins and future children. During this process I felt included and listened to. I wanted to name my relatives whose lives have been negatively impacted by the IRS. I wanted to acknowledge and have recorded the loss of family ties, communities, cultural identity, language, health, wellness, self-worth coupled with the occurrences of spiritual, emotional, mental, physical and sexual abuse that were rampant throughout these schools. I wanted their names to be recorded and remembered and like many others, I wanted their stories to be acknowledged and included.

Some questions to consider in wholistic and ethical social inclusion from the mental/knowledge direction are:

- Who will assess capacity and readiness and determine education and training needed? How will this be done?
- Is there education being provided on the truth and history of Canada and Indigenous people?
- Is education development and Indigenous illiteracy being addressed? Are resources and material available and facilitated?
- What education and training preparations need to developed and delivered?
- How will education foster decolonization while restoring Indigenous peoples' culture, traditions, language and land?
- Who are the local Indigenous peoples, their languages and land base?
- Where learning tools, resources, teachers and educators are available?
- What Indigenous languages need to be included and resourced?
- What existing practices/research to build on?
- Any other thoughts...?

Understanding, knowledge, respect, wisdom and truth telling culminate and enhance the possibility that inclusion from a place of respect is possible. In any action of inclusion one needs to know intelligently that other peoples' knowledge is valid and deserving of space. Indigenous knowledge will guide the methodologies from which action can emerge. From this place of respect, knowing and being, inclusion becomes an experience felt by contrast with rhetoric espoused.

7. Physical: Places and Presence

The physical direction calls attention to presence, space and place and are guided by the sacred teaching of *bravery*. To physically walk with all these seven sacred teachings and to carry them in your whole being is to walk in bravery. To carry truth and honesty forward takes bravery. Bravery requires humility in being truthful especially when making amends is the action. Humility, love, truth, honesty, respect and wisdom are all related to being brave in our thoughts and actions. Standing up for inclusion takes bravery. Being the only one to see who is missing and speaking up takes bravery. Despite everything, Indigenous peoples know we belong and we know through our creation stories that we have a purpose in Creation. Presence and places are important considerations. Indigenous peoples want to see other Indigenous peoples' presence in places that are welcoming, warm and respectful.

Through the many barriers in history and moving forward, Indigenous peoples have made strides and set strong examples for the rest of Canada and the world. We have seen resistance movements through Oka, Idle No More, Indigenous women movements, Indigenous youth-lead walks for better schools and education, women water walkers for the water, and growing Aboriginal rights movements and they are impacting public and social policy. Today many First Nations and Indigenous peoples are more visible and are playing more significant roles in fostering change and leading movements that may well help restore humanity to people and restore respect for our life source, the earth. Indigenous women are a growing voice and presence is consciousness raising and have been leaders in activism and social movements. The Idle No More[8] movement became a national mobilizer for peoples' attention to join a peaceful revolution to stand up for rights, land, water and living conditions in Canada among Indigenous peoples. The presence and evidence of Indigenous peoples in social movements and walks of bravery and courage, fights for change, and challenges to injustice is indeed growing.

Internally in Indigenous communities we are building culturally-based frameworks for the social inclusion of all members in our communities. These models exist within Indigenous organizations such as healing and wellness centres and are created from Indigenous knowledge, traditions and protocols. For example, in Ontario and across Canada, Native child welfare developments are growing and developing governance models from their own wholistic knowledge bundles from their Nations territories and traditional knowledge. One local example in southwestern Ontario is Mnnaasged[9] where wholistic approaches to healing and restoring Indigenous knowledge and values at the centre of agency development. Mnaasged's Executive Director, Carrie Tabobondung (an Anishinaabekwe from Wasauksing First Nation, Ontario), states that she has seen "so many incredible changes in child welfare on the outside but mostly we've grown as an organization together on the inside" (Tabobondung, 2015). Culturally-infused models governed by the seven sacred principles create a consciousness of mutual respect which in turns fosters inclusion of members of all age groups and members from various belief systems. The value of inclusion is not new in Indigenous knowledge systems. Today, it is more of a matter of re-building and restoring our values into how we build social systems. I believe in our Creation stories which tell us that we, Indigenous people, belong here and without us Creation would be incomplete. Hope, faith, truth and courage carry me forward to continue in areas where I strive to open up doors and windows and to remove obstacles toward inclusion and authentic social change.

A strong presence and visibility is a part of inclusion. We must see that we are being included. When one sits at a table to discuss anything Indigenous, a glance around the room ought to reveal other Indigenous people, stake holders, Elders, youth, women, men, leaders, and grandmothers/fathers present. Who this is about ought to be present. The presence of people and the presence of their voice is an indication that inclusion is authentic. The TRC walk I referred to earlier was a powerful experience of presence. Presence of the people, presence of the testimonies, stories and relatives, presence of memory and telling, and presence of process counters invisibility and exclusivity of truths. Reconciliation requires truth of sharing, truth of accounts, truth of accountability and truth of presence. Reconciliation is only possible when the truth is shared and accepted as the truth. People will march and people will walk. When people collectively walk together, a power of presence and undeniable truths are visible. The excluded seek inclusion by creating visibility in marching, chanting, going hungry and rallying at closed gates wanting voices to be heard and included in policy and funding. Bravery and courage are teachings that carry acts of dissention toward inclusion.

In considering the physical direction issue surrounding space and place warrant attention. Here are a few questions to guide inclusion of presence which is guided by bravery and courage:

- Whose Indigenous territory, land and place are you on?
- Whose traditional/ancestral territory & Nation needs to be acknowledged?
- Is it reasonable to consider meeting in Indigenous spaces?
- Is meeting in Indigenous organizations or communities a possibility?
- What are the human resources that are accessible to ensure inclusion with Indigenous peoples is enacted?
- Hire people to research and explore Indigenous models and examples: research best practices and provide examples.
- What funding resources are available to support inclusion efforts?
- What physical resources are available?
- Is anything missing, forgotten or overlooked?
- Any other ideas…?
- So what do you think? As an Indigenous person, asking and inviting people to share their thoughts is an inclusive basic principle.

As a follow up note to the collective lists and guides to consider inclusion with Indigenous peoples, I remind the reader that these are guides. I'm sure with ongoing dialogue, there is more to consider and more possibilities to emerge. My hope is that the lists in each of the elemental arenas will usher in thoughts and ideas and foster a wholistic perspective. The goal after all is

[8] Website: www.idlenomore.ca

[9] Go to www.mnaasged.ca for more information on this Indigenous child welfare organization.

wholistic and ethical actions for social inclusion with Indigenous peoples.

8. Some Final Thoughts

Social inclusion with Indigenous peoples, or any diverse group for that matter, is challenging—don't get me wrong. It's a process and with each effort and attempt, as we learn and try again, a shift occurs and growth emerges. I presented many layers of skepticism, hope, spirit, heart, mind and presence to foster considerations toward a wholistic direction of social inclusion. These were further supported by the ethical guidance of the Seven Sacred Teachings. The Anishinaabe creation story (Benton-Benai, 1988) affirms that Creation would be incomplete without Indigenous peoples. Today I know I belong. I know I am not alone and I want to include and honor all of my children, family, teachers, Indigenous scholars, critical thinkers, fellow travelers and truth seekers. We all are working to heal, restore, recover and reclaim our place in society along with the restoration and resurgence of Indigenous knowledge in strategies and approaches is growing and being asserted (Hart, 2014; Simpson, 2011). We are all in this together. The reality for Indigenous peoples in Canada and North America is that we are diversely blended in our identities, social and political locations. Arriving at an authentically inclusive wholistic and ethical place and space of social inclusion is a challenging task. Years ago, while on my own search and re-search (Absolon, 2011) to understand the myriad of confusion, I came across Leroy Little Bear's (2000) article on *Jagged Worldviews Colliding* and have referenced his insights in my work. In this article, his wisdom continues to ring true as he sums up the ex/inclusion collision nicely in the following:

> "Colonization created a fragmentary worldview among Aboriginal peoples. By force, terror and education policy, it attempted to destroy the Aboriginal worldview—but it failed. Instead, colonization left a heritage of jagged worldviews among Indigenous peoples. No one has a pure worldview that is 100 percent Indigenous or Eurocentric; rather, everyone has an integrated mind, a fluxing and ambidextrous consciousness and back again. It is this clash of worldviews that is at the heart of many current difficulties with effective means of social control in postcolonial North America. It is also this class that suppresses diversity in choices and denies Aboriginal people harmony in their daily lives." (p. 85)

Because Leroy Little Bear articulates the anguish of many of us, I tend to refer back to his wise words in describing the impacts and challenges today. Colonization has impacted *all of us* profoundly and we all have a role to play and work to do to restore inclusion and humanity to the world without harm. Understanding how we've been impacted and finding our truths, healing and humanity in the process is a life journey. The four directional circle journey is only one example of how my Anishinaabe culture and many other Indigenous knowledges informs how we can approach and consider inclusion. There are many other cultural frameworks informed by each Nations Indigenous knowledge and context. I encourage all Indigenous peoples to build and restore our place in society and Creation from the knowledges steeped in our cultures.

Patterns, puzzles and layers are what characterize who we are today and what work lays ahead in making meaning from it all. They are beautiful and complex. Efforts for social inclusion may be met with layers of suspicion, mistrust, self-doubt, anger, hurt, fear and worry. I believe and have hope that when action is guided by authentic knowledge along with principles of love, humility, truth, honesty, respect , bravery and wisdom these layers, wounds and barriers will be replaced with actions that move one's spirit, heart, mind and body into a place of humility, love, truth, honesty, respect, wisdom and bravery. The circle is a powerful teaching. These seven sacred principles are strong values gifted through powerful traditional ceremonies. They are medicine for *mino bimaadsiwin*, a good way of life. When we strive for that wholistic and balanced good life, goals of social inclusion are possible. *Miigwech!*

Acknowledgments

I wish to acknowledge all the teachers and mentors' whose teachings and examples make this world richer and more inclusive for all peoples. I acknowledge all those who do their best to walk, research and write with love, humility, truth, honesty, bravery, respect and wisdom toward addressing injustices for inclusion, healing and restoration. I acknowledge my colleagues, my family and partner for all their support. To the editors of this journal, I am grateful for your kind support. Miigwech to all of Creation and all my relations!

Conflict of Interests

The author declares no conflict of interests.

References

Aboriginal Field of Study. (2015). *Lyle S. Hallman Faculty of Social Work. MSW Aboriginal field of study* (Program Pamphlet). Kitchener: Wilfrid Laurier University. Retrieved from www.wlu.ca

Absolon, K. (2010). Indigenous wholistic theory: A knowledge set for practice. *First Peoples Child and Family Review*, 5(2), 74-87.

Absolon, K. (2011). *Kaandossiwin: How we come to know*. Winnipeg: Fernwood Publishing.

Absolon, K. (2009). Navigating the landscape of practice: Dbaagmowin of a helper. In R. Sinclair, M. Hart, & G. Bruyere (Eds.), *Wicihitowin Aboriginal social work in Canada* (pp. 172-199). Winnipeg: Fernwood Publishing.

Benton-Banai, E. (1988). *The Mishomis book*. Hayward, WI: Indian Country Communications Inc.

Cajete, G. (1994). *Look to the mountain: An ecology of Indigenous education*. Durango, CO: Kivaki Press.

Cote-Meek, S., Dokis-Ranney, K., Lavallee, L., & Wemigwans, D. (2012). Building leadership capacity amongst young Anishinaabe-kwe through culturally-based activities and creative arts. *Native Social Work Journal, 8*, 75-90.

Deloria, V, Jr. (1973). *God is red*. New York: Dell.

Dickason, O., & Newbigging, W. (2015). *A concise history of Canada's First Nations* (3rd ed.). Toronto: Oxford University Press.

Dion, S. (2009). *Braiding histories. Learning from Aboriginal Peoples' experiences and perspectives*. Vancouver: University of British Columbia Press.

Dumbrill, G., & Green, J. (2008). Indigenous knowledge in the social work academy. *Social Work Education, 27*(5), 489-503.

Dumont, J. (1976). Journey to daylight: Through Ojibway eyes. *Laurentian University Review, 8* (2), 31-43.

Freeman, B., & Lee, B. (2007). Towards an Aboriginal model of community healing. *Native Social Work Journal, 6*, 97-120.

Freire, P. (1996). *Pedagogy of the oppressed*. New York: Continuum.

Goudreau, G., Cote-Meek, S., Madill, H., & Wilson, S. (2008). Hand drumming: Health-promoting experiences of Aboriginal women from a Northern Ontario urban community. *Journal of Aboriginal Health, 4*(1), 72-83.

Graveline, J. F. (1998). *Circle works: Transforming Eurocentric consciousness*. Halifax, NS: Fernwood Publishing.

Graveline, J. F. (2010). Oh Canada. Our Canada. One of four against. *Critical Social Work, 11*(1), 81-88.

Gray, M., Coates, J., & Yellow Bird, M. (Eds.). (2008). *Indigenous social work around the world. Towards culturally relevant education and practice*. Burlington: Ashgate Publishing.

Green, J. (2009). Gyawaaglaab (Helping one another): Approaches to best practices through teachings of Oolichan fishing. In R. Sinclair, M. Hart, & G. Bruyere (Eds.), *Wicihitowin Aboriginal social work in Canada* (pp. 222-233). Winnipeg: Fernwood Publishing.

Haring, R. C., Freeman, B., Guiffrida, A. L., & Dennis, M. L. (2012). Relationship building for a healthy future: Indigenous youth pathways for resiliency and recovery. *Journal of Indigenous Social Development, 1*(1), 1-17.

Hart, M. A. (1996). Sharing circles: Utilizing traditional practice methods for teaching, helping and supporting. In S. O'Meara & D. A. West (Eds.), *From our eyes: Learning from Indigenous peoples* (pp. 59-72). Toronto: Garamond Press.

Hart, M. (2002). *Seeking Mino-Pimatisiwin. An Aboriginal approach to helping*. Winnipeg: Fernwood Publishing.

Hart, M. (2014). Introduction. Indigenous knowledges: Resurgence, implementation, and collaboration in social work. *Journal of Indigenous Social Development, 3*(2), 1-4.

Jackson, E. L., Coleman, J., Strikes With A Gun, G., & Sweet Grass, D. (2015). Treading, stitching, and storytelling: Using CBPR and Blackfoot knowledge and cultural practices to improve domestic violence for Indigenous women. *Journal of Indigenous Social Development, 4*(1), 1-27.

Linklater, R. (2014). *Decolonizing trauma work. Indigenous stories and strategies*. Winnipeg: Fernwood Publishing.

Little Bear, L. (2000). Jagged worldviews colliding. In M. Battiste (Ed.), *Reclaiming Indigenous voice and vision* (pp. 77-85). Vancouver: UBS Press.

Little Bear, L. (2012). Traditional knowledge and humanities: A perspective by a Blackfoot. *Journal of Chinese Philosophy, 31*(4), 518-527.

Nabigon, H. (2006). *The Hollow Tree. Fighting addiction with traditional Native healing.* Montreal and Kingston: McGill-Queen's University Press.

Nabigon, H., & Wenger-Nabigon, A. (2012). "Wise Practices": Integrating traditional teachings with mainstream treatment approaches. *Native Social Work Journal, 8*, 43-55.

Official Languages and Bilinguialism Institute. (n.d.). Site for language management in Canada. Retrieved from https://slmc.uottawa.ca/?q=native_peoples_languages

Pinderhuges, E. (1998). *Understanding race, ethnicity and power. The key to efficacy in clinical practice*. New York: Free Press.

Simpson, L. (2011). *Dancing on our turtle's back. Stories of nishnaabeg re-creation, resurgence and a new emergence*. Winnipeg: Arbeiter Ring Publishing.

Tabobondung, C. (2015). Message from Executive Director. Retrieved from www.mnaasged.ca

Truth and Reconciliation Commission. (2015). Retrieved from http://www.trc.ca/websites/trcinstitution/index.php?p=3

Twigg, R. C., & Hengen, T. (2009). Going back to the roots: Using the medicine wheel in the healing process. *First Peoples Child and Family Review, 4*(1), 10-19.

Verniest, L. (2006). Alleying with the medicine wheel: Social work practice with Aboriginal peoples. *Critical Social Work*, 7(1). Retrieved from http://www.uwindsor.ca/criticalsocialwork

Wesley-Esquimaux, C. C., & Smolewski, M. (2004). *Historic trauma and Aboriginal healing: The Aboriginal*

Healing Foundation research series. Ottawa, ON: The Aboriginal Healing Foundation.

Wilson, S. (2008). Research as ceremony. Halifax: Fernwood Publishing.

About the Author

Dr. Kathleen E. Absolon

Dr. Kathleen Absolon is member of Flying Post First Nation. Her blend inlcudes both Anishinaabe and British ancestry. She is an Associate Dean and Associate Professor in the Aboriginal Field of Study, Faculty of Social Work, Wilfrid Laurier University. She is an Indigenous practitioner, educator and researcher. She published *Kaandossiwin: How We Come to Know* (2011) among other works related to wholistic knowledges, community practice and Indigenous methodologies.

2

Diverse Outcomes: Social Citizenship and the Inclusion of Skilled Migrants in Australia

Juliet Pietsch

School of Politics and International Relations, Australian National University, Canberra, ACT 0200, Australia;
E-Mail: juliet.pietsch@anu.edu.au

Abstract

The sociology of citizenship is concerned with the social and economic conditions of citizens of a national community. Drawing on T. H. Marshall's contribution to the theory of social citizenship this article argues that some groups of migrants and ethnic minorities in Australia, particularly those from non-British and European Backgrounds, face a number of social and institutional barriers which prevent them from reaching their full potential as members of Australia's multicultural community. Evidence from the Australian Bureau of Statistics Census data shows different socioeconomic outcomes for migrants from British and European backgrounds compared with migrants from Asian backgrounds, despite having similar educational qualifications and length of time living in Australia. As such, it is argued that achieving social membership and inclusion continues to be a struggle for particular groups of migrants. A deeper commitment to the core principles of citizenship that is beyond mere notions of formal equality is needed if Australia is to address this important social issue.

Keywords

Australia; inclusion; migrants; social citizenship; socioeconomic status

Issue

This article is part of the issue "International Migration and Ethnic Integration", edited by Yaojun Li (University of Manchester, UK) and Anthony Heath (University of Oxford, UK).

---

1. Introduction

Social theorists have long been interested in the concept of citizenship which links individual entitlement on the one hand and ideas and attachment to a particular community on the other (Kymlicka & Norman, 1994). Debates about citizenship and multiculturalism are often sparked by social or political events or crises, which bring to the fore perceptions of weak ties among a particular racial, ethnic or religious group to the nation. For example, following the 9/11 terrorist attacks in the United States and Europe's 2015 refugee crisis, numerous political leaders around the world have denounced multiculturalism as a failure, and have instead emphasised the need for migrants to demonstrate their loyalty to the laws, values and traditions of their country. The resurgence of support for far-right wing parties and other populist representatives in the West demonstrates the growing amount of pressure on governments to withdraw from progressive and inclusive social citizenship policies for new migrants.

In order to enjoy full membership, members of migrant and ethnic minority groups have frequently had to adopt the majority culture through societal pressures to assimilate. Some groups have found this easier than others due to cross-cultural differences in terms of language, culture, political background and religion. Drawing on theories of social citizenship, this research shows that since the 1990s there is evidence of differential socioeconomic outcomes for European and non-European migrants in Australia, particularly in terms of income and professional employment opportunities relative to education. In doing so, this research looks at whether 'race' in the form of being 'white' or 'non-white' is a barrier to social inclusion. Stephen Castles (2000, p. 41) shows that through a process of social segmentation and social exclusion, various migrant and ethnic minority groups tend to remain in disadvantaged labour market positions, which is then passed on to subsequent generations. It is therefore necessary to look at practices of systematic social exclusion, which can lead to social segmentation and differential outcomes for particular groups of migrants and ethnic minority groups.

In Australia, at first glance, the absence of migrants from non-British or European backgrounds is noticeable in leadership positions within national institutions and organisations, suggesting that, even though Australia has adopted a multicultural citizenship model, attitudes of racial and ethnic superiority may continue to pervade Australian institutions and organisations. For example, according to Soutphommasane (2014), the poor representation of Asian Australians in federal politics "appears to replicate a pattern of invisibility that exists within Australian culture". This pattern of invisibility similarly exists in other institutions and organisations, particularly at senior levels where important decisions are often made. While nearly 14 percent of Australians come from non-British and European backgrounds, such cultural diversity is not represented within the senior leadership positions in Australian institutions and organisations (AHRC, 2016). This can have flow-on effects in terms of the social exclusion of citizens from migrant backgrounds in shaping the future of Australia. To find out whether social bias and discrimination might be playing a role, using Australian Bureau of Statistics (ABS) Census data between 1970 and 2011, this article examines whether there are any differences in the socioeconomic outcomes of groups that have similar levels of education and have lived in Australia for a similar length of time. First, this article examines theories of social citizenship as a framework for the empirical analysis of the ABS Census data.

2. Theoretical Background

The social construction of citizenship in Western democracies which predominantly focuses on the legal and political responsibilities of citizens frequently overlooks the obligations that states have towards their citizens in terms of providing an inclusive social citizenship that addresses the reality of racial inequality and social class. British Sociologist T. H. Marshall divided citizenship into three dimensions, namely *civic*, *political* and *social* rights (Marshall, 1950, 1977, 1981). Social rights were institutionalised in the form of the Welfare state and included a range of social entitlements such as education, health, employment benefits and employment opportunities (Esping-Andersen, 1990). In the incorporation of social rights within the Welfare state, it was argued that citizenship could alter patterns of social inequality. In developing the work of T. H. Marshall, sociologists have since redefined citizenship "as a set of social practices which define the nature of social membership" (Turner, 1993, p. 4). While there are many criticisms of T. H. Marshall's understandings of citizenship such as the fact that it is historically and culturally specific to Western cultures and framed solely within the confines of the nation-state (Barbalet, 1988; Hindess, 1993; Janoski, 1998; King & Waldron, 1988; Ong, 2005), there is no doubt that in Western democracies groups of citizens with civil and political rights are denied basic social rights such as equality of opportunity, employment and income due to various forms of discrimination and racial prejudice.

In culturally plural societies, migrants and ethnic minorities struggle to attain full membership and social inclusion. Talcott Parsons originally defined social inclusion as the process by which previously excluded groups attain full citizenship or membership in a society (Parsons, 1994, p. 145). Since then, studies have shown a multidimensional approach to understanding full membership and social inclusion. The World Bank (2007) for instance defines social inclusion in terms of financial, physical, human and social capital and emotional and functional satisfaction. Other studies define social inclusion in terms of material resources, social relations, civic activities, basic services, neighbourhood inclusion, achievement, participation and social connection (Greef, Verté, & Segers, 2015; Ogg, 2005). Migrants and ethnic minorities can be denied social inclusion due to their cultural background, linguistic differences, political or religious background or the distance between their country of origin and host country (see Dahlstedt & Bevelander, 2010). This article further looks at social inclusion in terms of income and occupational status opportunities, both of which can impact on leadership opportunities and levels of autonomy within an organisation. To be a full member in society, migrants and ethnic minorities need to have opportunities to not only participate in society but also shape the future of a society by utilising their various strengths and skills.

One of the significant barriers for migrants and ethnic minorities is the growing demands for linguistic assimilation in terms of English or national language proficiency, accent, style and pronunciation which some researchers have viewed as a form of racial discrimination (Colic-Peisker, 2005; Creese & Kambere, 2003; Hill, 2008; Piller & Takahashi, 2011). In fact, Piller and Takahashi (2011, p. 371) observe that "social inclusion policies are often blind to the ways in which language proficiency and language ideologies mediate social inclusion in linguistically diverse societies". For instance, in Australia and in other diverse multicultural societies, migrants and ethnic minorities wishing to attain citizenship must demonstrate English language proficiency in the form of passing a citizenship test written in English. This is just one hurdle towards full membership. In applying for a professional job or a position of leadership, some groups of migrants and ethnic minorities also need to overcome social bias due to their place of birth, skin colour, distinctive accent, etc. While place of birth is not always known, visible and audible markers such as skin colour and accent are often used as replacements for social bias (see McCrone & Bechhofer, 2008). For those with minority group ascribed characteristics, social inclusion and full membership may become an unreachable goal unless the majority accepts various forms of ascribed cultural and linguistic diversity as equal.

3. Citizenship and Social Inclusion

Together with formal modes of citizenship, socioeconomic achievement relative to opportunity is a necessity for the social inclusion and full membership of migrant and ethnic minority groups. Despite detecting a general pattern of upward socioeconomic mobility over time, research finds that some migrant and ethnic minority groups are less likely to experience upward socioeconomic mobility over time than others, thus providing evidence of social exclusion. In fact, in some cases, they may experience downward mobility because of a number of social and institutional barriers (Basran & Zong, 1998). A number of reasons emerge from research into the experience of migrants to explain these disparities. First, some areas of the labour market could be influenced by direct and indirect discrimination (Fox, 2013). In these areas, dominant groups in society exclude other groups from positions of influence. Weber (1978) referred to this phenomenon as a form of 'social closure', whereby one group excludes the other from scarce resources, and in doing so, is able to maintain the dominant group's privilege and social position.

Research evidence suggests that across Western migrant societies, race and birthplace origins can have an effect on whether or not some groups will experience upward socioeconomic mobility (Bauder, 2003; Frank, 2013; Valtonen, 2001; Weedon, 2002). This has been shown to be the case for 'non-white' ethnic minorities who, despite having very high levels of education, are particularly vulnerable to social exclusion. For example, with an overall shift from unskilled to skilled migration, higher levels of socioeconomic status as well as access to professional and managerial occupations are to be expected among first-generation migrants, thus negating the traditional pattern of overall income increase in later generations. However, this assumes that new skilled migrants do not face direct or indirect discrimination in the workforce. Inglis and Model (2007) find that, in contrast to people with European ancestry, 'non-white' migrants and ethnic minorities often remain disadvantaged for several generations. To examine whether there is a pattern of this occurring in Australia, in the next section this article examines the socioeconomic outcomes of Asian and European migrants with similar education backgrounds and length of stay in Australia. All things being equal, it is expected that both groups should have similar outcomes in terms of income and occupational status.

4. Diverse Entry Outcomes for Skilled Migrants

First, it is important to look at overall migration patterns in Australia in order to establish a contextual understanding of the diverse socioeconomic outcomes of different groups of migrants in Australia. Results from the ABS Census in Figure 1 show that over time the patterns of migration from the United Kingdom have remained fairly steady, with very little change over four decades of expansive immigration programs. However, as a proportion of the overseas-born population, their numbers have steadily declined from 41 percent of the overseas-born population in 1976 to 21 percent in 2011. There has been a similar pattern of steady immigration from other parts of Europe. However, since the 1970s, the proportion of Australia's overseas-born population in each major European group has declined. The sharpest declines in the proportion of the overseas-born population have been from the United Kingdom, Italy, former Yugoslavia, and Greece. For example, the Italian-born now comprise three percent of the Australian overseas-born population, compared with 11 percent in 1971; the Greek-born now comprise two percent of the Australian overseas-born population, compared with six percent in 1976. The decline in European migration is partly attributed to economic growth in Europe, which has rendered emigration to Australia less attractive than in the immediate post-war period.

The pattern of migration of people born in Asian countries has moved in the opposite direction. For instance, Figure 1 shows the exponential rise in numbers of migrants from Asian countries. Much of this increase can be attributed to the rapid growth in migration from China and India. As a proportion of Australia's overseas-born population, the Chinese-born population has increased from less than one percent in 1971 to six percent in 2011 (see Table 1). One of the contributing factors to this increase was the Australian government's decision to grant temporary and permanent residency status to students from the People's Republic of China in the aftermath of the Tiananmen Square protests of 1989, which then brought their family members to Australia through the family reunion scheme. The Indian-born population has similarly increased from one percent of the overseas-born population in 1971 to six percent in 2011 (see Table 1). Overall, in 2011 migrants born in Asian countries comprised 37 percent of the overseas-born population of Australia, not far behind the numbers of European-born migrants, who made up 40 percent of the overseas-born population. In Table 1 it can be seen that within the Asian group the top source countries are China, India, Vietnam, Philippines and Malaysia.

In terms of Australia's population more broadly, the results in Table 2 show the overall birthplace origins of the Australian population. The findings show that Australia's migrant population is much more diverse than in the 1970s when the majority of migrants came from the United Kingdom or countries in Europe. In recent times, Australia continues to accept significant numbers of United Kingdom and European migrants, however, there has been a significant increase in the numbers of migrants from Asia (up to 9.2 percent in 2011) and other

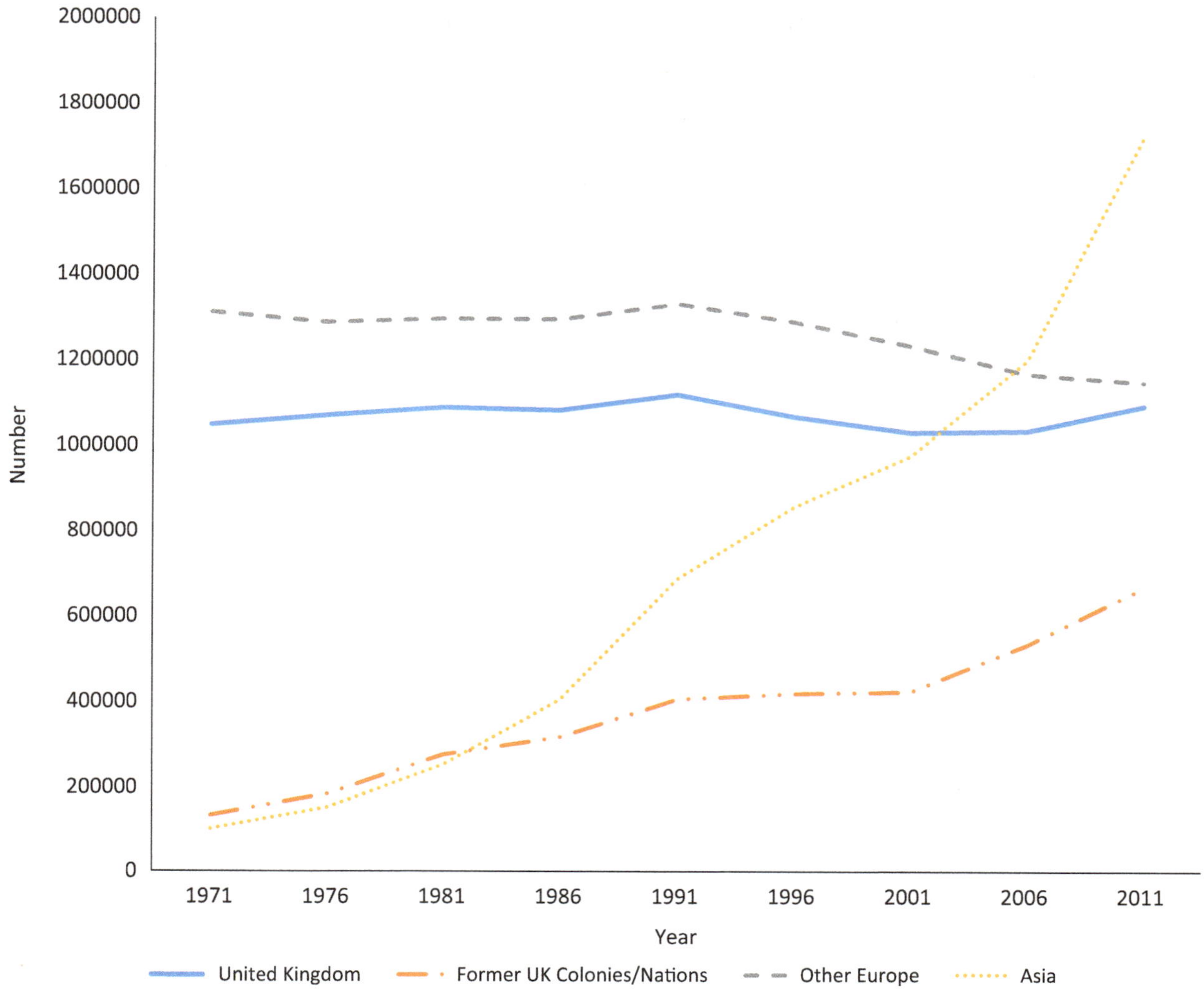

Figure 1. Population of migrants born overseas in Australia, 1971–2011.

Table 1. Population of migrants to Australia from main source countries in Asia, percent, 1971–2011.

	1971	1976	1981	1986	1991	1996	2001	2006	2011
China	0.7	0.7	0.9	1.2	2.1	2.9	3.5	4.7	6.0
India	1.1	1.4	1.4	1.5	1.6	2.0	2.3	3.3	5.6
Vietnam	0.0	0.1	1.4	2.6	3.3	3.9	3.8	3.6	3.5
Philippines	0.1	0.2	0.5	1.0	2.0	2.4	2.5	2.7	3.2
Malaysia	0.6	0.8	1.1	1.5	1.9	2.0	1.9	2.1	2.2
Sri Lanka	0.0	0.6	0.6	0.7	1.0	1.2	1.3	1.4	1.6
Korea	0.0	0.1	0.2	0.3	0.6	0.8	0.9	1.2	1.4
Indonesia	0.3	0.4	0.4	0.5	0.9	1.1	1.1	1.2	1.2
Total Overseas-Born Population (n)	2,578,963	2,608,109	3,003,798	3,247,423	3,756,441	3,876,709	4,105,637	4,416,029	5,294,150

Source: ABS (2011a).

regions including the Middle East, Africa and the Pacific Islands (up to 7.4 percent in 2011).

So far, the Census data shows that Australia's racial and ethnic make-up is gradually changing over time with an increase in migrants from non-British and European backgrounds, many of whom might be classified as 'non-white' in North American or British classification systems. In Australia, it is difficult to accurately measure the numbers of 'non-white' migrants and ethnic minorities beyond the first-generation because in the Census the Australian-born are only asked if they have parents born overseas and not where their parents come from.

Table 2. Birthplace origins of the Australian population, percent, 1971–2011.

	1971	1976	1981	1986	1991	1996	2001	2006	2011
Australia	79.8	80.6	78.2	77.6	75.5	74.5	72.6	70.9	69.8
United Kingdom	8.2	8.0	7.5	6.9	6.7	6.0	5.5	5.2	5.1
Former UK Colonies/ Nations	1.0	1.4	1.9	2.0	2.4	2.4	2.3	2.7	3.1
Other Europe	10.3	9.6	8.9	8.3	7.9	7.3	6.6	5.9	5.4
Asia	00.8	01.1	01.7	02.6	04.1	04.8	05.2	06.1	09.2
Other			01.9	02.5	03.4	05.0	07.8	09.2	07.4
Total Australian population (n)	(12,755,620)	(13,437,725)	(14,576,294)	(15,602,198)	(16,850,288)	(17,752,874)	(18,769,240)	(19,855,287)	(21,507,719)

Source: ABS (2011a).

However, the Census includes a question about ancestry among the Australian-born and those born overseas. In looking at the results in Table 3, the figures show that 0.9 percent of the Australian-born and up to 33 percent of first-generation migrants identify as having an Asian, Middle Eastern or Sub-Saharan African ancestry of which most (though not all) could be classified as 'non-white'. Overall, the Asian pan-ethnic group represent the fastest growing 'non-white' group in Australia. As such the remainder of this article focuses on the experiences of Asian migrants in particular and compares their experiences with migrants from the United Kingdom and other parts of Europe, of whom the majority in Australia have British or European ancestry.

In order to demonstrate the diverse socioeconomic outcomes among European and Asian first-generation migrants in Australia, the following results present comparisons in education, income and occupation of three separate migrant cohorts from the United Kingdom, Europe and Asia. Table 4 reveals that a higher proportion of migrants from Asia than from other countries hold a bachelor or postgraduate degree, which could be attributed to the fact that a greater proportion of recent migrants to Australia are arriving as highly skilled migrants who have met the requirements of the competitive points system. Nevertheless, even when the education levels of Asian migrants before the 1990s are taken into account, it is apparent that migrants from Asia are more likely to hold a university qualification than migrants from other countries. More than 28 percent of Asian migrants within each of the migration waves other than Vietnam hold a university qualification (see Table 4). A smaller proportion of migrants born in the United Kingdom and Europe arriving in the migration wave before the 1990s hold university degrees.

Given the higher levels of educational attainment among migrants born in Asia, one would expect there to be a higher proportion of Asian migrants than European migrants in high-income professional occupations, particularly among those groups who arrived before the 1990s. However, the findings in Figure 2 show diverse outcomes for two groups from different regions with a

Table 3. First mentioned ancestry origins of the Australian population, 2011.

	Born in Australia		Born Overseas	
	(n)	(%)	(n)	(%)
Oceanian	(4,592,267)	37.5	(581,983)	7.4
North-West European	(6,774,794)	55.3	(3,051,313)	38.6
Southern and Eastern European	(467,499)	3.8	(1,330,608)	16.8
North African and Middle Eastern	(43,850)	00.4	(409,155)	05.2
South-East Asian	(7,285)	00.1	(525,321)	06.6
North-East Asian	(35,675)	00.3	(894,412)	11.3
Southern and Central Asian	(7,966)	00.1	(627,908)	07.9
Peoples of the Americas	(7,049)	0.1	(118,184)	1.5
Sub-Saharan African	(3,560)	00.0	(149,927)	01.9
Other	(16,203)	0.1	(45,481)	0.6
Not Stated	(291,698)	2.4	(166,895)	2.1
Total overseas born (n)	(12,247,846)	100	(7,901,187)	100

Source: ABS (2011a).

Table 4. Migrants in Australia with a university education, by year of arrival, percent.

	<1990s	1991–2000	2001–2011	(n)
UK				
England	20	30	22	(125,778)
Scotland	18	32	27	(16,388)
Wales	23	36	31	(4,692)
Northern Ireland	21	42	34	(3,366)
Other Europe				
Italy	5	21	24	(7,300)
Former Yugoslavia	6	17	12	(12,493)
Germany	14	28	26	(11,016)
Greece	5	11	9	(4,328)
Netherland	12	31	23	(7,061)
Ireland	22	37	29	(8,535)
Poland	23	37	48	(10,655)
Malta	4	14	12	(1,494)
Asia				
China	28	41	48	(54,866)
India	36	58	60	(66,376)
Vietnam	20	13	17	(25,532)
Philippines	38	34	36	(40,418)
Malaysia	48	47	38	(25,815)
Sri Lanka	34	40	40	(19,974)
Korea	40	42	32	(10,901)
Indonesia	31	44	37	(8,445)

Source: ABS (2011a).

similar education and period of arrival in Australia indicating that for some groups there might be barriers to reaching their full potential. In terms of income, for those who have lived in Australia since before the 1990s, the outcomes for Asian migrants and migrants from the United Kingdom are fairly similar, showing that over time Asian migrants eventually catch up to other groups and even overtake other groups such as those from other parts of Europe.

For new migrants, the story is very different. New migrants from the United Kingdom tend to receive a much greater return on their education than new migrants from Asia. Over 30 percent of recent arrivals from the United Kingdom are employed in the highest-income bracket. The proportions of new migrants from Asian countries in the highest-income bracket are much smaller, with only 14 percent of Asian migrants in the highest-income bracket. It is possible that the differences in entry earnings capacity among recent Asian cohorts could be explained by the heightened emphasis on English language ability. However, given that skilled migrants from Asia, especially those with a university education, are usually fluent in English, this is less likely to explain the variation. Instead, it is more likely that other factors could be playing a role such as skin colour, accent or simply employer-based discrimination.

Another explanation might be related to the fact that many Asian migrants are students without Australian citizenship. However, while the majority of overseas students from Asia do not have citizenship, the results in Figure 2 only look at the experiences of migrants with citizenship. In looking at whether there are differences among those with citizenship and those without citizenship, the results in Figure 3 show that a higher proportion of new migrants from the United Kingdom and other parts of Europe earn a high income compared to the Asian cohort. Only six percent of recent arrivals from Asia without citizenship earn a high income compared to 28 percent of those from the United Kingdom and 19 percent of those from other parts of Europe. Asian migrants who arrived before 1990 end up doing comparatively better but it appears that it takes longer to achieve similar or better outcomes in terms of income status than their European counterparts.

The differences in outcomes might be explained by a number of other factors. For example, it is possible that the earlier cohort of Asian migrants to Australia who arrived before 1990 came from different origin countries than those who have arrived later. For example, we might expect those from English-speaking Hong Kong to have better outcomes than recent arrivals from non-English speaking countries in Asia. There are also likely to be differences among those from English-speaking Northern European countries and those from non-English speaking European countries in Southern and Eastern Europe. To explore this in a more detail, a re-

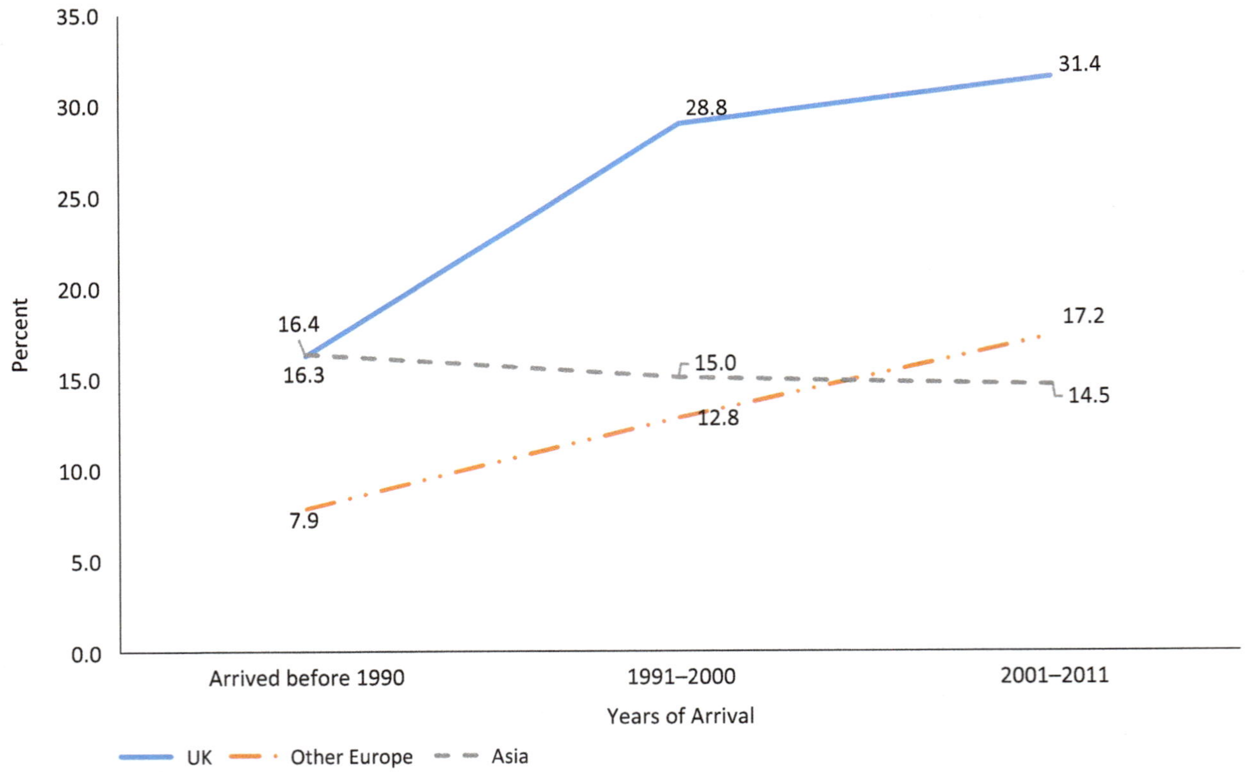

Figure 2. Percentage of migrant citizens on high incomes by year of arrival.

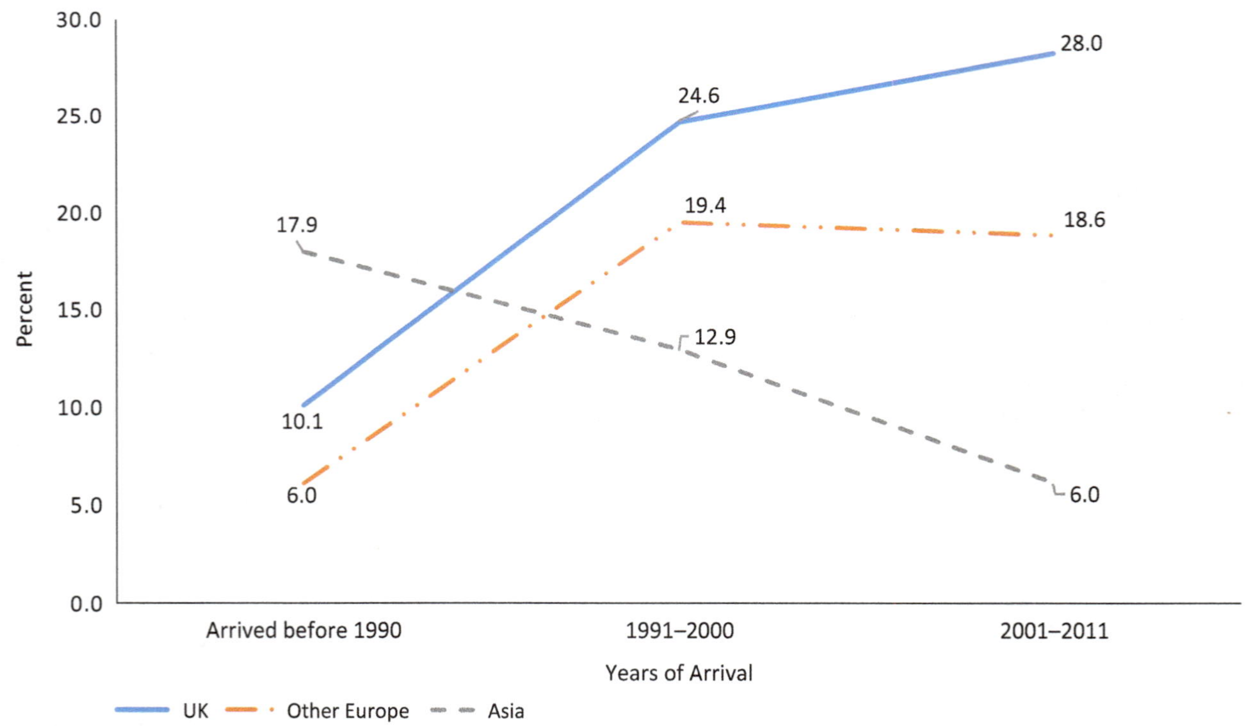

Figure 3. Percentage of migrants without citizenship on high incomes by year of arrival.

gression analysis is conducted to control for background factors such as English proficiency, timing of arrival, age, education, gender and citizenship status to determine whether there is a correlation between country origins and income status.

Table 5 draws on a sample from the 2011 Census, which is provided in the confidential unit record files (CURFs) and is based on a one percent sample of the Census population. The effects of country origins and timing of arrival is clearly evident in the multivariate results shown in Table 5. In terms of birthplace, migrants from South Asia and North-East Asia, as well as Southern and Eastern Europe, are less likely to earn a high income compared to migrants from the United Kingdom and Northern Europe. Newer arrivals are also less likely to earn a high income compared to migrants from previous migration waves, as the earlier findings demonstrate.

Up to 45 percent of the total sample of South Asians and 70 percent of new arrivals from South Asia have completed a bachelor degree or higher such as a postgraduate degree. This compares with 38 percent of the total sample of North-East Asians and 70 percent of new arrivals from North-East Asia. Among the total sample of Northern Europeans, only 24 percent have completed a bachelor degree or higher and among the new arrivals from the Northern Europe only 55 percent have completed a bachelor degree or higher. This is significantly less than the proportions of those with a bachelor degree or higher from South Asia and North-East Asia (70 percent). With such differences in the percentage of those with university education qualifications between those from Asia and those from Northern Europe, one would expect a positive relationship between Asian country origins and income status. Instead, the opposite is the case, indicating the possible existence of racial or ethnic discrimination.

Table 5. OLS Regression Model estimating effects of origins and background on income, Census, 2011.

	(B)	**(β)**	**Sig.**
Constant	2.61		0.00
Birthplace			
South-Asia	**−0.68**	**−0.09**	**0.00**
North-East Asia	**−1.22**	**−0.16**	**0.00**
South-East Asia	−0.04	−0.01	0.86
Southern and Eastern Europe	**−0.67**	**−0.07**	**0.00**
Ancestry of Parent 1			
Southern and Central Asia	0.27	0.04	0.14
North-East Asia	0.26	0.04	0.26
South-East Asia	0.39	0.04	0.10
Southern and Eastern Europe	**0.35**	**0.04**	**0.03**
Ancestry of Parent 2			
Southern and Central Asia	−0.17	−0.01	0.56
North-East Asia	−0.38	−0.01	0.33
South-East Asia	**0.68**	**0.02**	**0.01**
Southern and Eastern Europe	−0.07	0.00	0.76
Language Spoken at Home			
Southern Asian Languages	**0.44**	**0.06**	**0.03**
Eastern Asian Languages	0.59	0.08	0.04
South-East Asian Languages	−0.10	−0.01	0.73
Southern European languages	**0.55**	**0.07**	**0.00**
Northern European Languages	**1.28**	**0.10**	**0.00**
English Proficiency			
Very Well or Well	**1.44**	**0.12**	**0.00**
Timing of Arrival			
Arrived 2000 or before	**1.02**	**0.17**	**0.00**
Arrived 2001–2005	**0.71**	**0.08**	**0.00**
Background			
Age	**−0.09**	**−0.09**	**0.00**
Education	**0.53**	**0.23**	**0.00**
Gender	**1.37**	**0.22**	**0.00**
Citizenship	**0.84**	**0.13**	**0.00**
Adjusted R^2	0.18		
N	(11,979)		

Source: ABS (2011b). (N = 11,979). B: Unstandardised regression coefficient. β: Standardised regression coefficient. See Table A.1 in the Appendix for coding of variables.

In terms of occupational status, Table 6 finds a similar outcome. Given that a higher percentage of migrants from Asia in the CURF sample have a university education compared to migrants from Northern Europe, one might expect a higher percentage of migrants from Asia to be employed in a professional occupation. However, the findings in Table 6 indicate the opposite to be the case with a negative relationship between South Asian and North-East Asian birthplace origins and professional occupation status. For instance, the odds ratios (Exp (B)) are less than 1, showing that those from South Asia and North-East Asia are less likely to be employed as professionals compared to those from Northern Europe, even after controlling for language spoken at home, English proficiency, timing of arrival, education, age and citizenship status. The odds ratios are also highly significant (sig.=.000). This pattern suggests that migrants from the United Kingdom and Northern Europe, despite having lower levels of educational attainment, are more easily able to move into high-income professional occupations shortly after their arrival in Australia.

5. Discussion

The findings presented reveal that there are several barriers to a high income and occupational status among new

Table 6. Logistic Regression Model estimating effects of origins and background on occupation, census, 2011.

	B	SE	Sig.	Exp(B)
Constant	−4.06	0.21	0.00	0.02
Birthplace				
South-Asia	**−0.93**	**0.14**	**0.00**	**0.40**
North-East Asia	**−0.70**	**0.23**	**0.00**	**0.50**
South-East Asia	−0.12	0.22	0.57	0.88
Southern and Eastern Europe	−0.08	0.15	0.59	0.92
Ancestry of Parent 1				
Southern and Central Asia	**0.53**	**0.17**	**0.00**	**1.70**
North-East Asia	0.24	0.21	0.26	1.27
South-East Asia	0.08	0.23	0.73	1.08
Southern and Eastern Europe	−0.05	0.16	0.75	0.95
Ancestry of Parent 2				
Southern and Central Asia	0.00	0.29	0.99	1.00
North-East Asia	−0.13	0.37	0.73	0.88
South-East Asia	0.07	0.24	0.79	1.07
Southern and Eastern Europe	−0.43	0.23	0.06	0.65
Language Spoken at Home				
Southern Asian Languages	0.03	0.19	0.89	1.03
Eastern Asian Languages	**0.61**	**0.26**	**0.02**	**1.84**
South-East Asian Languages	−0.26	0.26	0.32	0.77
Southern European languages	**0.26**	**0.12**	**0.03**	**1.30**
Northern European Languages	**0.81**	**0.13**	**0.00**	**2.25**
English Proficiency				
Very Well or Well	**1.30**	**0.18**	**0.00**	**3.66**
Timing of Arrival				
Arrived 2000 or before	**0.32**	**0.09**	**0.00**	**1.37**
Arrived 2001–2005	**0.21**	**0.08**	**0.01**	**1.24**
Background				
Age	0.02	0.01	0.11	1.02
Education	**0.70**	**0.02**	**0.00**	**2.02**
Gender	**0.14**	**0.05**	**0.01**	**1.15**
Citizenship	**0.27**	**0.07**	**0.00**	**1.31**
Nagelkerke R square	0.25			
N	8,386			

Source: ABS (2011b). (N =11,979). B: Coefficient for the Constant. SE: Standard Error Around the Constant. Exp(B): Odds Ratio. See Table A.1 in the Appendix for coding of variables.

migrant groups, even for those groups with high levels of education, which result in ethnic labour market segmentation and social exclusion. In terms of income, new migrants from Asia in Australia are less likely to enter professional or managerial positions with a high income than new migrants from Northern Europe. Because the ABS Census survey does not ask whether migrants obtained their educational qualifications in Australia, it is difficult to determine whether there is an issue with the recognition of overseas qualifications or whether racial and ethnic discrimination is affecting the socioeconomic outcomes of migrant groups.

Research in Canada has shown that employers in Canada tend to favour migrants from English-speaking countries with comparable training systems (Hawthorne, 2007). Consequently, 'non-white' ethnic minorities from Asia often find that their skills are either not recognised or devalued. A similar phenomenon occurs in Australia, given that the qualifications and requirements to work in Australia depend on the type of occupation. Assessing overseas qualifications for employment purposes is usually a separate process to applying for a job where, as in all occupations, the employer decides whom they will employ. This tends to ensure that, as in Canada, employers can devalue legitimate qualifications and skills (i.e. human capital) held by 'non-white' migrant and ethnic minorities from Asia.

Comparative research has shown that employers tend to be less inclined to hire a migrant than a locally-born candidate (Heath & Cheung, 2007; Lindbeck & Snower, 1988). These forms of discrimination are thought to originate from the idea that people generally identify more with people who look like themselves (Lancee, 2012). For example, in his seminal work, Becker (1971) argued that 'personal preferences' or 'tastes for discrimination' on the part of employers and organisations were the main reasons for labour market discrimination.

In a 2012 study on discrimination in Australia, Booth et al. compared employer attitudes to Anglo Saxon Australians with employer attitudes to Indigenous Australians, Italian Australians, Middle Eastern Australians and Chinese Australians (Booth, Leigh, & Varganova, 2012). As part of their experiment, the researchers applied for entry-level jobs using distinctively Anglo Saxon, Indigenous Australian, Italian, Chinese and Middle Eastern surnames. Their study found that applications submitted to employers with Anglo Saxon names had a mean callback rate from potential employers of 35 percent. Applications with Italian surnames had a slightly lower callback rate of 32 percent, and those with distinctively Chinese and Middle Eastern surnames had mean callback rates of 21 and 22 percent respectively. Chinese applicants in Sydney hoping to get an interview would have to put in 92 percent more applications than applicants with Anglo Saxon names (Booth et al., 2012, p. 567). Racial and ethnic discrimination, therefore, may prevent highly educated migrants from gaining professional employment opportunities with high incomes and potential leadership opportunities.

Another approach to explain the labour market differences found in this research is to consider social capital theory, which implies that migrants who are equipped with social resources (i.e. social networks and resources of others) perform better in the labour market (Aguilera, 2002; Flap & Völker, 2004; Franzen & Hangartner, 2006). Social capital in terms of social networks and the resources of others provides an important gateway into the labour market. One way to further understand the influence of social capital is by distinguishing between 'bonding' and 'bridging' capital (Leonard & Onyx, 2003; Putnam, 2000; Schuller, 2007; Woolcock & Narayan, 2000). Bonding capital refers to social networks formed 'within' groups and bridging capital refers to social networks formed 'between' groups. According to Lancee (2012, p. 159), the acquisition of bridging capital tends to result in higher income and occupational status whereas the acquisition of bonding capital (such as those formed by established family or co-ethnic networks) does not.

On the surface, it seems that migrants from countries with similar cultural, political and historical ties to Australia's 'white' British and Northern European majority are more quickly and more easily able to transfer their education, skills and experience. This may partly explain why Asian migrants face greater challenges in gaining meaningful employment in line with their educational qualifications, skills, and experience in the initial period after their arrival. It does not, however, explain the whole picture. This is because many Asian migrants have in fact gained appropriate qualifications since arriving in Australia, or hold quality qualifications from internationally recognised higher education institutions in Western democracies. Alternatively, many have been successfully awarded qualification recognition by the Australian government or a peak industry body for holding one or more qualifications from internationally recognised higher education institutions within their own country. However, as mentioned, the requirements to work in Australia depend on the occupation and local employer organisations. The employer alone decides whom they will employ, regardless of the applicant's qualifications and skills. This leaves new migrants highly vulnerable to the attitudes of employers.

In summary, the findings presented suggest that there are a number of barriers to a high socioeconomic status among new migrant groups, even for those groups with high levels of education, which result in racial and ethnic labour market segmentation. In terms of income, new migrants from Asia in Australia are less likely to enter professional and managerial positions with a high income than new migrants from the United Kingdom. Because the ABS Census survey does not ask whether citizens obtained their educational qualifications in Australia, it is difficult to determine whether there is an issue with the employer recognition of foreign qualifications or whether racial and ethnic discrimination is affecting the socioeconomic outcomes of migrant groups. However, the results do suggest that racial and ethnic discrimination may prevent highly educated migrants from non-British or European backgrounds from gaining professional employment opportunities with high incomes and potential leadership opportunities. It is therefore important to ensure that university-educated and experienced non-British and European migrants are not denied full membership in terms of social citizenship and are able to contribute meaningfully within Australia's leadership ranks and the future direction of the country.

Acknowledgments

The author would like to thank A/Prof. Christine Inglis (University of Sydney), Emeritus Prof. Anthony Heath (University of Oxford) and the anonymous reviewers for their helpful comments and advice on sections of this paper.

Conflict of Interests

The author declares no conflict of interests.

References

Australian Bureau of Statistics. (2011a). *Australian Census 2011*. Canberra: Australian Bureau of Statistics.

Australian Bureau of Statistics. (2011b). *Australian Census 2011*. Expanded Confidentialised Unit Record File (CURF), Remote Access Data Laboratory (RADL). Findings based on use of ABS Microdata.

Aguilera, M. (2002). The impact of social capital on labor force participation: Evidence from the 2000 social capital benchmark survey. *Social Science Quarterly*, *83*(3), 854–874.

AHRC. (2016). *Leading for change: A blueprint for cultural diversity and inclusive leadership*. Sydney. Retrieved from https://www.humanrights.gov.au/our-work/race-discrimination/publications/leading-change-blueprint-cultural-diversity-and-inclusive

Barbalet, J. (1988). *Citizenship*. Milton Keynes: Open University Press.

Basran, G., & Zong, L. (1998). Devaluation of foreign credentials as perceived by visible minority professional immigrants. *Canadian Ethnic Studies*, *30*(3), 6–22.

Bauder, H. (2003). 'Brain abuse'or devaluation of immigrant labor in Canada. *Antipode*, *35*(4), 699–717.

Becker, G. (1971). *The economics of discrimination* (2nd ed.). Chicago: Chicago University Press.

Booth, A., Leigh, A., & Varganova, E. (2012). Does ethnic discrimination vary across minority groups? Evidence from a field experiment. *Oxford Bulletin of Economics and Statistics*, *74*(4), 547–573.

Castles, S. (2000). Underclass or exclusion: Social citizenship for ethnic minorities. In E. Vasta (Ed.), *Citizenship, community and democracy* (pp. 22–44). London: Palgrave Macmillan.

Colic-Peisker, V. (2005). 'At least you're the right colour': Identity and social inclusion of Bosnian refugees in Australia. *Journal of Ethnic and Migration Studies*, *31*(4), 615–638.

Creese, G., & Kambere, E. N. (2003). What colour is your English? *Canadian Review of Sociology and Anthropology*, *40*(5), 565–573.

Dahlstedt, I., & Bevelander, P. (2010). General versus vocational education and employment integration of migrants in Sweden. *Journal of Migrant and Refugee Studies*, *8*(2), 158–192.

Esping-Andersen, G. (1990). *The three worlds of welfare capitalism*. Cambridge: Polity Press.

Flap, H., & Völker, B. 2004. *Creation and returns of social capital*. London: Routledge.

Frank, K. (2013). Immigrant employment success in Canada: Examining the rate of obtaining a job match. *International Migration Review*, *47*(1), 76–105.

Franzen, A., & Hangartner, D. (2006). Social networks and labor market outcomes: The non-monetary benefits of social capital. *European Sociological Review*, *22*(4), 353–368.

Fox, J. (2013). The uses of racism: Whitewashing new Europeans in the UK. *Ethnic and Racial Studies*, *36*(11), 1871–1889.

Greef, M. D., Verté, D., & Segers, M. (2015). Differential outcomes of adult education on adult learners' increase in social inclusion. *Studies in Continuing Education*, *37*(1), 62–78.

Hawthorne, L. (2007). Foreign credentials recognition and assessment: An introduction. *Canadian Issues*, *Spring*, 3–13.

Heath, A., & Cheung, S. Y. (Eds.). (2007). *Unequal chances: Ethnic minorities in Western labour markets*. Oxford: Oxford University Press.

Hill, J. H. (2008). *The everyday language of white racism*. Malden, MA: Wiley-Blackwell.

Hindess, B. (1993). Citizenship in the modern West. In B. Turner (Ed.), *Citizenship and social theory* (pp. 19–36). London: SAGE Publications.

Inglis, C., & Model, S. (2007). Diversity and mobility in Australia. In A. Heath & S. Y. Cheung (Eds.), *Unequal chances: Ethnic minorities in Western labour markets* (pp. 45–103). Oxford and New York: Oxford University Press.

Janoski, T. (1998). *Citizenship and civil society*. Cambridge: Cambridge University Press.

King, D., & Waldron, J. (1988). Citizenship, social citizenship and the defence of welfare provision. *British Journal of Political Science*, *18*(4), 415–443.

Kymlicka, W., & Norman, W. (1994). Return of the citizen: A survey of recent work on citizenship theory. *Ethics*, *104*(2), 352–381.

Lancee, B. (2012). *Immigrant performance in the labour market: Bonding and bridging social capital*. Amsterdam: Amsterdam University Press.

Leonard, R., & Onyx, J. (2003). Networking through loose and strong ties: An Australian qualitative study. *Vol-*

untas: International Journal of Voluntary and Non-Profit Organizations, *14*(2), 189–203.

Lindbeck, A., & Snower, D. (1988). *The insider outsider theory of employment and unemployment*. Cambridge: The MIT Press.

Marshall, T. H. (1950). *Citizenship and social class and other essays*. Cambridge: Cambridge University Press.

Marshall, T. H. (1977). *Class, citizenship and social development*. Chicago and London: University of Chicago Press.

Marshall, T. H. (1981). *The right to welfare and other essays*. London: Heinemann.

McCrone, D., & Bechhofer, F. (2008). National identity and social inclusion. *Ethnic and Racial Studies*, *31*(7), 1245–1266.

Ogg, J. (2005). Social exclusion and insecurity among older europeans: The influence of welfare regimes. *Ageing & Society*, *25*(1), 69–90.

Ong, A. (2005). Citizenship. In D. Nugent & J. Vincent (Eds.), *A companion to the anthropology of politics* (pp. 55–68). Oxford: Blackwell.

Parsons, T. (1994). Full citizenship for the Negro American: A sociological problem. In B. Turner & P. Hamilton (Eds.), *Citizenship: Critical concepts* (pp. 139–141). London and New York: Routledge.

Piller, I., & Takahashi, K. (2011). Linguistic diversity and social inclusion. *International Journal of Bilingual Education and Bilingualism*, *14*(4), 371–381.

Putnam, R. (2000). *Bowling alone: The collapse and revival of American community*. New York: Simon and Schuster.

Schuller, T. (2007). Reflections on the use of social capital. *Review of Social Economy*, *65*(1), 11–28.

Soutphommasane, T. (2014, July 11). Are Asian Australians Trapped under a bamboo ceiling? Opinion article. *The Guardian*. Retrieved from https://www.theguardian.com/commentisfree/2014/jul/11/are-asian-australians-trapped-under-a-bamboo-ceiling

The World Bank. (2007). *Social exclusion and the EU's social inclusion agenda: Paper prepared for the EU8 social inclusion study*. Retrieved from http://siteresources.worldbank.org/INTECONEVAL/Resources/SocialExclusionReviewDraft.pdf

Turner, B. (1993). *Citizenship and social theory*. London: SAGE Publications.

Valtonen, K. (2001). Cracking monopoly: Immigrants and employment in Finland. *Journal of Ethnic and Migration Studies*, *27*(3), 421–438.

Weber, M. (1978). *Economy and society: An outline of interpretive sociology*. Berkeley and Los Angeles: University of California Press.

Weedon, K. (2002). Why do some occupations pay more than others? Social closure and earnings inequality in the United States. *American Journal of Sociology*, *108*(1), 55–101.

Woolcock, M., & Narayan, D. (2000), Social capital: Implications for development theory, research and policy. *World Bank Research Observer*, *15*(2), 225–249.

About the Author

Juliet Pietsch is Associate Professor at the School of Politics and International Relations, Australian National University. Her research focus is in the area of public opinion, immigration politics and the political integration of migrants and ethnic minorities in Australia.

Appendix

Table A.1. Coding of variables for Table 5 and Table 6.

Variable	Scoring
Income	12-point scale, Low Income=1, High Income=12
Birthplace	
South-Asia	Southern and Central Asia=1, Else=0
North-East Asia	North-East Asia=1, Else=0
South-East Asia	South-East Asia=1, Else=0
Southern and Eastern Europe	Southern and Eastern Europe=1, Else=0
Reference Category is North-West Europe	
Ancestry of Parent 1 Southern and Central Asia	Southern and Central Asia=1, Else=0
North-East Asia	North-East Asia=1, Else=0
South-East Asia	South-East Asia=1, Else=0
Southern and Eastern Europe	Southern and Eastern Europe=1, Else=0
Reference Category is North-West Europe	
Ancestry of Parent 2	
Southern and Central Asia	Southern and Central Asia=1, Else=0
North-East Asia	North-East Asia=1, Else=0
South-East Asia	South-East Asia=1, Else=0
Southern and Eastern Europe	Southern and Eastern Europe=1, Else=0
Reference Category is North-West Europe	
Language Spoken at Home	
Southern Asian Languages	Southern Asian Languages=1, Else=0
Eastern Asian Languages	Eastern Asian Languages=1, Else=0
South-East Asian Languages	South-East Asian Languages=1, Else=0
Southern European languages	Southern European languages=1, Else=0
Northern European Languages	Northern European Languages excl. English=1, Else=0
Reference Category is English	
English Proficiency	
Very Well or Well	Very Well, Well=1, Not Well, Not at All=0
Timing of Arrival	
Arrived 2000 or before	Arrived 2000 or before, Else=0
Arrived 2001–2005	Arrived 2001–2005, Else=0
Reference Category is Arrived 2006–2011	
Background	
Age	1=18–24, 2=25–29, 3=30–34, 4=35–39, 5=40–44, 6=45–49, 7=50–54, 8=55–59, 9=60–64, 10=65–69, 11=70–74, 12=75-79, 13=80-84, 14=85 and over.
Education	Certificate=1, Diploma=2, Bachelor's Degree=3, Graduate Diploma=4, Postgraduate Degree=5.

3

"Too Smart to be Religious?" Discreet Seeking Amidst Religious Stigma at an Elite College

Kateri Boucher and Jaime Kucinskas *

Department of Sociology, Hamilton College, New York, NY 13323, USA; E-Mails: kboucher@hamilton.edu (K.B.), jkucinsk@hamilton.edu (J.K.)

* Corresponding author

Abstract
To advance understandings of how religion manifests in subtle, nuanced ways in secular institutions, we examine student religiosity and spirituality at an elite liberal arts school marked by a strong intellectual collective identity. Using mixed research methods, we examine how the college's structures and dominant culture influence students' religiosity and spirituality. Despite an institutional commitment to promoting students' self-exploration and inclusion of social "diversity," we found both campus structures and mainstream culture deterred open spiritual and religious exploration and identification. The structure of the college and its dominant secular, intellectual culture reinforced: (1) a widespread stigma against religious and spiritual expression, (2) a lack of dialogue about the sacred, (3) discreetness in exploring and adhering to sacred beliefs and practices, and (4) a large degree of religious and spiritual pluralism. Our findings additionally illustrate that early exposure to the campus culture's critical regard for religion had a long-lasting impact on students' religiosity. A majority of students kept their religious and spiritual expressions hidden and private; only a marginalized minority of students embraced their expressions publically. To increase students' comfort with religious and spiritual exploration, we propose that colleges foster intentional peer dialogues early in the college experience. Furthermore, we recommend that campus communities prioritize religious and spiritual literacy and respect.

Keywords
college; diversity; higher education; lived religion; religiosity; spirituality

Issue
This article is part of the issue "Religious Diversity and Social Inclusion", edited by Gary Bouma (Monash University, Australia).

---

1. Introduction

Members of elite academic institutions are more likely to express discomfort with religion than people at other schools (Jacobsen & Jacobsen, 2012). This is due in part to the historical secularization of higher education and science, and the perception among many at elite secular colleges and universities that science and religion are conflicting perspectives (Evans & Evans, 2008; Reuben, 1996; Smith, 2003). To better understand how people bring their religious lives into secular institutions in nuanced and often hidden ways, and to make "invisible religion" more visible in secular institutions (Cadge & Konieczny, 2014), we examine student religiosity and spirituality at an elite, secular liberal arts campus.[1] College is an important site to examine because, upon arrival at college, students must choose whether to embrace or leave behind religious identities learned from their families (Peek, 2005). College is also

[1] In keeping with Jacobsen and Jacobsen (2012), we characterize an "elite" school as one that is historically selective in its admissions, academically rigorous, and relatively well-known on a national level.

a time when many students become aware of how their religious and spiritual identities are regarded by wider society.

Our study contributes to a growing body of scholarship on college students' religiosity and spirituality (Jacobsen & Jacobsen, 2012; Pew Research Center, 2015; Smith & Snell, 2009). We expand upon extant scholarship by interviewing various constituencies on campus, including administrators, faculty, and students to best understand the multiple cultural and structural levels which influence college students' religious and spiritual exploration on a secular campus.

We find that, despite institutional aims to promote tolerance for diversity and inclusion of students with diverse identities, the College's structures and dominant culture stigmatizes and deters religiosity. As sociologists Elizabeth Armstrong and Laura Hamilton discuss in their (2014) book *Paying for the party*, colleges and universities have institutional pathways which shape student experiences. At the liberal arts college we examined, the most common pathway for students to take was a secular one, as reinforced by academic life and the party scene. In and out of the classroom, most students, faculty, and administrators united around a mission of intellectual rigor. In this context, religion was viewed as highly suspect and implicitly contradictory to the mainstream campus culture which valued being a rational intellectual and a critical thinker. Due to the stigmatization of religion and its marginalized place on campus, few students engaged in public religious and spiritual exploration and dialogue. Most students instead hid their religious and spiritual pursuits, and explored them privately in individualistic ways.

2. Student Religiosity at Secular Colleges and Universities

Student religiosity typically declines somewhat in college (Astin et al., 2004). Although students may disaffiliate from formal religious institutions during their college years, they tend to grow spiritually and may adopt spiritual identities (Astin, Astin, & Lindholm, 2011; Lane et al., 2013; Lindholm, 2006). However, there is a great deal of variation in student religiosity and spirituality based on the kind of college or university that students attend (Cherry, DeBerg, & Porterfield, 2001; Freitas, 2010). Students at faith-based colleges are immersed in a more pervasive religious culture, and they tend to engage in spiritual and religious practices more than those at secular institutions (Kuh & Gonyea, 2015). In contrast, many students at secular public universities are disengaged from religion (Freitas, 2010). Other scholarship identifies how liberal arts colleges can be pervaded by a "narrative of religious intolerance" (Lane et al., 2013).

Although much research has been conducted on student religiosity at religious schools (Bouman, DeGraaf, Mulder, & Marion, 2005; Ma, 2010; Richter, 2001), we know less about how students on secular campuses, and in particular at elite colleges and universities, explore religiosity and spirituality. Consequently, in this study we focus on how student religiosity and spirituality manifest at an elite secular liberal arts school, which we expect will have low religious tolerance (Lane et al., 2013; Jacobsen & Jacobsen, 2012).

Because studies of student religiosity in higher education fail to examine the complex, multi-level, cultural, and structural contexts that students are embedded in (Maryl & Oeur, 2009), we intentionally explore these factors. First, we examine how various constituencies, ranging from top administrators to students, view religion on campus. Second, we explore the extent to which religiosity is supported by the school and present in popular convening spaces. Lastly, we examine how students become aware of the overarching normative campus orientation toward religion, and the ways in which they consequently explore the sacred.

Based on the few studies that exist (e.g. Lane et al, 2013; Jacobsen & Jacobsen, 2012), we expect that a general sense of religious intolerance among the students will affect the degree to which they felt comfortable sharing their religious backgrounds, beliefs, and practices. We also expect students to experience difficulty in reconciling their public, intellectual identities with religious identities (Smith, 2003; Speers, 2008).

3. Data Collection and Research Methods

This project began in a Sociology of Religion course taught by one of the authors. The class raised questions about student religiosity on elite secular campuses which had not been addressed in the extant literature. As a result, the author teaching the course trained the class in interviewing methods and helped them collect twenty-eight interviews with students on a small, elite, liberal arts campus in the fall of 2014. Participants were randomly chosen from a telephone list of the school's population. Interviews took place on campus in person, with the average interview lasting approximately thirty minutes. Participants were asked about their spiritual and religious histories, practices, and about campus culture regarding religion and spirituality.[2]

In the spring of 2015, we continued collecting data on campus religiosity. Interviewees were chosen based on purposive sampling. The authors invited student leaders from nine religious and spiritual organizations on campus to participate in the study. Faculty and administrators were invited based their leadership role in the campus community. Faculty participants were tenured and recommended by various members of the

[2] Descriptive statistics of these students' religious and spiritual profiles are shown in the Appendix.

community. During the second wave of data collection, we conducted nineteen interviews in total; we interviewed nine student religious leaders and eleven members of the faculty and administration. Student leaders were asked the same questions as students in the first wave, as well as questions about their experiences leading student groups. Professors and administrators were asked open-ended questions about how they perceived religious life on campus and their involvement with it.

All interviews were transcribed. Actual names and identifying information were replaced with pseudonyms and other descriptors. We then open-coded for: campus religious culture, student spiritual, religious, and secular identities, stigmas toward religion and spirituality, and respondent sociodemographics.[3] After identifying our initial primary categories, we completed a focused coding of all interviews. This additional coding included categories relating religion and spirituality to: the College administration and mission, initial experiences on campus, social interactions, academic experiences, social life, preconceived assumptions among students, dialogue on campus, pluralism and diversity, and religious and spiritual visibility/invisibility.

In addition to the interviews, we conducted a content analysis of the College's website. Through the website, the authors specifically explored the College's mission statement, as well as pages on student life, religious life, and social diversity on campus. We also analyzed the College's Senior Surveys (Higher Education Research Institute, 2013, 2014), which were administered to graduating seniors by the Higher Education Research Institute.

4. Hidden Religious and Spiritual Identities and a Lack of Dialogue

Our research exposed a stark discrepancy between students' public and private expressions of religiosity and spirituality. Most community members believed that the campus atmosphere was not particularly religious or spiritual. However, nearly three fifths of our randomly selected respondents identified as spiritual, religious, or both. In addition, 75% of the 2013 graduating seniors reported a specific religious affiliation.[4] This contradiction can be explained by our finding that many students' spiritual and religious practices were kept relatively private from their peers.

When students first arrived at the College, many of them quickly became aware of how religion was generally viewed negatively on campus. For example, senior Ali Roland, a leader of a student spirituality group, explained:

> "At the beginning of freshman year, even before the ideas [of religion and spirituality] were breached...there would be discussions within the friend groups, and if you did believe something, you would feel so uncomfortable. Because people would automatically be like 'Oh, you believe in God? Like, what are you, stupid?"

In addition, Grace Crowley, a senior leader of the Hillel group and former new member recruitment chair commented on how, "in the first week, and the first month, so many people want to get involved. But then they figure out the whole scene and figure out that maybe [Hillel] isn't that "cool" of a thing to do..." Roland and Crowley suggest that the subtle and explicit criticism of religious students' beliefs early in their college experience leads many students to hide their religious and spiritual backgrounds, beliefs, and practices for the rest of their time at the college.

Many students who arrived on campus identifying as religious or spiritual said that they began to avoid public displays of religiosity, and did not talk with their peers about their religious or spiritual backgrounds. One student explained, "In a very secular community such as [the College], I think people would be wary to describe themselves as religious or spiritual, whether or not they actually feel that way inside." Administrator Susan Nichols added:

> "I think that you could walk on this campus and think of yourself as a deeply religious person, and very quickly, just by observing conversations, decide—I'm going to be quiet about that. I'm not going to tell people that's an important part of who I am."

Even among their friends, students did not talk about their religious or spiritual lives. In fact, at the end of the interviews, a few of our respondents admitted that this was the first time they had discussed their religion or spirituality while at the College. Because students believed that the majority of the College students were not spiritual or religious, they assumed their friends and peers were secular.

Students and faculty members alike expressed surprise upon finding out that a student was religious. Meryl Parker, a faculty member, explained:

> "Whenever anybody 'announces' a religious identification in any way, my level of surprise makes me think that I just assume that everybody here is not religious, or not in any significant way. And then when somebody [explicitly] identifies as religious...I'm always kind of taken aback. And I definitely look at that student a little bit differently when I think about their self-identification with a religious group."

---

[3] Descriptive statistics of respondents from Wave 2 are available upon request.

[4] College Senior Survey 2013.

Parker's reflection shows that even some faculty members assume that most students on campus are not religious. Furthermore, when students deviate from the secular norm by making a religious identification obvious, they can be perceived differently and receive differential treatment from both faculty members and peers.

Respondents thought that the lack of religious dialogue on campus reflected the campus community's difficulty with approaching challenging dialogues in general. Yunus Farjad, a junior leader of the Muslim Students Association, explained, "If one has an opinion that goes against the majority of [the College's] students, they might feel pressured to not express it." Farjad, among many other respondents, found that the College community is not open to the expression of opinions or beliefs that might "rock the boat," as another respondent described.

5. Religious Discomfort and Stigmatization on Campus

The vast majority of the students, faculty members and administrators reported that the campus culture was not friendly to theism or organized religion. Various respondents described religious students on campus as being viewed as "weird," "backwards," or "off-putting." Students and faculty members alike shared experiences which suggested that the culture of religious discomfort is conveyed in both subtle, prejudicial and explicit, discriminatory ways.

5.1. Subtle Intolerance

Although many respondents reported a negative stigma towards religion on campus, it was often difficult for them to articulate their experiences with it. An anti-religious orientation often manifested implicitly in interactions between members of the community. Grace Crowley, senior leader of Hillel, the Jewish student group on campus, said students' discomfort with religion is, "not an outward thing...but it's like 'Oh, you're going to *Hillel*?' It's a look, or a glance, or a tone."[5] Similarly, senior Reuben Gamely described, "You know, it's like 'oh that person's *religious'* and that's like, *'oh.'* People don't identify as religious because it has a negative connotation...When you hear that someone is religious it has an off-putting effect." Crowley and Gamely reveal some of the subtle ways through which students at the College criticize their peers' religiosity and participation in student religious groups.

Administrators and faculty members also noticed that interactions between students conveyed undertones of intolerance. Dean Susan Nichols explained, "It's the subtle ways that we convey to one another—that's a goofy thing you're thinking. It's usually not words." Similarly, Christian faculty member Jamie Kim recalled that, when talking about religious identification, "Sometimes it's like 'Well, that's cool,' but sometimes it's like 'Oh...you're *that.*'"

These examples from students, faculty, and administrators indicate that religious students on campus sense a disapproval of their religious and spiritual identities through subtle gestures or cues. Students' perceptions of others' discomfort with religion led many students to not publicly affiliate with religion or engage in religious practices for fear of being judged.

5.2. Stereotyping and Overt Discrimination

In addition to subtle stigmatization of religion, some students and faculty described explicit stereotyping and discrimination on campus. For example, many respondents referenced an opinion article published in the spring of 2015 by a conservative publication on campus. The article argued that Islam as a religion is inherently violent, and that there is a high prevalence of extremism and violence among Muslims. In response, Fatima Choudhary, a junior leader of the Muslim Students Association, said she, "wasn't so much upset because of what they said, because [she] knew it wasn't true," but what bothered her most was that "this was such a widely available publication that is put everywhere on campus so any student can pick it up. A student who doesn't know much about Islam can pick it up and think, 'Oh, this is an official publication of [the College]. It must be legitimate.' And then when they read it, they'll believe it." Although Choudhary and the other Muslim students were used to being stereotyped in the mainstream conservative media, it concerned them to hear such direct stereotyping from a group of their peers on campus. Choudhary said that, in the wake of the article's publication, she became much more aware of her identity as a Muslim on campus, and more cognizant of how few other Muslim students there were at the College.

Jewish students also spoke of anti-Semitism from their peers at the College. In one incident, someone cut a hole out of the campus *sukkah* tent, a holy space for Jewish students during the *Sukkot* holiday. The same year, a friend of senior Hillel leader Zoe Holtzman found the message "Eradicate the Jews" written on a whiteboard on her door. Holtzman explained that Campus Safety investigated both of these incidents, but "nothing happened" and the perpetrators were never caught. Holtzman reflected on the sense of fear and insecurity the events incited, "Anybody who calls for things like that against people like yourself...It's going to kind of rattle you, and make you say, 'Wow, someone is really out there to get us,' right?" This experience suggests that Jewish students have felt uncomfortable and even unsafe on campus as a result of threats by their peers. Furthermore, because the perpetrators were never

[5] Bold type signifies emphasis by the respondent.

caught, Jewish students had to walk around campus every day not knowing which of their peers had committed these explicitly anti-Semitic acts.

These experiences demonstrated that the campus culture was not just apathetic or disinterested in religion. At times, members of the campus community were explicitly discriminatory and hostile towards organized religion. Although these incidents occurred intermittently, they directly threatened religious minorities on campus, made their identities more salient, and made them feel like outsiders. Such episodes not only made religious minorities feel misunderstood and more marginalized on campus, but among some, it instilled a fear of future interactions with their peers.

6. The Marginalization of Religion in Mainstream College Life

Respondents discussed how religion is stigmatized in the two main places that students regularly convene on campus: in the classroom and at parties. Because involvement in academics and the party culture were viewed as necessary parts of the student college experience by most students—and religion and theism were often viewed as incompatible with intellectual life and partying—religious students were marginalized and judged as deviant.

6.1. Academic Life

At elite liberal arts colleges, academics are a central part of college life. Like other liberal arts colleges, the College we examined generally promoted tolerance of social diversity in academic life. The College website (2013) stated that, "Woven throughout [the College]'s curriculum is the study of the world's races, cultures, religions and ideologies." However, students portrayed their classroom experiences as lacking conversation about religion, and at times even discouraging it. Students and faculty repeatedly stated how the intense intellectual atmosphere deterred religious exploration and acceptance.

Some respondents thought that faculty members ignored or demeaned religion in the classroom. Students and faculty members who identified as religious were particularly aware of critical attitudes toward religion in the classroom. Ji-Yun Lee, a leader of the College Christian Fellowship, said, "I've been in classes where the default mode was definitely 'religion is stupid.'" Jamie Kim, a faculty member and the advisor to the College Christian Fellowship, related that on campus, "You'll even hear faculty members with Ph.D.s who have biases against religion..." Although he hoped that faculty members would be open and accepting of religious beliefs, Kim suggested this was not always the case.

Many students perceived an implicit conflict between religious faith and scientific rationality. Students believed that you could not be both religious and intellectual, so students with religious identities were marginalized and viewed as unable to fully participate in academic life. A senior who did not identify as religious or spiritual, described, "The majority of kids I know here aren't religious. And even if they are practicing a religion, they're still...intellectual enough not to live by it." Ali Roland, a senior, similarly described how many students held the view that religion and intellect were implicitly opposed:

> "There's also this idea that...as students at [the College], we're too smart to be religious. Like we're too smart to put our faith into a higher power. Like I said, especially with an elite college like [College name], there's just this belief that being religious implies a lower intelligence level. I don't know if it's really spoken about that much."

In this context, there was considerable normative pressure to first be an engaged member of the prestigious college. To be a part of the College's elite privileged membership, one had to have a salient secular intellectual identity. To do otherwise would undermine one's perceived intelligence, which was one of the most valued traits at the College. These findings support our hypothesis that many students at this elite liberal arts school would have trouble reconciling their religious and intellectual identities. Because intellectual identities were central to being a part of the collective college identity, and religious identification was seen as oppositional to intellect, religious identities were marginalized and made suspect.

6.2. The Party Scene

At the College, partying was viewed by students as a central part of the mainstream social scene. Ninety percent of the graduating seniors in 2014 spent at least an hour partying in a typical week. In contrast, only ten percent of seniors prayed or meditated for at least an hour a week.[6] Unfortunately for religious students, most students we spoke with thought the party scene was not only incompatible with religiosity, but that the party crowd was particularly critical and dismissive of religion. It was a part of student social life in which religious students felt most marginalized, alienated, and judged.

Non-religious respondents assumed that religious students maintained strict religious commitments which did not allow for partying. Senior Henry Silber said that being at college involved the temptation to do "things that religions don't usually condone." Blake Rosenberg, a senior, explained, "People separate

[6] College Senior Survey 2014.

themselves from religion because it stops them from having a good time." Silber and Rosenberg's responses are indicative of a campus culture that perceives student religious identification as deviant and suspect, because it is viewed as a voluntary choice to not participate in the "fun" aspects of mainstream college life.

Religious students thought that the stigmatization of their religious traditions was particularly likely to happen at parties. Religious stigma was often expressed in the form of discriminatory jokes. Ji-Yun Lee, a self-identified Christian student, said that people in "party crowds" were more likely to make fun of Christians, or make Jesus jokes. Most of the religious students we spoke with said that they were not comfortable at campus parties.

Faculty also mentioned that the students who partied frequently were particularly likely to judge religious students. Faculty member Zach Sandler noted that religious students are generally regarded as "weird" by their peers, and that the stigma against religious students is related to the stigma against students who refrain from drinking alcohol. Similarly, administrator Harshad Bhat described that, "The minute a student says, 'I can't drink because of my culture, my faith,' now they're in that extreme crazy group, because it's proving this point that religion is backwards." Bhat's explanation further suggests that religious expression and practice were already assumed to be strange or deviant, and they were viewed as especially so when they interfered with students' ability to party.

7. The Perceived Lack of Structural Support for Religious Practice and Spiritual Exploration

7.1. Falling Short on the Institutional Mission

The College espoused an explicit commitment to support holistic student development and self-exploration, like many liberal arts institutions. It also sought to promote inclusion and tolerance of diverse social identities. These missions are clearly stated on the College's website and in its other publications. The College is guided by the motto "Know Thyself," which intimates a commitment to students' personal development and an intentional fostering of unique, individual identities. Religious and spiritual respondents thought that the motto could serve as a personal motivation for spiritual exploration. One student, when asked what religion means to him, shared: "It means knowing myself better. One of the big reasons I came to [the College] was because of Know Thyself." A senior administrator also believed that the motto could serve as a "perfect vehicle to give students permission to explore their religion and spirituality while they are here."

However, other respondents found that this motto was not an accurate reflection of students' experiences on campus. Rick O'Connor, a faculty member, noted that a more apt description of the College motto would be, "'Know Thyself, except don't talk about the religious part of yourself.'" Similarly, Sarah Wilder, a Protestant senior, shared: "Honestly, I think that a more accurate version of what the College actually achieves, or seeks to achieve, is...'Know Your Resume.'" Faculty and students alike believed that the College did not sufficiently endorse and support religious and spiritual life on campus.

Although the College's mission advocated a commitment to diversity and self-exploration, the College lacked an explicit commitment to the inclusion of religious and spiritual identities. For example, a page on the College's website on diversity," stated, "At [the College] you can be yourself—and be respected for who you are". A diversity fact sheet on the same page includes sections on racial and ethnic diversity, geographic diversity, and socioeconomic diversity.[7] Although the webpage explicitly encouraged multiple forms of diversity, it made no mention of religion or spirituality.

Despite a nominal promotion of diversity in its mission, students felt that the College and the campus community did not always support diversity in practice, especially when it came to religious diversity. Student leaders of religious and spiritual groups believed that members of the College saw religious diversity as potentially "dangerous" or "risky" to explicitly encourage.

7.2. Administrative Support and Limitations

Many religious students reported a lack of support from the administration for fostering religious exploration and inclusion. While these respondents generally thought the administration was tolerant and accepting of religious groups, they did not believe that the administration considered it important to actively engage with religion or spirituality.

Religious student leaders perceived a subtle lack of support from the administration. Ji-Yun Lee, a leader of a student Christian group, said, "I get the feeling that the administration is not too hot on us." Zoe Holtzman, senior leader of the Hillel group, commented, "I don't want to say that the administration is anti-religion...but they're not for religion." Holtzman and Lee's perspectives were echoed by other religious students, particularly those identifying as Christian or Jewish. Students in both groups thought that that they had to take their own initiative to help their religious groups thrive on campus.

Religious students additionally believed that the College had insufficient space and limited resources for the religious groups on campus. In particular, the majority of the Jewish student respondents expressed disappointment due to limited space available to them for

[7] Accessed May 15, 2015.

worship and practice. They were primarily concerned about the lack of a Kosher-friendly kitchen. Zoe Holtzman kept a Kosher diet at the College for her first three years. "That was really hard," she admitted. "Because of my limited options, I was getting really sick." Although no other respondents had tried keeping Kosher while on campus, many of them expressed concern that the College does not support Jewish students in this practice.

The challenges of limited space and resources are faced by all colleges and universities. However, these challenges are made especially difficult at a small school like the institution we studied, where there may only be a few students belonging to a particular religious group. Furthermore, religious groups were often comprised of students from a wide range of traditions and practices. Administrator Susan Nichols addressed the structural challenges to supporting religious students' needs:

> "There are challenges...for example, it can be hard to find mentors who have that background, availability, and interest. We've had different people over the years who have worked with our Jewish community or Muslim students. And when it's just a handful of students, you can't really justify hiring a full-time person. So piecing it together in a way that works and feels meaningful for students can be a challenge."

While Nichols and other administrators have put thought into how best to support the College's diverse religious population, they are aware that, given the structural limitations characteristic of a small college, not all students will be satisfied with the support for their identities and interests.

Our research demonstrated that some administrators are thoughtfully considering the needs of religious and spiritual groups on campus and attempting to uphold the college's mission of diversity. However, there was a disconnect between their efforts and students' perceptions of results, which led religious students to think that the administration did not prioritize their needs.

8. Religion and Spirituality on Campus

8.1. Spiritual Pluralism

Although cultural and structural factors combined to discourage public, shared discussions and experiences of the sacred, transcendent experiences were still part of students' lives on campus. Such experiences, however, often manifested in private, personal, and non-traditional forms. Regardless of specific religious or spiritual identification, students crafted their own unique sets of sacred beliefs and practices. One student, for example, identified as Catholic and believed in God, but did not specifically identify as "religious." Another student considered herself agnostic and was not tied to any particular religion. Yet, she admitted to finding herself praying sometimes. A third student described herself as both agnostic and "culturally Catholic." The latter term, she explained, she had created as a category to describe her own particular approach to Catholicism.

Although about two fifths of randomly selected student respondents did not explicitly identify as spiritual or religious, most engaged with spirituality in some way. In fact, three-fourths of the same respondents reported having had recent spiritual experiences. Many students spoke of experiencing spirituality through non-traditional avenues. Freshman and self-identified atheist Nikki Wilson said that for her, "Spirituality has a lot to do with nature....I remember one of the first days I got here, me and my roommate went to the [wooded area on campus]. It was probably the closest I've gotten to spiritual because we just sat there for a really long time, and it was really quiet..." Despite Wilson's tranquil moments in nature, she does not identify as "spiritual." Rather, she is drawn to nature and associates it with spirituality.

Blake Rosenberg, a senior and self-identified "agnostic/discordian," spoke of many aspects of his life that he considers sacred and divine. He referenced working at the community farm on campus, which he describes as a "holistic connection" that he cannot find anywhere else. When he writes, he says: "It is similar to a prayer, but instead of choosing God as my audience, I choose someone I know." Additionally, washing dishes offered him a similar spiritual experience. Rosenberg described his experiences as transcendent moments, without necessarily connecting them to a belief in God or a "spiritual" self-identification.

Another student, Henry Silber, was raised Jewish but considered himself neither spiritual nor religious. He "usually" doesn't believe in a higher power. However, Silber discussed the ways that reading and listening to music were spiritual experiences: "If there's a passage that's really incredible, or a piece of music that's jaw-dropping, I think that's a form of experiencing the divine. Like something pure, and beautiful....It makes me want to find something deeper." Even though Henry was not intentionally engaging in religious or spiritual practices, he experienced the spiritual through non-traditional avenues.

These three respondents did not label themselves as "spiritual" or theistic, yet they each cited spiritual or divine experiences in their lives on campus. All of these experiences were unique, personally meaningful, and deviated from conventional forms of organized religion.

8.2. Embracing Religiosity in Marginal Safe Spaces: Student Religious Groups

Although the general campus culture which stigmatized religion led the majority of students to keep their religious identities and expressions hidden, a small minority of students embraced their religious expressions publically. The College's head chaplain estimated that about ten percent of the College's students participated in a religious or spiritual group on campus. Perhaps because these students were a marginalized minority on campus, they were very grateful for the support they received from each other and from the chaplaincy.

Leaders of religious groups spoke of the difficulty in arriving at the College without sufficient community support. Counterintuitively, this lack of initial support actually contributed to some students' religious involvement. Ji-Yun Kim, a senior and leader of the College Christian Fellowship, spoke of her challenging arrival to the College:

> "I would have to say that I kind of struggled for a while, because there are so few Christians here. And there wasn't a lot of leadership....Normally there's a staff worker who leads the fellowship, but we don't have that here. And so that was hard."

Kim's struggles caused her to feel isolated, and she began to reconsider her identity as a Christian. However, she explained that as a direct result of the adversity she faced, "[her] faith skyrocketed" because she "had to take it into [her] own hands."

Zoe Holtzman shared a similar story: "It was really hard at first. I was pretty unhappy for about the first year." She wasn't satisfied with the availability of *Shabbat* services, and did not feel supported by her peers in her Jewish faith. But by her senior year, she had gained a different perspective: "What I've noticed here is that when you don't have people like you around you, you have to fight more for what you believe in and you have to identify more with that." For Holtzman, the anti-Semitic incidents on campus actually motivated her membership in the Hillel group. The discrimination the Jewish community faced "made us want to push Jewish life on campus more, and show that we're still a strong Jewish community that doesn't get derailed by those kinds of threats." Overt forms of discrimination from peers served as catalysts for the Hillel students to re-claim their place on campus.

Although the stigma towards religious groups on campus caused most students to veil or reject their own religious identities, the social climate on campus caused a contingency of students to become even more active and invested in their religious identities. Both Holtzman and Kim's experiences suggest that being in the midst of a campus culture that is not primarily religious caused them to further embrace their own religious identities.

Student religious groups became havens for many of their members by the end of their college experiences. Holtzman explained that by her senior year at the College, she thought of the Hillel group as her family. Similarly, Sarah Wilder, a Protestant senior, shared that a Protestant discussion group "is a place where I've opened up many times about things where I wouldn't elsewhere." The chaplaincy was another important source of support for religious students. Caitlin O'Connor, an agnostic Catholic, shared that she may not have stayed at the College if it had not been for the head chaplain's constant support and guidance. Overall, religious students' experiences showed how valuable student religious groups and mentors can be in providing support; such support was seen as especially important in the face of a campus culture critical of religion.

9. Discussion

This study examined a secular elite liberal arts college in order to make "invisible religion" more visible (Cadge & Konieczny, 2014) and to trace the cultural and structural facets of campus life which support or impede student religiosity. Although our findings are from a single small liberal arts college, based on past research, we suspect the subtle and explicit ways through which religious and spiritual life are repressed in public spaces on campus are likely to occur at other liberal arts colleges and elite secular universities (Freitas 2010; Jacobsen & Jacobsen, 2012; Lane et al. 2013).

Despite how the College's mission officially promoted the inclusion of people with diverse social identities, many students perceived a lack of peer, faculty, and administrative support for religious and spiritual exploration. The College additionally lacked a pathway for the majority of the student body to meaningfully explore religion or spirituality in a supportive environment. In mainstream social pathways on campus—such as in academic life and in the party scene—religion and spirituality were not only absent, but were viewed with suspicion. Students repeatedly spoke of how important being smart was to maintaining an identity as part of the prestigious College. They viewed religiosity as based on "belief" or "faith" rather than reason, and perceived an inherent conflict between religion and being an intellectual. Partying, a valued part of the student college experience for most non-religious students, was also viewed as incompatible with religious practice; religiosity was seen by non-religious students as an irrational, deviant impediment to having fun and getting the full college experience. Our findings correspond with Donna Freitas' (2010) study, which found that students often fail to reconcile religiosity with college party culture.

Despite the taken-for-granted, secular, mainstream campus culture, many students were involved in a discreet, individualized seeking of the sacred. While students were often hesitant to publicly self-identify as religious or engage in religious dialogue, behind closed doors they were more willing to share personal stories and experiences regarding their spiritual and religious backgrounds, beliefs, and practices when given the opportunity.

A minority of students embraced a public religious identity and maintained small marginalized communities in which they could embrace and discuss their religious and spiritual lives. In the face of discrimination and prejudice from the larger campus community, some religious students deepened their commitments to their faith tradition and their small student religious communities. This finding suggesting that some students will embrace, strengthen, and assert their religious identities when confronted with adversity mirrors sociologist Lori Peek's (2005) scholarship on the *declared religious identities* of Muslim students after the September 11 terrorist attacks. In the face of religious stereotyping and criticism, some Muslim students developed a stronger commitment to their faith and expressed their religiosity in more public ways.

At the liberal arts college we investigated, dominant secular norms and structural institutional pathways combined to discourage religious practice and spiritual exploration among the students. Because the structural opportunities for religious practice and dialogue were limited and socially marginalized, students were more likely to develop discreet, private religious and spiritual beliefs and practices. With the largely invisible nature of student religiosity and spirituality on campus, few students explicitly requested greater administrative support of religious and spiritual initiatives. Consequently, the administration did not prioritize these measures. Thus, students' religious and spiritual lives remained largely concealed and private, and the cycle of invisible religion perpetuated.

Like many other liberal arts colleges, the College aimed to foster a community with dialogue and openness regarding various forms of diversity. In order to better fulfill this mission regarding religion and spirituality specifically, we suggest that student leaders and administrators at secular colleges and universities focus on creating safe spaces for "deliberative dialogues" early on in students' college experiences (Lane et al., 2013, pp. 348). Intentional open dialogue would help foster a greater openness among students in exploring religion and spirituality, and aid in preventing and addressing religious intolerance. We recommend that these dialogues begin as early as freshmen orientation. After undergoing an identity-sensitivity training that includes a component on religiosity and spirituality, orientation leaders should be given the space to facilitate safe, inter-faith dialogues among new students. We believe that early support in sharing one's story will have a lasting effect on students' comfort in publicly sharing their religious and spiritual identities and expressions during the rest of their time on campus.

Our study also reveals surprisingly high amounts of discriminatory attitudes and actions against students from all of the three major religious traditions represented at the College—Christianity, Judaism, and Islam. Safe spaces for practice and dialogue allowed these religious groups to form their own supportive communities, even in the midst of a culture of discrimination. These findings underscore the importance of prioritizing the creation of safe spaces for religious and spiritual groups to convene and practice in colleges and universities. We recommend that faculty and administrative members work with religious student groups to ensure that each group has a designated space on campus in which they can gather and maintain their religious practices.

In addition, our study has illustrated the importance of having religiously diverse faculty and staff members. Students cited the valuable role that faculty and staff mentors can play in increasing students' comfort levels on campus and providing support. Finding a full-time staff member can be a challenge, especially at a small college. If full-time staffing is not possible, we recommend that administrative members work with student leaders to consider alternative options, such as hiring a part-time staff member, or forming connections with religious leaders in the area.

Initiatives fostering religious dialogue and literacy are being intentionally developed on other college campuses across the nation. President Obama launched "The President's Interfaith and Community Service Campus Challenge," in 2011, which encouraged many colleges and universities to commit to fostering religious and spiritual respect and education (U.S. Department of Education, 2011). Prestigious Ivy League schools, such as Yale and Princeton, have become national leaders in developing programs of religious pluralism and spiritual exploration. Such programs are promising but, as we suspect based on our results and other research (e.g. Freitas, 2010; Lane et al., 2013), still relatively rare or marginal at most secular colleges and universities. Because college is a critical time of identity formation for many students, such programs are very important not only for supporting religious and spiritual students, but also for promoting inclusion of people of all religions into campus social life. While at college, students may also be exposed to a greater diversity of identities in their peers than ever before. Colleges should take advantage of this opportunity to help students develop relationships with people from other faith traditions.

Future research should follow youth in their transitions from college to the workplace to examine the extent to which hidden religious and spiritual orientations are carried on into the world of work. We predict that the attitudes, beliefs, and practices that students develop with respect to their own spiritual and religious lives, and that of others, during their college years will affect their attitudes in subsequent life experiences in their workplaces and other often secular institutions. Future research should also examine how religious tolerance developed during one's youth, or the lack there of, shape one's treatment of members of other faith traditions during adulthood.

Conflict of Interests

The authors declare no conflict of interests.

References

Armstrong, E. A., & Hamilton, L.T. (2013). *Paying for the party*. Cambridge: Harvard University Press.

Astin, A. W., Astin, H. S., & Lindholm, J. A. (2011). *Cultivating the spirit: How college can enhance students' inner lives*. San Francisco, CA: Jossey-Bass.

Astin, A. W., Astin, H. S., Bryant, A. N., Calderone, S., Lindholm, J. A., & Szelenyi, K. (2004). *The spiritual life of college students*. Los Angeles: Higher Education Research Institute.

Bouman, J., DeGraaf, D., Mulder, M., & Marion, J. V. (2005). Connecting the mind, heart, and hands through intentional community at Calvin College. *Journal of College and Character, 6*. doi:10.2202/1940-1639.1463

Cadge, W., & Konieczny, M. E. (2014). "Hidden in plain sight": The significance of religion and spirituality in secular organizations. *Sociology of Religion, 75,* 551-563.

Cherry, C., DeBerg, B. A., & Porterfield, A. (2001). *Religion on campus.* Chapel Hill: University of North Carolina Press.

Evans, J. H., & Evans, M. S. (2008). Religion and science: Beyond the epistemological conflict narrative. *Annual Review of Sociology*, *34,* 87-105.

Freitas, D. (2010). Sex and the soul: Juggling sexuality, spirituality, romance, and religion on America's college campuses. Oxford: Oxford University Press.

Higher Education Research Institute. (2013). Senior survey.

Higher Education Research Institute. (2014). Senior survey.

Jacobsen, D., & Jacobsen, R. H. (2012). *No longer invisible: Religion in university education.* Oxford: Oxford University Press.

Kuh, G. D., & Gonyea, R. M. (2005, July 11). *Exploring the relationships between spirituality, liberal learning, and college student engagement*. New York: Teagle Foundation. Retrieved from http://www.teagle foundation.org/teagle/media/library/documents/ resources/20050711_k_gonyea.pdf

Lane, A. M., Allis, S., Allman, N., Pettys, A., Quinlan, M., & Siefert, B. (2013). "Religion is not a monolith": Religious experience at a Midwestern Liberal Arts College. *Journal of College and Character, 14,* 341-350. doi: 10.1515/jcc-2013-0043

Lindholm, J. A. (2006). The "interior" lives of American college students: Preliminary findings from a national study. In J. Heft (Ed.), *Passing on the faith: Transforming traditions for the next generation of Jews, Christians, and Muslims* (pp. 75-102). New York: Fordham University Press.

Ma, S. Y. (2010). The Christian college experience and the development of spirituality among students. *Christian Higher Education, 2,* 321-339. doi: 10.1080/15363750390246097

Maryl, D., & Oeur, F. (2009). Current knowledge and directions for future research. *Journal for the Scientific Study of Religion, 48,* 260-275. doi: 10.1111/j.1468-5906.2009.01446

Peek, L. (2005). Becoming Muslim: The development of a religious identity. *Sociology of Religion, 66,* 215-242. Retrieved from http://www.jstor.org/stable/4153097

Pew Research Center. (2015). *America's changing religious landscape: Christians decline sharply as share of population; unaffiliated and other faiths continue to grow*. Washington, DC: Gregory Smith.

Reuben, J. A. (1996). *The making of the modern university: Intellectual transformation and the marginalization of morality.* Chicago: University of Chicago.

Richter, R.J. (2001). Correlation of psychological well-being and Christian spiritual well-being
at a small Christian liberal arts college in the urban Midwest. *Wisconsin Lutheran College.*

Smith, C. (2003). *The secular revolution: Power, interests, and conflict in the secularization of American public life.* Oakland: University of California Press.

Smith, C., & Snell, P. (2009). *Souls in transition: The religious and spiritual lives of emerging adults: The religious and spiritual lives of emerging adults*. Oxford: Oxford University Press.

Speers, S. (2008). The secular thesis revisited: Religious life on the secular college campus today. *Journal of College and Character, 10.* doi:10.2202/1940-1639.1056

U.S. Department of Education. (2011). *Center for faith-based and neighborhood partnerships*. President's Campus Challenge. Washington, DC: U.S. Department of Education.

About the Authors

Kateri Boucher
Kateri Boucher is a Sociology student at Hamilton College in the class of 2017. She is currently doing research on civic agriculture in Quito, Ecuador and on urban farms in the United States.

Dr. Jaime Kucinskas
Jaime Kucinskas is Assistant Professor of Sociology at Hamilton College. Her research interests span the sociology of religion, inequality, social movements, and cultural change. In her current research, she examines how people experience the sacred in their everyday lives at work and in other secular institutions. Kucinskas has published in the American Journal of Sociology, the Journal for the Scientific Study of Religion, and Sociology of Religion.

Appendix

Table 1. Religiosity and spirituality of randomly selected respondents (*N*= 28).

	Total	Percent
Religious Self-Identification		
Religious and Spiritual	8	28.6
Religious	3	10.7
Spiritual but not Religious	5	17.9
None	12	42.9
Denomination		
Protestant	2	7.1
Catholic	7	25.0
Jewish	4	14.3
Episcopalian	1	3.6
None	14	50.0
Belief in a Higher Power		
Yes	16	57.1
No	6	21.4
Not sure	6	21.4
Frequency of Prayer		
Daily	7	25.0
Weekly	1	3.6
Monthly	1	3.6
Yearly	3	10.7
Never	16	57.1
Frequency of Attending Religious Services		
Weekly	10	35.7
Monthly	2	7.1
Never	16	57.1
Spiritual Experiences		
Had at least one kind of spiritual experience		
Meditation	21	75.0
Nature	7	25.0
Running/Sports	5	17.9
Other	2	7.1
None	7	25.0

4

Framing Social Inclusion as a Benchmark for Cycling-Inclusive Transport Policy in Kisumu, Kenya

Walter Alando * and Joachim Scheiner

Department of Transport Planning, Faculty of Spatial Planning, Technische Universität Dortmund University, 44227 Dortmund, Germany; E-Mails: walter.alando@tu-dortmund.de (W.A.), joachim.scheiner@tu-dortmund.de (J.S.)

* Corresponding author

Abstract

Cycling in many cities of the Global South faces unending exclusion from street spaces despite the on-going transport policy reforms. This exclusion worsens the marginalisation of the poor majority who use this mode. In this paper, we formulate social inclusion as a policy tool for reconciling transport policy to the cycling needs of Kisumu, Kenya. We draw from social quality theory and Lefebvre's right to the city concept to assemble the ideals of social inclusion. These ideals form the benchmark for a qualitative content analysis of the policy pronouncements contained in the Kenya Vision 2030 and the Integrated National Transport Policy to ascertain the opportunities presented by these policies for cycling inclusion. Findings from interviews held with transport professionals in government and private practice support this content analysis. Results show that while the Kenya Vision 2030 focuses on economic growth, the Government has prioritised the implementation of its projects, thus diminishing the fragile opportunity for cycling inclusion presented by the transport policy. To consolidate this opportunity, we propose different policy recommendations to improve the terms for cyclists to claim and produce street spaces.

Keywords

cycling; Kisumu; social exclusion; transport-led exclusion; transport planning

Issue

This article is part of the issue "Transport Policy and Social Inclusion", edited by Miriam Ricci, Graham Parkhurst and Juliet Jain (University of the West of England, UK).

---

1. Introduction

Providing street-spaces that support utility cycling remains an elusive target of transport policy in many Sub-Saharan African cities. In Kisumu, Kenya in particular, this challenge seems to be compounded by mixed commitment to cycling that is generated by the parallel pursuit of economic growth and transport policy reform agenda. While cycling combines the advantages of speed and affordability for its users, the concurrent pursuit of these economic and transport policy agenda has not influenced street-space allocation in ways that support its use. Consequently, transport infrastructure and service expansion projects that aim to improve safety, connectivity and accessibility (GoK, 2009) have instead created street-spaces that exclude cycling. This exclusion worsens the social exclusion of the poor majority who rely on cycling to access opportunities and to generate income by offering bicycle taxi services (Mutiso, 2010; UN-HABITAT, 2004).

Finding a way of addressing this transport exclusion is the central concern of this paper. The paper specifically explores the extent to which social inclusion can be packaged to form a policy frame for reconciling transport planning in Kisumu to the city's neglected cycling needs. Social inclusion is understood to be 'the process of improving *not only* the terms for individuals and groups that are disadvantaged on the basis of their identity to take part in society, *but also...the process of improving their* ability, dignity, and opportunity *available for them to do so'* (World Bank, 2013, pp. 3-4, emphasis added). Guided by this conception, the paper pursues two objectives: i) to assemble a literature-based frame for analysing social inclusion in transport, and ii) to find out the extent to which Kenya's economic development blueprint is consistent with its transport policy and the implications of this extent of consistency for cycling-inclusive transport planning in Kisumu.

The paper draws on the inclusionary principles espoused by social quality theory (Maesen & Walker, 2002) and Lefebvre's right to the city concept (Lefebvre, 1996) to assemble the key tenets that guide its analysis of Kenya's economic development blueprint (i.e. Kenya Vision 2030) and transport policy for the opportunities they hold for cycling inclusion in Kisumu. We discuss these policies in section 4.

The remainder of this paper is organised in six sections. The next section presents a theoretical basis for employing social inclusion in the current paper. Section 3 contextualises transport exclusion in Sub-Saharan African cities while section 4 puts Kisumu, the study city into perspective. The methodology is presented in section 5. Section 6 builds a theoretical analysis that generates the themes against which the provisions of the extant policies that shape transport planning in Kisumu are analysed in section 7. The implications of policy results for the inclusion of cycling are also presented in section 7. The conclusions and policy proposals are given in Section 8.

2. Theoretical Framework

2.1. Social Quality Theory

Social quality theory emerged in Europe in response to the withdrawal with which policymaking tackled the social dimension of development. Its central argument is that traditional economic analysis, with its neoliberal inclination, is insufficient to explain the changing nature of daily circumstances such as production, employment and distribution systems (Walker & Maesen, 2003). The theory decries the inability of economic growth on its own to solve social challenges such as limited access to social services and rising poverty (Walker & Maesen, 2003). Focusing on economic growth as the sole indicator of development is argued to conceal the totality of development, by subordinating the social and cultural dimensions of people's needs and preferences (Maesen & Walker, 2002; Walker & Maesen, 2003).

The theory holds that because the individual is the core unit of the society, meaningful development therefore ought to be that which creates conditions that enable individuals to effectively be part of the society. Development policies should hence produce conditions that enhance individual wellbeing and potentials while at the same time creating room for them to participate in the social and economic life of their societies (Beck, Maesen, & Walker, 1997; Maesen & Walker, 2012). This argument is used as a basis for analysing the extent to which policies enhance the ability to cycle in Kisumu.

While the initial development of the theory aimed to redress weak social welfare and industrial relations in Europe, its scope has now widened beyond this narrow theme and geographical concern. Within Europe, the theory has been tested in various policy areas including urban development (Maesen & Walker, 2002). Other applications outside Europe have also emerged, with the most well-documented ones being in East Asia (e.g. Lin, Ward, & Maesen, 2009). In this paper, we explore the use of the theory in transport planning.

Social quality theory offers a theoretical and methodological tool for measuring human wellbeing that goes beyond the conventional quality of life measures such as social indicators (e.g. Baud, Sridharan, & Pfeffer, 2008) and human needs and basic needs (e.g. Doyal & Gough, 1991). While these individualised indicators offer a robust approach to assessing quality of life at the individual level, they are less useful when community and other social relations are the focus of analysis (Siltaniemi & Kauppinen, 2005). Moreover, the conventional quality of life paradigm presupposes the existence of certain social structures and relationships, thus precluding a critical analysis of how social structures and relationships relate with exclusion and wellbeing (Siltaniemi & Kauppinen, 2005; Ward, Meyer, Verity, Gill, & Luong, 2011). In contrast, social quality theory takes the premise that the individual is part of the larger society. Thus individual wellbeing is the product of the tension between individual development preferences and societal development needs on the one hand and the tension between community development aspirations and the development aspirations defined by groups, institutions or formal organisations on the other (Maesen & Walker, 2002). The challenge therefore is to temper these tensions such that the individual is enabled to actualise. Section 7 examines the extent to which government policies have coincided with cycling needs and the opportunities this avails for enabling cycling.

Four hypotheses that are fundamental for enabling individuals to participate in their societies are proposed by social quality theory. These include socio-economic security, social inclusion, shared norms, and autonomy (Walker & Maesen, 2003). The first two hypotheses are particularly relevant in the quest for inclusive street-spaces that this current paper is concerned with. The first hypothesis holds that people must have access to socio-economic security in order to protect them from poverty and other forms of deprivation. Accordingly, this paper investigates the extent to which transport planning has created inclusive streets that directly facilitate bicycle taxi operators to earn their living while indirectly enabling poor households to free up portions of their incomes that are tied on transport expenditure. We show in section 4 that transport expenditure is a major source of financial burden for poor households. With regard to social inclusion, the theory holds that people must experience social inclusion or minimum levels of social exclusion from key social and economic institutions. In this regard, we explore the extent to which transport planning has created street-spaces that accommodate all modes irrespective of the socio-economic statuses of their users. This discussion is developed in sections 6 and 7.

This sub-section has shown that development effort is incomplete until excluded individuals are facilitated to participate in normal social activities. The next sub-section pushes this idea further by arguing that inclusion is a right, rather than a privilege.

2.2. The Right to the City

The concept of the 'right to the city' was first formulated in 1968 by Henry Lefebvre as a call for a radical alternative to capitalism (Lefebvre, 1996). He criticised the continued disenfranchisement of urban residents by the political and economic agenda that were pursued under capitalism at the time (Lefebvre, 1996; Marcuse, 2009). Specifically Lefebvre argued that the preoccupation of capitalism with managing individual consumption impeded its ability to tackle larger social essentials, which were not necessarily material products (Lefebvre, 1996). The capitalist model was argued to be wrought with internal contradictions and crises, which produced injustice as a result of its failure to tackle non-materials concerns of the society (Marcuse, 2009; Soja, 2010). This injustice denied urban residents the right to appropriate and produce the city.

As a departure from capitalism which tackled what could arguably be termed as the symptoms of development challenges, Lefebvre focused on the root causes of these challenges to present a new perspective for understanding them. He took the radical stance that a meaningful solution could be found by addressing unjust structural relations that denied urban residents the right to appropriate and to produce urban spaces (Lefebvre, 1996). This stance presents a departure from welfare protection and market (de)regulation and other interventions, which focused on satisfying 'want' (Marcuse, 2009) rather than dismantling the underlying structures that generated injustice. Lefebvre's presentation of the right to the city as a cry and a demand demonstrates a resolve for meaningful change that not only enables urban residents to access resources but also empowers them to determine how resources are produced. In the words of Marcuse (2009), the right to the city therefore presents a 'demand' for resources that should be justly accessible to the excluded and a 'cry' by the alienated for the right to determine how these resources are produced.

On the basis of the foregoing understanding, the current paper explores the extent to which social inclusion can be packaged as a policy frame for advancing the right of cyclists to access street-spaces and to influence how street-spaces are produced through their active travel behaviour.

This section has presented a theoretical argument that identifies the participation of excluded individuals as not only a precondition for all-inclusive development but also a right that needs to be recognised and be upheld. In the next section, we take a look at transport exclusion and its possible research directions in Sub-Saharan African (SSA) cities.

3. Contextualising Transport Exclusion in Sub-Saharan African Cities

The last fifteen years have witnessed a renewed attention to social exclusion in transport research (e.g. Church, Frost, & Sullivan, 2000; Kenyon, Lyons, & Rafferty, 2002; Lucas, 2011; Scheiner, 2010). A common theme through this research is the conception of exclusion as suppressed travel due to disadvantaged socio-geographical locations of residential places (Church et al., 2000; Shergold & Parkhurst, 2012), limited access to the car and public transport (Kenyon et al., 2002; Shergold & Parkhurst, 2012), and socio-demographics such as gender, age and race (Engels & Liu, 2011; Shergold & Parkhurst, 2012). Transport exclusion is therefore arguably a form of social exclusion given that it occurs because of the social status of the excluded.

While the socio-economic and demographic indicators discussed above are useful in enabling a normative categorisation of exclusion, they nonetheless do not take account of different travel behaviour (Shergold & Parkhurst, 2012). This gap raises doubts about their capability to explain transport exclusion that arises because of the choices that travellers make. Specifically, the results of these indicators remain unclear on the differences in exclusion experienced across travel modes and travel routes, although these choices present unique conditions that can be argued to impact differently on exclusion.

In view of the foregoing revelation, we argue that focusing on the empirical travel behaviour and policy processes that produce spaces where travel choices are made would lend a richer understanding of exclusion. Within the context of Europe, Scheiner (2010), for instance, alludes to this position even though his study does not directly focus on social exclusion. Based on the notion that households choose residential locations that suit their travel behaviour, he employs empirical travel data to show a positive association between vertical social inequality and limited activity spaces that those in the lower social ranks can access. Such results are concealed when inclusion strategies focus on normative categorisation of exclusion based on socio-demographic and geographical indicators.

It is even more difficult for these indicators to fully account for transport exclusion in Sub-Saharan African cities unless they are adapted to do so. This is because of the unique circumstances that define exclusion in these cities. These circumstances include the predominance of non-motorised transport (Gwilliam, 2003; Salon & Aligula, 2012), persistent absolute poverty and consequent low car ownership levels (Lucas, 2011), and the tension between the rapid sprawl of residential locations and the predominant mono-functional urban land-use regime (UN-HABITAT, 2014). All these contrast to factors that cause exclusion in developed cities, where the current proxies of exclusion have been developed. The interplay of these circumstances creates a situation where as many as 80% of daily trips in SSA cities are made using non-motorised options (Diaz Olvera, Plat, & Pochet, 2013; Salon & Aligula, 2012). In addition, exclusion also takes a gender dimension. Cases have been reported where the most vulnerable women, children, the old, and physically disabled are constrained from making out-of-home trips due to poor road conditions (Diaz Olvera et al., 2013), unaffordability (Salon & Gulyani, 2010), and poor and unreliable public transport (UN-HABITAT, 2014). We therefore argue that richer results of exclusion could be obtained if the definition of transport exclusion in the context of these Sub-Saharan African cities incorporated these conditions.

The foregoing revelations present a need to extend the scope of transport exclusion to incorporate the conditions that cause exclusion in Sub-Saharan African cities. Policy efforts that aim to address transport exclusion in these cities must ideally address these factors. The next section now puts Kisumu into the context of this transport exclusion by presenting its transport situation and policy environment.

4. Putting Kisumu into Perspective

Kisumu city is the main commercial, administrative, and educational hub of Kisumu County. There are 46 other administrative counties across Kenya. The city has an estimated population of 400,000 inhabitants and a land mass of about 297km^2, making it the third largest city in Kenya after Nairobi and Mombasa (GoK, 2010a). The city is administered by Kisumu County Government that is also in charge of different dimensions of urban planning in the city.

Due to its function as the principal urban centre in the region, Kisumu has continued to attract a sustained inflow of population that comes in search of opportunities (Maoulidi, 2012). However, the production of the very opportunities that attracts this population to the city has hardly kept pace with its inflow, thus making unemployment, poverty, and poor access to services a daunting planning challenge for the city (Nodalis, 2014). Unemployment and poverty rates are estimated at 30% and 48% of the city's total workforce and households respectively (Nodalis, 2014). The bulk of this poor population resides in the slums and informal settlements of the city (Nodalis, 2014).

Although inadequate access to transport services is an important dimension of poverty (Kim & Dumitrescu, 2011), little research attention has gone into the transport disadvantage that faces the poor of Kisumu. Instead, efforts to tackle poverty in the city have focused on improving the delivery of socio-economic opportunities such as employment, housing, water, and education (e.g. Nodalis, 2014). Meanwhile, studies of cities of comparable socio-economic conditions reveal that the poor spend as much as 25% of their disposable incomes on meeting recurrent transport costs, partly due to lack of affordable alternatives (Kim & Dumitrescu, 2011; Odero, Sibanda, Njenga, Mbathi, & Opiyo, 2009). Furthermore, they make fewer trips yet they spend more time travelling and are the most predisposed to road-crashes when compared to their high income counterparts (de-Langen & Tembele, 2001; Kim & Dumitrescu, 2011). In Kisumu, these challenges are compounded by poor road conditions, which cut off most of the city's slum and peri-urban settlements from public transport service.[1]

Utility cycling among the poor of Kisumu is thus a pragmatic response to unemployment and inadequate access to faster and affordable alternatives to walking. Although the poor are the predominant bicycle users, other income groups also cycle, either privately or using bicycle taxis (Kola, Onyango, & Oindo, 2012). The modal share of cycling is estimated at 16% (Makajuma, 2006). It is thought that the recent emergence of motorcycle taxis has caused a general decrease in this modal share because its operators are mostly former bicycle taxi riders who have switched to operating motorcycles.[2] However, a new pattern characterised by a rise in the number of private cyclists has also emerged as some travellers who relied on bicycle taxis resort to using their own bicycles.[3] Generally, motorcycles are even more expensive than public transport which is equally expensive for a majority of the poor. Despite this undying significance of cycling in Kisumu, the city authority has failed to support cycling in terms of infrastructure and traffic rules. This failure occasions not only its exclusion from the streets but also the social exclusion of its riders, passengers and operators.

The recent formulation of the Kenya Vision 2030 (KV2030) and the Integrated National Transport Policy (INTP) presents an opportunity for interrogating government commitment to inclusive transport that ad-

[1] Field interview with County Chief Officer in charge of transport, 27.08.2015

[2] Field interview with practising NMT expert, 20.08.2015

[3] Field interview with practising NMT expert, 20.08.2015

dresses the foregoing disadvantage that faces cycling in Kisumu. Although these two documents are national government documents, the structure of government in Kenya (GoK, 2010b) provides that they are implemented at the local level. The influence of these documents in shaping the development of Kisumu is further emboldened by its selection as one of the priority cities under the KV2030 plan (GoK, 2007).

The Kenya Vision 2030 is an economic development blueprint that aims to turn Kenya into a middle-income country by the year 2030 (GoK, 2007). It was launched in 2008. The document envisages sustained economic growth, social justice and political accountability as the basis for realising its vision. It provides a long-range vision for these sectors and proposes to achieve their specific targets by implementing priority projects that it identifies within a successive five-year medium-term planning framework.

Relevant to the current paper is the recognition of the role of transport infrastructure in accelerating business and improving livelihoods. In this regard, the government seeks to develop and maintain a safe, integrated, and efficient transport network as its transport vision (GoK, 2007). In order to realise this vision, the document prioritises the development of Bus Rapid Transport and the light railway system in Nairobi and later in other priority cities such as Kisumu (GoK, 2007). The document also targets to develop an Integrated National Transport Master Plan to guide infrastructure development across all Kenyan cities, including Kisumu. Curiously though, the KV2030 does not acknowledge the INTP, which was prepared two years before KV2030 was initiated and only launched in 2009 after undergoing some amendments to align it to the KV2030. This raises curiosity about the consistency between the two documents and the implications of this consistency for inclusive transport. This issue is explored further in section 7.

5. Methodology

The study begins by a theoretical analysis to enable it build a framework for employing social inclusion in problematizing transport disadvantage in the context of Sub-Saharan African cities. This is followed by a qualitative content analysis of the KV2030 and the INTP to identify the extent to which the thematic concerns generated from the theoretical analysis are tackled by the extant policies. Where possible, the study makes reference to the transport proposals of Kisumu Integrated Strategic Urban Development Plan (ISUD)[4] to demonstrate the situation in Kisumu. This content analysis is sparingly supported by results of field observations and qualitative analysis of interviews held with relevant government officials and transport experts.

5.1. Data

The main data used in the analysis is the content of KV2030, INTP and ISUD documents. Copies of these documents were obtained from Kisumu County Government. To supplement this data, the study held semi-structured interviews with the chief officer in charge of transport at Kisumu County Government and one Non-Motorised Transport expert. These respondents were purposively selected because of the rich information they possessed on the subject matter of our investigation because of their official responsibilities and experience in transport in general and cycling in particular (Singh, 2006). The interviews were held in August 2015, with the main theme being the opportunities and challenges that faced cycling and its users under the present planning framework in Kisumu and the on-going policy reforms. An interview schedule that was tailored along the emerging issues enumerated in section 6 was prepared to guide these interviews.

Field observations were made on an on-going basis to get a grasp of the challenges that faced cycling on the streets and to cross-check the findings from the interviews.

5.2. Analysis

The theoretical analysis presented in section 6 generated 5 main themes that formed the categories that were used in the subsequent analyses in section 7. These themes centred on problematizing transport disadvantage in general, contextualising exclusion, visibility of exclusion, conception of spaces of exclusion, and response to the ideals of inclusion. The content analysis is organised according to these themes that enabled us to formulate our preconceptions and pre-knowledge (Mayring, 2014) of what inclusive policies and processes should entail. The content of KV2030 and INTP documents were then analysed to find out the extent to which they tackled these thematic concerns and the opportunity they availed for cycling inclusion. According to Mayring (2014), a content analysis is not a standardised instrument; it should rather be flexible enough to suit the material in question and issues at hand. The content-related arguments take preference over procedural arguments because validity is regarded more highly than reliability (Mayring, 2014). Table 1 (Miles & Huberman, 1994) presents a summary of how the three policy documents have tackled the thematic concerns raised.

6. Linking Social Inclusion to Transport Discourse

6.1. Problematizing Transport Exclusion through Social Inclusion

Social inclusion is increasingly presented to be a basic condition for achieving sustainable urban transport

[4] The ISUD is the strategic plan that guides the development of the city for the period 2013 to 2030.

(Khayesi, Monheim, & Nebe, 2010; Lucas, 2012; World Bank, 2013). Although it is conceptually differentiated from social exclusion (Labonte, 2004), it arguably offers a basis for problematizing the plight of individuals and groups that are excluded by transport systems (Church et al., 2000; Lucas & Musso, 2014). This opportunity is presented by its conception as both a means to ending social exclusion and concurrently an end to be pursued in its own right. The central aim of social inclusion is to strengthen the participation of excluded individuals and groups in social processes by improving their ability and dignity as well as the opportunities available for them to participate (World Bank, 2013).

The foregoing conception projects social inclusion as the central target of efforts that aim to achieve the tenets of the social quality theory and the right to the city. In fact, the very emergence of the concept of social inclusion is itself a response to the challenges of social exclusion and by extension the restrictions that this exclusion places on the right to the city (Allman, 2013; Harvey, 2012; Labonte, 2004). Specifically, its growing use is motivated by the need to reduce the relative disadvantages that face individuals or groups because of their weaker social statuses, that limit their ability to participate in normal social activities (Sen, 2000). These disadvantages have been argued to limit their enjoyment of the right to the city (Harvey, 2003, 2012).

Despite the potential of social inclusion in problematizing transport disadvantage, it has received little research attention, particularly in medium-sized Sub-Saharan Africa cities (Lucas, 2011). It seems that transport exclusion itself is still not very clearly understood in these cities. In this paper, we therefore operationalise normal social activities to refer to participation in mobility and accessibility by all modes of transport. We use this understanding to interrogate how Kenya's development blueprint and transport policy problematize the transport challenge in general and the extent to which this problematization accommodates cyclists.

6.2. The Context of Exclusion Matters

The fundamentals of social quality theory and the right to the city concept seem to converge at the view that social inclusion forms the common denominator that is necessary to support participation in social processes. This is especially so if one considers that social inclusion outlines the terms and nature of this participation that underpin the achievement of the tenets of the theory and the concept. In the case of social quality theory, social inclusion is directly identified as a precondition that enables individuals to be part of the society (Maesen & Walker, 2012). Similarly, the right to the city concept also argues for social inclusion, not only in appropriating existing resources but also in determining how these resources are produced (Marcuse, 2009).

But facilitating social inclusion requires an unambiguous understanding of who the excluded are and the factors that exclude them. Existing literature on social exclusion has thus far narrowly limited the scope of disadvantage that defines exclusion and the excluded individuals and groups to the contexts of the challenges that face countries from where this literature emanates. These include mainly countries of Europe, Asia and to some extent Australia and the USA. Consequently, income status, race, gender, sexual orientation, ethnicity, religion, physical disability status, and caste dominate as the basis for defining exclusion (e.g. Øyen, 1997; Sen, 2000; World Bank, 2013). These forms of exclusion are typical in the context of these countries and are by no means exhaustive, more so with regard to the transport disadvantage in SSA cities. A more realistic investigation of exclusion in SSA cities must hence begin by recognising this context-specificity of the phenomenon (Silver, 2007).

The foregoing unruly nature of social exclusion demands that the phenomenon is conceptualised to reflect its context-specific drivers and forms in SSA cities if it is to be useful in understanding transport disadvantage in these cities. At the same time, while some of the dimensions of exclusion used in existing literature resonate with exclusion in the context of SSA cities, they must be adapted to reflect the unique circumstances in these cities. For instance, although cyclists in many SSA cities are predominantly the poor (Pochet & Cusset, 1999; UN-HABITAT, 2004), indirectly addressing their transport disadvantage through tackling poverty is not likely to yield their inclusion. This is because their exclusion has more to do with street-spaces, which hardly cater for cycling and less to do with their poverty status. Poverty in this case only adds to their invisibility during street-space allocation but does not in itself trigger their exclusion from the streets. Indeed, research shows that not all cyclists are necessarily poor (Bechstein, 2010; Nkurunziza, Zuidgeest, & van Maarseveen, 2012; Salon & Aligula, 2012). This example demonstrates the ease of blurring the real drivers of exclusion when its conception gives undue prominence to the socio-economic statuses of the excluded. Useful insights into different dimensions of transport exclusion could be obtained by shifting attention to the planning processes, products and outcomes that occasion exclusion (Cameron, 2006; Schwanen et al., 2015).

This paper therefore attempts a direct conception of the exclusion of cyclists for what it is—exclusion from the streets. We employ this conception to focus the problematization of the transport disadvantage discussed in the previous section to cycling concerns in Kenya in particular. We interrogate the extent to which current policies enable the disadvantage that faces cyclists to be identified as well as the extent to which these policies facilitate cyclists to participate in mobility and to influence street-space allocation through their active travel behaviour.

6.3. Unrelenting Exclusion amid 'Progress' in Transport

Within transport research, the use of social inclusion has been inspired by transport-related marginalisation that persists despite the progress witnessed in transport service and infrastructure development (Jones & Lucas, 2012; Kenyon et al., 2002). This progress is evidenced by road expansion, improvements in public transport, and a concurrent rapid growth in motorisation (Gwilliam, 2003; Watson, 2014; WHO, 2015). While these developments are desirable to the extent that they enable goods, services and people to reach destinations, their benefits are evidently skewed against non-motorised modes such as cycling because the planning strategies that generate them are not sensitive to the needs of non-motorised modes (Gwilliam, 2003; Watson, 2014; WHO, 2015). These auto-oriented strategies not only make it hard and unsafe for non-motorised modes to access cities (Gwilliam, 2003; Watson, 2014; WHO, 2015); they also lead to increased number of accidents that disproportionately affect non-motorised modes (WHO, 2015). These disadvantages ultimately lead to reduced accessibility to opportunities such as jobs, education and health services for those who cannot afford motorised modes (Diaz Olvera, Didier, Pochet, & Maidadi, 2012; Salon & Gulyani, 2010). The appropriateness and effectiveness of these auto-oriented transport planning strategies to generate positive social impacts for low income groups remains doubtful (Grieco, Ndulo, Bryceson, Porter, & McCray, 2009; Lucas, 2011; McCray, 2004; Watson, 2014).

The result of this mismatch between progress in transport conditions on the one hand and its outcomes for non-motorised modes on the other draws particular attention to cycling in medium-sized Sub-Saharan African cities. While cycling commands a significant modal share in most of these cities (Bradbury & Howe, 2002; Quarshie, 2004; UN-HABITAT, 2010), the modernist planning regime that is prevalent throughout the region oddly stifles its use by failing to recognise it and to cater for its infrastructure needs alongside those of motorised modes (Asingo & Mitullah, 2007; Steyn, 2012; Watson, 2014). This failures exposes cycling to unsafe competition with motorised modes over street-spaces that are designed to facilitate motorised transport (Kim & Dumitrescu, 2011; Odero et al., 2009; UN-HABITAT, 2004). It is unsurprising therefore that cyclists accounted for about 9.1% of the fatalities reported in Kenya between 1994–2008, making it the third most dangerous mode after driving and walking (Ministry of Transport, 2009, cited in Odero et al., 2009). In Kisumu specifically, cycling further faces active government ban (Alal, 2014) although it remains one of the most popular travel modes in the city (Makajuma, 2006). These disadvantages meted on cycling intensify the exclusion of the poor majority who use the mode for commuting, intra-urban connection and as a tool for income generation by operating it as bicycle taxis (Bradbury & Howe, 2002; UN-HABITAT, 2004).

Transport exclusion however restricts not only the physical access to opportunities; it also directly stifles efforts to bridge social inequality gap in many SSA cities. It is estimated that as many as 50% of the inhabitants of some of the cities live below the poverty line and can afford neither private cars nor public transport (UN-HABITAT, 2014). In the case of Kisumu, the failure to provide for cycling not only generates the physical exclusion of its users; it also excludes bicycle taxi operators from their source of livelihood. As mentioned earlier, this failure also strains household budgets by locking large proportions of their incomes to transport expenditure.

This current paper therefore questions the extent to which the extant policies make this exclusion visible and the opportunities that such visibility offers for cycling inclusion.

6.4. In Search of Inclusion in Excluded Spaces and Processes

Urban streets have historically been the object of the struggle for the right to the city for modes other than the car (e.g. Attoh, 2012; Furness, 2010; Murthy, 2011). This struggle is shaped by transport exclusion that results from growing motorisation that is reinforced by state planners' conception of street-spaces as corridors of motorised traffic rather than spaces of multi-modal use (Banister, 2002; Murthy, 2011). The neoliberal agenda (Harvey, 2012) and the modernist approach to transport planning (Hobson, 1999; Watson, 2009, 2014) are at the centre in propagating this exclusion. On the one hand, this neoliberal agenda is responsible for commodifying urban spaces (Harvey, 1982, 2012), thus reducing street-space allocation to an exercise of maximising economic value rather than the use value of street-spaces. On the other hand, the modernist planning agenda devalues non-motorised modes by prioritising automobiles in its pursuit for 'modernity' (Furness, 2010). The resulting exclusion of non-motorised modes takes many forms. Key among these are outright stigmatisation of the modes (Furness, 2010; Salon & Aligula, 2012) and a blatant failure to allocate street-spaces that support their use (Furness, 2010).

Cycling inclusion remains a difficult target under this modernist planning regime. This is because its ensuing negative social representation (Khayesi et al., 2010; Pochet & Cusset, 1999) prohibits transport planning in its current form from allocating street-spaces that can facilitate its use. At the same time, cycling stands no chance for inclusion in commodified spaces because it generates no economic return that is readily quantifiable using the current transport evaluation tools such as the Cost-Benefit Analysis (Jones, Moura, & Domingos, 2013). It is therefore relevant to explore the extent to which policy efforts that aim to include cycling can centre their ideals on the active travel behaviour of cyclists in terms of their mode choices, route choices and the attendant challenges. Moreover, it is also relevant to explore the extent to which such policies can consolidate the right of cyclists to produce street-spaces as they already do, albeit without state recognition. In this connection, the current paper questions how spaces of exclusion are produced by the policies and explores the challenges and opportunities availed by these policies for cycling inclusion.

6.5. *Ideals of Inclusion*

Addressing the limitations imposed on cycling by the planning agenda discussed in the previous section requires clarity on the ideals that social inclusion strives for. It has been suggested that social inclusion must strive to achieve and safeguard ability, dignity and opportunity as its basic ideals (World Bank, 2013). Ability in its broader sense is recognised as an innate quality (Fodor, 1975) that must nonetheless be socially mediated (Prinz, 2005). In this context, we present the existing cycling culture in Kisumu as an innate quality that requires deliberate planning support in order to enable it play an effective role in enabling mobility and income generation or saving. Dignity on the other hand concerns respect and recognition with which cyclists are treated in policy and practice. Low dignity attached to cycling by state planners renders the mode invisible in official statistics and consequently unattended to both in terms of policy and of infrastructure provision (Khayesi et al., 2010). Lastly, inclusionary efforts must also aim to enhance the opportunities for cycling by reducing the physical barriers to cycling. These barriers are occasioned by a lack of supportive infrastructure and traffic conditions (Alando, Brussel, Zuidgeest, & Durgi, 2013). In this paper, we explore the difficulties that cyclists are exposed to by the failure to provide infrastructure and traffic conditions that support cycling. These ideals form a basis for assessing the policies for the opportunities that they avail for cycling inclusion.

This section has attempted to interweave the connection between social inclusion and transport disadvantage in an effort to construct a frame for assessing the extent to which KV2030 and the INTP are inclusive. The next section now dialogues the two policies to find the extent of their convergence on inclusion and the implications of this extent for cycling inclusion.

7. Dialoguing the Kenya Vision 2030 and the Integrated National Transport Policy: Implications on Inclusion

This section carries out a qualitative content analysis of the policy pronouncements contained in the KV2030 and INTP to find out the opportunities they hold for cycling inclusion in Kisumu. The content analysis is guided by the categories identified in section 6. Accordingly, the policy documents were analysed to find out how the messages they contained had tackled the thematic concerns that were raised in that section (Mayring, 2014).

Table 1 summarises the findings. Where possible, the study makes reference to ISUD plan to demonstrate its points.

Table 1. The extent to which policy and practice have tackled key thematic concerns of inclusion.

Concern	KV2030	INTP
Problematizing transport disadvantage	• Hindrance to mobility and economic participation • Modernist • Overall road crashes and pollution • Traffic congestion • High cost of transport	• Hindrance to accessibility • Inadequate transport integration • No vision for transport sector • Poor quality transport services
Contextualising transport exclusion	• Regional disparity in road network coverage	• Inappropriate modal split • Transport unaffordability • Planning biased against NMT • Lack of infrastructure provision for NMT
Visibility of exclusion	• No mention of NMT even in delegated form • Only recognises regions of the country that are excluded from roads for motorised transport	• Explicit acknowledgement of bias against NMT modes in general
Production of spaces of exclusion	• Capital infrastructure projects	• Integrated transport
Response to the ideals of inclusion	• Focused on priority projects (capital projects) • Road is synonymous with space for cars • Benchmarking with international 'best practices' • Pursuit of aesthetics in infrastructure design	• Need for integrated transport including NMTs recognised

7.1. Problematizing Transport Disadvantage

The two policy documents agree on the existence of transport disadvantage that impedes different mode users from full participation in transport activities. However, there is a divergence in the manner in which this disadvantage is problematized by the two documents.

First, the KV2030 perceives this disadvantage in terms of the hindrance it places on mobility, participation in national economy and the international competitiveness of the country. Thus transport disadvantage is problematized in terms of the need to improve transport infrastructure in order to *'facilitate firms and citizens in their wealth-creation efforts'* (p. 17). Attendant to this is the need to reduce traffic congestion, high cost of transport, road crashes and pollution, all of which are focused on improving the conditions for motorised modes. At the same time, there is a visible pressure to develop transport infrastructure facilities that are among other things *'aesthetically appealing'* in order to *'to provide cost-effective world-class infrastructure facilities and services in support of the Vision'* (p. 17). This confirms the pressure of modernisation (Steyn, 2012; Watson, 2009, 2014) that limits transport strategies from being realistic to the practical challenges that face SSA cities. While it is expected of a national policy document like KV2030 to develop targets like these, *inadequate room allowed for policies other than KV2030 to influence development at the local level*[5] raises doubts about the ease of recognising the challenge that faces cycling under this arrangement.

On the other hand, the INTP demonstrates an integrated outlook in the way it problematizes transport disadvantage. Specifically, it identifies poor quality transport services, lack of a vision for the transport sector, which particularly disadvantages non-motorised modes (p. 46), and inadequate transport integration. The policy acknowledges that these challenges impede accessibility for non-motorised modes like cyclists just like they do for motorised modes. A clear opportunity to problematize the challenge facing cycling is therefore availed by this policy. However, this problematization is not likely to lead to the prioritisation of cycling issues in Kenya in general and Kisumu in particular unless KV2030 is reoriented to give room for other policies to influence development priorities at the local level. This can be achieved through the five-year-medium-term-planning framework that is provided for under KV2030 (GoK, 2007). Steyn (2012) has shown the need to reconcile such conflicting forces in order to allow the inclusion of the excluded urban citizens.

7.2. Contextualising Transport Exclusion

The theoretical analysis presented in section 6 demonstrates that exclusion means different things in different contexts and that there is a need to understand this exclusion in transport terms in order to tackle it. There is a mix of social concerns that are raised by the two policies and which can form a basis for cycling inclusion. However, these concerns are scattered and sometimes not even directly related to transport.

The most prominent transport exclusion concern that emerges from KV2030 is presented in terms of regional disparities in road network coverage. Accordingly, the policy seeks to *'implement infrastructure projects that will stimulate demand in hitherto neglected areas targeting increased connectivity and reduced transport and other infrastructure costs'* (p. 19). This prioritisation of transport strategies at the regional scale does not however elicit the inclusion cycling because of practicality of using the mode over such long distances. The strategy is thus in every practical sense for motorised transport. It is instructive that the neglected regions mentioned in the policy document are the Arid and Semi-Arid areas of the country and not the neglected slum areas of it cities, most of which equally need a deliberate transport strategy. Salon and Gulyani (2010) for instance demonstrate that most of the urban poor who can hardly afford the cost of transport reside in these settlements.

The social pillar of the KV2030 presents an opportunity through which the inclusion of disadvantaged modes could be contextualised in secondary cities like Kisumu. Specifically, the pillar seeks to implement policies *'that minimise the differences in income opportunities and access to social services'* (p. 196). This target identifies urban slums and pockets of extreme poverty as some of the areas that need this attention. The policy intention fits the situation in Kisumu where cycling is not only a mode for accessing destinations, but also a tool for income generation. However, the policy does not recognise the central part played by transport in income generation and enabling access. The opportunity presented by the policy for the inclusion of cycling is thus lost since the policy prioritises improved education, health, water and sanitation, among other human resource investments as its strategies (p. 198). Moreover, although transport is a major component of household expenditure (Kim & Dumitrescu, 2011), the policy does not address this connection in its bid to *'create a socially just and equitable society without extreme poverty'* (p. 199).

The INTP on the other hand contextualises the transport disadvantage that faces cycling in a more direct way that can elicit attention to this disadvantage. It identifies inappropriate modal split, transport unaffordability, bias against non-motorised modes by planners and lack of infrastructure provision for non-motorised modes. While these disadvantages resonate with the cycling situation in Kisumu, *'they are not likely to be addressed as long as they remain separated from*

[5] Field interview with Practising NMT expert, 20.08.2015

the priorities of the KV2030'[6]. According to the experts, lack of priority to cycling by KV2030 has been a hindrance to acknowledging the need to cater for cycling in terms of infrastructure and traffic rules. It should be pointed out that KV2030 projects have taken precedence over most other projects when it comes to government funding and support. A possible strategy to deal with this lack of harmony between KV2030 and the cycling priorities would be to acknowledge the social aspect of transport in the social pillar of KV2030. This would ingrain exclusion issues in the transport sector to the social pillar so that they get prioritised in government plans.

7.3. Visibility of Exclusion

This analysis sought to understand the extent to which the two policies made the exclusion of cyclists visible and the opportunities that such visibility offered for cycling inclusion. Differences were found between the two policies.

To begin with, KV2030 does not refer to non-motorised modes, neither in terms of acknowledging their problems nor in laying out strategies to deal with the challenges they face. This lack of mention makes the mode completely invisible from any intervention that is initiated by the KV2030. The only closest mention of exclusion relates to excluded regions and slum settlements. However, as already discussed before, the latter areas are not mentioned for transport interventions. The implication of this invisibility of cycling concerns in KV2030 is that the mode will continue to face exclusion for as long as the current arrangement that prioritises KV2030 projects remains.

In contrast, the INTP demonstrates a clear articulation of cycling concerns. These have already been discussed earlier. However, it is notable that the policy explicitly acknowledges the bias against non-motorised modes in general. The policy acknowledges that public transport in urban areas remains unaffordable to many members of working households despite the country's elaborate road network (p. 45). The policy also acknowledges that transport development in Kenya in general has focused its attention on roads for motorised transport, yet these are only accessible to a small minority since the majority remain poor. What is interesting is that despite this knowledge of this phenomenon that is arguably a case of social exclusion, non-motorised modes in general are not recognised in law to qualify them for government funding and other forms of support (GoK, 2009). This lack of recognition perpetuates lack of safety for cycling as it has to use road-spaces that are designed for motorised transport.

The articulation of the challenge that faces non-motorised modes described above brings out the social component of transport disadvantage. This is particularly so with regard to how it impacts on the transport cost for the poor, excludes them from the street-spaces, and makes it unsafe for the poor to use the streets. Packaging the solution to this challenge as a social inclusion agenda would arguably afford non-motorised modes in general and cycling in particular the visibility they require for the government to facilitate their use. It should be pointed out that the social pillar of KV2030 already tackles such social concerns although it is not explicitly linked to transport disadvantage. This makes this form of transport disadvantage invisible. The social concerns raised by INTP should hence be packaged as social inclusion concerns and be linked with the social pillar of KV2030 in order to afford them the necessary government attention. Doing this can lead to the prioritisation of cycling in Kisumu, which is hardly recognised or even catered for in spite of its active use by the poor majority.

7.4. Production of Spaces of Exclusion

Differences in the conception of the transport disadvantage presented in the previous sections elicit different infrastructure and traffic interventions. While the INTP advocates for integrated transport that includes streets that cater for cycling, KV2030 on the other hand focuses on capital infrastructure projects in its effort to address the transport disadvantage that it identifies. As mentioned already though, the targets of the KV2030 are priorised in determining not only the planning but also the execution of transport infrastructure projects. This leads to the production of spaces that exclude cycling. According to the planning authorities, *'accommodating pedal cycling [on the road] remains a challenge due to limited funds, lack of policy priority, and the emergence of motorcycles [which attracts more political attention] even though we understand its role in enabling the poor the move'.*[7]

Kisumu is currently implementing key transport infrastructure projects that are intended to improve its linkage with the neighbouring cities of Kakamega, Busia, and other cities along the Kisumu-Nairobi transport corridor. These projects are implemented within the framework of the flagship projects of KV2030 and are *largely driven by the pursuit of economic goals rather than social ones*[8]. It is notable that while the roads affected by these projects double as urban roads within the city boundaries, no clear provision has been made to accommodate cycling on their urban segments. This, despite the significance of cy-

[6] Field interview with Practising NMT expert, 20.08.2015 & County Chief Officer in charge of transport, 27.08.2015

[7] Field interview with County Chief Officer in charge of transport, 27.08.2015.

[8] Field interview with County Chief Officer in charge of transport, 27.08.2015.

cling in terms of employment for bicycle taxi operators and as an alternative mode of transport, particularly among the low-income earners of the city (Oballa, Mwaura, & Stellmach, 2012). Instead, the car-oriented street design has now cut off access, thereby preventing cyclists from turning at some important junctions in the city.[9] This makes it riskier to cycle on these roads and casts doubts on whether the projects have cyclists in mind in their quest to increase safety, connectivity and accessibility.

The foregoing production of street-spaces that exclude cyclists is not improved by the ISUD either. Instead the plan seems to borrow heavily from KV2030 and therefore a continuation of its desire for capital infrastructure projects. Cycling concerns do not receive any attention beyond the recognition of the role of cycling in enabling accessibility and the need to provide for it in terms of infrastructure and traffic conditions (Nodalis, 2014, p. 36). This is curious because the plan should offer concrete strategies on how to include the mode in order to enable it play the roles that the plan acknowledges. Instead, the plan only duplicates the capital projects proposed for Nairobi under the KV2030 without much regard to the unique cycling culture of Kisumu.

While it would have been expected that this ISUD plan would contextualise the KV2030 and tackle the unique local level planning challenges and opportunities, it fails to do so. The plan does not offer any concrete proposals on how to progressively include cycling within the street spaces of Kisumu but instead evadingly recommends that the present modal mix should be organised by providing dedicated lanes and stops and waiting areas (p. 36). In view of this insecure treatment of cycling concerns, we argue in this paper that presenting these concerns as challenges of social exclusion could generate the urgency needed to integrate the concerns into future infrastructure developments projects. This integration can occasion the production of more inclusive street-spaces. Doing this would pre-empt the difficulty of doing so once this opportunity is lost.

Responding to the infrastructure and traffic needs of the bicycle is also complicated by the use of the term 'non-motorised' modes to refer to cycling and walking, and indeed sometimes even more modes. Whereas the KV2030 fails to recognise the role of non-motorised transport, its introduction by the INTP requires enhanced clarity in order to allow its operationalisation. In Kisumu, the use of the term '*boda boda*' by planners to refer to both pedal bicycles and commercial motorcycles diminishes the possibility of producing street-spaces that include cyclists even further. This lack of clarity about the exact meaning of 'non-motorised modes' and '*boda boda*' in the context of Kisumu has engendered ambiguity with regard to the few non-motorised lanes that have been provided on the Kisumu-Busia and Kisumu-Nairobi roads under the on-going roads projects. It remains unclear who the intended users of these spaces are. These lanes have been claimed by bicyclists, pedestrians, hawkers, and motorcyclists,[10] thereby making all of them vulnerable to accidents just like they would have been if the lanes did not exist. There is therefore a need to operationalise these terminologies in order to clear the current ambiguities that emerge from their use. Moreover, it also emerges that the production of streets that include cycling cannot be tackled in isolation of these other modes and activities that claim the same spaces as the bicycle. Addressing these concerns is however beyond the scope of the current paper.

7.5. Response to the Ideals of Inclusion

The theoretical analysis revealed the need to mediate cycling in order to address its concerns. Whereas KV2030 responds to the projected growth in travel demand through capital infrastructure projects, the recognition of modes other than motorised by the INTP presents an opportunity for mediating cyclists to meet their travel demand using the bicycles. However, practicalizing this recognition remains a challenge due to the current influence of the KV2030, which focuses on stimulating economic growth rather than social inclusion. Because of this inclination, the KV2030 looks at inclusion indirectly as a means to enabling participation in the economy, rather than directly as an end in itself. Moreover, the kind of participation it envisages is by motorised modes, rather than non-motorised ones like cycling. Again, the focus of KV2030 on benchmarking its transport infrastructure standards with international best practices and developing infrastructure that is aesthetically appealing in design (p. 38) are clearly informed by the need to facilitate motorisation rather than cycling and other forms of non-motorised modes. It therefore remains doubtful if the current arrangement where the provisions of the KV2030 are prioritised can mediate cycling in Kisumu and other Kenyan cities.

The foregoing challenge is worsened by the ISUD, which proposes the expansion of existing roads and the creation of more roads to create room for the projected growth in motorised transport in Kisumu. It appears that the accessibility concerns of cyclists will continue to remain secondary unless transport planning is reoriented to enable cycling. *'[So far] cycling lanes are only considered in areas where road corridors [reserves] can accommodate it...often what remains after motorised transport has been catered for'*[11]. This attitude not only diminishes the importance of cycling; it also generates incoherent cycling network that does not encourage

[9] Field observation.

[10] Field observation.

[11] Field interview with Practising NMT expert, 20.08.2015.

cycling. There is clearly a need to demystify the inferior social construction of cycling that occasions this diminished attention to it, and to design the roads to allow safe multiple-modal use.[12]

The ISUD plan evidently renders the growth of the city car-dependent, as can be seen in the proposals to decentralise the city to outlying areas in the outskirts of the current city centre (Nodalis, 2014). The proposed relocation of public transport termini to these new nodes will certainly lead to growth in the use of private cars as these nodes are far from the city centre where most daily services such as government, banking, and social services are located. All these proposals come at a time when the city has not exhausted the space it has close to the city centre. It is curious that no provision has been made to accommodate the infrastructure and traffic needs that will arise due to the use of the bicycle to connect these nodes. These proposed changes in land-use structure, in addition to the natural triggers of travel demand, will necessitate the use of different modes by travellers of different socio-economic groups. There will hence be a need to revise the priorities of the KV2030 through the five-year medium-term-plans in order to accommodate emerging issues that the preparation of the KV2030 never foresaw[13].

8. Conclusion and Policy Recommendations

This paper has attempted to develop social inclusion as a frame for cycling-inclusive transport planning in Kisumu. Basing its arguments on social quality theory and the right to the city concept, the study developed key criteria upon which it assessed the Kenya Vision 2030 and the Integrated National Transport Plan for the extent to which their pronouncements were inclusive of cycling and its street-space needs. The aim was to identify the gaps that the policies presented as well as the opportunities that they availed for making social inclusion an imperative of transport policy. The paper shows that both the Kenya Vision 2030 and the Integrated National Transport Policy hold some potential for fronting the need for cycling-inclusive streets through social inclusion. While the Kenya Vision 2030 holds the power to influence action at the local city level, it is nonetheless weak when it comes to directly advocating for inclusive transport. On the other hand, the Integrated National Transport Policy identifies challenges that can be packaged as social inclusion concerns. However, its policy pronouncements are less prioritised in comparison to those of the Kenya Vision 2030. This diminished priority makes the INTP less influential in shaping pro-cycling interventions in Kisumu. These dissenting strengths of the two policy documents are not likely to generate the inclusion of cyclists unless they are harmonised. The current paper seizes the opportunity presented by the social nature of exclusion that faces cycling to present social inclusion as a frame for reconciling these contrasting strengths and to articulate the need for cycling-inclusive transport planning. Facilitating cyclists through their social inclusion is argued in this paper as a way of not only enabling them to participate in the mobility in ways that they can afford but also a way of recognising that they have a right to access the city by bicycles.

This study makes a number of key policy recommendations that it hopes can elicit better inclusion of cyclists through a more proactive policy formulation and implementation.

To begin with, there is a need to harmonise the two policies in order to build on their synergies. In this regard, it is relevant to directly identify transport disadvantage as a social concern and to make it one of the priority concerns of the social pillar of Kenya Vision 2030. This would accord it equal priority with the other targets of the Kenya Vision 2030. There will be need for such harmonised policies to emphasise inclusion as a goal in itself rather than a means to participation in the economy. This is because the opportunity for cycling inclusion would be lost if inclusion is presented merely as a means to participating in economic pursuits. These recommendations are relevant at policy formulation level and would call upon the national government to implement.

It is also relevant that the harmonisation of these two policies recognises that the use of bicycles on street-spaces is a right that ought to be protected by the state. These street-spaces however have multiple claims. Policies that seek to include cycling must as such link with land-use and other transport strategies to ensure that efforts to include cycling are not derailed by such multiple claims. This study also recommends that the use of social inclusion in advancing the cycling-inclusive policies should consider the context-specific factors that exclude cyclists, such as the conditions of the street-spaces and the processes of allocating these street-spaces. These factors should be used hand in hand with the socio-geographic indicators that have been used traditionally to study social exclusion. These set of recommendations would call upon both the national government as well as Kisumu County Government to implement given that they concern both policy formulation and implementation. This paper also recognises the role of local cyclists, bicycle taxi operators, and bicycle advocates in ensuring that recommendations relating to the right to access the city is recognised and upheld by the city authority.

Acknowledgements

The authors acknowledge the German Academic Exchange Program and the Kenya National Council for

[12] Field interview with Practising NMT expert, 20.08.2015.
[13] Field interview with Practising NMT expert, 20.08.2015.

Science, Technology and Innovation for funding this study. The opinions expressed in the paper however remain the responsibility of the authors.

Conflicts of Interests

The authors declare no conflict of interests.

References

Alal, M. (2014, January 28). Kenya: Kisumu Boda Bodas Plan Demos over Ban From CBD. *The Star*. Retrieved from http://allafrica.com/stories/201401280610.html

Alando, W., Brussel, M., Zuidgeest, M., & Durgi, D. (2013). Exploring the utility of the spatially-constrained accessibility measure in integrating urban cycling and land-use in Pune, India. In *Proceedings of the 14th N-AERUS / GISDECO conference, September 12-14 2013*. Enschede, Netherlands.

Allman, D. (2013). The Sociology of Social Inclusion. *SAGE Open*, *3*(1).

Asingo, P. O., & Mitullah, W. V. (2007). *Implementing road transport safety measures in Kenya: Policy issues and challenges*. *Working Paper No. 545*. Nairobi: Institute for Development Studies.

Attoh, K. A. (2012). The Transportation Disadvantaged and the Right to the City in Syracuse, New York. *Geographical Bulletin*, *53*(1), 1-19.

Banister, D. (2002). *Transport planning*. London: Spon.

Baud, I., Sridharan, N., & Pfeffer, K. (2008). Mapping Urban Poverty for Local Governance in an Indian Mega-City: The Case of Delhi. *Urban Studies*, *45*(7), 1385-1412.

Bechstein, E. (2010). *Cycling as a supplementary mode to public transport: A Case Study of Low Income Commuters in South Africa*. Paper read at the 29th Southern African Transport Conference, 16-19 August 2010. Pretoria, South Africa.

Beck, W., Maesen, L., & Walker, A. (1997). Introduction. In W. Beck, L. Maesen, & A. Walker (Eds.), *The social quality of Europe*. The Hague: Kluwer Law International.

Cameron, A. (2006). Geographies of welfare and exclusion: social inclusion and exception. *Progress in Human Geography*, *30*(3), 396-404.

Church, A., Frost, M., & Sullivan, K. (2000). Transport and social exclusion in London. *Transport Policy*, *7*(3), 195-205.

de-Langen, M. de, & Tembele, R. (2001). *Productive and liveable cities: Guidelines for pedestrian and bicycle traffic in African cities*. Lisse: A. A. Balkema Publishers.

Diaz Olvera, L., Didier, P., Pochet, P., & Maidadi, S. (2012). Motorbike taxis in the "transport crisis" of West and Central African cities. *Echogeo*, *20*, 2-15.

Diaz Olvera, L., Plat, D., & Pochet, P. (2013). The puzzle of mobility and access to the city in Sub-Saharan Africa. *Journal of Transport Geography*, *32*, 56-64.

Doyal, L., & Gough, I. (1991). *A theory of human need*. Basingstoke: Macmillan.

Engels, B., & Liu, G.-J. (2011). Social exclusion, location and transport disadvantage amongst non-driving seniors in a Melbourne municipality, Australia. *Journal of Transport Geography*, *19*(4), 984-996.

Fodor, J. A. (1975). *The Language of Thought*. Harvard: Harvard University Press.

Furness, Z. (2010). *One less car: Bicycling and the politics of automobility*. Philadelphia: Temple University Press.

GoK. (2007). *Kenya Vision 2030*. Nairobi: Ministry of Planning and National Development.

GoK. (2009). *Integrated National Transport Policy: Moving a Working Nation*. Nairobi: Ministry of Transport.

GoK. (2010a). *The 2009 Kenya Population and Housing Census: Counting Our People for the Implementation of Vision 2030*. Nairobi: Kenya National Bureau of Statistics.

GoK. (2010b). *The Constitution of Kenya, 2010*. Nairobi: Government of Kenya.

Grieco, M., Ndulo, M., Bryceson, D., Porter, G., & McCray, T. N. (2009). *African, Transport and the Millennium Development Goals: Achieving an Internationally Set Agenda*. Cambridge Scholars Publishing.

Gwilliam, K. (2003). Urban transport in developing countries. *Transport Reviews*, *23*(2), 197-216.

Harvey, D. (1982). *The limits to capital*. London, New York: Basil Blackwell Publisher Limited.

Harvey, D. (2003). The right to the city. *International Journal of Urban and Regional Research*, *27*(4), 939-941.

Harvey, D. (2012). *Rebel cities: From the right to the city to the urban revolution*. London: Verso.

Hobson, J. (1999). *New towns, the modernist planning project and social justice: The case of Milton Keynes, UK and 6th October, Egypt*. London: Development Planning Unit, University College London.

Howe, J. (n.d.). Boda Boda: Uganda's low capacity transport services.

Jones, H., Moura, F., & Domingos, T. (2013). Transport Infrastructure Project Evaluation Using Cost-benefit Analysis. *Procedia: Social and Behavioral Sciences*, *111*, 400–409.

Jones, P., & Lucas, K. (2012). The social consequences of transport decision-making: Clarifying concepts, synthesising knowledge and assessing implications, *21*, 4-16.

Kenyon, S., Lyons, G., & Rafferty, J. (2002). Transport and social exclusion: investigating the possibility of promoting inclusion through virtual mobility. *Journal of Transport Geography*, *10*(3), 207-219.

Khayesi, M., Monheim, H., & Nebe, J. M. (2010). Negotiating "Streets for All" in Urban Transport Planning: The Case for Pedestrians, Cyclists and Street Vendors in Nairobi, Kenya. *Antipode*, *42*(1), 103-126.

Kim, P., & Dumitrescu, E. (2011). *Share the road: Invest in walking and cycling*. Nairobi: UNEP.

Kola, M. O., Onyango, G. M., & Oindo, B. O. (2012). The Status of Public Transportation in unplanned suburbs of Kisumu Municipality, Kenya. *International Journal of Arts and Commerce*, *1*(1).

Labonte, R. (2004). Social inclusion/exclusion: Dancing the dialectic. *Health Promotion International*, *19*(1), 115-121.

Lefebvre, H. (1996). The right to the city. In E. Kofman & E. Lebas (Eds.), *Writings on cities.* Oxford: Blackwell.

Lin, K., Ward, P., & Maesen, L. (2009). Social quality theory in perspective. *Development and Society*, *38*(2), 201-208.

Lucas, K. (2011). Making the connections between transport disadvantage and the social exclusion of low income populations in the Tshwane Region of South Africa. *Journal of Transport Geography*, *19*(6), 1320-1334.

Lucas, K. (2012). Transport and social exclusion: Where are we now? *Transport Policy*, *20*, 105-113.

Lucas, K., & Musso, A. (2014). Policies for social inclusion in transportation: An introduction to the special issue. *Case Studies on Transport Policy*, *2*(2), 37-40.

Maesen, L., & Walker, A. (2002). Social Quality: The Theoretical State of Affairs. *European Foundation on Social Quality*, 1-24.

Maesen, L., & Walker, A. (2012). *Social quality: From theory to indicators*. New York: Palgrave Macmillan.

Makajuma, G. (2006). *Urban transport market determinants in Kenya. Analysis of modal choice and fare competition* (MSc). Delft: UNESCO-IHE.

Maoulidi, M. (2012). *Kisumu Millennium Development Goals Multi-sector Household Survey: Final Report.* New York: Millennium Cities Initiative.

Marcuse, P. (2009). From critical urban theory to the right to the city. *City*, *13*(2/3), 185-197.

Mayring, P. (2014). Qualitative Content Analysis: Theoretical foundation, basic procedures and software solution. Retrieved from http://nbn-resolving.de/urn:nbn:de:0168-ssoar-395173

McCray, T. M. (2004). An issue of culture: the effects of daily activities on prenatal care utilization patterns in rural South Africa. *Social Science & Medicine*, *59*(9), 1843-1855.

Miles, M. B., & Huberman, A. M. (1994). *Qualitative Data Analysis*. Thousand Oaks, CA: SAGE Publications.

Murthy, K. (2011). Urban Transport and the Right to the City: Accessibility and Mobility. In M. Faetanini (Ed.), *Urban Policies and the Right to the City in India. Rights, Responsibilities and Citizenship.* New Delhi: UNESCO.

Mutiso, W. K. (2010). *'Boda boda' bicycle taxis and their role in urban transport systems. Case studies of Nakuru and Kisumu, Kenya* (MSc). University of Cape Town, South Africa.

Nkurunziza, A., Zuidgeest, M., & van Maarseveen, M. (2012). Identifying potential cycling market segments in Dar-es-Salaam, Tanzania. *Habitat International*, *36*(1), 78-84.

Nodalis. (2014). *Kisumu Integrated Strategic Urban Development Plan: Planning for Kisumu's Future*. Paris: Nodalis.

Oballa, B., Mwaura, J., & Stellmach, T. (2012). *Rapid urban planning studio report kisumu*. Nairobi: UN HABITAT.

Odero, K., Sibanda, G., Njenga, P. R, Mbathi, M., Musyimi, & Opiyo, R. O. (2009). *Share the road: Minimum standards for safe, sustainable and accessible transport infrastructure in Nairobi*. Nairobi: UNEP.

Øyen, E. (1997). The contradictory concepts of social exclusion and social inclusion. In C. Gore & J. B. Figueiredo (Eds.), *Social exclusion and anti-poverty policy.* Geneva: International Institute of Labour Studies.

Pochet, P., & Cusset, J. M. (1999). Cultural barriers to bicycle use in Western African cities: The case of Bamako and Ouagadougou, *23*(2), 43-50.

Prinz, J. (2005). Are emotions feelings? Special issue on "Emotion experience", *12*(8), 9-25.

Quarshie, M. (2004). *Cycling in Ghana: An indepth study of Accra*. Accra: Centre for Cycling Expertise.

Salon, D., & Aligula, E. M. (2012). Urban travel in Nairobi, Kenya: Analysis, insights, and opportunities. *Journal of Transport Geography*, *22*, 65-76.

Salon, D., & Gulyani, S. (2010). Mobility, Poverty, and Gender: Travel 'Choices' of Slum Residents in Nairobi, Kenya. *Transport Reviews*, *30*(5), 641-657.

Scheiner, J. (2010). Social inequalities in travel behaviour: trip distances in the context of residential self-selection and lifestyles. *Journal of Transport Geography*, *18*(6), 679-690.

Schwanen, T., Lucas, K., Akyelken, N., Cisternas Solsona, D., Carrasco, J.-A., & Neutens, T. (2015). Rethinking the links between social exclusion and transport disadvantage through the lens of social capital. *Transportation Research Part A: Policy and Practice*, *74*, 123-135.

Sen, A. (2000). *Social exclusion: Concept, application, and scrutiny*. Social Development Paper No. 1. Asian Development Bank.

Shergold, I., & Parkhurst, G. (2012). Transport-related social exclusion amongst older people in rural Southwest England and Wales. *Journal of Rural Studies*, *28*(4), 412-421.

Siltaniemi, A., & Kauppinen, M.-L. (2005). The View from the International Council on Social Welfare. *European Journal of Social Quality*, *5*(1), 275-288.

Silver, H. (2007). *The process of social exclusion: The dynamics of an evolving concept* (CPRC Working Paper No. 95). Rhode Island, USA.

Singh, Y. K. (2006). *Fundamental of Research Methodology and Statistics*. New Delhi: New Age International.

Soja, E. W. (2010). The city and spatial justice. In B. Bret,

P. Gervais-Lambony, C. Hancock, & F. Landy (Eds.), *Espace et justice. Justice et injustices spatiales.* Nanterre: Presses universitaires de Paris Ouest.

Steyn, G. (2012). Modernity and informality: Conflicting forces shaping urban form in Kisumu, Kenya. *International journal for housing science*, *36*(3), 170-179.

UN-HABITAT. (2004). *Kisumu City Development Strategy (2004 - 2009).* Nairobi: UN-HABITAT.

UN-HABITAT. (2010). *Sustainable mobility in African cities.* Nairobi: UN-HABITAT.

UN-HABITAT. (2014). *The state of African cities 2014: Re-imagining sustainable urban transitions*. Nairobi: UN-HABITAT.

Walker, A., & Maesen, L. (2003). Social quality and quality of life. In *Proceedings of ESPA-NET Conference*, 13-15 November 2003.

Ward, P. R., Meyer, S. B., Verity, F., Gill, T. K., & Luong, T. C. (2011). Complex problems require complex solutions: the utility of social quality theory for addressing the Social Determinants of Health. *BMC public health*, *11*, 630.

Watson, V. (2009). 'The planned city sweeps the poor away...': Urban planning and 21st century urbanisation. *Progress in Planning*, *72*(3), 151-193.

Watson, V. (2014). African urban fantasies: dreams or nightmares? *Environment and Urbanization*, *26*(1), 215-231.

WHO. (2015). *Global Status Report on Road Safety 2015*. Geneva: WHO.

World Bank. (2013). *Inclusion Matters: The Foundation for Shared Prosperity*. Washington, DC: World Bank.

About the Authors

Walter Alando

Walter Alando is an urban planner and a lecturer of urban planning at Maseno University, Kenya. He is currently undertaking his PhD research at the Department of Transport Planning, Technische Universität Dortmund, Germany. His research focuses on transport exclusion, inclusive cities, cycling infrastructure planning, and land-use and non-motorised transport integration.

Dr. Joachim Scheiner

Joachim Scheiner received his PhD in geography at Freie Universität Berlin. He is now a professor in transport studies at the Faculty of Spatial Planning, Technische Universität Dortmund, Germany. His research focuses on travel behaviour in the context of residential mobility, spatial development and societal change.

Intentions to Move from Homelessness to Social Inclusion: The Role of Participation Beliefs, Attitudes and Prior Behaviour

Julie Christian [1,*], Dominic Abrams [2], David Clapham [3], Daniella Nayyar [1] and Joseph Cotler [1]

[1] School of Psychology, University of Birmingham, Birmingham, B15 2TT, UK; E-Mails: j.n.christian@bham.ac.uk (J.C.), dxn497@student.birmingham.ac.uk (D.N.), jxc338@bham.ac.uk (J.C.)
[2] School of Psychology, University of Kent, Canterbury, CT2 7NP, UK; E-Mail: d.abrams@kent.ac.uk
[3] Henley Business School, University of Reading, Reading, RG6 6UD, UK; E-Mail: d.f.clapham@reading.ac.uk

* Corresponding author

Abstract
A key aim of homelessness services is not only to ensure that homeless people attain a secure home, but that this is a pathway to wider social inclusion. However, relatively little is known about the psychological elements that are essential for homeless people to engage with these pathways, nor whether these elements combine in ways that are predictable from previous research. In the present work, we examined both demographic and behavioural precursors, and contemporaneous psychological predictors, of a set of 49 homeless men's intentions to engage with a programme to move them toward long-term housing and social inclusion. Contrary to predictions based on subjective utility and rational choice theories, we found that normative pressure and did not directly predict the men's intentions. Instead, we found that intentions were predicted by their attitudes towards the services, and their specific beliefs about the benefits of particular courses of action (efficacy beliefs), and to a more restricted extent their experience (sociodemographics); and in those with high prior service use histories, only participatory beliefs guided future service use intentions. These findings suggest that it is important to focus on intentions as a highly relevant outcome of interventions, because beliefs about interventions can break the link between past behaviour or habitual service use and future service use. Such interventions may be particularly effective if they focus on the evaluative and efficacy-related aspects of behaviour over time and better understand the benefits the men evaluated the services as offering them.

Keywords
attitudes; homelessness; service use; social inclusion

Issue
This article is part of the issue "Homelessness and Social Inclusion", edited by Isobel Anderson (University of Stirling, UK), Maša Filipovič Hrast (University of Ljubljana, Slovenia) and Joe Finnerty (University College Cork, Ireland).

---

1. Introduction

One of the recurring themes in the debate on homelessness in Britain has been the difficult and fractured nature of the pathways out of homelessness and, therefore the move from social exclusion to social inclusion through the acquisition and maintenance of permanent housing. There has been concern that many pathways out of homelessness are characterised by recurring episodes of housing instability and high dropout rates from different forms of intermediary provision, which casts some doubt on the usefulness of existing forms of provision (Anderson, 2010; Clapham, 2005). As background, provision for homeless people in the UK is mainly based on the 'continuum of care' or 'staircase' approach (Johnsen & Teixeira, 2010) in which homeless people progress from one form of provision to another on the basis of their perceived ability (as assessed by professional staff) to move on to the next stage. To reach the final stage of permanent housing, homeless people have to show to professionals that they are able to cope on their own and are 'tenancy ready'. This system creates many barriers and difficulties for many homeless people to overcome in accessing services and moving through the 'continuum of care' that can test their skills, knowledge and determination. Therefore, within this system it is important to know what factors are important in influencing the chances of success.

The difficulties inherent in the 'continuum of care' approach have led to calls for the adoption of the 'housing first' principles. Under the 'housing first' principles and guidance, the provision of adequate permanent housing is the first priority and cornerstone for further social intervention designed to deal with any ongoing health or social problems, or lack of capabilities to cope in mainstream accommodation. The 'housing first' approach requires less of homeless people before they achieve permanent housing. In explaining the difficulties that homeless people face in achieving successful outcomes of permanent housing in the current situation, the housing literature has tended to attribute the failure rates to housing management practices, or the quality of neighbourhoods or the accommodation provided (Pawson & Munro, 2010; Warnes, Crane, & Coward, 2013). As such, the focus has been on the physical quality of the houses that homeless people move on to, the support offered through housing management services, and the quality of the neighbourhood in both physical and, particularly social terms.

A different perspective focuses on homeless persons' own experiences and understanding of their situations. Much of this work has focused on interactions with services, because it is a social context that allows us an opportunity to explore the daily experiences of homeless people find themselves in. Thus, there has been growing interest in the impact of social and psychological factors of those using the programmes, seeing them as part of a multi-faceted solution. Such research often focuses on the presence or absence of an appropriate social network or on family cohesion, believing norms to be an important determinant of service use and 'future housing success'. However, the individual homeless persons' perception of their own choices and their own psychological situation has remained somewhat neglected. One example of a factor that has been overlooked is that of homeless people's self-efficacy—their sense of their ability to achieve an intended or desired result outcomes (Bandura, 1997)—could reasonably be expected to bear on their service use behaviours. Discussion of the role of self-efficacy, and other psychological enablers or inhibitors has been sparse in the housing crisis literature (compared with that of more obvious material or familial factors). The limited focus on psychological variables is regrettable given that they provide powerful proximal predictors of social participation—which is to say, it is the way people make sense of their situation, not just the objective situation itself, that helps to explain differences in the way people behave (Schultz & Oskamp, 1999).

In addition to the lacuna in conceptual and empirical focus on psychological components of service use, there also remains a dearth of systematic evaluation evidence on the impact of support services on fostering social inclusion for homeless people. More needs to be known both about the ways that interventions have impact (both positive and negative), and which aspects best encourage homeless people's desire to make use of services that will help them achieve social participation. The aim of this paper, therefore, is to report and consider evidence that illuminates the potential impact and the role of efficacy and other related psychosocial factors on homeless people's intentions to use services that can increase aimed at aiding their resettlement in longer-term accommodation, and thereby also enhancing their social participation and inclusion. We first provide some theoretical background regarding these psychological variables, then introduce the research itself and statistically test hypotheses about the link between demographic and psychological variables on the one hand, and service-use intentions on the other.

1.1. Efficacy & Psychosocial Factors Linked to Housing and Services Uptake

Social inclusion and exclusion is not simply an economic or social structural phenomenon, it is also experienced most powerfully and directly as a psychological phenomenon—in people's daily experiences (see Abrams & Christian, 2007). Homeless people are confronted by multiple forms of exclusion, but it can be argued that the psychological dimension is critical in forming their intentions and subsequent actions, in part because the interpersonal information provides a working understanding for their experiences of the structural-level. To address this, researchers have adopted mainstream psychological approaches to explore homeless people's coping strategies, because motivations to seek housing and employment are thought to be rooted in people's expectations and previous personal experiences. Determination to seek housing is also arguably linked to how people perceive events that unfold in the world, and their ability to tackle adverse circumstances. However, only a handful of studies, focusing on personal outcomes, have looked closely at the role of efficacy and interventions for homeless people (Epel, Bandura, & Zimbardo, 1999; Park & Kim, 2014), which is surprising given that 'efficacy' is often viewed as synonymous with empowerment and/or wellbeing in the housing and homelessness literatures (see Clapham, Christian, & Foye, 2016). Within the domain of homelessness, Epel et al. (1999) found, in a population of US homeless people, that those who had been previously employed and who had a higher level of educational achievement also had a more positive future orientation (a higher ability to plan for the future) despite current personal circumstances. While it is possible to argue that a number of personal and situation factors may increase or decrease a strong sense of personal efficacy (self-belief), Epel et al. (1999) too suggest that enhanced personal efficacy leads to greater feelings of empowerment over barriers to housing, and ultimately to more sustained house seeking behaviours and, eventually, to social inclusion.

Within the literature, an efficacy style framework has also been applied in conjunction with social identity theory (SIT) and the more general self-categorization perspective (Abrams & Hogg, 1990; Tajfel & Turner, 1979), as well as a model of social attitude formation, the Theory of Planned Behaviour (TPB, Ajzen, 1991) to investigate social perceptions, motives, and sense of 'self'. Here, beliefs about the self were not solely task-based, but the factors were rider reaching such as *perceived benefits of service use* (i.e., attitudes towards service use), the extent to which homeless people perceived they had personal agency over their service interaction (i.e., perceived control), and the 'influence of social and cultural norms' (i.e., identification and normative influence) were explored in populations of homeless people in the UK and the US. In a series of multinational studies, Christian and colleagues (Christian & Abrams, 2004; Christian & Armitage, 2002; Christian, Armitage, & Abrams, 2003; Christian, Clapham, & Abrams, 2011) conclude that homeless people's social engagement is predicted both by the extent to which they perceive they have 'some control over their service participation', and by the extent to which they feel able to 'identify' with the staff at facilities. Across studies with over 700 homeless participants, increases in their 'perceived control' led to a greater sense of empowerment. Moreover, the influence exerted by social norms on participation behaviour appears to be linked to the stability of homeless people's support networks. Friendship groups (friendships with other homeless people) were less stable than those with support worker groups and therefore the latter were easier to identify with. The findings suggest that there may well be a hierarchy of social relationships in which staff could be seen as more stable social referents, but that this might change over time as circumstances fluctuate (also see Christian & Abrams, 2003; Snow & Anderson, 1987). The results suggest that a combination of factors, efficacy as well as normative-based variables, interact with the social context to determine whether people uptake service opportunities (see, Christian & Abrams, 2004). Unclear, however, is the role of prior behaviour (which could be either previous service use and measures of housing instability) in shaping intentions—with some research supporting a direct link from prior behaviour to intentions, and other studies suggesting no direct links but providing evidence for an intentions-behaviour relationship—leaving questions about potential impact of this factor within this domain.

In the present work we extend previous research (Christian & Abrams, 2003, 2004; Christian et al., 2011) by exploring the potentially distinct but additive contributions of efficacy-based beliefs, attitudes, and normative influences (social influence and social identification with friendship groups) in predicting both current and future housing service use. We are also conscious of the complex nature of the circumstances facing homeless people. Therefore, an important contribution of the present work is to disentangle how contemporaneous psychological variables (attitudes, efficacy and so on) relate to future service use intentions after accounting for the individual's context, defined in terms of differences in the length of time that particular individuals have spent with coping with housing instability, as well as their length of residence at the shelter in which they are currently residing. Arguably, both these indices of past behaviour could be a basis of service use 'habits', which may or may not fully explain continuing and intended active engagement with the housing services and their use (i.e., no relationship between prior behaviour and intentions); or alternatively the findings could demonstrate desire to engage on the part of the men and provide evidence of contextual/structural issues which might present barriers to service use (i.e., no relationship between current behaviour and intentions). As such, the present correlational study seeks to understand to what extent psychosocial variables may play a role in enabling people to break free of their situation and past circumstances in determining future service use intentions, an indicator of their eventual pathway to social participation and inclusion.

2. Method

2.1. Selection and Recruitment

Prior to conducting the study, service facilities were contacted based on information from experts working with the homeless population in Birmingham (also see, Christian & Abrams, 2003; Toro et al., 1999; Snow & Anderson, 1987). The main principles for consideration of these facilities were the location and size of the population served, mainly due to the differences in services offered from different sized facilities. The sample of homeless people was drawn from both large and small facilities, because smaller facilities tended to offer either supported housing or floating support to their homeless clients, whereas larger facilities generally provide both services to their clients. It was considered to be important that both forms were taken into account.

Once facilities agreed to take part in the investigation, two approaches were used to recruit homeless people. First, posters providing information about the study were displayed in common areas; and second, members of staff also approached clients and asked whether they might be willing to take part in the research (see, Christian et al., 2003). Similar procedures have been previously used (Akilu, 1992; Christian & Armitage, 2002; Christian et al., 2011; Toro et al., 1999). Potential participants, asking opting in, were then included in the interview schedule.

2.2. Participants

Forty-six homeless men from Birmingham, England, ranging in age from 21 to 62 years (M = 38.63, SD = 11.54) took part in the study. They were predominantly: White British (59%) and single persons (87%). Additionally, there was almost an equal split for participants between those with employment/academic qualifications (24), versus those without academic/employment qualifications (22). Of these, 27 participants had experience working as labourers or with 'unskilled jobs', while 19 participants reported having skilled employment backgrounds. The profile of the participants reflects the patterns reported in the single homeless literature (Anderson, 1994; Burrows, 1997; Busch-Geertsema, Edgar, O'Sullivan, & Pleace, 2010; Fitzpatrick, Johnsen, & White, 2011; Fitzpatrick, Kemp, & Klinker, 2000). All participants had used services prior to the study, and on average, the participants had spent six months in their current temporary accommodation, residing at the shelter from which they were sampled.

2.3. Measures

2.3.1. Pilot Study

In accordance with the framework (TPB; Ajzen, 1991; Bandura, 1997; SIT, Abrams & Hogg, 1987) used to guide the research, a pilot study was conducted prior to main study, pilot interviews were conducted with ten homeless people. The purpose of these was to gather the content for both the interviews, and to determine whether homeless people felt that use of services led to them securing long-term accommodation, thus ensuring the ecological validity. Interviews used open-ended response formats and lasted an average of one hour. The resulting interview measure consisted of the following items:

Behavioural Intentions
Behavioural intention items were: "I intend to use a housing programme this month", "I am likely to use a housing programme this month", "The chances are that I will use a housing programme this month," (scored 1 = *strongly disagree* through to 5 = *strongly agree*). The mean of the 3 items was taken as a reliable measure of intention to use a housing programme ($\alpha = 0.67$).

Attitude
Participants were presented with the statement: "Using a housing programme this month would be". Two response options were provided: important/unimportant; positive/negative," on 5-point scales. The mean of the 2 items was taken as a measure of attitude towards the use of a housing programme ($\alpha = 0.78$).

Norms
Participants were asked if they felt that friends and families influenced their decision to participate in housing programmes. Only referent beliefs were assessed, because in pilot phases of the work, participants were clear that there was not a relationship between referent beliefs and their motivation to comply. For example, "Those who are important to me think that I should use a housing programme this month" (referent belief) (scored 1 = *disagree completely* through to 5 = *agree completely*). The item was used as a measure of social norms.

Perceived Control
A single item tapped perceived control: "How much control do you feel you have over your housing and housing searches?" (scored 1 = *disagree completely* through to 5 = *agree completely*).

Efficacy: Participatory Behavioural Beliefs
Three items were used to measure participants' participatory beliefs. These items clustered around 'attendance', 'meeting with key workers' (support staff), and their role in activities with Local Government to gain housing. The questions focused on assessing whether the participants felt that they had the skills/confidence necessary to engage in these behaviours to meet their housing related goals, or whether they felt that they were unable to do so (i.e., perception of skills needed related to specific tasks required as identified by them). Items were scored 0 (never) to 5 (very often). The mean of the 3 items was used as a measure of efficacy: participatory behavioural beliefs ($\alpha = 0.61$).

Social Identification
Two items measured social identification. These included statements such as, "In general, the social groups I belong to are an important part of my self-image". Each were scored 1 (disagree completely) to 5 (agree completely). The mean of the 2 items was taken as a measure of identification with a social group ($\alpha = .91$).

To help to tease apart the nature of the social relationships that might be important for participants, we also asked about the range and numbers of social contacts, friendships and what they found important features of them, and whether they thought social groups were based on location (i.e., "I have friends in Bournemouth; I have a mate in London." Social groups were not categorical in terms of construal around a 'role' as linked to activities, such as political participation or community network, rather they were linked to geographical locations whether all within one city, Birmingham, or in several locations ranging from London to southern regions of England and Wales). Information was gathered using scoring 1 (low end of scale/no contacts) through to 5 (high end of the scale/several contacts). In addition, open ended questions were also thematically coded and assigned categorical values for analysis.

Sociodemographic Characteristics and Prior Service Use Patterns
Causes of homelessness, views of people's ability to over-

come housing instability in Britain, length of time spent in the current homeless hostel, level of education/type of employment training, age, ethnicity, and marital status were recorded using open-ended questions. Ethnicity and marital status were binary (0,1) coded for the purpose of statistical analyses. Length of time spent homeless, however, was coded in number of days spent homeless.

2.3.2. Procedures and Administration

Administration of Structured Interview

Consistent with procedures outlined in the literature, homeless people were approached at tables in facilities, or they were randomly selected from daily registers (Toro et al., 1999; also see, Christian et al., 2011). All participants were told that their responses would be kept confidential, and that their assistance would not affect their future opportunities to take part in the services programmes. Prior to taking part in the interviews, homeless people were asked if they would be willing to take part in a series of interactions and told that these meetings would include an interview and intervention classes. If potential participants agreed, then they were provided with more information about the study and a first interview was arranged. Interview schedules were administered verbally and on a one-to-one basis in a quiet area within service facilities. This widely accepted procedure minimizes the effects of literacy on responding (Toro & Wall, 1991). Interviews took approximately 45 minutes to complete.

Measure of Current Behaviour

To capture an 'objective measure' of current service use behaviour, service providers were contacted eight weeks after the interviews had been completed. They were asked whether each of the men was still residing at the hostel. A binary coding system was employed and participants were assigned '0' if they were not still residing at the hostel (because they had moved into other accommodation (longer term)), and '1' if they were still in residence. (This measure was used in conjunction with prior service use histories and length of time spent without permanent accommodation.)

3. Results

3.1. Preliminary Findings

It may be surprising given the barriers that homeless people face in the 'continuum of care' approach that, in general, homeless people had positive views of services, and they also felt that most people facing housing issues within British society overcome these difficulties (M = 4.36 overcome housing difficulties on a 5-point scale). Moreover, they indicated that they did not spend 'a lot' of time worrying about their access to housing (M = 1.39 level of worry on a 5-point scale). They men felt that they had 'average' amounts of control over their lives generally (M = 3.5 on a 5-point scale) in spite of their circumstances. On the whole, they reported fairly positive views towards (their) housing instability and its resolution, with their concerns largely focused on the process and not access to housing. These themes are reflected in the correlations presented (see below).

3.1.1. Are Perceived Benefits of Services Hindering Inclusion?

In this study, we sought to explore perceptions of service utilisation. The overall pattern emerging demonstrates that attitudes, participatory behaviours and norms are interrelated, indicating that the homeless men are primarily motivated by what they perceived the benefits and outcomes of their service utilisation to be (see Tables 1 and 2, which provides correlations amongst the variables). Interestingly, for those still residing at the hostels in which they were interviewed ($n = 29$; still residing after interview), there was a strong relationship between homeless people's attitudes and their intentions to continue participation, such that the more benefits that they saw as coming from taking part in housing services, the more likely they were to intend to take part in them. Also consistent with our expectations, intentions to use housing services were associated with a stronger perceived control over one's circumstances ($r = .42$, $p = .004$). Participants also felt that they would benefit most from an intervention programme, as tapped by asking them about whether they would find further services to supplement current service to be helpful in their acquisition of permanent accommodation, if they could see the benefits of the service they were using ($r = .417$, $p = .008$).

As we have pointed out, perceived benefits of their service use (attitudes), future service use intentions, perceived control, and participatory beliefs were all interrelated, supporting the theory approaches informing the work. In Table 2, we used the average length of stay/contact with the current service as a way to divide (median split procedure) the sample into low and high service use categories to explore differences in future service use intentions. (Although the sample sizes are not equal, the distribution of high and low members across services is, which is why there are no mean differences found amongst locations). For those in the low prior service use category (i.e., 90 days maximum), there is a relationship between prior use and future service use intentions, with those having had the shortest histories of contact with services being those people forming the strongest intentions. More robust future use intentions were also associated with shorter lengths of time spent without permanent accommodation. Other factors correlated with higher future use intentions were age and ethnicity—meaning that younger men, of British Caucasian origin, reported having stronger intentions for future use. This is, in contrast, to those who had longer periods of contact with services (excess of 90 days and up

Table 1. Descriptive statistics and intercorrelations ($n = 46$).

	Mean	SD	1	2	3	4	5	6	7	8	9	10	11
1. BI	4.39	0.99											
2. ATT	3.97	1.21	.403**										
3. SN	2.11	1.69	.205	.367*									
4. PBB	3.44	1.62	.420**	.163	.073								
5. Control	3.52	1.56	.170	.054	.007	.037							
6. SI	3.03	1.64	.189	.317*	.017	.117	.067						
7. MI	1.89	0.88	−.78	−.351*	−.007	−.149	−.153	−.122					
8. Current Use	0.83	0.38	−.165	.157	−.084	−.031	−.179	.045	−.124				
9. Prior Behaviour	192.11	284.49	−.260	−.147	−.145	−.058	−.321*	−.196	−.069	.158			
10. Time Homeless	1652.59	2067.07	.053	.029	.054	−.026	.084	.020	−.062	.078	.220		
11. Age	38.63	11.54	−.248	.046	−.120	−.183	.041	−.102	−.242	.106	.211	.355*	
12. Ethnicity	59% white		.358*	.089	−.068	.163	.055	.099	−.054	−.035	−.022	.014	−.310*

Notes: * $p < .05$; ** $p < .01$; 1. BI = Behavioural Intentions; 2. ATT = Attitudes; 3. SN = Subjective Norms; 4. PBB = Participatory Behavioural Beliefs; 5. Control = Perceived Control; 6. SI = Social Identity; 7. MI = Number of Social Groups Reporting Being a Member of; 8. Current Use = moved on or still residing in hostel; 9. PB = length of time spent residing at current hostel (in days); 10. Length of time spent as homeless (reported in days).

to 3 years). Within this population of men, attitudes and intentions are almost synonymous ($r = .849$, $p = .001$), showing the close link between perceived benefits and future intentions. Also, there were negative relationships between attitudes and social norms, as well as between time spent without permanent accommodation and perceived benefits of services (i.e., with their attitudes). In these cases, longer spells of homelessness reduced the number benefits viewed as linked with housing services and fewer benefits were associated with more social pressures to engage in service use.

3.1.2. Is Service Use Behaviour a 'Habit': The Role of Prior Behaviour?

Turning attention to the absence of a significant correlation between the men's current behaviour and future service use intentions, while inconsistent with what we might expect (see Armitage & Connor, 2001; Christian et al., 2011), the moderate relationship between prior behaviour and future use intentions means that there is still quite good capacity for predicting what people are likely to do. For this reason, we explore the prediction of intention from a number of variables identified through the correlation analysis, and we test our prognostication using a multiple regression analysis. With future service use intentions as the dependent variable, on Step 1, we entered ethnicity and prior behaviour (length of time spend at without permanent accommodation) to control for the effects of personal experiences amongst the men and the influence this might have on shaping their future use. Then, on Step 2 we entered attitudes and participatory behaviours. In this way, we can test the relative contributions of each of these psychosocial variables, and the extent to which these outweigh the influence of personal habits, or circumstances (i.e., length of time), or background (ethnicity) in forming future service use intentions.

The regression analysis (see Table 3) showed that prior behaviour (length of time homeless) and ethnicity explained 12.6% of the variance, F_{change} $(2, 42) = 3.02$, $p = .059$, with a significant effect for ethnicity. (This allows us to control for the impact of any influence from prior behaviours before exploring the contributions of other background variables. Once these are examined we move to examine the impact of psychosocial variables). The addition of attitude and participatory behavioural beliefs accounted for a further 24% of the variance, F_{change} $(2, 40) = 7.55$, $p < .005$, so that the model as a whole accounted for 36.5%. Overall, the findings suggest that prior and current experiences were much less important in shaping intentions, with emphasis instead given to attitudes, perceived benefits and to a lesser extent to the men's ethnicities[1].

Given the relationship between future use intentions and prior use, we also conducted the regression analysis using the responses of those in the lower service use population[2]. Variables were entered in the same ordering as described above.

The regression analysis (see Table 4) showed that prior behaviour (length of time homeless) and ethnicity explained 27.6% of the variance, F_{change} $(2, 29) = 5.52$, $p = .009$, with a significant effect for both factors. The addition of attitude and participatory behavioural beliefs accounted for a further 14.4% of the variance, F_{change} $(2, 27) = 3.363$, $p < .05$, so that the model as a whole accounted for 42%. Overall, the findings suggest that the homeless experiences and ethnicity were much less important in shaping future use intentions ($p = .068$ and $.062$ respectively), with emphasis on participatory beliefs ($p = .02$).

[1] If we treat ethnicity as a random factor rather than as a measured variable, then p = n.s.

[2] With an n-size of 33, we have power at .95 (with the effect size).

Table 2. Descriptive statistics and intercorrelations for high and low prior service use populations: High prior use above diagonal ($n = 13$) and low prior use below diagonal ($n = 33$).

	Mean	SD	1	2	3	4	5	6	7	8	9	10	11	12
1. BI	4.38 (4.40)	1.02 (.98)	—	.849**	−0.457	0.273	.535	0.216	−0.46	−0.18	0.03	0.517	0.086	0.255
2. ATT	3.08 (4.03)	1.12 (1.25)	0.245	—	−.669*	0.092	.548	0.231	−0.443	−0.184	−0.038	.595*	−0.029	0.152
3. SN	2.00 (2.15)	1.07 (1.71)	−0.106	−0.352	—	−0.023	.000	−0.167	0	0.191	0.286	−0.153	0.068	0.371
4. PBB	3.61 (3.36)	1.49 (1.68)	.474**	0.193	−0.393	—	.134	−0.116	−0.149	0.391	0.124	−0.276	0.039	0.045
5. Control	3.60 (3.48)	1.55(1.58)	.031	−.118	.038	−.314	—	.259	−.803*	.312	.045	.420	.162	.008
6. SI	2.00(3.04)	1.75(1.61)	0.178	.351*	0.487	0.204	−.009	—	−0.261	0.342	−0.183	0.117	−0.4	0.469
7. MI	2.00(1.84)	1.00(.83)	0.102	−0.308	0.11	−0.16	.128	−0.053	—	−0.096	0.067	−0.532	−0.378	−0.165
8. Current Use	92%	78.8%	−0.166	0.259	0.004	−0.14	−.314	−0.032	−0.300	—	0.219	−0.343	0.165	−0.228
9. Prior Behaviour	176 days	231 days	−.360*	−0.172	0.065	−0.12	−.445*	−0.201	−0.133	0.131	—	0.058	0.121	0.101
10. Time Homeless	500 days	445 days	−.372*	−0.178	0.183	−0.134	−.440	0.006	0.09	−0.001	.696**	—	0.235	−0.07
11. Age	36 years	43 years	−.384*	0.107	0.135	−0.295	−.015	0.013	−0.236	0.039	0.431	0.281	—	−0.433
12. Ethnicity	61% White-British	54% White-British	.400*	0.074	0.032	0.201	.070	−0.053	−0.009	0.005	−0.407	−0.017	−0.299	—

Notes: * $p < .05$; ** $p < .01$; 1. BI = Future Service Use Intentions; 2. ATT = Attitudes; 3. SN = Subjective Norms; 4. PBB = Participatory Behavioural Beliefs; 5. Control = Perceived Control; 6. SI = Social Identity; 7. MI = Number of Social Groups Reporting Being a Member of; 8. Current Use = moved on or still residing in hostel; 9. PB = length of time spent residing at current hostel (in days); 10. Length of time spent as homeless (reported in days).

Table 3. Hierarchical multiple regression analysis predicting future service use intentions.

Step/Predictor		R	R^2	F_{Change}	df_a	B	SE
1.	Ethnicity	.355	.126	3.022	2,42	.695*	.287
	Length of Time Spent Homeless					−2.464	.000
2.	Ethnicity	.605	.365	7.554	2,40	.529*	.254
	Length of Time Spent Homeless					−2.525	.000
	Attitude					.266*	.105
	Participatory Behavioural Beliefs					.198*	.078

Notes: Dependent measure: future service use intention; * $p < .05$.

Table 4. Hierarchical multiple regression analysis predicting future service use intentions ($n = 33$; low prior service use included).

Step/Predictor		R	R^2	F_{Change}	df_a	B	SE
1.	Ethnicity	.525	.276	5.52**	2,29	.362*	.313
	Length of Time Spent Homeless					−2.22*	.000
2.	Ethnicity	.648	.420	3.363	2,27*	.286	.296
	Length of Time Spent Homeless					−1.95	.000
	Attitude					.675	.089
	Participatory Behavioural Beliefs					2.35*	.089

Notes: Dependent measure: future service use intention; * $p < .05$; ** $p < .01$.

4. Discussion

The general point emerging from these findings is that effective services need to understand and target the whole person, but that there may be important time periods to understand when and how people are willing to form intentions and to use services aimed at aiding them. In this study, based on an application of theory of planned behaviour (Ajzen, 1991) and efficacy principles (Bandura, 1997), the homeless men suggest that they have identified of skills or behaviours that might overcome the perceived barriers to reaching longer-term accommodation (participatory behaviours), but they also identify and deal with the presence of potential structural systems/organizational issues that could be inhibiting satisfactory housing outcomes and perpetuate the cycle of social exclusion (absence of a link between intentions and current behaviour). Here, we note the complexity of service use and homeless people's lives. Additionally, picking up on the latter we examine the prior behaviour-current behaviour-intention relationship. However, we explore possible patterns of those using services versus those who have moved on. The results of this highlight that barriers to housing might not be the same barriers or hurdles that impact decisions whether to take part in services; the barriers might be very different. The perceptions of different barriers have implication for whether the men were able to form intentions and to sense of efficacy over the tasks that might be relevant to them participating in their own rehousing processes. Then, we show that use of housing services is not a habitual act on the part of homeless people, because there a change in the frequency of behaviour (current behaviour is guided by a cost benefit analysis in which the men actively gauged the benefits of participation (also see Christian & Abrams, 2003).

To better understand this point about engagement and predicting future service use intentions, let's examine the role of participatory behavioural beliefs (Bandura, 1997). First, the evidence suggests that homeless people's understanding of the phases needed to gain permanent accommodation, and their assessment of whether they possess the skills required to successfully complete the tasks/steps, together are key elements in their intentions about whether to try to advance their situation to gain permanent accommodation. Similarly, the perceived benefits (Ajzen, 1991) of the delivery of the service use were important. The more positively they evaluated the service delivery (higher attitude scores), the more likely they were to report positive participatory beliefs, showing the close link between content and delivery in determining future use (service use intentions) (Eagly & Chaiken, 1993). While the data are only cross sectional, they map on to other longitudinal data, which also showed that determinants of initial service use were not the same determinants reported after 12 months of engagement (Christian et al., 2003).

Breaking this pattern down in terms of thinking about the process, it is possible that two things could be happening. The first, and most likely, is that perceptions of the use of services and what is needed to overcome barriers to continued participation are not the same, and should not be conceptualized of as such. These barriers could be contextual (and thus the absence of a link with current behaviour) and tie into the local housing environment. But, there might also be a combination of contextual factors and personal resource issues that go on here too (and hence the reason why length of time without accommodation is not related but rather length of engagement with service). Therefore, it might be seeing two populations for the following reasons: homeless people with more positive attitudes to services might stay or development other links within the services, and those with more negative attitudes might move-on, because the resources needed might not be gleaned through engagement but by benefits and resources in achieving satisfactory housing outcomes. In other words, if those desiring to 'move on' perceive more benefits as drawn from outside of the service, they could see more opportunities laying elsewhere than those men who are more content with the service. That is, the experience of homeless people not using services, but achieving positive housing outcomes, might need to be captured and incorporated in intervention programmes' design in order to facilitate understanding of this. A second possibility is that the men's 'perceived service requirements/needs' are not static but dynamic and change over time, and indeed the potential benefits may also change over time, and therefore this should be considered by those designing and monitoring service delivery (this might also be why longer contact with services decreases intentions for future use. It is possible that needs are being met through other avenues and resources whether personal network or structural in nature and not the service. The flip side is that if the services are aiming for this, then the decrease in future intentions should be recorded positively as an achieved goal).

In the debate about the relative merits of the 'continuum of care' and 'housing first' models, the findings show the importance of psychological variables in enabling homeless people to overcome the many hurdles placed in their way to achieving permanent housing. The fewer the hurdles, the more likely it is that homeless people will have the necessary skills, knowledge and determination to overcome them. Also, the early reward of permanent housing in the 'housing first' approach is more likely to be reflected in more positive evaluations of service outcomes and so increase the intention to participate in programmes, both factors that proved important in determining outcomes in the present study.

As well as the practical and policy implications, there are a number of important theoretical contributions. Bentler and Speckart (1981) and Bagozzi (1981) have suggested that the best predictor for future behaviour is past behaviour, highlighting the central role that prior behaviour is likely to play in guiding choices, actions, and motives of people. This contrasts strongly with Ajzen's (1991) argument that effects of prior behaviour should be absorbed in the attitude, subjective norm, and perceived behavioural control components within the Theory of Planned Behaviour. Prior behaviour should therefore not exert an independent influence on behaviour or future behaviour. Here, however, we would argue that current behaviour might be restrained by social structures, so the reason we are not seeing a direct link is not because the men are not intending to engage, but because there are barriers that are beyond what they perceive. (We indicate that they are beyond their perceptions, because findings suggest that they feel they have knowledge to help in the resettlement process.) What is interesting is that prior behaviour appears to have an optimal window for facilitating task-related efficacy and intentions for future service use. Shorter and more intensive contact seems to be more effective for active engagement, whereas longer sustained periods of contact change the pattern associated with intentions and cost/benefit analysis carried out by the men. Importantly, this does not seem to be connected to the length of time spent without permanent accommodation Given that these services rely on a co-creation model, it highlights that homeless people see their needs, and contributions, as important in charting the directions in which help might be developed—including the notion that these might not be static but more dynamic in nature.

One unexpected finding in this study was that we did not observe a strong role of norms or identification with intentions or behaviours. This differs from our prior work (Christian & Armitage, 2002; Christian et al., 2011) and that of others (Snow & Anderson, 1987). One factor that maps onto this difference is that the present context is housing whereas previous work focused on outreach services. It is possible that housing intentions have a more individualistic focus—ultimately concerned with the person's own personal situation. The present evidence suggests that if norms and identity have an influence on intentions it may be rather indirect. For example, norms were related to attitudes but not directly to intentions. In contrast, it seems likely that use of outreach services involves a focus on provision that is often shared with others such as food, other material or emotional supports and so forth. Therefore, the role of norms and identity may be more proximal to the behaviour given the immediacy of the context. However, further research, and ideally longitudinal evidence, is needed to understand how and when group identity and shared social norms may be implicated in housing intentions.

This highlights some interesting methodological points and constraints on the application of our findings. The current study provides a concrete step towards understanding more about the relationship between psychosocial variables and future service use, but it does not shed light on when those perceived benefits are likely to change (relationship between attitudes and current and prior behaviour), or why there is a disparity between current behaviour with prior behaviour to that of future use. The complexities of this would likewise have to be unpacked using more qualitative and narrative forms of data collection. Additionally, we realize that this is a restricted sample size and that we have not include women's views. It is likely in another location and with a mixed gender sample we would find some variations in the patterns. But equally such an application would answer important questions about the influence of the structural context. It is possible that locations such as London, for example, will follow the same emergence of routines between services, either because members of staff move between organizations, or because the framework and participation in professional networks shapes the provision that is offer. Suffice to say that such application would be a welcome—and would be an important contribution.

The present findings suggest that focusing on homeless people's evaluations of their prospects and choices, and their beliefs about the effectiveness of pursuing various options for action can play an important role in their developing effective intentions. This does not, of course, mean that they will be able to overcome the very real material and practical barriers to inclusion and finding housing that undoubtedly exist, but at least it does mean that some of the psychological obstacles may be overcome and homeless people could be enabled to persist more with action that is likely to be effective. In turn, we know that things that increase social inclusion also increase well-being, and feed into a virtuous cycle that helps to build social capital and other important non-financial resources (Abrams & Christian, 2007; Abrams, Hogg, & Marques, 2005). In summary, the present research offers an optimistic prospect for those planning interventions that can support homeless people. The past is not an inevitable portent of the future and the right kind of support does seem to hold the potential for helping homeless people to perceive and aim for better outcomes.

Acknowledgements

We would like to thank Mr. Damien Neadle for his assistance in the preparation of this piece; and Shemeica Thomas, Leyla Williams, Tracey Beech, Amanda Yaffe, and Sara Hussey for their assistance with data collection. We are especially grateful to all of the men and facilities taking part in this study—thank you! And, finally, we would like to express our gratitude to the EPSRC for funding to the first author (EP/P002021/1).

Conflict of Interests

The authors declare no conflict of interests.

References

Abrams, D., & Christian, J. (2007). A relational analysis of social exclusion. In *Multidisciplinary handbook of social exclusion research* (pp. 211–232). Chichester: John Wiley & Sons.

Abrams, D., & Hogg, M. A. (1987). Language attitudes, frames of reference, and social identity: A Scottish dimension. *Journal of Language and Social Psychology*, *6*(3/4), 201–213.

Abrams, D. E., & Hogg, M. A. (1990). *Social identity theory: Constructive and critical advances*. Berlin: Springer-Verlag Publishing.

Abrams, D., Hogg, M. A., & Marques, J. M. (2005). A social psychological framework for understanding social inclusion and exclusion. In D. Abrams, J. M. Marques, & M. A. Hogg (Eds.), *The social psychology of inclusion and exclusion* (pp. 1–26). London: Psychology Press.

Ajzen, I. (1991). The theory of planned behaviour. *Organizational Behaviour and Human Decision Processes*, *50*(2), 179–211.

Akilu, F. (1992). Multi-method approach to the study of homelessness. In P. Kennett (Ed.), *New approaches to homelessness* (Working Paper 104). Bristol: SAUS Publications.

Anderson, I. (1994). *Access to housing for low income single people: A review of recent research and current policy issues*. York: The Centre for Housing Policy, University of York.

Anderson, I. (2010). Services for homeless people in Europe: Supporting pathways out of homelessness. In E. O'Sullivan, V. Busch-Geertsema, D. Quilgars, & N. Pleace (Eds.), *Homelessness research in Europe. Festschrift for Bill Edgar and Joe Doherty* (pp. 41–63). Brussels: FEANTSA.

Armitage, C. J., & Conner, M. (2001). Efficacy of the theory of planned behaviour: A meta-analytic review. *British Journal of Social Psychology*, *40*(4), 471–499.

Bagozzi, R. P. (1981). Attitudes, intentions, and behaviour: A test of some key hypotheses. *Journal of Personality and Social Psychology*, *41*(4), 607.

Bandura, A. (1997). Self-efficacy: Toward a unifying theory of behavioural change. *Psychological Review*, *84*(2), 191–215.

Bentler, P. M., & Speckart, G. (1981). Attitudes "cause" behaviours: A structural equation analysis. *Journal of Personality and Social Psychology*, *40*(2), 226.

Burrows, R. (1997). The social distribution of the experience of homelessness. In R. Burrows, N. Pleace, & D. Quilgars (Eds.), *Homelessness and social policy* (pp. 50–68). London: Routledge.

Busch-Geertsema, V., Edgar, W., O'Sullivan, E., & Pleace, N. (2010). Homelessness and homeless policies in Europe: Lessons from research. In *Conference on homelessness* (Vol. 9, p. 10).

Christian, J., & Abrams, D. (2003). The effects of social identification, norms and attitudes on use of outreach services by homeless people. *Journal of Community & Applied Social Psychology*, *13*(2), 138–157.

Christian, J., & Abrams, D. (2004). A tale of two cities: Predicting homeless people's uptake of outreach programs in London and New York. *Basic and Applied Social Psychology*, *26*(2/3), 169–182.

Christian, J., & Armitage, C.J. (2002). Attitudes and intentions of homeless persons towards service provision in South Wales. *British Journal of Social Psychology*, *41*, 219–231.

Christian, J., Armitage, C. J., & Abrams, D. (2003). Predicting uptake of housing services: The role of self-categorization in the theory of planned behaviour.

Current Psychology, 22(3), 206–217.

Christian, J., Clapham, D., & Abrams, D. (2011). Exploring homeless people's use of outreach services: Applying a social psychological perspective. *Housing Studies, 26*(5), 681–699.

Clapham, D. F. (2005). *The meaning of housing: A pathways approach*. London: Policy Press.

Clapham. D. F., Christian, J., & Foye. C. (2016). *The concept of well-being in housing research*. Paper presented at the European Network for Housing Research Conference: Governance, Territory and Housing, Belfast.

Eagly, A. H., & Chaiken, S. (1993). *The psychology of attitudes*. San Diego, CA: Harcourt Brace Jovanovich College Publishers.

Epel, E. S., Bandura, A., & Zimbardo, P. G. (1999). Escaping homelessness: The influences of self-efficacy and time perspective on coping with homelessness. *Journal of Applied Social Psychology, 29*(3), 575–596.

Fitzpatrick, S., Johnsen, S., & White, M. (2011). Multiple exclusion homelessness in the UK: Key patterns and intersections. *Social Policy and Society, 10*(4), 501–512.

Fitzpatrick, S., Kemp, P., & Klinker, S. (2000). *Single homelessness: An overview of research in Britain*. York: Joseph Rowntree Foundation.

Johnsen, S., & Teixeira, L. (2010). *Staircases, elevators and cycles of change: 'Housing First' and other housing models for homeless people with complex support needs*. Crisis: London.

Park, S. I., & Kim, S. (2014). Mediating Effect of self-efficacy in the relationship between anger and functional health of homeless men. *Journal of Korean Academy of Nursing, 44*(4).

Pawson, H., & Munro, M. (2010). Explaining tenancy sustainment rates in British social rented housing: The roles of management, vulnerability and choice. *Urban Studies, 47*(1), 145–168.

Schultz, P. W., & Oskamp, S. (1999). *Social psychology applied perspectives*. US Imports & PHIPEs.

Snow, D. A., & Anderson, L. (1987). Identity work among the homeless: The verbal construction and avowal of personal identities. *American Journal of Sociology, 92*, 1336–1371.

Tajfel, H., & Turner, J. C. (1979). An integrative theory of intergroup conflict. *The Social Psychology of Intergroup Relations, 33*(47), 74.

Toro, P. A., & Wall, D. D. (1991). Research on homeless persons: Diagnostic comparisons and practice implications. *Professional Psychology: Research and Practice, 22*(6), 479.

Toro, P. A., Wolfe, S. M., Bellavia, C. W., Thomas, D. M., Rowland, L. L., Daeschler, C. V., & McCaskill, P. A. (1999). Obtaining representative samples of homeless persons: A two-city study. *Journal of Community Psychology, 27*, 157–177.

Warnes, A. M., Crane, M., & Coward, S. E. (2013). Factors that influence the outcomes of single homeless people's rehousing. *Housing Studies, 28*(5), 782–798.

About the Authors

Julie Christian is a Lecturer in Social Psychology. She has worked in both housing and psychology departments, holding Fellowships at London School of Economics and Political Science and at Cardiff University, before being appointment at Birmingham. Julie has an established track record in researching attitudes, social identity, housing and homelessness. She was an Associate Editor for the Journal of Community and Applied Social Psychology. And, as an extension of her research, she holds executive board positions.

Dominic Abrams is Professor of Social Psychology and the Director of the Centre for Group Processes at the University of Kent, Canterbury. A Chartered Psychologist, he is a Fellow of SPSSI, SPSP, and the UK Academy of Social Sciences. He is co-founding editor of the journal *Group Processes and Intergroup Relations*. He has published extensively in the areas of social identity theory and intergroup relations, particularly working on the relationship between social inclusion and social identity.

David Clapham is Professor of Planning at the University of Reading in the UK. He is the author of *Accommodating Difference and The Meaning of Housing* published by Policy Press in 2015 and 2005 respectively. He was editor of the journal *Housing, Theory and Society* for 10 years up to 2015.

Daniella Nayyar achieved her Bachelor's degree in Human Psychology from the School of Life and Health Sciences at Aston University in 2013. She is currently working towards her Ph.D. exploring environmental and individual differences in performance and learning.

Joseph Cotler holds both Bachelor and Masters degrees, and is currently a Ph.D. candidate in Social Psychology at the University of Birmingham. His work examines differences in social identification amongst multiple group types and subsequent outcome behaviours.

6

The Effect of Transport Accessibility on the Social Inclusion of Wheelchair Users: A Mixed Method Analysis

Raquel Velho [1,*], Catherine Holloway [2], Andrew Symonds [3] and Brian Balmer [1]

[1] Department of Science and Technology Studies, University College London, Gower Street, London, WC1E 6BT, UK;
E-Mails: raquel.velho.12@ucl.ac.uk (R.V.), brian.balmer@ucl.ac.uk (B.B.)
[2] Department of Computer Science, University College London, Gower Street, London, WC1E 6BT, UK;
E-Mail: c.holloway@ucl.ac.uk
[3] Institute of Orthopaedic and Musculoskeletal Sciences, University College London, Stanmore, HA7 4LP, UK;
E-Mail: andrew.symonds.12@ucl.ac.uk

* Corresponding author

Abstract
In recent years the accessibility of London buses has improved with the introduction of ramps and wheelchair priority areas. These advances are meant to remove physical barriers to entering the bus, but new conflicts have arisen particularly over the physical space aboard. We aimed to research the barriers faced by wheelchair users in public transport using a mixed methods approach to establish the breadth of issues faced by wheelchair users. To this end we quantified the push-force used alight a bus and a study to understand the coping mechanisms used by people to propel up a ramp. This quantitative approach found push forces which resulted in a load of 2 to 3 times body weight being transferred through people's shoulders, forces which can be directly linked to shoulder injury. This could disable the user further, preventing them from being able to push their wheelchair. Alongside the quantitative study, we conducted qualitative research comprising of a number of in-depth interviews with wheelchair users about the barriers they face in public transport. Our main claim, highlighted through this interdisciplinary collaboration, is that proposed 'solutions' to accessibility, such as ramps, often generate problems of their own. These barriers can affect the life of wheelchair users, impacting on their confidence and causing social isolation. These can be long-term in nature or immediate.

Keywords
accessibility; disability; interdisciplinarity; public transport; science and technology studies; Transport for London; wheelchair

Issue
This article is part of the issue "Transport Policy and Social Inclusion", edited by Miriam Ricci, Graham Parkhurst and Juliet Jain (University of the West of England, UK).

---

1. Introduction

> "If I were to ask you to describe transport accessibility for wheelchair users in London as it is today with three words, what are the three words you would choose?"
> "Well-intentioned. Inadequate. Uninspiring." (Peter)

With three adjectives, Peter painted a less than ideal image of London's public transport from his perspective. A 25-year-old lawyer who works and lives in Central London, he carefully chose where to live in the European capital to ensure an easier commute, requiring only a short underground journey on the famous Tube network. His is one of several stories and ways of talking about transport and its impact on people's lives, particularly the influence that transport (in)accessibility might have on wheelchair users' social inclusion. In this article, we want to consider transport and inclusion with wheelchair users' accessibility to the network as the primary focus by using two, quite different, disciplinary approaches—sociology and engineering. The aim is to highlight how both approaches demonstrate, in different ways, how solutions proposed to improve accessibility may also generate future problems for wheelchair users.

In 2005, the main transport authority in London, Transport for London, introduced low-floor buses with boarding ramps for wheelchair users. These buses would eliminate some obvious physical obstacles (compared to the previous model of buses, the Routemaster, which had a step) and permit wheelchair users to board and alight buses, ensuring their inclusion to one mode of the public transport network. However, as we will discuss below, this implementation was not the end of accessibility problems as wheelchair users can also face other issues. Indeed, with wheelchair users being able to physically use the bus, other conflicts began to appear generated by these improvements.

This research was initially developed as a pilot study in 2013 as a collaboration between the UCL departments of Civil, Environmental and Geomatic Engineering and of Science and Technology Studies. The intention was to think about accessibility from both perspectives, quantitative and qualitative, with the aim of seeing whether these two ostensibly incommensurable disciplines could inform each other and provide new insights into transport accessibility for wheelchair users. The aim of this article is to explore the initial results of this interdisciplinary collaboration. To begin, we will briefly describe the policies and regulations which frame transport accessibility in the UK and, more specifically, London. We will then address the question of accessibility with a mixed methods approach, developed below in two separate sections: the first offers a quantitative analysis from an engineering and biomechanics perspective. The second section takes on a qualitative approach, based on the field of Science and Technology Studies. In the last section we ask what new insights were acquired through the collaboration of engineers and social scientists, and discuss the rigidity of the transport system in London as it affects wheelchair passengers.

2. Background

Public transport is incredibly important to disabled people in Great Britain. In a recent report analysing secondary data by Jolly, Priestley and Matthews (2006) it was found disabled people attach a greater importance to and almost half are totally reliant on public transport for each journey they take. The main reason for public transport reliance is a lack of access to a car. However, disabled people travel a third less than the general public (Miller, Gillinson, & Huber, 2006). When public transport is not accessible then mobility can not happen, which in turn can isolate people from the economic, political and social life of the community (Kenyon, Lyons, & Rafferty, 2002). There are 1.2 million wheelchair users in England (National Health Services Modernisation Agency, 2004). Wheelchair users have specific access needs as most find gaps and steps difficult to overcome, therefore a ramp is needed to overcome the naturally occurring gap between the footway and the bus. Specific to London, guidelines have been developed for accessible bus stop design, and accessible buses (Mayor of London, 2006). A key guideline in this document is the need for a wheelchair accessible space and an interface between the bus and footway which results in a ramp gradient of less that 12% (7 degrees). It is believed this gradient is a compromise between reducing the necessary push force needed to ascend or descend the ramp, and the requirements of the built environment.

Accessibility is a term which means different things to different audiences, generally due to the scale over which it is being measured. At a micro-level accessibility can be measured using the Capability Model (CM), which focuses on measuring the Provided Capabilities of the person when undertaking a task and comparing these to the Required Capabilities of the task (Holloway & Tyler, 2013). In this respect the CM looks to understand accessibility by understanding the interactions between the person and the environment. Holloway and Tyler explore the CM with regards to attendant wheelchair propulsion noting that when an assistive technology such as a wheelchair is used by someone this then enhances their provided capability set (for most tasks). In a similar manner the bus ramp can be assumed to reduce the required capabilities thereby increasing accessibility. The CM looks to address how people accomplish these tasks, these 'coping strategies' can range from simply avoiding an activity or adapting the movement required to complete the task. The engineering component in our research uses the Capability Model as its framework to discuss the difficulties wheelchair users have while boarding and alighting a bus. It uses peak and average tangential force when pushing up a standard bus ramp to quantify the provided capability. A model of how a person pushes is developed and the forces occurring at the shoulder are used as a secondary measure of provided capability, while the muscle activity patterns of pushing are used to describe the coping strategies.

On the other hand, accessibility can also be understood from a qualitative perspective as a potential factor for inclusion. Here, we need to listen to people's own experiences of the public transport system to grasp the barriers they face. In our research, the social sciences approach based its framework on the field of Science and Technology Studies, which has built up a substantial body of literature that analyses scientific processes and technological innovation not as 'things in themselves' but as institutions comprised of both things and people. As such, any new or changing technology must be considered alongside the variety of users, producers, maintainers, regulators and other groups which come into being or change with the technology itself (Bijker, 1997; MacKenzie & Wajcman, 1985).

The public transport system lends itself aptly to an STS analysis, particularly given the work of Actor-Network Theory (ANT) scholars, some of whom have already worked on transport networks (Galis & Lee, 2014; Latour, 1996). In ANT, a system such as the transport network is perceived as being composed of more than just 'things'. It has its buses, trains, tracks, gears, engines, roads, but it also embraces a much wider variety of actors, from the drivers and staff to the passengers, but also includes diverse groups such as regulators, engineers, mechanics, and others. Moreover, the size of London's public transport system, the placement of its stations, bus stops, the employment of thousands of staff members and the way it transfers millions of passengers, we can see it as a large sociotechnical system with the ultimate goal of carrying its users across the city (Hughes, 1987). A key advantage of viewing the transport system in this way is that it foregrounds the fact that different actors will view the system differently, for instance, a 'perfectly reasonable regulatory standard' from the perspective of managers may be a 'pointless impediment' from the perspective of wheelchair users. Moreover, some of these perspectives may be particularly prominent and visible, whilst others are rendered invisible and marginal (Star, 1991).

STS has also developed some literature which works with disability and disabled people (Blume, 2009; Blume & Hiddinga, 2010; Winance, 2006), but much of this work is concerned primarily with the development of prostheses and how it interacts with the disabled person (and vice-versa) or with definitions of (dis)ability. Our work, however, will be primarily directed towards thinking about the shaping of the public transport network in London, an example of a sociotechnical system, in which a constellation of human and non-human actors come together to permit passengers to reach their destinations. Additionally, underlying this system there is a history of choices that have been made pertaining to its design and elaboration—choices that impact the users in a variety of ways, both overtly and covertly (Winner, 1980, Woolgar 1991). This observation highlights that the system could be different. Different choices could (and can) be made (Bowker & Star, 2000; Lampland & Star, 2009; Star, 1991). Our interviews with wheelchair users sought to re-insert their voices and experiences as active participants within this socio-technical system.

3. Methods

During the pilot study, we recruited a number of wheelchair user volunteers to come to the Pedestrian Accessibility Movement Environment Laboratory (PAMELA) where they would engage in two activities. The first consisted of asking participants to board and alight a bus with the gradient set to 7 degrees. The experiments were recorded using the CCTV cameras onboard the bus and these were analysed to determine the components of the task which caused difficulty. In particular, time to complete tasks, number of pushes and number of attempts were recorded. Having participated in the engineering component of our research, the participants were invited back into the reception of the PAMELA facility. They were then engaged in indepth, semi-structured interviews covering themes around their experience of the London public transport system. These interviews were recorded, transcribed, and then coded using data analysis software according to recurring themes using standard qualitative methods (Silverman 2006; Weber, 1990). Interviewees' names have been anonymised, using pseudonyms of their choice. Unlike quantitative survey techniques, qualitative research does not seek a statistically representative sample but instead seeks to explore, in depth, people's experiences and the meanings they attach to those experiences (Berg, 2001; Seale, 2004).

As our sample sizes for the pilot study were initially small (four participants), the data we are using here has been supplemented for both branches. For the engineering component, we ran an additional study in the PAMELA facility with seven male participants with a history of spinal cord injury. We had initially aimed to have an equal gender split but we struggled to recruit people for the study and failed to recruit any females unfortunately. Each participant used a manual wheelchair as their primary form of mobility. Participants were asked to propel a manual wheelchair on a stretch of level paving, up a 6.5% incline and up a 12% incline. On the qualitative side, a series of 18 semi-structured interviews with wheelchair users in London were undertaken in the summer of 2015. This additional data brings the total number of interviews with wheelchair users in this paper to 22, covering a wide variety of impairments, age, gender, and employment status.

4. The Engineering/Biomechanics Approach

4.1. Pilot Study

As the numbers were so few in the pilot study, the aim was to understand how people completed the task as opposed to quantifying exactly how difficult it was. The follow-on study which just took a single component of the task—the ramp push—was then conducted to understand exactly how hard the task is. In this instance, wheelchair users were asked to board and alight a bus three times, each time in a way which was easiest for them. For all participants, video was recorded using the standard CCTV cameras on-board a bus (see Figure 1).

The video data was analysed using video observation software and the GPS clock displayed on the top left corner of each recording. A proxy for provided capability of task time was used to understand how difficult the task of boarding and alighting was for the wheelchair user. Task time was calculated for each trial from this analysis and a description of how each person boards and alights a bus was developed. In addition the coping mechanisms used by people were observed.

There was no difference in alighting time with each person consistently exiting the bus in 4 seconds. However, differences in technique and ability meant that there was a clear difference in boarding time, which is shown in Figure 2. In particular participant MM needed to use the handrails to pull herself onto the bus and CH failed on two attempts to board the bus on the first time on two of the runs. With regards to coping strategies people adapted their pushing style in different manners. For example in Figure 1 it can be clearly seen that CH leant forward to maximize the pushing time. However, others used the yellow grab handles or shorter faster pushes to complete the task.

It was apparent by these coping strategies that people were struggling to manage the task. It was decided, following this pilot, to complete a more controlled assessment to compare the amount of force used (provided) to board a bus (a short, steep ramp) with a longer, less steep ramp and also flat footway pushing to understand the potential accessibility barrier posed by a bus ramp. This was conducted in the detailed biomechanical study.

4.2. Detailed Biomechanical Study

The detailed biomechanical study is fully described in Holloway et al. (2015). However, the methods are summarised here to aid the reader. Seven male participants with a history of a Spinal Cord Injury attended PAMELA facility. Each participant used a manual wheelchair as their primary form of mobility. Participants were asked to propel a manual wheelchair on a stretch of level paving, up a 6.5% incline and up a 12% incline, which was chosen to replicate the incline found on a London Bus access ramp. During the propulsion tasks, forces applied to the wheelchair push rim to estimate the provided capabilities of the user. In addition upper limb joint movement and shoulder joint muscle activity were recorded and used as inputs to a computer model of the upper limb, to estimate forces experienced at the shoulder joint. Shoulder joint forces have been shown to be correlated to shoulder pain and injury, therefore we think it is essential to understand the forces produced in undertaking the accessibility tasks both in terms of quantifying provided capabilities and also understanding the effect of coping strategies. It should be noted that all participants were free of shoulder pain at the time of this study and had not had a recent shoulder injury or pain.

Figure 1. Showing a screen grab of each of the video playback angles used for task time analysis.

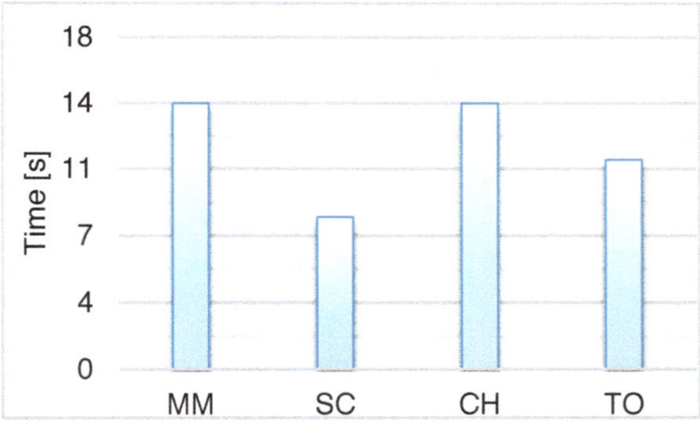

Figure 2. Boarding time (averaged over 3 runs) for each person.

4.2.1. Results of Detailed Biomechanical Study

Provided Capabilities: The total propulsion forces applied to the wheelchair push rim were significantly affected by the tasks. Climbing the 6.5% incline people used significantly greater force than level propulsion (106.90N vs. 50.36N), and climbing the 12% incline people used a significantly greater force than climbing the 6.5% incline (139.63N vs. 106.90N). These forces translated into significant increases in shoulder joint forces experienced during the incline propulsion tasks. During level propulsion, peak shoulder joint forces were under one body weight. During the 6.5% incline, peak shoulder forces were over two times body weight and during the 12% incline task, peak shoulder forces were over three times body weight.

Coping strategies: How each individual managed to generate the push force varied and this is reflected in the different muscle activity. Generally there were significant increases in peak muscle activity levels during the incline tasks compared to level propulsion. During level propulsion, peak muscle activity levels around the shoulder joint were on average 26% of maximum. When climbing the 6.5% incline, peak muscle activity levels were on average 63% of maximum and when climbing the 12% incline, peak muscle activity levels were on average 77% of maximum. Interestingly it would appear that when going up a 6.5% slope the deltoid, which is the very large muscle at the top of arm reaches a maximum, and as the person attempts to go up a 12% slope they are forced to increase the amount of muscle activity in smaller muscles such as the infraspinatus.

5. The Social Science Approach

5.1. Findings

During the interviews, we spoke to wheelchair users about the barriers that they face and the impact that this has on their daily life. Through the 21 conversations, we attempted to understand the origins of problems these users might face and whether we could attempt a classification of these barriers. Through coding the interviews, we generated three heuristic categories of problems narrated by the interviewees as distinct moments and barriers: spatial, technical, and social. Here, we would like to reinforce that these classifications are actor's categories. For example, while accounting their experiences, our interviewees would narrate the barriers as distinct moments, e.g. "One day, I had a problem because of the ramp. Another day, I had a problem because of the lack of space."

5.1.1. Technological Barriers

> "I've been to so many bus depots because the ramps were broken and I can't get off. You end up going to a depot." (Adam)
>
> "I accept that it's improved and improvements that have been made have been amazing in some respects, but on the other hand, it's still as if.... It's still as stressful if not more stressful because the wonder of technology is the wonder that it ever works." (Michael)

In order for the space on the bus to even become an issue as a passenger, a wheelchair user must first be able to board it at all. Transport for London prides itself in its fleet of low-floor buses, all of which have mechanical ramps to be deployed for a wheelchair user to be able to board and alight. This change in the rolling stock of London buses in 2005 was a true turning point for accessibility throughout the city. It is, of course, dependent on this technological artefact functioning as intended: a broken ramp, which might break either before or after the wheelchair has boarded the bus, can mean a passenger having to wait hours or take a long detour. What emerged in our interviews is a sense of the wide variety of ways things could go wrong on buses and throughout the transport system.

Wheelchair users are dependent on boarding ramps when it comes to the London Overground and Underground train stations that are accessible from street-level to the platforms. Here, however, it is not just an issue of the ramp working. These are low-tech versions of the fitted, mechanical ramps on buses and are dependent on others deploying them correctly:

> "The chap with the ramps did arrive and he went to put the ramp for me get off with the doors open. The driver of the train either hadn't seen him or didn't want to see him because they were running behind schedule, or whatever, so the doors shut with the ramps in a half position, me inside, and actually clunked the chap on the platform so he fell over." (Basil)

It becomes particularly interesting to think about the ramp as a potentially problematic factor in accessibility for wheelchair users when we think back to the research done by engineers. Despite none of our interviewees having mentioned developing joint pain as a result of ramp inclination, this is still a problem which engineers have pointed out. In addition, some wheelchair users have mentioned the steepness of ramps as a problematic factor in accessibility as it makes their boarding of the bus more difficult, and their alighting more dangerous.

There is a variety of technological 'bits and bobs' which also frustrate and hinder wheelchair users beyond the practicality of the ramps, both manual and electric. For instance, inside the buses, a special button by the wheelchair priority area is supposed to be used to alert the driver that they would like to get off at the next stop. This allows the drivers to get ready to deploy the ramp, and makes a sharp siren noise to get their attention. The siren noise is also activated continuously while the ramps are being put out and coming back in, perhaps to alert other passengers and passers-by on the street of what is happening. Interviewees such as Alex and Sophie have expressed some discomfort at this because it calls attention to them, and even expressed the experience as akin to public humiliation:

> "[Imitates alarm noise] And everyone looks, everyone stares, and I'm like, yeah, I'm just getting on the bus." (Alex)
>
> "So I don't like the fact that there's the siren that starts wailing at you, or at everybody, when you're about to get on or about to get off the bus. It's all a bit of a big faff, but you get used to it. I mean, public humiliation seems to be...you've got to be able to deal with it if you're disabled anyway, because people will look at you, people will...etc." (Sophie)

Despite such barriers not affecting the physical acts of boarding and disembarking, they impact on wheelchair users' wellbeing, their impressions of the public transport system and, in the above quote, compound Sophie's existing sense of being stigmatised. These negative experiences play into their personal perceptions but also on their desire to use the network and overcome potentially being confined to their home and to engage in activities beyond their local community.

5.1.2. Spatial Barriers

> "You're in a chair and you can't move and you can't get out of the space so they tend to close up around you." (C.S.)
>
> "You'll hear this time and time again, there's generally only one wheelchair space, but it's also the space that can be used for toddlers, buggies, suitcases, and things like this." (Basil)
>
> "And also sometimes you know, they have rails that are probably in the way of the user to manoeuvre within the space." (Um Hayaa)

Space is an inevitable part of the background whenever people speak in general about transport: moving around the city; going from Northeast to Southwest; or the mileage from one stop to another (Vertesi, 2008). For wheelchair users, another kind of space was present in our interviews: personal or manoeuvrable space. In the above quotes, the 'space' referred to is the 'wheelchair priority area', a demarcated location on the bus which is specifically designated for these passengers' use. It is prescribed as "the only place wheelchair users can travel safely" (Transport for London, 2014, p. 70) and these passengers are required to place themselves facing opposite to the direction of travel.

Despite the title of 'wheelchair priority space', interviewees reported that it is often a key source of anxiety before travelling. The issues around it are many, from the size of their own wheelchairs and difficulty manoeuvring in or out of the space, to the sadness of not being able to travel with a friend who is also a wheelchair user, or even the much publicised debate around buggy and pushchair users or luggage sharing the space (Bellisario, 2012; Moss, 2013). The direction of travel can also provide a degree of frustration and discomfort. In these cases, the users described how they subvert the wheelchair space by travelling in a way that suits them best:

> "For me, I prefer to go face-in and hold on to the rails, I find that fine. The reverse side, I sometimes get that sick feeling." (M.)
>
> "I suffer sometimes with travel sickness and so I find it easier sometimes to sit the opposite way to how you're supposed to sit in the wheelchair space." (Michael)

Despite this subversion of the space, this can also be the source of anxiety, as both interviewees laughed nervously and mentioned they probably should not be saying that. They expressed that some bus drivers understand, but that it is often a risk in terms of their, and other passengers', safety. Interestingly, here we find another example of a potential solution to wheelchair users' travelling needs which is also proving to be more complicated than initially intended. Like the ramp, the wheelchair priority area was meant to facilitate accessibility but is also a source of anxiety.

5.1.3. Social barriers

> "Obviously, you've heard about the problems with wheelchairs vs. buggies on that space. That's not the only problem that you'll actually find. You'll find that you've got people standing in the space who don't necessarily want to move, or you've got people who've got luggage in the space who don't want to move, or you've got older people who've got their shopping trolley in the space. That's always very problematic." (Marie)
>
> "It is like a battle of wheels, buggy versus wheelchair. It should never, never be that way. It should never be that way." (Faith)

The category of social barriers—by which we specifically mean barriers created by other people—was particularly evident when interviewees discussed what has perhaps been the most prominent debate in the UK media around transport accessibility, the "wheelchair vs. buggies" priority debate. In 2012, Doug Paulley sued FirstGroup in Yorkshire after having been denied access to a bus because the space was occupied by a mother with a pushchair (Press Association, 2014). Three years and one overruling later, the case has escalated and will be heard by the Supreme Court in the UK. It was previously established that the wheelchair area should be used on a first-come, first-served basis but for the wheelchair users we interviewed this can sound outrageous when they are only given one space to ride on the bus.

> "A buggy can fold, they have that option." (M.)
> "And when I see things like that, my reaction is, it's not about who's more important, it's about who has a choice; so I do not have a choice about my use of the wheelchair whereas a baby can be got out of its buggy." (Diana)

After research done in 2012, Transport for London launched a campaign that November to address the issue, with campaign posters on buses and at bus stops in bold black and red letters asking, "Buggy users, please make way for wheelchair users". Interviewees' perceptions on the impact of that campaign were mixed, but conflicts with bus drivers were also mentioned as a source of anxiety. In some cases, they reported, drivers are unclear on the rules of whether a wheelchair user and a buggy are allowed to share the space, or in some cases drivers simply do not stop the bus at all for a wheelchair user to board it.

> "I've had buses drive past me without even stopping, you know, and I've been sent to the end of the route occasionally because they've forgotten I'm actually on the bus." (Michael)

Yet these conflicts with buggy users and drivers are not the only social barriers for wheelchair users. A large number of interviewees expressed concern at social attitudes towards disabled people in London. Negative reactions towards them take a variety of forms such as awkward "nosy questions", invading their personal space by pushing their wheelchair without asking, or even outright verbal and physical abuse. Participants described these social issues as a mix of a lack of public awareness around disability and, according to some interviewees, a media push towards depicting disabled people as "scroungers". To some, this stigmatisation is being done with the government's support:

> "I think we've only got the rights that we fought for and it takes constant ambition to add onto these fights because in the interest of saving money our government has, I believe, quite deliberately and callously waged a media campaign depicting us as a drain on the state and an unacceptable one at that." (Leda)

Although our focus in this article is on barriers, it is important to add that these negative views were also matched by comments from the interviewees that there was a willingness to help. Moreover, in three interviews the wheelchair users explicitly stated that they had no issues with buggies at all.

5.1.4. Isolation

These three different sources of barriers to using the public transport system create a sense of anxiety and frustration in the wheelchair users we interviewed, but perhaps more problematic is the social consequence of this fear. For instance, when asked what happens when a trip goes wrong and they are faced with a barrier, Marie described how all you can do is complain to the transport authority and, in response, receive a generic email. She explained that this "puts you off" travelling:

> "It isolates you even more because your world is getting smaller, and smaller, and smaller, all the time...." (Marie)

A functioning, accessible, transport system, particularly in a city as large and crowded as London, is the difference between being able to get around, and isolation. Options to public transport would include taxis or personal cars, which are described as "luxury" items but also, in some cases, as the only viable option.

> "If I use an adapted vehicle, it's much better, much easier, than being pressured to wait in the cold at the bus stop hoping that the first bus will accommodate my needs." (Um Hayaa)

Um Hayaa had to resort to private transport to pick up her daughter from a variety of after school activities, otherwise she would have had to take three different buses, each trip fraught with the anxiety of broken ramps, impatient drivers, and not enough space. However, she had to make an investment choice to purchase a vehicle, one which not all wheelchair users are able to make. Sophie, who also makes use of a private vehicle, described how aware she is that it is a privilege not to worry about public transport. Beyond the costs of a private car, wheelchair users often have to worry about the costs related to their mobility aid itself. She explains:

> "Disability is a luxury that not many people can afford, and that's the problem. People don't realise how expensive everything gets. Either how isolated life is if you don't have the money and/or the equipment, which, equipment means money. And that's why people are so scared of disability." (Sophie)

The general narrative around the public transport network in London for wheelchair users that emerged in our interviews centres on anxiety, pre-planning, battles, and effort. The consequence of these impediments, it is suggested, is greater isolation for these groups. In the words of one of our interviewees:

> "I'm sure you know, getting out and about changes people's lives, and it makes things.... Being social makes you much more alive, much healthier, and public transport is really good for that if you've got that option[.]" (Alan)

6. Discussion

6.1. Well-Meaning Solutions

When Transport for London writes about accessibility in its network, many figures are cited, from its bus fleet being 98% low floor access (the few exceptions being some older Routemaster models still used on Heritage routes) to a quarter of the Tube stations and half of the Overground stations having step-free access. All of these figures are to be welcomed. The image of this network is quite positive, and wheelchair users do seem to benefit extraordinarily. But this should not allow us to ignore that the reality of the network does not always match these numbers, and wheelchair users still face the variety of barriers described above.

In addition to the barriers wheelchair users themselves describe as facing, the engineering section of our research has found that with each push the make, they further wear their shoulder and eventually, nearly all will have upper limb injuries, some so severe they will be unable to independently push themselves. A number of factors effect the development of injuries and the associated pain. These include: the cyclical nature of the wheelchair push cycle (Kotajarvi et al., 2004; Mercer et al., 2006), the low gross mechanical efficiency of wheelchair pushing—only 10% of effort goes directly into making a person move forwards (De Groot, Veeger, Hollander, & van der Woude, 2002) and challenging surfaces (Holloway et al., 2012). To give an indication of the scale of the problem, the incidence of shoulder pain is reported to range from 42% (Dalyan, Cardenas, & Gerard, 1999) to 66% (Fullerton, Borckardt, & Alfano, 2003), with the most commonly reported injury damage to the rotator cuff muscles (Akbar et al., 2010).

It was found that upper limb demand and injury risk were significantly greater during incline wheelchair propulsion in comparison to level propulsion, which means that ramps at a greater incline for boarding and alighting buses and trains can further add to the risk. As the gradient of the incline increased, upper limb demand and injury risk increased. During level propulsion, on average, muscles around the shoulder were working at 27% of their maximum and joint forces were less than one body weight. During the 12% incline task, on average, muscles around the shoulder were working at 77% of their maximum, and joint forces were above three times body weight. The results demonstrate that a common daily task such as accessing a bus places a high demand on the upper limbs of a manual wheelchair user. Push force is an important factor in assessing the accessibility of transport for wheelchair users as it has been shown to be directly proportional to forces which occur at the shoulder. The shoulder is the most commonly injured joint for wheelchair users with injury rates ranging from 42% (Dalyan, Cardenas, & Gerard, 1999) to 66% (Fullerton et al, 2003). Shoulder pain can be so severe that it leaves the person without an independent form of mobility. It has been noted previously that the method of assessment of accessibility can affect the resulting guidance, and that even when guidance is followed it can be challenging to wheelchair users (Holloway & Tyler, 2013). Guidance such as *Manual for Streets 2* (Department for Transport, 2007) used by the UK to help produce accessible pedestrian infrastructure are not always produced based on empirical evidence, and are often developed via case studies or rule of thumb practice which. In a society where sensing technology is becoming ubiquitous, there is an opportunity to both collect more diverse and also dynamic datasets and to use these to assess infrastructure policy changes. Projects such as Wheelmap (www.wheelmap.org) and Accessible Routes form Crowd-sourced Cloud Services (www.arccs.org) are beginning to develop web and mobile tools to enable more dynamic modelling of accessibility. The challenge will be to understand how such crowd-sourced data can be used effectively to inform and evaluate policy, and indeed to see if it can be shared across traditional policy sectors e.g. health (rehabilitation) and transport (accessibility).

This data from the engineering component of our research is enlightening when paired with the narratives put forward by the wheelchair users themselves. As pointed out in section 5.2.1., though our interviewees did not specifically indicate developing an injury as a particular hinderance in their use of the public transport system, ramps did figure prominently as a potential barrier. Yet it seems ironic that the enabler of their access to public transport can also be a problematic factor. The same thing can be seen with the other aspects of 'accessibility': the alarms which signal ramp deployment are seen as unwanted attention, the wheelchair priority areas become contested spaces with pushchairs and luggage, etc. What our interdisciplinary collaboration has helped highlight is this paradox where well-meaning solutions do not simply solve the problems with accessibility. The engineering approach has shown this through ramp inclination when even where guidance is followed, injuries can still occur, while the sociological perspective has teased this out from wheelchair users' description of the barriers they face. We would like to make it clear that we are not criticising the improvements that have been made as such, but rather that they should be taken as a lesson where, rather than thinking in terms of solutions as an end-point we should speak of ongoing conversations and of adjustments to the network. However, this becomes difficult if the public transport system is seen as a stabilised network.

6.2. Standardisation and Rigidity

It would come as no surprise to STS scholars that, despite the heuristic classification of the different barriers made by our interviewees into social, spatial, and technical origins, the problem is not always so clear-cut. Indeed, most STS scholars make the point that these classifications are rarely, if ever, obvious (Bowker & Star, 2000). In other words, despite the problem seeming to be due to a technical issue, it can also be related to spatial and social dimensions. Broken or faulty ramps are a good example of this blurring of categories. This technology was developed with sensors which withdraw if an obstacle is detected. If the ramp does not deploy appropriately when an obstacle is detected, is the barrier for the wheelchair user spatial or technological? The ramp does not work (technical) but is this because of spatial features such as the presence of street furniture, or the design of the curbs (either too low or too high)? Similarly, the debate around the wheelchair priority area can lend itself to a similar question: is the problem social (negotiating priority with other passengers on the bus) or is it spatial (the space is not big enough)?

The difficulty in drawing these lines is testament to how tightly knitted these different aspects of the network are, which brings us back to the notion of sociotechnical systems referred to in the background section above. In a system where there are numerous types of agents, human and non-human, physical and non-tangible (such as legislation), intense collaboration between all of them is imperative to make it a cohesive whole. Yet this very cohesiveness is dependent on another process, that of standardisation and consolidation. Hughes describes consolidation as the moment in the life of a sociotechnical system in which there are few competing systems (Hughes, 1987). Transport in London has definitely reached such a period in its development as it is controlled by a single higher authority, Transport for London. Historically, much work goes into reaching this moment of consolidation, mainly by passing through the development of standards, which function as a unifying language, to ensure that all different actors and agents of the system are communicating and compatible (Bowker & Star, 2000; Lampland & Star, 2009; Scott, 1998; Timmermans & Berg, 1997). Generally, this has been a successful process for most users of the London transport system, so why are experiences so irregular for wheelchair users?

Given the age of various means of transport in London, we can say that the process of standardisation and stabilisation have been ongoing for at least a century. The London Underground celebrated its 150-year anniversary in 2013. These processes happened throughout a period where the perception of disability and impairment were different. Disability Studies scholars argue that through the Victorian era and up until the 1960s, there was a medical model of disability which individualised impairments and placed the burden of care on the disabled person and/or their family. This model normalised the absence of disabled people from social settings, giving the idea that it was a person's impairment which hindered their inclusion into society. In the 1960s, the social model of disability made its first appearances with a series of disabled rights activist groups arguing that disability has its origins in social notions (Blume & Hiddinga, 2010; Davis, 1999; Linton, 1998; Shakespeare, 2006). The Union of the Physically Impaired Against Segregation defined disability as "the disadvantage or restriction of activity caused by a contemporary social organisation which takes no or little account of people who have physical impairments and thus excludes them from participation in the mainstream of social activities" (Union of the Physically Impaired Against Segregation, 1976).

It is only in the past two decades that accessibility has been added to the transport agenda in the UK, with the backing of legislation such as the Disability Discrimination Act of 1995, now superseded by the Equality Act 2010. Much of the negative experiences related by wheelchair users are arguably due to an initial lack of inscription of their needs into the transport network, which up until the past decades did not consider them as potential passengers, as well as a slow shift of social perceptions and assumptions about disabled people in general (Beckett & Campbell, 2015; Shakespeare & Watson, 1997). As Star argues: "A stabilised network is only stable for some, and that is for those who are members of the community of practice who form/use/maintain it" (Star, 1991, p. 42). For the moment, wheelchair users are still somewhat 'non-standard 'agents within this sociotechnical system and do not (yet) experience a stabilised network.

We argue that, perhaps precisely because wheelchair users are non-standard agents, they experience the transport system through its fragments rather than its entirety. For this reason, the narratives given by interviewees often point to different and diverse factors (space, people, technology) rather than the system as a whole (as ANT scholars tend to do). The use of standards as necessary to regulate and stabilise the system is what is now locking out these users from experiencing it as such. This is reminiscent of what Scott (1998) described in *Seeing Like a State*, where the establishment of norms and regulations from a top-down approach does not necessarily translate in a positive and productive manner for those on the ground, such as the development of accessibility regulation still straining the bodies of wheelchair users and causing harm, as is shown by our engineering section. This feeds back to what was discussed in section 6.1. on prescribing solutions as an end-all, when for the many actors who interact with these proposals they may generate problems in and of themselves.

We would also like to briefly point out that it is important to remember that wheelchair users are not 'passive'. While these barriers strain their journey through the system, they also develop their own tactics for dealing with these issues. Our interviewees have provided some examples, such as M. in a quote above mentioning that she gets into the space facing forwards and holding onto the rails. Other examples from out interviews include wheelchair users carrying toolkits to fix ramps, 'bunny-hopping' off a bus or train, using their wheelchairs on escalators, or even organising activists group to campaign for improved accessibility. This is a rich area of research that merits further exploration in the future as it can provide some insight and suggestions for improvement in transport policy.

7. Conclusion

In this article we intended to think about accessibility through an interdisciplinary lens, using both an engineering and a sociological approach, and consider the new insights this collaboration might bring. Transport is an essential service to the population which ensures people's inclusion in society as it provides the link between the private (the home) and the public (the museum, coffee shop, Parliament, etc.) spheres. In the case of our participants, we can see that issues around the accessibility of public transport can lead to anxiety and social isolation, but also to physical injury. The collaboration between disciplines helped to highlight that what can be framed as a solution to barriers in accessibility can also generate problems in itself, such as ramps becoming broken or straining wheelchair users' bodies and causing harm. This is often due to the 'add-on' nature of some of these fixes onto a system that has already been mostly stabilised in the past century. Despite STS and ANT theories telling us that these systems are more complicated, our interviewees described the issues they face as physical, spatial, or social which we suggest is due to their experiences being fragmented.

For this reason, policy-making in transport, including the establishment of legislation, regulations and best-practice guides, should be developed in as plural a manner as possible where, rather than speaking in terms of 'solutions', ongoing conversations about improvements are held. The physical and spatial environment needs to be understood and people's abilities can be measured to provide better guidance. This should also be supplemented by the understanding that transport is an extremely large network which encompasses not only things, technologies and policies, but also a wide variety of people and social interactions. A plural approach to investigating the limits and weak points of public transport networks, including engineering, biomechanics, sociology, city planning, among others, can permit a wider range of solutions to be proposed.

Acknowledgments

All authors thank the numerous participants in our research. The first author also thanks the Brazilian CAPES Foundation for the funding of her doctoral research.

Conflict of Interests

The authors declare no conflict of interests.

References

Akbar, M., Balean, G., Brunner, M., Seyler, T. M., Bruckner, T., Munzinger . . . Loew, M. (2010). Prevalence of rotator cuff tear in paraplegic patients compared with controls. *J Bone Joint Surg Am*, *92*(1), 23-30.

Beckett, A. E., & Campbell, T. (2015). The social model of disability as an oppositional device. *Disability & Society*, *30*(2), 270-283.

Bellisario, R. (2012, July 10). Refused access: Fighting for the right to travel on the buses. *The Guardian*. Retrieved from http://www.theguardian.com/society/2012/jul/10/fighting-right-travel-buses

Berg, B. L. (2001). *Qualitative research methods for the social sciences*. Boston, MA: Allyn and Bacon.

Bijker, W. E. (1997). *Of bicycles, bakelites and bulbs: Toward a theory of sociotechnical change*. Cambridge, MA: The MIT Press.

Blume, S. (2009). *The artificial ear: Cochlear implants and the culture of deafness.* Rutgers University Press.

Blume, S., & Hiddinga, A. (2010). Disability Studies as an academic field: reflections on its development. *Medische Antropologie*, *22*(2), 225-236.

Bowker, G. C., & Star, S. L. (2000). *Sorting things out: Classification and its consequences.* Cambridge, MA: The MIT Press.

Dalyan, M., Cardenas, D. D., & Gerard, B. (1999). Upper extremity pain after spinal cord injury. *Spinal Cord*, *37*(3), 191-195.

Davis, L. J. (1999). Crips strike back: The rise of disability studies. *American Literary History*, *11*(3), 500-512.

De Groot, S., Veeger, H. E. J., Hollander, A.P. & van der Woude, L. H. V. (2002). Consequence of feedback-based learning of an effective hand rim wheelchair force production on mechanical efficiency. *Clinical*

Biomechanics, 17(3), 219-226.

Department for Transport. (2007). *Manual for Streets*. London, UK: Thomas Telford Publishing. Retrieved from http://www.dft.gov.uk/pgr/sustainable/manfor streets

Fullerton, H. D., Borckardt, J. J., & Alfano, A. P. (2003). Shoulder pain: A comparison of wheelchair athletes and nonathletic wheelchair users. *Medicine & Science in Sports & Exercise, 35*(12), 1958-1961.

Galis, V., & Lee, F. (2014). A Sociology of treason: The construction of weakness. *Science, Technology & Human Values, 39*(1), 154-179.

Holloway, C. (2011). *The effect of footway crossfall gradient on wheelchair accessibility* (Doctoral dissertation). University College London, London.

Holloway, C., Richards, R., Smitham, P., Gall, A. & Tyler, N. (2012) The effect of everyday outdoor tasks on wheelchair propulsion patterns: results linking EMG analysis and a new lightweight force sensing wheel. In *(Proceedings) 51st Annual Scientific Meeting of the International Spinal Cord Society, London, 2012.*

Holloway, C., & Tyler, N. (2013). A micro-level approach to measuring the accessibility of footways for wheelchair users using the capability model. *Transportation Planning and Technology, 36*(7), 636-649.

Holloway, C. S., Symonds, A., Suzuki, T., Gall, A., Smitham, P., & Taylor, S. (2015). Linking wheelchair kinetics to glenohumeral joint demand during everyday accessibility activities. In *2015 37th Annual International Conference of the IEEE Engineering in Medicine and Biology Society (EMBC)* (pp. 2478–2481). http://doi.org/10.1109/EMBC.2015.7318896

Hughes, T. P. (1987). The evolution of large technological systems. In W. E. Bijker, T. P. Hughes, & T. J. Pinch (Eds.), *The social construction of technological systems: New directions in the sociology and history of technology* (pp. 51-82). Cambridge, MA: The MIT Press.

Jolly, D., Priestley, M. & Matthews, B. (2006). *Secondary analysis of existing data on disabled people's use and experiences of public transport in Great Britain*. University of Leeds, UK: Disability Rights Commission.

Kenyon, S., Lyons, G., & Rafferty, J. (2002). Transport and social exclusion: Investigating the possibility of promoting inclusion through virtual mobility. *Journal of Transport Geography, 10*(3), 207-219.

Kotajarvi, B. R., Sabick, M. B., An, K. N., Zhao, K. D., Kaufman, K. R., & Basford, J. R. (2004). The effect of seat position on wheelchair propulsion biomechanics. *J Rehabil Res Dev., 41*(3B), 403-14.

Lampland, M., & Star, S. L. (2009). *Standards and their stories: How quantifying, classifying, and formalizing practices shape everyday life*. Ithaca, USA: Cornell University Press.

Latour, B. (1996). *Aramis, or, the love of technology*. Cambridge, MA: Harvard University Press.

Linton, S. (1998). Disability studies/not disability studies. *Disability & Society, 13*(4), 525-539.

MacKenzie, D. A., & Wajcman, J. (1985). *The social shaping of technology: How the refrigerator got its hum*. Milton Keynes, UK: Open University Press.

Mayor of London. (2006). Accessible bus stop design guidance. *Transport for London*. Retrieved from http://content.tfl.gov.uk/accessibile-bus-stop-design-guidance.pdf

Mercer, J. L., Boninger, M., Koontz, A., Ren, D., Dyson-Hudson, T., & Cooper, R. (2006). Shoulder joint kinetics and pathology in manual wheelchair users. *Clinical Biomechanics, 21*(8), 781-789.

Miller, P., Gillinson, S., & Huber, J. (2006). *Disablist Britain: Barriers to independent living for disabled people in 2006*: Scope.

Moss, A. (2013, November 1). Wheelchair users' fight for bus space. *BBC*. Retrieved from http://www.bbc.co.uk/news/uk-england-24614134

National Health Services Modernisation Agency. (2004). *Improving services for wheelchair users and carers—Good practice guide*. London: Department of Health. Retrieved from http://www.dh.gov.uk/en/Publicatio nsandstatistics/Publications/Publications PolicyAndG uidance/DH_4103389

Press Association. (2014, November 21). Disabled man forced off bus by refusal to move pram sparks equality test case. *The Guardian*. Retrieved from http://www.theguardian.com/society/2014/nov/11/disable d-man-forced-off-bus-refusal-move-pram-sparks-equ ality-test-case

Scott, J. C. (1998). *Seeing like a state: How certain schemes to improve the human condition have failed*. London: Yale University Press.

Seale, C. (2004). *Social research methods: A reader*. London: Routledge.

Shakespeare, T. (2006). The social model of disability. *The disability studies reader, 2*, 197-204.

Shakespeare, T., & Watson, N. (1997). Defending the social model. *Disability & Society, 12*(2), 293-300.

Silverman, D. (2006). *Interpreting qualitative data: Methods for analyzing talk, text and interaction*. London: SAGE.

Star, S. L. (1991). Power, technology and the phenomenology of conventions: On being allergic to onions. In J. Law (Ed.), *A sociology of monsters: Essays on power, technology and domination* (pp. 26-56). London: Routledge.

Transport for London. (2014). *Big red book*. London: Transport for London.

Timmermans, S., & Berg, M. (1997). Standardization in action: Achieving local universality through medical protocols. *Social Studies of Science, 27*(2), 273-305. doi:10.2307/285471

Union of the Physically Impaired Against Segregation. (1976). Fundamental principles of disability. In M. Oliver (Ed.), *Understanding Disability: From Theory to Practice* (pp.19-29). Basingstoke, UK: Palgrave Macmillan.

Vertesi, J. (2008). Mind the gap: The London underground map and users' representations of urban space. *Social Studies of Science*, *38*(1), 7-33.

Weber, R. P. (1990). *Basic content analysis*. Newbury Park, CA: SAGE.

Winner, L. (1980). Do artifacts have politics? *Daedalus*, *109*(1), 121-136.

Winance, M. (2006). Trying out the wheelchair: The mutual shaping of people and devices through adjustment. *Science, Technology & Human Values*, *31*(1), 52-72.

Woolgar, S. (1991). Configuring the user: the case of usability trials. In J. Law (Ed.), *A sociology of monsters: Essays on power, technology and domination* (pp. 66-75). London: Routledge.

About the Authors

Raquel Velho is a doctoral candidate in the Department of Science and Technology Studies, University College London where her research investigates the resistance-practices wheelchair users develop while using the public transport system in London in order to tackle a diversity of barriers in their journey. She obtained her Master's degree in Science, Technology, Medicine and Society from Imperial College London and is interested in the intersection of sociology of technology and disability studies.

Catherine Holloway is a senior lecturer at University College London's Interaction Centre where she researches how to better design assistive technologies and accessibility more widely. Catherine is the Director of the Biomedical Instrumentation Group at UCL's PAMELA facility and the CEO of Movement Metrics, a social enterprise to develop sensors and metrics to measure activity of persons with disabilities.

Andrew Symonds received his BSc in Physiotherapy in 2004 from Kings College London and his MRes in Healthcare Engineering for an Ageing Population from University College London in 2013. He is currently working as a PhD student at the University College London Aspire Centre for Rehabilitation Engineering and Assistive Technology. His PhD work is focused on the biomechanical analysis of over ground manual wheelchair propulsion.

Brian Balmer is Professor of Science Policy Studies, Department of Science and Technology Studies, University College London where his research combines historical and sociological approaches to understanding the nature of expertise, particularly in relation to the life and biomedical sciences. He has published widely on the role of volunteers in biomedical research, military technology and society, and biotechnology policy.

7

Identification Paradoxes and Multiple Belongings: The Narratives of Italian Migrants in the Netherlands

Marjo Rouvoet [1], Melanie Eijberts [2] and Halleh Ghorashi [1,*]

[1] Department of Sociology, Faculty of Social Sciences, Vrije Universiteit Amsterdam, 1081 HV Amsterdam, The Netherlands; E-Mails: marjo1989@gmail.com (M.R.), h.ghorashi@vu.nl (H.G.)
[2] Amsterdam University College, 1098 XG Amsterdam, The Netherlands; E-Mail: m.eijberts@auc.nl

* Corresponding author

Abstract
In a time identified by many as one of "multicultural backlash," we can observe a growing negative discourse on the integration of migrants with Islamic backgrounds in most European countries. Criticisms are rooted in the assumptions that cultural and religious differences are the source of social problems and that these migrants are unwilling to integrate. The aim of this article is threefold. First, it criticizes the linear and simplistic assumptions of integration informing the present negative dominant discourse in the Netherlands. Second, it shows that sources of belonging are more layered than the often-assumed exclusive identification with national identity. Third, it broadens the scope of discussion on integration (which is now mainly fixated on Islamic migrants) by showing the somewhat similar experiences of Italian migrants on their path toward integration and belonging within the Dutch context. Through this study, we argue that the process of ethnic othering in the Netherlands is broader than the often-assumed cultural difference of non-Western migrants.

Keywords
discourse; identification; integration; migrants

Issue
This article is part of the issue "International Migration and Ethnic Integration", edited by Yaojun Li (University of Manchester, UK) and Anthony Heath (University of Oxford, UK).

1. Introduction

At the turn of the 21st century, we observed excessive negative attention—or as some call it a "moral panic" (Parekh, 2008; Vasta, 2007)—toward migrants with an Islamic background. In most European states there has been a so-called "multicultural backlash," with the Netherlands often mentioned as an example because of its shift from a tolerant integration policy toward a restrictive, assimilative policy (Vasta, 2007; Vertovec & Wessendorf, 2009). The Dutch discourse of migration has been dominated by the arrival of the so-called guest workers in the late 1950s (Ghorashi, 2010a), despite a longer and diverse history of immigration to the Netherlands. Postwar economic growth and the need for unskilled labor forced the Dutch government to look beyond its borders, fostering labor contracts, first with Italy and Spain and later with Turkey and Morocco (Wilterdink, 1998). This background contributed to the persistent image of immigrants as being low educated and low skilled even as the reality of migration to the Netherlands became much more diverse. Despite this dominant image and the continuity in the policies from the 1970s until now (particularly in terms of attention for economic integration), we can see a clear shift in the Dutch discourse, particularly in how migrants' cultures have been approached in policies and politics. In the 1970s, migrants (then guest workers) were encouraged to maintain their cultural traditions and identities, with the idea that they would eventually return to their country of origin. In the 1980s, when the idea of returning was revealed to be unrealistic, there was a shift in policies toward promoting integration in addition to, but not replacing, the preservation of one's own culture. During that time, integration and the cultures of ethnic groups were not considered mutually exclusive. But by the turn of the century, we saw that the cultures and religions of non-Western ethnic others (including both migrants and their children) were increasingly considered to be the main source of social problems and disruption of social cohesion in society (Schinkel & van Houdt, 2010). This has been the backbone of the growing restrictive and assimilative turn in Dutch discourse. Loyalty to Dutch identity is increasingly presented as a dilemma for non-Western migrants: either they choose the Netherlands or they choose their home country (Scientific Council for Government Policy [WRR], 2007). This shift in the Dutch discourse, from integration to assimilation with an emphasis on loyalty toward Dutch national identity, is argued to be the result of the perceived failure of integration during the "multicultural era" (Schinkel & van Houdt, 2010; Vasta, 2007).

We aim to show that the complexity of the integration process goes beyond the binary division of success and failure. Our study shows that the process of integration is multilayered, ambiguous, and even paradoxical, not, as many assume, linear. We also aim to broaden the discussion on migrants' integration in the Netherlands by focusing on an under-researched group in the context of migration, namely, European migrants within Europe, particularly the experiences of Italian migrants in the Netherlands. Most studies on migrants in the Netherlands focus on Turkish or Moroccan migrants (Prins, 2011; Vedder & Virta, 2005; Vermeulen & Penninx, 2000). This study focuses on the experiences of integration and belonging of two waves of Italian migrants who came to the Netherlands after 1960. With this choice we hope to add nuance to the assumption that the "integration problem" is a problem of non-Western ethnic groups who are considered to be others with very different cultures and religions. The main assumption within the multicultural backlash is that the cultural and religious contrast and apparent incompatibility of Western self and non-Western other is the major source of the decline in social cohesion and unrest. Anthias (2013, p. 2) rightly argues that this strong "culturalization of social relations" leads to the reification of difference as dangerous and blinds us to other broader sources of exclusion. The lack of studies on migrant groups considered to be closer to the European self-reinforces this assumption. For that reason, the aim of this research is to show the broader sources of exclusion, deconstructing the culturalist foundation of the present discourses of integration.

Finally, we aim to look beyond national identity as a single source of belonging. Several studies show that migrants today increasingly maintain ties with more than one nation, facilitated by technology (Castles & Miller, 2009; Glick Schiller, Basch, & Szanton Blanc, 1995). However, knowledge remains limited about the layered identification process within a new host society over time and the sources of belonging beyond national identity (see also Zontini, 2015). Using in-depth open interviews, we show the struggles of two generations of Italian migrants in the Netherlands to become a part of that society. We use the WRR's (2007) concepts of functional and emotional identification to demonstrate the layers, dynamics, and tensions of different forms of identification over time. Moreover, the in-between position of these migrants (as both the European self and the non-Dutch other) provides us with challenging material for unraveling a number of assumptions, including linear integration.

2. Theoretical Framework

Duyvendak and Scholten (2010) argue that studies on immigration and integration are often squeezed into simplified theoretical models, whereas, in practice, the process is more complex, paradoxical, multisided, and multilayered. A model that is often used by policymakers is Esser's (2003) four dimensions of integration. These dimensions are presented as subsequent stages, where successful completion of the successive *Culturation*, *Positioning*, and *Interaction* dimensions will eventually lead to the final phase of *Identification*, where the immigrant feels she or he belongs to the new society. The importance of cultural adjustment (including language proficiency) to the society has become a benchmark of Dutch integration policies, visible in policy documents and in public statements (Entzinger, 2009). The prominence of policies as well as studies assuming integration as a linear process or a straight-line approach is being increasingly criticized, claiming that integration is a complex and multilayered process that, in practice, includes paradoxes (Alghasi, Eriksen, & Ghorashi, 2009; Brenninkmeijer, Geers, Roggeband, & Ghorashi, 2009; Eijberts, 2013).

A good example to illustrate this critique is language as part of culturation. In a linear approach to integration, language is the key factor in the integration process because it contributes to societal inclusion by enhancing job opportunities (positioning) and facilitating contact with natives (interaction; Esser, 2003). However, other studies have shown the double-edged sword of language, meaning that it can be a source of both inclusion and exclusion. Ghorashi and van Tilburg (2006) found that refugee women from Afghanistan and Iran considered the Dutch language essential to obtaining a job in the Netherlands, but even when they were able to speak Dutch fluently, employers continued to perceive this as "not good enough" (positioning). Through their autobiographical research, Davis and Nencel (2011, p. 5) argue that, as immigrants—in their case, from the United States—they still have to deal with comments about their accent or grammar on a daily basis, despite their Dutch fluency and their living in the Netherlands for most of their lives (interaction).

Another example is the assumption that, once migrants are integrated into society economically and socially, thus having passed the positioning and interaction stages, they will eventually enter the stage of identification with their host society (Esser, 2003). Buijs, Demant and Hamdy (2006) oppose this line of reasoning by showing how radicalized Muslim youths are not among those who are socially isolated or economically deprived; instead they are more active and involved in society and, as a result, sensitive to feelings of unfair treatment by the host society. The researchers describe this as the "integration paradox": when migrants are actually eager to integrate into dominant society, they are most sensitive to feelings of exclusion (Buijs et al., 2006, p. 202; see also Ghorashi, 2010b).

Despite these critiques, the linear model is still prominent in the Dutch discourse on integration, and it still guides policymaking. There is growing pressure for migrants to adjust themselves to what it means to be Dutch (Ossewaarde, 2007; Schinkel & van Houdt, 2010). According to the WRR (2007), a Dutch scientific board that advises the government, this current understanding of integration and its link to belonging to the Dutch national identity should be revised to embrace the complexity of the process. First, considering belonging to be based solely on connection to a specific national identity limits the scope of belonging to a rather static notion of identity (e.g., identifying as Dutch; Eijberts, 2013). This is particularly problematic because the construction of Dutchness as such is exclusionary toward migrants and thus does not stimulate belonging (Davis & Nencel, 2011; Ghorashi, 2003; Ghorashi & Vieten, 2012; Vasta, 2007). Second, the national framing of belonging blinds us to the multiple ways and levels of creating and maintaining bonds with a society (WRR, 2007). One of the most imaginable identification routes for many is identification with the city they live in. Kasinitz, Mollenkopf and Waters (2002) have shown that immigrants in New York are more likely to identify as New Yorkers than as Americans. The authors argue that identification with the city is more open to diversity, whereas being American is less accessible because of its association with whiteness (Kasinitz et al., 2002). Another growing route of identification is the transnational sense of belonging that is becoming more imaginable for different diaspora groups (Ghorashi, 2016). Meer and Modood (2013, p. 309) argue that the transnational capacity of Islam, for example, provides youth with "emancipatory qualities" to create a sense of belonging and connection transcending the duality of choice between the territorial limitations of their past and present countries.

3. Methodology

We chose qualitative methods for this study, specifically, in-depth interviews with a biographical angle. This particular approach enabled us to understand participants' dynamic and multilayered perspectives. Respondents' narratives provided space for understanding the processes of negotiation in the past and the present, helping us to grasp the meanings that respondents attached to the central themes of this research (integration and belonging) and to get a picture of their experiences and challenges (Kvale, 1996). To facilitate the required openness, we avoided asking direct questions about "integration," as this could limit the research due to the variety of personal interpretations and narrow concepts people may have about the topic. Instead, respondents were asked to share their experiences and talk about their lives in the Netherlands. Through follow-up questions we tried to obtain specific descriptions that helped us better understand the meanings they attached to these experiences. The biographical angle, as expressed in the chronological structure of the interviews, enabled us to capture the diversity of stories about participants' choices and experiences in the Netherlands in different phases of their lives. The narratives gave us the opportunity to discover what was important to the narrators about their points of connection or disconnection to places and people in their lives, what and whom they identify with, and the meanings they attached to experiences (Bryman, 2008; Kohler-Riessman, 1993; Riley & Hawe, 2005).

3.1. The Sample

Interviews were conducted from January through June 2013. A combination of purposive sampling and snowball sampling was used. We looked at Italian migrants who have been in the Netherlands for at least 20 years to enable analysis of what changes have taken place in their identification with the Netherlands as well as their sources of belonging. We did not include more recent migrants, assuming that a certain length of stay was necessary to study belonging, which develops over time. The respondents had to meet certain conditions to be included: they had to be Italians living in Amsterdam at the time of the interview. All respondents had to be first-generation migrants who arrived in the Netherlands during either the 1960s and 1970s (first wave) or the 1980s and 1990s (second wave). This division allowed us to consider the impacts of time (age and length of stay) and context (policies) in the positioning of these two groups of Italian migrants. We were interested in the similarities and differences between the two groups. The phases covered in the interviews were the period before their migration, the first years after their migration, the present, and the future. In total, 22 interviews were conducted, 12 from the first wave and 10 from the second wave.

Interviews lasted 1–5 hours. Some of the longer interviews were conducted at two different times. To secure respondents' anonymity, we used pseudonyms. Respondents comprised 13 males and 9 females. Males were largely overrepresented in the first wave because, at that time, Italian males were more likely to come to the Netherlands (Tinnemans, 1991). Most participants in the first group came from southern Italy and had low educational backgrounds and professional histories of unskilled or low-skilled labor (Lindo, 2000, p. 130). In the second wave, conversely, there were more women, and most of the respondents came from northern Italy and generally had higher educational backgrounds. This second group had more diverse backgrounds as well as different motivations for coming to the Netherlands. Some came for work, but most came because they had fallen in love with a Dutch partner.

3.2. Analysis

To understand the multiplicity of positions in relation to integration and belonging, we used identification as a sensitizing concept in analyzing the data. Jenkins (2004) argued that using identification as a concept provides opportunities to follow the dynamic and ongoing process of positioning while enabling researchers to locate different levels in the process. Throughout the analysis, we worked interpretatively and inductively, guided by what the respondents shared. An essential first step was to find patterns of similarity in the interviews (Kohler-Riessman, 1993). All interviews were transcribed, and a preliminary thematic analysis took place after half the interviews were conducted.

Through further analysis and by consulting theoretical and empirical literature about integration, we distinguished the two most dominant identification patterns present in the narratives, which the WRR (2007, p. 14ff) labels as functional and emotional identification. Functional identification refers to the functional aspects of participation in a new society, like having voluntary or paid work with which you identify and are identified with by other members of society. There is thus a greater focus on the individual and not so much on ethnic group membership. Functional identification entails having common goals as an institution or a society and interdependency (e.g., being invested together in improving the well-being of a society's elderly members). There can be multiple functional identifications that can aid one's social and economic integration in society (e.g., teacher and soccer player in a club). Emotional identification refers to having a "sense of belonging" (WRR, 2007, p. 16) associated with certain places and spaces. As the WRR points out and as we mentioned earlier, public discourse and policymaking in the Netherlands often emphasizes emotional identification, which is seen as a measure of ultimate loyalty—with the underlying premise that you can only emotionally identify with and feel loyalty toward one nation, thus often demanding of migrants an impossible choice. Functional identification, according to the WRR, does not receive a lot of attention, even though it can also provide an important bond with the host society (WRR, 2007, p. 14), as our findings below confirm. When using the terms functional and emotional identification, the WRR does not discern between self-identification and how one is identified by others, using both interchangeably for ascribed and achieved identification. However, as we shall see below, this difference is crucial in uncovering the complexities and layers of Italian migrants' experiences in the Netherlands.

4. Empirical Data

4.1. Sources of Functional Identification

In contrast to the emphasis on emotional identification with the nation that is found within public and policy discourses in the Netherlands (see also Duyvendak, 2011), and partly due to the nature of the first wave of migration, work experiences (but also membership in a group or committee) were mentioned as a major source of identification with the Netherlands. Dante's story is a good illustration of this. Dante came to the Netherlands in the 1960s, intending to stay for just one year. Once back in Italy, however, his "head was still in the Netherlands." He returned to the Netherlands, married a Dutch woman, and had several jobs, which he talked about extensively throughout the interview. He emphasized his efforts to be active and "do good things," such as volunteer work with elderly people. He proudly explained that he had also received appreciation for his work, illustrating how important it was for him to contribute to society through his work, to feel needed and appreciated by society.

The importance of work was also mentioned by several second-wave migrants, even though their motivations to migrate were more varied. Eva, who arrived in the early 1990s, said she migrated, not for economic reasons, but to increase her Dutch husband's chances for a good career in the Netherlands, thereby leaving her own good job behind in Italy. At first she did not feel at home in the Netherlands. However, "the more I worked, the better I felt." Working helped her reconnect with a part of herself, but also with members of Dutch society. As a teacher, she was surrounded by students who came to learn something from her and who appreciated what she taught them, which illustrates the potential power and value of functional identification—for Dutch society as well.

Many respondents talked about compliments they received at work, and how this helped them feel less foreign and more like a colleague, pointing to the importance of functional identification and work as such in being able to build bridges. Although work proved to be a strong source of identification with the Netherlands, the experiences were not all positive. This is because members of the majority group saw our respondents primarily as Italian ethnic others rather than as potentially valuable employees and full-fledged members of society. Matteo, a first-wave migrant, recounted how he had encountered discrimination at his job because of his ethnicity. This is in line with Lindo's (2000) findings that Italian migrants initially encountered prejudice from colleagues and employers, which faded when Moroccan and Turkish labor migrants arrived (see also Wessendorf, 2007). Second-wave migrants mostly experienced a "subtle" form of discrimination, as this quote from Angelo, who worked in the construction industry, demonstrates:

> In the beginning almost nobody spoke to me. It is just...yes, a bit set aside. You are at the table with colleagues and, uh, they talk about many things, but nobody talks to me, since they knew I did not speak the language. So you are really isolated. Just all those jokes [about me], you know...in the beginning, yes, all make jokes.

Van Laer and Janssens (2011) argue that jokes are mentioned as one the manifestations of "subtle discrimination," a form of discrimination that is less easily recognized, and which has an ambiguous character because the one who commits it often does so unintentionally. Though the act may be unconscious, the consequences are real; the "victim" may experience lower emotional and physical well-being in the context of work. In Angelo's case, while language may have formed a barrier, by making jokes, his coworkers highlighted his ethnic otherness, thereby making it harder for him to feel included.

In summary, work (paid and voluntary) was a source of functional (self-)identification with the Netherlands for Italian migrants. They wanted to contribute to Dutch society. However, there were also experiences of (subtle) discrimination at work stemming from the majority group's fixation on ethnic othering, which impeded respondents' feelings of inclusion.

4.1.1. Language and Functional Identification

While language in Dutch policy discourses is considered an integral first step (a part of culturation) in the supposedly linear integration trajectory (Esser, 2003), it was not always a part of the integration trajectory of Italian migrants. When the first-wave migrants arrived to find work in the Netherlands, there were no expectations or facilities for them to learn the language, which might have heightened their identification as "other" by ethnic Dutch people and thereby initially impeded some migrants' functional (self-)identification and possibly even emotional identification with the Netherlands (as we shall see later). Since conditions were better for the second-wave migrants and not everyone in the second wave had to find a job immediately (because they tended to migrate for love), one might expect that, upon arrival, they would have quickly learned Dutch. Yet, 5 out of the 10 respondents preferred to speak in Italian or English and had low Dutch fluency. For them, it seemed that an English-speaking environment was an additional obstacle to practicing Dutch, which is illustrated in Barbara's story. Barbara is a second-wave migrant who came to the Netherlands "out of love." She did not need to work immediately and started taking Dutch classes. Despite the opportunity to learn Dutch at school, she encountered difficulties due to the lack of opportunities to practice Dutch:

> My only frustration was when I was going around and when I wanted to speak in Dutch, people were answering in English. So I made a lot of effort to speak Dutch, and I think the people wanted to be nice and help me, but it was not a great help, because I wanted to learn Dutch. And then...I found a job where I didn't have to speak Dutch. All of my jobs in the Netherlands,...were in international firms, where people didn't speak Dutch. So I speak Dutch, but I don't feel as confident as in English, because I hardly speak it. Unfortunately.

Since Dutch language proficiency has become such an important marker of successfully following the supposed linear integration path, the past and present challenges for first- and second-wave Italian migrants to learn Dutch has likely encumbered their functional identification by Dutch colleagues and employers, as indicated in the previous section and by other researchers (Ghorashi & van Tilburg, 2006). Therefore, an important source of belonging for migrants may be difficult to obtain, and this may even impede the formation of emotional (self-) identification with the Netherlands (WRR, 2007).

4.2. Emotional Sources of Identification

When it comes to emotional identification, we see that there are different spatial levels of identification (neighborhood, city, continent, world) and that belonging can be quite complex and multilayered. Nationality- and culture-wise, most respondents entirely or predominantly identified themselves as Italian, but this did not imply that they did not feel at home in the Netherlands. An illustration of this is Roberio, a first-wave migrant who married a Dutch woman. He explained that he felt at home in both Rome, his city of origin, and Amsterdam. He is fascinated by Amsterdam and loves its "allure," with all its museums, restaurants, and theaters. However, he emphasized that he felt 100% Italian at the same time. Thus, for Roberio, emotionally identifying as Italian and feeling at home in the Netherlands—that is, in Amsterdam—are not binary oppositions.

Other first-wave migrants expressed similar feelings about Amsterdam and talked at length about all the different streets and places they knew in the city. The same connection was also found among the second-wave migrants. Eva, the only woman who had lived outside the city in the eastern Netherlands before coming to Amsterdam, stated that Amsterdam was "a different world" compared to the rest of the Netherlands. "I don't feel different at all anymore. I am a foreigner, but not different." Jano's connection to Amsterdam took on a different aspect. He came to the Netherlands in the 1980s at the age of 17. He recounted feeling more at home in Amsterdam than in Italy due to his sexual orientation:

> I felt safe here. [More] than in Italy, I felt more free in my spirit. Because soon I understood that Amsterdam was a gay city. And I was already convinced that I was gay. And I thought: Yes, that's it...yes...

In addition to emotional identification at the city level, other levels were present as well. The neighborhood was mentioned by some as a strong source of emotional identification. Pasquale, one of the first-wave migrants, indicated he feels at home in the Jordaan neighborhood because he was received there with open arms.

At a higher/superordinate/transnational level, some identified with being European or as an international citizen. These identifications were mentioned exclusively by the second-wave migrants, which may be related to the gradually intensifying cooperation in the European Union and/or generational differences, for instance, the usage of technology and social media and easier access to affordable travel. Jano, for example, identified both with Amsterdam and as a European. He argued that, even though each country had its own characteristics, he considered all European countries to be related, based on their common history and Christianity. A more internationally oriented identification occurred among three of the second-wave respondents, one of whom identified herself as a world citizen, while the other two identified as expats instead of migrants. They mentioned that they felt less attached to one place solely, but to multiple places throughout the world. Barbara explained that she travels a lot and feels at home in three places now: the Netherlands, Rome, and New York.

In addition to places, we also identified sources of belonging connected to people. Family members served as an important source of belonging. This created tension for several migrants because they had children who were born and/or raised in the Netherlands, while their parents and other family members still lived in Italy. The lack of family support was especially missed by the women participants. However, children seemed to be a major reason for choosing to remain in the Netherlands, as participants often stated that they probably would have returned to Italy if they had had no children (for similar findings for Italian immigrants in the UK, see Zontini, 2015). They either decided to stay because their children felt at home in the Netherlands or because they considered the Netherlands a better place to raise their children.

A good example is Dori (a second-wave migrant), who feels emotionally divided between Italy and the Netherlands. She married a Dutch man, came to the Netherlands in the 1980s, and became pregnant. However, she felt homesick and returned to her family in Italy to give birth to her child. Nevertheless, she kept trying to return to the Netherlands. After six years, she finally decided to settle in the Netherlands to be with her partner and live together as a family. Her son is an adult now, and this has renewed her desire to return to Italy. She mentioned that she wants to spend her "old days" in Italy. She still identifies with being Italian and feels she will never be able to become Dutch like her husband, who was born "here." Nonetheless, she also feels at home in the Netherlands, stating: "I have two feet, one in the one part, the other in the other part," pointing to the fact that an emotional self-identification with being Italian can go hand in hand with a sense of home in the Netherlands, expressing different kinds of belonging.

Another example is Maria, a first-wave migrant, who came to the Netherlands as the wife of an Italian labor migrant and who also struggled with her emotional identification. Her children were born in the Netherlands, and her husband wanted to stay, but she longed to go back to Italy because she missed her Italian family. While working, this went "unnoticed," as she was active. "[I] was young, 21 years, and I liked the work. Run here, run there, work, everything...it was nice, the work was nice." Hence, her functional identification with her job in the Netherlands was able to override her emotional identification with Italy for a certain time. However, time went on and Maria found herself living in the Netherlands for 50 years, despite her desire to leave:

> You should not stay too long, if you want to leave later. After three to five years in a different country, you should try to go back. Otherwise, you don't make it anymore. Children arrive, and when children are born here, you have roots here, too.....These roots become deeper, then you do not leave anymore. I am happy here, but I am always alone.

In sum, most respondents indicated various levels of emotional identification, but when it came to the national level, most identified with Italy rather than the Netherlands. Within the Netherlands, the highest emotional identification was at the city level for first-wave migrants and a combination of the city level and/or European level for second-wave migrants. Moreover, respondents from both groups did not exclusively identify with being Dutch themselves, but their children did. This generational difference can become a source of tension, bringing the well-being and preferences of the children into conflict with those of their parents—when the parents desire to leave, but their children desire to remain (see Zontini, 2015). The following section shows how tensions in emotional identification are related to functional identification, and the significance of age.

4.3. Functional vs. Emotional Identification

One paradox we encountered in the narratives was that an emphasis on functional identification in the early stages of migration might conflict with emotional identification with Italy at a later stage. An example of this was recounted by Jano, who was retired. He had tried to enter into Dutch social life, but upon his retirement, he did not know anyone in his neighborhood or any other Dutch people, which he partly considered his own fault:

> So it also...was also our fault. Because we were both busy at work, full time, both of us. On holidays, we went to England and to Italy, so we didn't stay here, we didn't meet people on the street. We didn't have occasion to have a chat, and so on, and so on...

For Jano, an emphasis on work limited his time to learn Dutch, and his travels to Italy did not leave room for building contacts with Dutch people. Now that he is at home more, increased contact with his neighbors has fostered a sense of belonging at the neighborhood level: "We are no longer the foreigners, the weird people. We are part of this group of people. And that is a good feeling." In addition, he started Dutch conversation classes, which diminished his hesitancy to speak Dutch.

Not everyone is able to make these sorts of investments at a later stage of the migration process. In the first stages of her "integration," Maria and her Italian husband focused on work. Now that her husband has died and she has retired, Maria admitted she is ashamed that she cannot speak Dutch fluently, despite having been in the Netherlands for 50 years. She spoke of wanting to engage in small talk with the baker, for instance, but does not do so as she feels she will not be able to express herself understandably. She really regrets not having had time to study Dutch when she was younger because of her focus on work and on raising her children. Nowadays, however, due to a lack of schooling and old age, her brain is no longer "open," as she phrases it.

Hence, the proper positioning (Esser, 2003) in the labor market did not automatically lead to more interaction, that is, social integration, as is often assumed, even though, especially in their old age, the Italian migrants realize that is what they desire. Passing the successive stages of integration is no guarantee for developing an emotional identification with the Netherlands or even the often lesser-contested sense of belonging.

The second paradox we observed was that even those who did invest in contact with Dutch people (interaction) and learned to speak Dutch fluently (culturation) experienced problems with their emotional identification at a later stage. Chiara and Marta, two second-wave women who could be considered the most successfully integrated (they have a high Dutch fluency, good jobs and housing situations, and Dutch partners), were the only ones who indicated they did not really feel at home in the Netherlands. In the initial phases of their migration, they were ambitious to become part of the Dutch society, but after approximately 20 years, they have started to withdraw from Dutch social life, speaking about their emotional struggles with living in the Netherlands while still considering Italy their "home." Chiara mentioned that, upon her arrival in the Netherlands, the first thing she did was learn Dutch. She regularly receives compliments for her level of Dutch, and she explained that she tried hard to integrate into Dutch society. However, she consciously decided to stop "integrating" at a certain point because she wanted to maintain her Italian identity:

> You have to choose at a certain moment—do you want to be Italian? Because you cannot be schizophrenic, it drives you crazy. And then of course, around my 35th, I chose to bring my Italian identity forward. And that, because that is what I feel more comfortable with....Now, I am always busy with something Italian, with books, with people who speak Italian. And that gives me peace, that is nice....I think, I have really always tried my best to learn Dutch, integrate....I liked it, I had the energy for it...but at a certain moment then you recognize that it is exhausting, this urge to belong.

This illustrates that knowing the language, working, and seeking contact does not automatically lead to emotional identification with a new country. The paradox in the case of Chiara and Marta is that successful integration has led to higher emotional struggles with the Netherlands—which is also due to being seen as the ethnic other in daily interactions. Jano, for example, mentioned:

> I have always found my way in the Netherlands...the only thing which still irritates me...not so much irritating but rather annoying me, is that, when you tell people that you have been here for 32 years, you are still Italian to them. They always ask about Italy and then you think, God, it is as if I just arrived here yesterday.

Or as Marta puts is: "There is a feeling of Us and Them, you know. You are from outside, so you do not belong, these kind of things....There is always a feeling of reticence toward the other." This finding is in line with Davis and Nencel's (2011) conclusion that "meeting the implicit and explicit criteria of integration does not ensure that newcomers can be taken up into the national imaginary available for thinking about 'Dutch-ness' in the Netherlands" (p. 482). It also relates to those of Eijberts (2013) and Ghorashi (2010b), who both showed that a high level of integration could actually become a reason for a lower level of emotional identification if the expectation of being accepted as a full citizen is not met. Our data also underline other studies' findings of this so-called integration paradox (Buijs et al., 2006).

4.4. Embracing In-Betweenness

A strong line in the narratives was the simultaneous presence of Italy and the Netherlands and selective use of these two contexts to describe connections and loss, possibilities and impossibilities. Edward Said (1993, p. xxxi) refers to the condition of being both an insider and an outsider simultaneously as the condition of in-betweenness. Daniela, a second-wave migrant recounts this point:

> At a certain moment in time, that breaking loose, leaving everything behind you, was of course nice, and probably I needed to develop my individuality, develop myself as an individual. I did not fit anywhere, and I did not want to fit anywhere. However, at a certain point, I decided to live here, and then I thought, I recognized, that I indeed did not fit here. And that this was no longer a good feeling.

According to Daniela, the key to living as a migrant is accepting that you will never be entirely at peace, you will always have "flying roots":

> I accepted that my emotional house is not in the Netherlands....What is inside of me, is not here, it is there....You have to be tough enough to say: there are my emotions, here is my future and my work; you are a bit schizophrenic. But it is a nice way to be schizophrenic.

While one is active, mobile, and ambitious to build a future through hard work, this in-between position is associated with positive feelings, as several migrants regarded being a migrant as an enriching experience. However, this feeling might become less positive at an older age when the level of mobility is reduced and the resources to connect are less accessible (see Zontini, 2015). For the older generation who no longer work and whose children have left the house, the position of being in-between has made them feel more of an outsider, accompanied by a sense of social isolation. The solution for them, as long as their health and resources let them, is to take long vacations in Italy and live the lives of pensionatos. Even then, some have discovered that, in Italy, they feel like tourists, as living abroad for so long had changed their connection to Italy as well (see Zontini, 2015).

This sense of social isolation was illustrated by Rosa, a first-wave migrant who came to the Netherlands as the wife of Bernardo, an Italian labor migrant. First, she remarked that living in the Netherlands for 50 years had made her Dutch as well. Nevertheless, later she stated: "There is always something. Since I am Italian. Do you understand what I mean? I cannot really become Dutch."

Feeling different is strengthened by the lack of social contacts—Rosa indicates that lately she has "almost nobody anymore"—as well as an increasing number of unfriendly encounters. Although Rosa and Bernardo began their interview by emphasizing they never experienced problems with Dutch people, toward the end of the interview they recounted several instances of having been treated in an unfriendly manner due to their background. During a conflict with a neighbor, they were told to go back to their own country. This was an especially sore spot for Rosa, who repeatedly stated how much the comment hurt her. Bernardo said that Dutch people used to be nice, but that more recently they had become less friendly, which has been echoed by other migrant groups in previous research, as the public and political discourse on integration has become harsher in tone (e.g., Eijberts, 2013).

Unfriendly and unwelcoming remarks were often mentioned by the first-wave migrants. This was less true of the second-wave migrants, possibly due to their greater focus on functional identification or their stronger feeling of identification as European. In sum, although both waves of migrants found themselves in an in-between position, this had become a stronger source of confusion and isolation for the first wave. Rosa, for example, stated: "Sometimes I really think, what am I actually? Not Dutch and not Italian. I am a strange person." This outsider position, which some call a sense of social isolation, may increase as people age. Getting old had various consequences for this group. On different occasions, they indicated their frustration at being afraid or unable to deal with new technology that could help them to stay in touch with family and friends in Italy (see also Zontini, 2015); thus, for them it is more difficult to engage in transnational spaces, which could actually enhance integration in both countries. They do not feel as part of Dutch society and have lost connections with Italy both emotionally (because of the duration of their stay in the Netherlands) and physically (because of the lack of mobility they enjoyed when younger). Physical distance, combined with a lack of knowledge about new technology that could help bridge this distance virtually, has added to their sense of isolation. In this way, first-wave migrants feel both out of place and behind the times because of their age (Zontini, 2015).

5. Discussion

As demonstrated above, the narratives show paradoxical processes at work when Italian migrants talk about their lives in the Netherlands. Many had a very strongly developed functional (self-)identification in the Netherlands and wanted to contribute to society (especially in the earlier stages of their life and stay in the Netherlands). They wanted to be "needed," as one respondent said, and be a valuable contributor to the welfare of their organization and society. In this sense, they can clearly be seen as an asset to Dutch society. However, their colleagues did not always recognize their efforts and approached them primarily as ethnic others, which led to their feeling excluded and may have called their self-identification into question. According to the WRR (2007), functional identification can be one of the most powerful means to fostering social cohesion and integration. However, overemphasis on migrants as ethnic others may hamper its effects.

Furthermore, at the level of functional identification, we heard narratives that challenged the assumption that language, as part of culturation, serves as a critical bridge to integration, a dominant assumption in the literature and policy discourse of integration in the Netherlands (Entzinger & Biezeveld, 2003; Esser, 2006). We refer to this contrast as the *paradox of language*. In the past, policymakers saw no need to focus on language because the migration approach of that time focused on the temporary stay of guest workers (Entzinger, 2009). However, migrants may realize later in life that their lack of language knowledge means they were unable to invest in a social life in the Netherlands outside of work. Thus, while their lack of culturation in terms of language did not result in a lack of positioning, positioning in turn did not automatically lead to more interaction, challenging the assumed linear process of one following the other. However, in old age, social interaction with their neighbors was exactly what migrants desired, and the shift in importance from functional to emotional identification caused them to feel a longing for their country of origin.

However, with the second-wave migrants especially, it becomes clear that culturation in terms of language does not open all doors either. This group of Italian migrants enjoyed higher education, and most of them worked in international environments. Some identified as expats, which could be considered a way of distancing themselves from the dominant image of the guest worker who is low educated and traditional. Though the label "guest worker" does not fit the second group of participants (from the 1980s and 1990s), they are often associated with it. Because of the "negative" image of this label, there is a clear pattern of de-identification by the second group, emphasizing their difference based on education (being more educated than the average Italian who came in that period), salary (gaining more salary than the average Italian in that period), and choice (choosing to migrate rather than needing to). In this way, they are maintaining the image of mobile migrants or Eurostars (Favell, 2008), who are from higher classes compared to the earlier group of Italian migrants. Even though all of the second-wave migrants were motivated to learn Dutch, half of them had not succeeded in learning enough to feel comfortable speaking it. The main causes for this were having a schedule that prevented the combination of working and learning Dutch, and being in a Dutch-speaking environment with Dutch people who switched to English.

However, even those who received compliments for their Dutch (culturation) and who had successfully socioeconomically integrated (positioning and interaction) did not develop the emotional identification with the Netherlands predicted by Esser (2003) and the Dutch government. This might be partly due to the fact that these kinds of mobile migrants often combine their sense of mobility with a functional integration, as Favell (2008) has argued. Another argument could be that Amsterdam has been less permissive and open than it presents itself. In an ethnographic comparison between different European cities, Favell (2008) showed that Amsterdam is a deeply regulated and controlled city in which some processes of social and ethnic closure are ingrained in daily interactions. Thus, the linear assumption underlying Dutch integration policies does not even apply to European migrants in the Netherlands, who are considered culturally close. More importantly, the "integration paradox" applies to those who are most integrated, who have successfully passed all stages, in contrast to those who are less integrated and do not even feel at home.

Even more, in this study, we observed a rather different pattern—a clash between functional (e.g., economic) and emotional sources of identification. In the case of first-wave migrants, we showed that the exclusive emphasis on work in the first stages of migration could become a hindrance to emotional identification at a later stage. Their in-between position became a source of social isolation later in life. For the second-wave migrants, we found that those who had succeeded in learning fluent Dutch, who worked, and could be considered successfully integrated, as defined by Esser's (2003) first three dimensions of integration, indicated that they felt neither Dutch nor at home in the Netherlands. Knowledge of the Dutch language and active participation in the workforce led to exposure to the exclusionary aspects of not being Dutch, which had a negative impact on their sense of belonging (see also Eijberts & Ghorashi, 2016).

In addition to the paradoxes of language and integration, we also identified layered sources of emotional identifications. Identification as "being Dutch" has become an important measure of integration in the Netherlands (WRR, 2007). As we stated earlier, several studies have shown that the construction of Dutchness is exclusive of difference, which does not provide space for a sense of emotional belonging for migrants (Davis & Nencel, 2011; Ghorashi & Vieten, 2012; Vasta, 2007). This is confirmed by our research: migrants in our study did not (or could not) fully identify with a Dutch identity but instead predominantly identified as being Italian. However, their sense of belonging was certainly much broader than identification with a national identity. The most prominent source of emotional identification was at the city level. The multicultural character and openness of Amsterdam proved an important basis for identification. This matches Kasinitz et al.'s (2002) results of immigrants identifying as New Yorkers rather than as Americans. In addition to the city level, we also found emotional identifications with particular neighborhoods and at the European level. Notably, European identification was only present in the narratives of the second-wave migrants. Their identification as expats along with intensified European cooperation and attempts to construct a European identity may have contributed to this level of identification. Identifying as European gave them an opportunity to connect their worlds (the Netherlands and Italy) and choose the best of both worlds when relating to the condition of in-betweenness. In contrast, we found that the first-wave migrants actually faced the downside of what Said (1993) refers to as the in-between position. Their focus on work in the earlier years of their migration, their limited contacts with Dutch people combined with social contacts mainly in Italy and with Italians in the Netherlands seem to have become a source of isolation in their old age (feeling out of place and behind the times).

In addition to these different (either overlapping or conflicting) layers of belonging to places, we identified family as an important core of belonging in both Italy and the Netherlands. For both migrant groups, we saw some contradictions at play, such as between the place one lives in (the Netherlands) and the people with whom one identifies (Italian family members in Italy) or the place where one's children live (the Netherlands) and the place one wants to be (Italy).

6. Conclusions

This article aimed to demonstrate the complexity of the integration process and to broaden the scope of existing studies on migrants living in the Netherlands by including the experiences of Italian migrants. To understand Italian migrants' routes to identification in the Netherlands, we distinguished between functional and emotional identification (WRR, 2007). The narratives showed that the experiences of the participants were complex, nonlinear, multilayered and did not fit a linear definition of "integration." The narratives also showed that different forms of identification overlapped and clashed over time.

All respondents in our study had to deal with a new language, with finding their way in the Netherlands, and with re-figuring the question of who they are. A similarity in all the narratives, despite differences in age and migration background, was the in-between position of these migrants in Dutch society. The first-wave migrants in our study have a less positive narrative about this in-between position due to their age and isolation in Dutch society. They miss social contacts with their families in Italy, but when they are in Italy, they feel less at home, as over time they have come to feel like an outsider there as well. Yet, we saw that the second-wave migrants were better able to cope with this in-between position and profit from its positive aspects. As Eva put it: "...you have the ability...to look at both parts, from a distance. You can be more critical. That is fun. That is fun, yes." The second-wave migrants are part of many places at the same time, are connected virtually to the world (but also to their friends and families in Italy), and have the resources to be mobile. Identifying as European, for many of them, is a way to make sense of this mobility and the multiple sources of connection. As Antonsich (2012, p. 7) argues: "Europe answers the needs of the modern individual to travel, to communicate, to exchange information and experiences. This clearly resonates with the image of the mobile European citizen put forward by Verstraete (2010)." Nevertheless, we agree with Favell (2008) that this notion of mobility should not be overemphasized, because the interactions of these mobile migrants are situated within specific national settings that also include exclusionary practices, as we discussed above.

This study has also shown that the struggle for integration and belonging in the Netherlands is not limited to migrants with Islamic backgrounds. There are many similarities in the paradoxes (of language and socio-economic integration) present in the narratives of this research with those found in other studies on various generations of migrants and refugees with Islamic backgrounds (e.g., Eijberts & Ghorashi, 2016). We hope, with the results of this study, to weaken the "culturalist" foundation of the present discourse on integration. Moreover, we have provided a more comprehensive insight into the various ways identification takes place, beyond the singular source of national identification.

Conflict of Interests

The authors declare no conflict of interests.

References

Alghasi, S., Eriksen, T. H., & Ghorashi, H. (Eds.). (2009). *Paradoxes of cultural recognition in northern Europe*. Surrey: Ashgate.

Anthias, F. (2013). Moving beyond the Janus face of integration and diversity discourses: Towards an intersectional framing. *The Sociological Review*, *61*(2), 323–343. doi:10.1111/1467-954X.12001

Antonsich, M. (2012). Bringing the demos back in: People's views on "EUropean identity". *European Societies*. doi:10.1080/14616696.2012.724575

Brenninkmeijer, N., Geers, M., Roggeband, C., & Ghorashi, H. (2009). *Eergerelateerd geweld in Nederland, Onderzoek naar de beleving en aanpak van eergerelateerd geweld*. Den Haag: Sdu Uitgevers.

Bryman, A. (2008). *Social research methods* (3rd ed.). Oxford: Oxford University Press.

Buijs, F. J., Demant, F., & Hamdy, A. (2006). *Strijders van eigen bodem: Radicale en democratische moslims in Nederland*. Amsterdam: Amsterdam University Press.

Castles, S., & Miller, M. J. (2009). *The age of migration: International population movements in the modern world* (4th ed.). Basingstoke: Palgrave Macmillan.

Davis, K., & Nencel, L. (2011). Border skirmishes and the question of belonging: An authoethnographic account of everyday exclusion in multicultural society. *Ethnicities*, *11*(4), 467–488.

Duyvendak, J. W. (2011). *The politics of home: Belonging and nostalgia in Europe and the United States*. New York: Palgrave Macmillan.

Duyvendak, J. W., & Scholten, P. (2010). The invention of the Dutch multicultural model and its effects on integration discourses in the Netherlands. *Perspective on Europe*, *40*(2), 39–49.

Eijberts, M. (2013). *Migrant women shout it out loud*. Amsterdam: VU University Press.

Eijberts, M., & Ghorashi, H. (2016). Biographies and the doubleness of inclusion and exclusion. *Social Identities: Journal for the Study of Race, Nation and Culture*. doi:10.1080/13504630.2016.1244766

Entzinger, H. (2009). Different systems, similar problems: The French urban riots from a Dutch perspective. *Journal of Ethnic and Migration Studies*, *35*(5), 815–834.

Entzinger, H., & Biezeveld, R. (2003). *Benchmarking in immigrant integration*. Rotterdam: ERCOMER/Erasmus.

Esser, H. (2003). What substance is there to the term "Leitkultur"? In R. Cuperus, K. A. Duffek, & J. Kandel (Eds.), *The challenge of diversity: European social democracy facing migration, integration, and multiculturalism* (pp. 47–58). Innsbruck and Wien: StudienVerlag.

Esser, H. (2006). *Migration, language and integration* (AKI Research Review 4). Berlin: Social Science Research Centre Berlin. Retrieved from http://193.174.6.11/alt/aki/files/aki_research_review_4.pdf

Favell, A. (2008). *Eurostars and Eurocities: Free movement and mobility in an integrating Europe*. Oxford: Blackwell.

Ghorashi, H. (2003). Multiple identities between continuity and change: The narratives of Iranian women in Exile. Focaal: *European Journal of Anthropology, 42*, 63–75.

Ghorashi, H. (2010a). The right to be different: The position of Muslim migrants in the Netherlands. In R. Banakar (Ed.), *Rights in context: Law and justice in late modern society* (pp. 163–177). Surrey: Ashgate.

Ghorashi, H. (2010b). "Dutchness" and the migrant "other": From suppressed superiority to explicit exclusion? *Focaal, 56*, 106–111.

Ghorashi, H. (2016). Muslim diaspora in the West. In J. Stone, R. Dennis, P. Rizova, A. D. Smith, & C. Xiaoshuo Hou (Eds.), *Wiley Blackwell encyclopedia of race, ethnicity, and nationalism* (pp. 1481–1484). Oxford: Wiley Blackwell.

Ghorashi, H., & van Tilburg, M. (2006). "When is my Dutch good enough?" *Journal of International Migration and Integration, 7*(1), 51–70.

Ghorashi, H., & Vieten, U. M. (2012). Female narratives of "new" citizens' belonging(s) and identities in Europe: Case studies from the Netherlands and Britain. *Identities: Global Studies in Culture and Power, 19*(6), 725–741.

Glick Schiller, N., Basch, L., & Szanton Blanc, C. (1995). From immigrant to transmigrant: Theorizing transnational migration. *Anthropological Quarterly, 81*(1), 48–63.

Jenkins, J. (2004). *Social identity* (2nd ed.). London: Routledge.

Kasinitz, P., Mollenkopf, J., & Waters, M. C. (2002). Becoming American/Becoming New Yorkers: Immigrant incorporation in a majority minority city. *IMR, 36*(4), 1020–1036.

Kohler-Riessman, C. (1993). *Narrative analysis*. Thousand Oaks: Sage.

Kvale, S. (1996). *InterViews. An introduction to qualitative research interviewing*. Thousand Oaks: Sage.

Lindo, F. (2000). The silent success: The social advancement of southern European labour migrants in the Netherlands. In H. Vermeulen & R. Penninx (Eds.), *Immigrant integration: The Dutch case*. Amsterdam: Het Spinhuis.

Meer, N., & Modood, T. (2013). Beyond "methodological Islamism"? A thematic discussion of Muslim minorities in Europe. *Advances in Applied Sociology, 3*(7), 307–313.

Ossewaarde, M. R. R. (2007). The new social contract and the struggle for sovereignty in the Netherlands. *Government and Opposition, 42*(4), 491–512.

Parekh, B. (2008). *European liberalism and "the Muslim question"* (ISIM Papers No. 9). Amsterdam: Amsterdam University Press.

Prins, J. (2011). Marokaans Nederlandse jongeren aan het woord in focusgroepen. *Migrantenstudies, 2*(25), 176–183.

Riley, T., & Hawe, P. (2005). Researching practice: The methodological case for narrative inquiry. *Health Education Research, 20*(2), 226–236.

Said, E. W. (1993). *Culture and imperialism*. London: Vintage Books.

Schinkel, W., & van Houdt, F. (2010). The double helix of cultural assimilationism and neo-liberalism. *The British Journal of Sociology, 61*(4), 696–715.

Scientific Council for Government Policy. (2007). *Identificatie met Nederland. Report to the Government*. Amsterdam: Amsterdam University Press.

Tinnemans, W. (1991). *L'italianità: De Italiaanse gemeenschap in Nederland*. Amsterdam: Het Spinhuis.

Van Laer, K., & Janssens, M. (2011). Ethnic minority professionals' experiences with subtle discrimination in the workplace. *Human Relations, 64*(9), 1203–1228.

Vasta, E. (2007). From ethnic minorities to ethnic majority policy: Multiculturalism and the shift to assimilationism in the Netherlands. *Ethnic and Racial Studies, 30*(5), 713–740.

Vedder, P., & Virta, E. (2005). Language, ethnic identity, and the adaptation of Turkish immigrant youth in the Netherlands and Sweden. *International Journal of Intercultural relations, 29*, 317–337.

Vermeulen, H., & Penninx, R. (2000). *Immigrant integration: The Dutch case*. Amsterdam: Het Spinhuis.

Vertovec, S., & Wessendorf, S. (2009). *Assessing the backlash against multiculturalism in Europe* (MMG Working Paper 09-04). Göttingen: MPIMMG.

Wessendorf, S. (2007). Sushi-eating secondos and casual Latins: Political movements and the emergence of a Latino counter-culture among second generation Italians in Switzerland. *Journal of Intercultural Studies, 28*(3), 345–360.

Wilterdink, N. (1998). Mondialisering, migratie en multiculturaliteit. In C. H. M. Geuijen (Ed.), *Multiculturalisme* (pp. pp. 55–67). Utrecht: Lemma.

Zontini, E. (2015). Growing old in a transnational social field: Belonging, mobility and identity among Italian migrants. *Ethnic & Racial Studies, 38*(2), 326–341.

About the Authors

Marjo Rouvoet (MSc) has a masters in Social Research at the VU Amsterdam, the Netherlands. Her research field is migration, integration and national identity. Her affiliation with migration and integration is both academic as well as practical. Rouvoet worked as a volunteer in a Refugee Centre in Middelburg and lived and worked in a migrant-neighborhood in Amsterdam. She currently works as a policy officer in Dordrecht.

Melanie Eijberts (PhD) is a lecturer at Amsterdam University College, the Netherlands. She holds a BA in Social Sciences from University College Utrecht and a Diploma in American Studies from Smith College, Northampton, Massachusetts. She received her MSc in Comparative Studies of Migration, Ethnic Relations, and Multiculturalism from the University of Utrecht in 2006 and obtained a PhD degree from VU Amsterdam in 2013. She investigated the sense of belonging and integration strategies of women of Moroccan and Turkish descent in the Netherlands.

Halleh Ghorashi (PhD) is professor of Diversity and Integration in the Department Sociology at the Faculty of Social Sciences, VU Amsterdam, the Netherlands. She is also Visiting Professor at the Institute for Reconciliation and Social Justice, University of the Free State, South Africa. She has published extensively on topics such as identity, diasporic positioning, cultural diversity, and emancipation with a particular focus on the narratives of identity, (forced)migration and belonging in the context of growing culturalism.

8

Rural Homelessness in Western Canada: Lessons Learned from Diverse Communities

Jeannette Waegemakers Schiff [1], Rebecca Schiff [2,*] and Alina Turner [3]

[1] Faculty of Social Work, University of Calgary, Calgary, T2N 1N4, Canada; E-Mail: schiff@ucalgary.ca
[2] Department of Health Sciences, Lakehead University, Thunder Bay, L3V 0B9, Canada; E-Mail: rschiff@mun.ca
[3] Turner Research and Strategy Inc., Calgary, T2X 2P5, Canada; E-Mail: turneralina@gmail.com

* Corresponding author

Abstract
Until recently, there was little acknowledgement that homelessness existed in rural areas in Canada. Limited research and scarce data are available to understand the scope and dynamics of rural homelessness in Canada. As suggested in our previous work, there is a need for rural homelessness research to examine themes from a provincial perspective. The aim of this research was to contribute to expanding the knowledge base on the nature of rural homelessness at a provincial level in the Canadian province of Alberta. In order to understand the dynamics of homelessness in rural Alberta, we conducted interviews with service providers and other key stakeholders across Alberta. We examined homelessness dynamics and responses to rural homelessness in 20 rural communities across the province. Across all of the communities in the study, homelessness was reported however, the magnitude of the issue and its dynamics were distinct depending on the local contexts. We also identified several themes which serve as descriptors of rural homelessness issues. We note a number of recommendations emerging from this data which are aimed at building on the experiences, capacities, and strengths of rural communities.

Keywords
Canada; disaster management; domestic violence; homelessness; Housing First; immigrant; indigenous persons; rural; seniors; youth

Issue
This article is part of the issue "Homelessness and Social Inclusion", edited by Isobel Anderson (University of Stirling, UK), Maša Filipovič Hrast (University of Ljubljana, Slovenia) and Joe Finnerty (University College Cork, Ireland).

---

1. Introduction

With a few exceptions, most research and interventions that focus on homelessness have concentrated on those living in urban areas. The visibility of urban homelessness, the ability to readily estimate their numbers, differences in profile from singles to families, children and youth to seniors, has made it possible to describe population characteristics and begin to determine ways of addressing need. The same cannot be said of the rural experience.

Anderson and Sim (2000, 2011) note the significance of geographic location to social exclusion in housing. While there is a body of work from other countries such as the UK (see especially Cloke, Marsden, & Mooney, 2006; Cloke & Milbourne, 2012) and the United States (United States Government Accountability Office, 2010) which has more specifically focused on rural housing and social exclusion, there is little research available to understand the scope and dynamics of rural homelessness in Canada (Waegemakers Schiff, Schiff, Turner, & Bernard, 2015). The aim of this research was to contribute to expanding the knowledge base on the nature of homelessness in rural Canadian communities. We begin with a review of the state of knowledge on rural homelessness in Canada. As Waegemakers Schiff et al. (2015) suggest, there is a need for rural homelessness research to capture common emerging themes from a provincial rather than community-by-community perspective. As such, this study also focuses beginning to address this need through an provincial examination of homelessness dynamics and responses to rural homelessness across 20 diverse rural communities in Alberta Canada. Through this process, our research uncovered a few significant trends with regards to the nature of rural homelessness in Alberta. In particular, we identified three themes which serve as descriptors of rural homelessness issues and are considered in the context of Canadian and international literature on rural homelessness. These themes focused on: Significant sub-populations; economic dynamics and; rural housing market dynamics. We also identified two other unique issues which are mostly unrecognised in the literature on homelessness and might be important considerations in understanding rural homelessness dynamics.

2. Background: Rural Homelessness in Canada

Until recently, there was little acknowledgement that homelessness existed in rural areas in Canada (Waegemakers Schiff et al., 2016). Understanding of rural homelessness is minimal compared to that focussed on urban populations, and assessment of needs within the non-urban population is often overlooked. Rural homelessness was unacknowledged in this country, until reports from diverse rural areas of Canada began to emerge in the last decade which shed light on the unique context of the issue (Christensen, 2011; Robertson & White, 2007; Roy, Hurtubise, & Rozier, 2003; Standing Senate Committee on Agriculture and Forestry, 2008). The combination of vast, sparsely inhabited spaces, a harsh climate, and minimal to non-existent social services in remote areas, provides the setting and unique challenges for those who are without adequate housing in rural Canada. Recent reports reveal considerable concerns over dwellings that provided inadequate shelter from the elements, others being unfit for human habitation, and people doubled up and living in extremely overcrowded situations (Christensen, 2012).

A combination of counts and estimates of homeless persons throughout Canada report that every night, at least 30,000 Canadians experience homelessness. Among them, almost 3,000 'sleep rough' indicating that they sleep in cars, parks or on the street and are considered unsheltered. Another 14,400 stay in emergency shelters, which are usually temporary and provide overnight sleeping facilities but often no day-time accommodation (Gaetz, Donaldson, Ruichter, & Gulliver, 2013). Longer term stay is attributed to the 7,350 who stay in domestic violence shelters, although these facilities often have a 30- or 60-day maximum length of stay. A final group includes more than 4,460 who are provisionally accommodated in hospitals, prisons or halfway houses who have no permanent residence to return to upon discharge from the facility (Gaetz, Donaldson, Ruichter, & Gulliver, 2013). The foregoing reflects urban homelessness. There are no accurate reports of how many people are homeless absolutely or relatively, in rural Canada.

With a few exceptions, most research and intervention has concentrated on individuals and families living in urban areas; consequently, homelessness has most often been framed as an urban phenomenon. In cities and towns, homeless individuals seek a range of support services, including food, overnight shelter and financial help at organizations established to address these needs. These activities make the urban homeless a visible population in many respects. This visibility, the ability to more readily estimate their numbers, and differences in profile (singles families, youth and seniors, aboriginal, immigrant and refugee), has made it possible to describe population characteristics and begin to determine ways of addressing their described needs in Canadian cities (Peressini, McDonald, & Hulchanski, 1995).

In contrast, rural locations often do not have specific services for homeless people and consequently there are few places available for identification of those who may be in housing distress and consequently for data collection necessary for accurate counts. As a result, the extent of homelessness in different parts of rural Canada is simply unknown. Because rural homelessness is difficult to measure with any accuracy, measures of rural poverty and core housing need are often taken as proxy indicators. As such, they suggest that the rate of rural housing instability is similar to that in urban areas (Employment and Social Development Canada, 2011; United States Interagency Council on Homelessness, 2015). However, researchers in the United States (Fitchen, 1992; Lawrence, 1995) note that rural housing insecurity may be as ubiquitous as it is in urban settings, and homeless rates may be even higher than in urban areas when those living in substandard or unfit housing are included. Houses which would be routinely condemned in urban areas, fall outside of the view of local officials in rural areas and remain inhabited despite their unsafe condition (Robertson, Harris, Noftsinger, & Fischer, 2007).

While rural homelessness has received some attention in Australia (Grigg, Judd, Ryan, & Komiti, 2005), the United States (Fitchen, 1992; Lawrence, 1995; Robertson et al., 2007) and England (Cloke, Milbourne, & Widdowfield, 2000, 2001, 2003), what little is known about rural homelessness in Canada is confined to small body of academic literature and a group of local reports which generally focus on discrete communities and sub-regions in disparate parts of the country. Some have a general overview of rural homelessness in a given region and others are focused on discrete populations such as Aboriginal people (Belanger & Weasel Head, 2013; Kauppi, Pallard, McGregor, & Seyler, 2015), northern remote areas (Christensen, 2012), and those with a serious mental illness (Forchuk et al., 2010). The lack of consolidated information across the country hinders a clear understanding of the specificity and complexity of Canadian rural homelessness and thus hampers efforts to tailor programs and initiatives aimed at alleviating homelessness in rural environments (Waegemakers Schiff et al., 2016).

A recent review of the literature on rural homelessness in Canada (Waegemakers Schiff et al., 2016) suggests that there is a need for research to capture common emerging themes from a provincial rather than community-by-community perspective. They suggest that, due to the vastness of Canada and its immense regional variation, a provincial perspective is a more manageable stepping-stone to a detailed national understanding. In keeping with this recommendation, this research focused on a province-wide investigation of homelessness in rural Alberta. We examined homelessness dynamics and responses to rural homelessness in 20 rural communities across the province. In this process, we were able to provide a preliminary assessment of nature of this issue and local responses to rural homelessness across these communities.

3. Alberta Context

Alberta is primarily a rural province, with large expanses of sparsely settled areas, two major cities (pop. 1,250,000 and 812,000), and a few larger urban clusters. Although the size of France, Alberta is primarily a rural province, with large expanses of sparsely settled areas, multiple small communities (pop. less than 2,500 persons) which are surrounded by vast swatches of range land, farm land, arboreal forests as well as mountainous areas. Resultantly, we utilised a data gathering approach (see Methodology) that would represent all of these variations. The province is divided, for economic analysis, into fourteen regions, with two major urban regions (Capital and Calgary which were omitted from the study). The remaining 12 regions are mainly rural in nature, although six host cities of 35,000 to 130,000. Rural regions of the province also vary as dominated by either agricultural, energy sector (oil and gas) or recreational/tourist characteristics (see Figure 1).

4. Methodology

In order to understand the dynamics of homelessness in rural Alberta, we conducted interviews with service providers and other key stakeholders across Alberta. The participants for this study came from two sources; local representatives who had familiarity with the social services and housing demands in their communities as well as key government officials and stakeholders of larger province-wide organizations. For this study, we focused on Alberta's economic development regions (Figure 1) and targeted their rural settlements (Table 1). Using this selection, we then narrowed the targeted communities according to population size, densities, agricultural, energy sector (oil and gas) and recreational/tourist characteristics. Within these regions, 51 separate agencies were contacted and 20 communities participated in the study. The study was limited to rural communities with populations under 25,000 to align methods to a concurrent national study (Waegemakers Schiff & Turner, 2014). Study communities had an average of 7,000 residents. The 20 communities involved directly with the study were: Athabasca; Beaver County (Ryley); Brooks; Camrose; Chestermere; Claresholm; Coaldale; Cochrane; Didsbury; Fairview; Fort Mackay; High Level; Jasper; Lac La Biche; Redwater; Pincher Creek; Rocky Mountain House; Slave Lake; St. Paul; Wetaskiwin.

Within these communities we identified and contacted key individuals in government and the local social services coordinating organizations which are allied with

Figure 1. Alberta economic regions (2015). Source: Government of Alberta. Available at http://www.albertacanada.com/business/statistics/regional-economic-indicators.aspx

Table 1. Alberta economic development regions and associated study communities.

Economic Region	Community
Battle River	Camrose
Calgary	Chestermere; Cochrane
Capital	Beaver County; Wetaskiwin
Central	Didsbury
Mackenzie	High Level
North Central	Athabasca; Redwater
North East	Lac La Biche; St. Paul
Palliser	Brooks
Peace County	Fairview
Slave Lake	Slave Lake
South Central	Claresholm; Coaldale
South West	Pincher Creek
West Yellowhead	Jasper; Rocky Mountain House
Wood Buffalo	Fort Mackay

Family and Community Support Services office across the entire province and requested their participation. For all identified stakeholders and local representatives, phone calls and emails were followed with recruitment packages that contained both the interview guide, ethics approval and informed consent documents.

Between February to April 2014 we conducted interviews with key informants in 20 communities across all of these economic regions and 6 stakeholders at the provincial services level. The narrow time-frame minimized any potential impact of political and economic forces on the regions. Data were collected using a template for surveying rural communities that had been previously developed and used in a national survey of rural homelessness (Waegemakers Schiff & Turner, 2014), with the addition of a few modifying questions salient to the Western Canadian context. Homelessness was defined according to the Canadian Definition of Homelessness (Canadian Observatory on Homelessness, 2012). The study included both 'hidden' and visible forms of homelessness, such as rough sleeping, couch surfing, doubled up and sheltered populations. A graduate research assistant who was experienced in interviewing arranged and conducted most of the community interviews which were primarily telephone-based.

5. Data Analysis

For each community we created a profile based on key indicators (population size, percent of persons with low income, size of the Aboriginal population) and descriptors arising from the interviews with respect to housing conditions, migration dynamics, homelessness trends, and action on homelessness in the community. We supplemented these community descriptors with a data base that contained 19 key community variables including location, access to major centre, macroeconomic trends (community type as defined by Bruce et al. (2005), proximity to First Nations reserve(s), households in core housing need as identified in the national housing study (Canada Mortgage and Housing Corporation [CMHC], http://www.cmhc-schl.gc.ca/en/hoficlincl/homain/stda/data/data_013.cfm), homeless population estimates and trends, the local homelessness response including emergency shelters, rental subsidies, homeless action plan, system coordination across social services organizations, and awareness of and implementation of a *housing first* approach. These were quantified so that we could use a cluster analysis, based on the community profiles compiled from key indicators and descriptors, to aid in in thematic analysis through characterization of groups of communities according to common parameters.

6. Findings

Across all of the study communities in the study, homelessness was reported and this impression was confirmed by the provincial stakeholders. However, the magnitude of the issue and its dynamics were distinct depending on the idiosyncrasies of local contexts. Nevertheless, on the whole, most community representatives included in the study pointed to the existence of homelessness as something that has 'always been there' to a certain extent. Interviewees also noted that rural homelessness differs from the urban because of its 'hiddenness'. The rural homeless population was reported to be quite mobile, constantly moving from place to place. While interviewees noted issues of outmigration from urban centres to rural areas, and migration between rural communities, there was no identification of migration of the urban poor to rural areas as noted in Belgium by Meert and Bourgeois (2005).

Rural homelessness was described as a 'hidden phenomena,' characterized by families and individuals doubling up and couch surfing, or living in makeshift housing (unsafe housing, trailers, camping out, etc.). Doubling up and couch surfing were the most often-cited manifestations of rural homelessness. A small amount of visible homelessness was reported in the form of transient people loitering in town centres, rough sleeping and people sheltered in shelters in the few towns where these exist. On a per capita basis, some study communities reported quantifiable homelessness prevalence rates. For example, an interviewee from High Level estimated the community to have a homeless population of about 30 people; for a town with a population of 3,610, this would result in a homelessness prevalence rate of 0.8%. Comparatively, Calgary, which is known to have one of the highest urban homelessness rates nationally, reports an estimated 0.307% prevalence rate (Calgary Homeless Foundation, 2013). Smaller study communities that did not have shelters also reported in some instances that transportation was provided, usually through bus tickets, to locations where shelters exists. This practice also minimizes the extent of the homeless population as many of those transported out cannot easily return.

Our research also uncovered a few significant trends with regards to the nature of rural homelessness, program approaches, and policy responses in Alberta. In particular, we identified three themes which serve as descriptors of rural homelessness issues. These themes focused on: Significant sub-populations; economic dynamics and; rural housing market dynamics. We also identified two other unique issues which are mostly unrecognised in the literature on homelessness and might be important considerations in understanding rural homelessness dynamics. One of these issues was of a geographic nature, addressing the issue of parks and recreational areas. The other was of a temporal nature, relating to the impact of disaster situations on homelessness dynamics and service systems.

7. Notable Sub-Populations

Interviewees identified six distinct sub-populations of people experiencing homelessness in rural areas of the province. These included: victims of domestic violence; youth; newcomers; indigenous persons, chronic substance (alcohol) abusers, and chronically homeless people. Notably, interviewees did not mention those with mental health problems, despite the fact that they are a significant part of urban homelessness (Hwang, Stergiopoulos, O'Campo, & Gozdzik, 2012).

7.1. Victims of Domestic Violence

Domestic violence was cited as a key driver to housing instability and homelessness, not only as a direct factor in pathways into homelessness, but also for its long term repercussions. This is not surprising as Family issues and domestic violence are frequently cited as factors that precipitate rural homelessness (Glass, 2002; Kauppi et al., 2012; Lee, Budgell, & Skinner, 2007; Peters & Robillard, 2009). Community and provincial stakeholders noted the impacts of domestic violence for women, youth, children and seniors, leading to loss of housing and various forms of hidden homelessness. In rural Alberta contexts, the available options for those escaping abuse are much more limited than in urban centres; an issue that is reflected in some of the other Canadian literature (Callaghan & Turnbull, 1999; Yukon Anti-Poverty Coalition, 2011). Women fleeing violence have to leave their communities to escape their abusers, which also takes them out of their network of social supports.

A network of women's shelters is in place across 33 Alberta communities. About 45% (15) of these are located outside Alberta's main seven cities. The proximity and availability of women's shelters plays a key role in migration to access services as women and children have to leave their community to seek safety and support in localities with such services. Many sought supports in other rural communities with women's shelters. This is especially true for Indigenous people, as the Alberta Council of Women's Shelters reported that as many as 70% of domestic shelter users across the province are Indigenous women. This also reflects reports from other areas (Kauppi, 2012; Schmidt, Hrenchuk, Bopp, & Poole, 2015). Resultantly, in recent years, an increasing complexity of presenting issues for such centres is also reported.

Indigenous women face the additional challenges engendered by systematic racism and sexism upon arrival at their destination. Interviewees reported that landlords are often cautious to rent to women fleeing violence, particularly when they are Indigenous and have children with them for fear of damages to their units or 'partying' and over-crowding from relatives and friends doubling up. These reports are similar to those from Nunavut (Schmidt et al., 2015) and northern Ontario (Kauppi, Pallard, & Shaikh, 2013). One encouraging initiative suggests that solutions tailored to this group are emerging in rural Alberta. Landlords in Camrose are working with Indigenous women fleeing violence, making rental units available to them. Support workers advocate on behalf of the women and support housing stability. As a result, landlords are now 'lining up' to be part of the initiative as the women proved to be 'ideal tenants': stable, caring for the property, and paying rent on time.

7.2. Youth

Youth were another group that emerged as a notable sub-population of the rural homeless. Study communities reported homeless youth to be even less visible on the street, and most likely to couch surf and double up. Youth homelessness was often un-recognized from an official perspective, though interviewees remarked it to be a notable emerging issue. These reports are similar to those that come from many rural areas such as Nova Scotia (Karabanow, Naylor, & Aube, 2014), Ontario (Martin, 2013), and Manitoba (E. Peters & Craig, 2014).

Youth were reported to be homeless most often as result of abuse in the home, which led to notable movement and transience as they sought a safe place to live outside their familial home. The gendered experience of domestic and sexual violence impacts youth further. Sexual and gender identity, identified as a key driver in youth homelessness (Gaetz, 2014) adds yet another dimension in rural contexts. These dynamics often led to significant movement into urban centres. Youth serving agencies in Edmonton, for example, anecdotally report as many as 40% of youth they serve come from rural communities. The impetus for migration of rural homeless youth has become an important area for further study as reflected in the work from Nova Scotia (Karabanow et al., 2014) and Ontario (Martin, 2013), but need to expand to develop programmatic and policy solutions.

One youth shelter was reported in the rural Alberta case study communities (Camrose). As in urban contexts, the service response to rural youth homelessness is entwined with child intervention services and education, particularly given the high rates of abuse reported. For most youth, the lack of access to treatment for counseling, mental health and addictions locally was yet another service gap and is a problem in many rural areas (Kauppi et al., 2015; Forchuk et al., 2010). Here, ongoing challenges of service coordination are noted to limit the range and comprehensiveness of responses to the issue. There is a need for service coordination to ensure developmentally appropriate supports and housing options for homeless youth in rural Alberta.

7.3. Newcomers

There is currently little to no discussion in the Canadian literature of homelessness among immigrants or refugees in rural areas. One report provides a description of homelessness among a diverse group of participants from several ethno-cultural communities in Windsor/Essex County, Ontario (Anucha, 2006). While it did not specifically address rurality as a dynamic in their experiences, the report notes that newcomers' homelessness in the area is precipitated by housing unaffordability. Through interviews conducted in this Alberta study, economic immigrants, refugees, refugee claimants and Temporary Foreign Workers emerged as a notable sub-population experiencing hidden homelessness in some study communities. Where homelessness was reported among this group, it was most often described as a result of low income leading to doubling and over-crowding, or living in poor quality housing. Foreign workers accounted for a large proportion of those living in substandard living situations in certain regions. Many of these individuals are living together in groups in accommodations not suitable for many people. In certain areas, doubling up was reported to be a common trend due to the accommodations provided by employers.

For immigrant women experiencing domestic violence, the added element of rurality exacerbated their isolation and ability to access supports. For some, the prospect of leaving abusers to move to a larger urban centre when they have limited knowledge about Canadian social support and justice systems and competency in English leaves this group particularly vulnerable. When the spouse is also the woman's sponsor for immigration purposes, the situation is particularly more tenuous from a legal perspective as well (Walsh, Hanley, Ives, & Hordyk, 2015).

7.4. Indigenous Persons

Several local and regional reports from across Canada have noted over-representation of Indigenous people in the homeless population (Kauppi et al., 2009; Hallstrom et al., 2013; Stewart & Ramage, 2011) although the extent to which this applies in rural settings is unknown. Some rural literature has examined the context and process of migration and mobility between reserves and urban areas (Belanger, Weasel Head, & Owasago, 2012; Christensen, 2011; Peters & Robillard, 2009), though not specifically of the problems and dilemmas of their rural homeless experience. The majority of communities included in this study were located near Indigenous communities. In communities with relatively large Indigenous populations and/or proximity to reserves, the makeup of the homeless population consistently demonstrated an over-representation of Indigenous people. In areas where a high number of Indigenous communities and reserves exist near the town, there the majority of homeless people are reported to be Indigenous. In areas where no Indigenous over-representation was reported in the homeless population, limited proximity to Indigenous communities was also noted. There were however exceptions to this trend, as in the case of Fairview where Indigenous women made up as many as 75% of domestic violence shelter users despite no Indigenous communities being in close proximity.

In some areas, Indigenous people are deterred from using town services and encouraged to 'find their way down the highway' to larger cities; a trend which might be attributed to racist sentiments within smaller communities. The issue of racism as a confounding factor for rural homelessness among Indigenous people is also reported by Waegemakers Schiff et al. (2015). Many interviewees, who also noted their familiarity with local residents, reported that homeless Indigenous individuals were often the children of parents who survived the residential school system, and faced complex mental health and addictions issues, domestic violence and traumatic experiences, as well as Fetal Alcohol Spectrum Disorder (FASD), which is often undiagnosed, especially in adults.

Some literature and reports on homelessness among Indigenous people in Canada have focussed on migration between reserves and urban centres (Belanger & Weasel Head, 2013; Christensen, 2012; Carle & Belanger-Dion, 2003; Kauppi et al., 2009; Peters & Robillard, 2009). Interviewees reported frequent migration from Indigenous communities. They also described migration as motivated by a number of factors, including poor housing conditions on-reserve, lack of employment and education opportunities, as well as the need to access services (medical, judiciary, counseling, etc.). Several researchers studying migration patterns have reported similar motivations (Belanger & Weasel Head, 2013; Christensen, 2012; Peters & Robillard, 2009). Lack of safety, abuse, and violence were also reported by interviewees to be main drivers out of Indigenous communities. This is a particularly salient theme for Indigenous women and children fleeing violence on-reserve who seek support outside their home communities.

It is important to distinguish the contexts in which Indigenous rural homelessness plays out. On-reserve homelessness has distinct dynamics that should be noted. As this particular study was not intended to study on-reserve homelessness, we strongly urge that future research specifically examine this issue. In the interim we briefly describe the dynamics reported in one rural Indigenous town that is on a reserve.

7.5. Chronically Homeless Persons

Several reports from across Canada have noted the existence of chronic homelessness in rural communities, although at rates lower than those found in urban settings (Waegemakers Schiff et al., 2015). People experiencing chronic homelessness were reported as a smaller component of the homeless populations across the study communities and were characterized by complex mental health, addiction, and FASD issues. Those suffering from these disabilities were regarded as relatively small group, numbering less than ten in a typical community. This group was consistently facing housing loss due to these challenges, as subsidized housing and support services are limited in rural areas. The lack of supports available to manage underlying issues leads to further housing instability. For those who struggle with addictions or mental illness in rural Canada, lack of treatment and support services are reported as scarce and there is little (or none, depending on the location) supportive housing

(Callahan & Turnbull, 1999; Forchuk et al., 2010; Glass, 2002; Grodzinski et al., 2011; Lee et al., 2007; Nunavut Housing Corporation, 2013; Smith & Fuller, 2007; Stewart & Ramage, 2011).

Some special populations present specific dynamics influencing their homelessness. Among those with living with mental illness and addictions, there are chronically homeless populations in rural Alberta communities which have become well known to the small pools of landlords. People so identified are often placed on a 'no-rent list'. Particularly during economic growth periods, this group is described as most often 'squeezed out' of existing rental stock by incoming migrant workers. Some of the communities included in the study had a local women's shelter, however, none had emergency homeless shelters available to all adults or to families, to accommodate those in need of basic shelter services. As a result, rough sleeping was commonly reported, along with individuals and families living in makeshift shelters, trailers and tents.

Rough sleeping was reported across Alberta; particularly during warmer months. A small number of homeless people can be found in ditches, backyards, and parks or forested areas. This corresponds to other reports of the various ways the absolutely homeless cope in rural areas (Glass, 2002; Lee et al., 2007; Peters & Robillard, 2009). Notably, a significant proportion of chronically homeless and rough sleepers were reported to be Indigenous people, particularly in areas with proximity to First Nations or other Indigenous communities, which is also reported in other areas (Belanger & Weasel Head, 2013; Kauppi et al., 2015; Peters & Craig, 2014).

8. Economic Dynamics

Interviewees who reported homelessness to be a minor issue in their community were scarce. Most noted that homelessness was not only a major challenge to the social infrastructure of their locality, but even noted its prevalence and intensity to be increasing in recent years. This impact on communities is a dynamic that is mentioned (Young & Moses, 2013) but has not been well explored in the literature. Across the 20 study communities, the reported homelessness trends appeared to be closely tied to macro-economic shifts in the global economy impacting Alberta; particularly as related to the oil and gas industry. While some sites are intimately engaged in oil and gas, others were indirectly impacted by the ebbs and flows in prosperity characteristics of the industry. These communities act as service centres, or stop-points between resource-extraction sites and larger urban centres. This echoes what is also reported to drive housing affordability in the western Artic (Young and Moses, 2013). Not surprisingly, northern Alberta areas reported a much more intimate link with the oil and gas industry, which was attributed to be a main driver in their homelessness population. The ties particular communities have with resource extraction, especially in northern regions or on corridors between urban centres and these sites, have a marked impact on housing markets and homelessness dynamics.

There are a number of reasons behind the reported strained housing markets, which must be contextualized in relation to the larger economic contexts impacting the locality. For example, some centres were experiencing rapid growth brought on by regional economic development, often tied to the oil and gas industry. The influx of new workers created increased competition for scarce housing, driving prices well beyond affordability for those of modest or low income means. A provincial stakeholder reported strained vacancy rates due to the pressure of migration related to oil and gas industry in the region. The oil and gas industry placed significant strain by also recruiting landlords directly to house their workforce. Companies rent out available units at top dollar for their workers, leaving a depleted stock for both secondary industry workers earning significantly less and the community's lower income populations.

Home ownership is also caught in this cycle as housing investment speculation leads to rapid increases in house prices, which squeeze out middle and lower income families. In turn, the pressure on an already limited rental stock increases as migrant workers and local lower income renters compete for available units, driving up costs. As an interviewee from Rocky Mountain House noted, 'things get worse, when things are good'—referring to the fact that a booming economy creates stress on households. The impact of this housing crunch not only affects lower income, vulnerable groups, but also key workers who are unable to afford to live in such communities. These key workers include those in the social service, mental health, and addictions sectors among others; the shortage of such critical services providers hampers the service infrastructure in such centres. Unlike the larger urban centres where such issues are related to lack of social and support services (Kauppi et al., 2015), rural communities are much more sensitive to these economic swings and have fewer resources to mitigate the changing demands for these services (Kauppi et al., 2013).

Both provincial and local interviewees related homelessness to these dynamics. Notably, they reported that in general, local homeless populations resided in these study communities regardless of the ups and downs of the oil and gas industry. However, an emerging homeless population was identified as attracted by an economic boom. As unskilled migrants, often struggling with alcohol or drug issues, they brought an additional layer of complexity in psychosocial issues to the local homeless population in resource-dependent communities.

9. Rural Housing Market Dynamics

The housing markets in rural Alberta play a key role in homelessness dynamics. Purpose-built rental housing is very limited and the rate of development is significantly lower than that of larger urban centres. Most stock exists in the form of single family housing, spread out across a larger surface area than what is often seen in cities. While some study communities reported available housing to exist on the outskirts of town, the lack of public transportation limits lower income groups from accessing it.

The housing stock traditionally available to lower income groups, particularly those with complex mental health and addiction issues, is reported to take the form of rental units on the top floors of older commercial buildings in the town centre (usually on the main road going through the town). While a valuable and limited resource for those with limited incomes, these buildings are reported to be aging to the extent that many are on the slate for demolition. Other forms of housing include hotels and motels, which are rented for longer periods by oil and gas workers in some communities. However, low vacancy rates and high prices limit their accessibility for lower income families and individuals.

Another dynamic that plays out in farming communities involved in this study involves the longer process of corporatization that has pushed people into increasingly smaller areas available for cultivation. Over time, some of these families become squeezed out of available land, leading to over-crowding and living in poor quality housing. As result of these economic and housing market dynamics, low vacancy rates were reported in 13 of the 20 case study communities. Ten of these communities specifically noted rents were also on the rise locally, which is consistent with reported trends across Alberta (CMHC, 2013).

10. Unique Regional Issues

Two unique issues emerged in this research which are related to specific regional circumstances or events. The first issues identified was the impact of recreational areas on rural homelessness. Another issue which emerged was related to the impact and ability to respond to disasters and the impact on housing stability in rural areas.

10.1. Recreational Areas

An issue that has not been considered in the literature is the impact of recreational areas on homelessness dynamics. Alberta is home to several significant recreational areas which are fueled by both local use and a large tourist base. The recent rise in prosperity for many Albertans has also spawned an increase in secondary and recreational homes in rural areas near both summer and winter destinations. While there is a robust literature on locational impact of recreational (second home) ownership in Canada, and Alberta specifically (Bohlin, 1975; Halseth, 1998; McNicol & Glorioso, 2014), there has not been specific or detailed consideration of the impact of these trends on homelessness dynamics. Notable are larger communities that are located in or near national parks such as Banff, Jasper and Canmore. Other smaller communities are also affected including those located near provincial parks and recreation areas, such as Sylvan Lake, Pigeon Lake, and towns in the Crowsnest Pass. Those located in national parks boundaries have unique constraints that are distinct from those communities located near but outside of park boundaries. National parks have severe restrictions on additional residential building construction which restricts housing availability, especially for those with lower incomes. Service industry workers and their families are most often impacted by these dynamics. While we recognize that the economic factors that influence homelessness are analogous to those created by energy sector development in other areas, the influences in recreational and tourist areas have unique aspects that require a separate examination.

10.2. Disaster Homelessness

In addition to other important aspects of rural housing and homelessness, we identified a need to address the significant challenges created by natural disasters. Interviews revealed that natural disasters hold the potential not only to contribute to acute homelessness but also significantly impact existing homeless people and services in affected areas. Two events that were recent in the context of the study were identified by participants: the June 2013 flooding which ravaged the city of Calgary and parts of southern Alberta and significantly impacted several First Nations (Environment and Climate Change Canada, 2014) and the 2011 fires in the town of Slave Lake that destroyed most of the infrastructure and 30% of all homes in the town (CBC News, 2011). The more recent 2016 fire that ravaged the town of Fort McMurray had significant impact on that municipality's infrastructure and housing (The Globe and Mail, 2016); the impact on homeless persons was also reported by some media outlets (McDermott, 2016). Despite the significance of these events, there is little in the peer-reviewed literature which considers their impact on homelessness dynamics.

The June floods of 2013 severely impacted the Stoney and Siksika First Nations and further exacerbated already hidden homelessness and dire housing conditions in Morley, Eden Valley, and nearby Rocky Mountain House. Promised emergency housing did not substantially materialize in these communities and many of those forced from their homes were living in motels in Calgary, Canmore and nearby areas for extended periods. Some families were doubled or tripled up with up to 19 individuals attempting to live in a three-bedroom dwelling. In other instances, family sub-units rotated their place of residence among several houses occupied by relatives, a version of couch surfing that involves entire families. These events continue to exacerbate an already problematic housing and homeless problem on these reserves and continues several years after the disaster.

The experience of Slave Lake in the wake of the 2011 fires provide further learnings about the unique circumstances resulting from natural disasters. The housing situation faced by Slave Lake as a result of a massive fire led to more than 700 people were left homeless. Rebuilding has been a four-year plan and is now essentially complete. But in that time span, many lived in interim housing secured from the province, some on site and others in distant communities. This created unique set of circumstances whereby a large portion of the population could be considered homeless. At the same time, a strong economy fueled by the energy sector kept the local economy healthy and ensured rapid return of the local population. Most often, families were couch surfing and doubling up. Notably, there remained a reported 'base' homeless population that preceded the fire consisting of longer term homeless, who were struggling with mental health and addictions issues. Within the context of the disaster, homelessness-related supports and the needs of this group were reported to take a 'backseat' given the extent of the housing problem facing the general population.

The Slave Lake fire and June 2013 floods examples highlight the unique circumstances natural disasters can create in rural communities. As there is presently no work that explores this issue, a detailed consideration of the impacts of disasters on homelessness should be pursued to examine longer term effects of disasters on rural communities and consider impacts in future planning and emergency preparedness work. Because of the pervasive and specific housing challenges of indigenous people a specific consideration the uneven impacts of disasters on homelessness among Indigenous people, off and on-reserve should be undertaken.

11. Conclusions and Recommendations

The aim of this research was to respond to a need for rural homelessness research in Canada to examine issues from broader, provincial perspectives rather than community-by-community case study approach. As such, this study focused on an examination of homelessness dynamics and responses to rural homelessness in 20 rural communities, spanning the wide range of landscape geographies and economic regions in the province of Alberta.

In this study we became acutely aware of the ways in which international research on rural homelessness has similarities and differences, depending on geographical and political context. In comparison to the UK, where local authorities keep a closer count of those in housing need and research has been more precise (Cloke & Milbourne, 2012), and the US where housing assistance by way of rental subsidies and social programs extends a bit further into small towns (United States Government Accountability Office, 2010), the rural areas of Canada are vast, under-served, under-populated and have few resources. Moreover, the concept of rurality in a densely populated country such as the UK generally concerns itself with localities within ready access to urban areas and facilities, which significantly impacts the ways in which the needs of rural homeless people can be addressed. The vast stretches of Canadian and north western US states create additional challenges in location of homeless people, accessing and delivering services. One commonality which stretches across all of these geographies is the limited attention devoted to understanding the size of this population, the multiple aspects of, challenges and needs of the rural poor who are often on the edge of housing loss.

We identified a few significant trends with regards to the nature of rural homelessness in Alberta; some of which supports existing findings in other Canadian contexts and some of which add a new perspective to existing literature on rural homelessness in Canada. In particular, we identified a few issues which are mostly unrecognised in the literature on homelessness and might be important considerations in understanding rural homelessness dynamics. This includes the impact of economic dynamics and rural housing market dynamics on rural homelessness, the impact of recreational areas on rural homelessness, and the impact of natural disasters on homelessness populations and support systems in rural areas. We also note the importance of further exploration into homelessness related to the experiences of immigrants and refugees in rural areas; indigenous persons who choose to stay in rural areas, and chronically homeless people.

A number of recommendations emerging from this data are aimed at building on the experiences, capacities, and strengths of rural communities. A first and crucial step is the development of regional and systematic approaches as part of an intentional response to rural homelessness (Nichols & Doberstein, 2016). This would include coordinating resources and developing systemic regional strategies as well as the tailoring of strategies to groups of communities with similar challenges in service delivery. Similar to larger efforts in urban areas, such approaches should include a comprehensive housing and service infrastructure plan to address housing instability in smaller centers as part of broader regional responses Kauppi, Pallard, Lemieux, and Matukala Nkosi, 2012; Schiff & Brunger, 2015). The plans should also encourage exploration of innovative alternatives to shelter, which leverage local resources, and innovative adaptations of 'housing first' approaches in rural communities. There should also be consideration given to the integration of homelessness in future emergency preparedness initiatives to address 'disaster homelessness'.

We also note the need to identify strategies for enumerating rural homelessness. While the 2016 homeless Point-in-Time Count (initiated by the Government of Canada through the Homeless Partnering Strategy) will provide more accurate numbers on homelessness in key Canadian larger communities, rural communities do not have formalized data collection approaches with respect to homelessness to track the level of need for housing. Most respondents provided anecdotal estimates, but were unable to point to data collection and analysis processes. This was reported to be a key hurdle to making the case for investment in responses locally and to understanding the needs of the population. Without a comprehensive needs assessment to determine the magnitude of the issue locally, and the needs of the population, service providers and advocates were hampered significantly.

Regional and systematic approaches must respond to the needs of priority sub-populations: Indigenous persons, victims of domestic violence, youth, seniors and immigrant newcomers. Indigenous people on- and off-reserve require targeted approaches to overcoming complex jurisdictional barriers to services and supports (Christensen, 2011; Peters & Craig, 2014). Victims of domestic violence in many rural communities need alignment with housing and homelessness responses. Targeted responses to youth, seniors, and newcomers' housing stress and homelessness in rural communities also need to be developed.

There is a need to increase awareness of, and leadership for, rural housing and homelessness which will champion solutions at all levels of governance. Locally, rural communities of practice can be supported through targeted networking and capacity building activities in the areas of 'housing first' implementation, performance management, system planning, and research.

As many other authors cited in this article have noted, there has been scarcity of information about rural specific elements, although the recent spate of activity is beginning to address this gap. Emerging research priorities for a research agenda on rural homelessness should include: developing baseline information on rural homelessness; service infrastructure analysis to assess available resources and gaps systematically; probing macroeconomic impacts which affect homelessness dynamics in rural communities; increasing understandings of rural Indigenous homelessness, on and off-reserve and the role of migration; enhancing knowledge about rough sleeping and chronic homelessness in rural contexts; identifying potential policy responses and funding allocation models that meet the needs of rural residents and; tailoring housing first interventions in rural contexts, particularly to address the needs of priority sub-populations. Planning and implementation responses would be enhanced through the development of a combination of a research network to facilitate knowledge mobilization and a Canadian research agenda on rural homelessness.

Acknowledgments

The researchers would like to thank the Alberta Interagency Council on Homelessness, Ministry of Human Services and Alberta Centre for Child, Family and Community Research, who fully funded this study. We would like to thank the community representatives and provincial stakeholders who participated in this effort for their contributions and willingness to share their expertise and experience. A special thanks to Adrian de Zwart, MSW, for his research assistance support with this project.

Conflict of Interest

The authors have no conflict of interest to declare for this manuscript.

References

Anucha, U. (2007). *Exits and Returns: An Exploratory Longitudinal Study of Homeless People in Windsor, Essex County*. Canada Mortgage and Housing Corporation.

Anderson, I., & Sim, D. (Eds.). (2000). *Housing and social exclusion: Context and challenges*. Coventry: Chartered Institute of Housing and Housing Studies Association.

Anderson, I., & Sim, D. (Eds.). (2011). *Housing and inequality*. Coventry: Chartered Institute of Housing and Housing Studies Association.

Belanger, Y. D., Weasel Head, G., & Owasago, U. (2012). *Assessing urban Aboriginal housing and homelessness in Canada*. Retrieved from http://www.homelesshub.ca/ResourceFilesFinal_Belanger/_Housing_and_Homeless_-_6_May_2012.pdf

Belanger, Y. D., Weasel Head, G. (2013). *Urban Aboriginal homelessness and migration in Southern Alberta. Final report prepared for the Alberta Homelessness Research Consortium (AHRC)*. Edmonton, Alberta.

Bohlin, K. M. (1975). *The spatial and economic impact of recreational expenditures and sales in the Pigeon Lake area of Alberta* (Master's thesis). University of Alberta, Edmonton.

Bruce, D., Essex, S., Gilg, A., Yarwood, R., Smithers, J., & Wilson, R. (2005). The geography of housing needs of low income persons in rural Canada. In S. Essex (Ed.), *Rural change and sustainability: Agriculture, the environment and communities* (pp. 265–280). Cambridge, MA: CABI Publishing.

Calgary Homeless Foundation. (2013). *Migration's impact on homelessness in Calgary*. Retrieved from http://www.calgaryhomeless.com/wp-content/up/uploads/Backgrounder_Migration.pdf

Callahan, M., & Turnbull, I. (1999). *Muskoka, Ontario: Understanding homelessness in Muskoka*. Retrieved from http://homelesshub.ca/resource/muskoka-ontario-understanding-homelessness-muskoka

Canada Mortgage and Housing Corporation. (2013). *Rental market report: Alberta highlights*. Retrieved from http://www.cmhc-schl.gc.ca/odpub/esub/64483/64483_2013_B02.pdf?fr=1394817906330

Canadian Observatory on Homelessness. (2012). *Canadian definition of homelessness*. Homeless Hub. Retrieved from www.homelesshub.ca/homeless definition/

Carle, P., & Belanger-Dion, L. (2003). Rapport de recherche sur la population itinérante et sans domicile fixe des Laurentides. Mont-Tremblant, Québec.

CBC News. (2011). Fire destroys 40% of Slave Lake: High winds, low humidity challenge firefighting efforts. Retrieved from http://www.cbc.ca/news/canada/edmonton/fire-destroys-40-of-slave-lake-1.981352

Christensen, J. B. (2011). *Homeless in a homeland: Housing (in)security and homelessness in Inuvik and Yellowknife, Northwest Territories*, Canada. Montréal: McGill University.

Christensen, J. (2012). 'They want a different life': Rural northern settlement dynamics and pathways to homelessness in Yellowknife and Inuvik, Northwest Territories. *The Canadian Geographer/Le Géographe canadien*, *56*(4), 419–438.

Cloke, P., Milbourne, P., & Widdowfield, R. (2000). The hidden and emerging spaces of rural homelessness. *Environment and Planning A*, *32*(1), 77–90.

Cloke, P., Milbourne, P., & Widdowfield, R. (2001). The geographies of homelessness in rural England. *Regional Studies*, *35*(1), 23–27.

Cloke, P., Milbourne, P., & Widdowfield, R. (2003). The complex mobilities of homeless people in rural England. *Geoforum*, *34*(1), 21–35.

Cloke, P., & Milbourne, P. (2012). *International perspectives on rural homelessness*. New York: Routledge.

Cloke, P., Marsden, T., & Mooney, P. (2006). *Handbook of rural studies*. London: Sage.

Employment and Social Development Canada. (2011). *August 2011: Rural and remote homelessness*. Ottawa: Government of Canada. Retrieved from http://www.esdc.gc.ca/eng/communities/homelessness/publications_bulletins/august_2011.shtml

Environment and Climate Change Canada. (2014). *Alberta's flood of floods in Canada's top ten weather stories for 2013*. Retrieved from https://www.ec.gc.ca/meteo-weather/default.asp?lang=En&n=5BA5EAFC-1&offset=2&toc=hide

Fitchen, J. M. (1992). On the edge of homelessness: Rural poverty and housing insecurity. *Rural Sociology*, *57*(2), 173–193.

Forchuk, C., Montgomery, P., Berman, H., Ward-Griffin, C., Csiernik, R., Gorlick, C., . . . Riesterer, P. (2010). Gaining ground, losing ground: The paradoxes of rural homelessness. *Canadian Journal of Nursing Research*, *42*(2), 138–152. Retrieved from http://www.ingentaconnect.com/content/mcgill/cjnr/2010/00000042/00000002/art00013

Gaetz, S., Donaldson, J., Richter, T., & Gulliver, T. (2013). *The state of homelessnness in Canada*. Retrieved from: http://homelesshub.ca/resource/state-homelessness-canada-2013

Gaetz, S. (2014). *Coming of age: Reimagining the response to youth homelessness in Canada*. Toronto: The Canadian Homelessness Research Network Press.

Glass, A. (2002). *Faces of homelessness in a rural area: Housing issues and homelessness in the West Kootenay Boundary region*. Retrieved from http://homeless.samhsa.gov/ResourceFiles/Faces_of_Homelessness_in_a_Rura l_Area-_Housing_Issues.pdf

Grigg, M., Judd, F., Ryan, L., & Komiti, A. (2005). Identifying marginal housing for people with a mental illness living in rural and regional areas. *Australian and New Zealand Journal of Psychiatry*, *39*(11-12), 995–1000. Retrieved from http://www.blackwell-synergy.com/doi/abs/10.1111/j.1440-1614.2005.01703.x

Grodzinski, E., Londerville, J., Sutherns, R., & Bentham, C. (2011). *Rural homelessness study. Report prepared for the County of Wellington*. Retrieved from http://www.wellington.ca/en/socialservices/resources/wellingtoncountyruralhomelessnessstudy.pdf

Hallstrom, K., Coates, W., Mindel, K., Richter, S., & Finseth, N. (2013). *Open door needs assessment report*. Retrieved from http://www.camroseopendoor.com/uploads/1/8/5/7/18576650/open_door_needs_assessment_report.pdf

Halseth, G. (1998). *Cottage country in transition: A social geography of change and contention in the rural-recreational countryside*. Montréal: McGill-Queen's Press.

Hwang, S. W., Stergiopoulos, V., O'Campo, P., & Gozdzik, A. (2012). Ending homelessness among people with mental illness: The At Home/Chez Soi randomized trial of a Housing First intervention in Toronto. *BMC Public Health*, *12*(1), 787. doi:10.1186/1471-2458-12-787

Karabanow, J., Naylor, T., & Aube, C. (2014). From Place to Space: Exploring Youth Migration and Homelessness in Rural Nova Scotia. *Journal of Rural & Community Development*, *9*(2), 112–127.

Kauppi, C., Gasparini, J., Henri Pallard, L., Garg, R., Montgomery, P., Webster, S., . . ., & Secretariat, H. P. (2009). *Migratory and transient homelessness in Northern Ontario: A study of the pathways to becoming homeless in Sudbury and its related impacts*. Sudbury, Ontario, Canada: Social Planning Council of Sudbury.

Kauppi, C., Pallard, D. H., Lemieux, S., & Matukala Nkosi, T. (2012). *Homelessness in Timmins. January 2011 Final report*. Sudbury, Ontario, Canada: Poverty, Homelessness and Migration.

Kauppi, C., Pallard, H., & Shaikh, A. (2013). Migration and homelessness: Exploring attachment to place amongst francophone, Anglophone and Indigenous people in Northeastern Ontario. *Spaces & Flows: An International Journal of Urban & Extra Urban Studies*, *3*(1). 97–107.

Kauppi, C., Pallard, H., McGregor, D., & Seyler, K. (2015). Homelessness and housing in a Northeastern Ontario, Canada, First Nation: A community-based project. OIDA *International Journal of Sustainable Development*, *8*(4), 51–66.

Lawrence, M. (1995). Rural homelessness: A geography without a geography. *Journal of Rural Studies*, *11*(3), 297–307.

Lee, D., Budgell, M., & Skinner, J. (2007). *Happy Valley-*

Goose Bay community plan for addressing homelessness and transitional housing. Retrieved from http://www.nlhhn.org/PDF/HV-GB_Community Plan.pdf

Martin, F. (2013). *To go or to stay: Migration decisions and homelessness in East Central Ontario*. Retrieved from http://static1.squarespace.com/static/521e0ebfe4b0f88e5934ce70/t/52a08c99e4b061dbb499e0b8/1386253465559/To+Go+Or+To+Stay+%28english%29.pdf

McDermott, V. (2016, June 7). Groups unsure how many of Fort McMurray's homeless population will return. *Fort McMurray Today*. Retrieved from http://www.fortmcmurraytoday.com

McNicol, B., & Glorioso, R. (2014). Second home leisure landscapes and retirement in the Canadian Rocky Mountain community of Canmore, Alberta. *Annals of Leisure Research*, *17*(1). 27–49.

Meert, H., & Bourgeois, M. (2005). Between rural and urban slums: A geography of pathways through homelessness. *Housing Studies*, *20*, 107–125.

Nichols, N., & Doberstein, C. (2016). *Exploring effective systems respoonses to homelessness*. Toronto: Homeless HUB Press.

Nunavut Housing Corporation. (2013). *The GN long-term comprehensive housing and homelessness strategy*. Retrieved from http://homelesshub.ca/resource/gn-long-term-comprehensive-nunavut-housing-and-homelessness-strategy

Peressini, T., McDonald, L., & Hulchanski, D. (1995). *Estimating homelessness: Towards a Methodology for Counting the Homeless in Canada*. Canada Mortgage and Housing Corporation. Retrieved from http://www.urbancentre.utoronto.ca/pdfs/researchassociates/1996_Peressini-McD-JDH_Estimating-Homelessness.pdf

Peters, E., & Craig, S. (2014). *Aboriginal homelessness in Flin Flon, Manitoba*. Retrieved from http://ion.uwinnipeg.ca/~epeters/Flin%20Flon%20Final%20Report-2.pdf

Peters, E. J., & Robillard, V. (2009). 'Everything you want is there': The place of the reserve in First Nations' homeless mobility. *Urban Geography*, *30*(6), 652–680.

Robertson, K., & White, M. (2007). *Mapping homelessness in rural Nova Scotia: A study of community resources*. Ottawa, Ontario, Canada: Service Canada.

Robertson, M., Harris, N., Noftsinger, R., & Fischer, P. (2007, March). Rural homelessness. Paper presented at the Toward Understanding Homelessness: The 2007 National Symposium on Homelessness Research. Washington. Retrieved from https://aspe.hhs.gov/sites/default/files/pdf/120751/report_0.pdf

Roy, S., Hurtubise, R., & Rozier, M. (2003). *Itinérance en Montérégie: Comprendre le phénomène et identifier les besoins*. Collectif de recherche en itinérance, Montréal. Retrieved from http://extranet.santemonteregie.qc.ca/depot/document/3028/resumeMonteregie.pdf

Schiff, R., & Brunger, F. (2015). Northern housing networks: Building collaborative efforts to address housing and homelessness in remote Canadian aboriginal communities in the Context of rapid economic change. *Journal of Rural and Community Development*, *10*(1). Retrieved from http://www.jrcd.ca/viewarticle.php?id=1217&layout=abstract

Schmidt, R., Hrenchuk, C., Bopp, J., & Poole, N. (2015). Trajectories of women's homelessness in Canada's 3 northern territories. *International Journal of Circumpolar Health*, 74: 29778. doi: 10.3402/ijch.v74.29778

Smith, N., & Fuller, S. (2007). Homelessness in rural PEI, 'Research report'. Retrieved from: http://homelesshub.ca/resource/homelessness-rural-pei

Standing Senate Committee on Agriculture and Forestry. (2008). Beyond freefall: Halting rural poverty. Ottawa: Government of Canada.

Stewart, C., & Ramage, S. (2011). A pan-Northern Ontario inventory of homelessness problems and practices: Northern Ontario service deliverer's association. Sudbury: Northern Ontario Service Deliverer's Association.

The Globe and Mail. (2016). The Fort McMurray fire: What's happening now, and what you've missed. Retrieved from http://www.theglobeandmail.com/news/alberta/the-fort-mcmurray-disaster-read-the-latest-weekend/article29930041

United States Government Accountability Office. (2010). *Rural homelessness: Better collaboration by HHS and HUD could improve delivery of services in rural areas*. Washington, D.C.: United States Government Accountability Office.

United States Interagency Council on Homelessness. (2015). *Opening Doors. Federal strategic plan to prevent and end homelessness*. Washington, DC. Retrieved from https://www.usich.gov/resources/uploads/asset_library/USICH_OpeningDoors_Amendment2015_FINAL.pdf

Waegemakers Schiff, J., & Turner, A. (2014b). *Housing first in rural Canada: Rural homelessness and housing first feasibility across 22 Canadian communities*. Retrieved from http://homelesshub.ca/resource/housing-first-rural-canada-rural-homelessness-housing-first-feasibility-across-22-canadian

Waegemakers Schiff, J., Schiff, R., Turner, A., & Bernard, K. (2015). Rural homelessness in Canada: Directions for planning and research. *The Journal of Rural and Community Development*, *10*(4), 85–106.

Walsh, C. A., Hanley, J., Ives, N., & Hordyk, S. R. (2015). Exploring the experiences of newcomer women with insecure housing in Montréal Canada. *Journal of International Migration and Integration*, *17*(3), 1–18.

Young, M. G., & Moses, J. M. (2013). Neoliberalism and homelessness in the Western Canadian Arctic. *Canadian Journal of Nonprofit and Social Economy Research*, *4*(2), 7.

Yukon Anti-Poverty Coalition. (2011). *A home for everyone: A housing action plan for Whitehorse*. Retrieved from http://www.yapc.ca/assets/files/a-home-for-everyone.pdf

About the Authors

Jeannette Waegemakers Schiff is a faculty member in Social Work at the University of Calgary. Her academic areas span individual practice, program evaluation and administrations, and research in mental health and homelessness. She is a member of the Canadian Homeless Research Network and the organizing steering committee of the Canadian Observatory on Homelessness. She provides program evaluation and consultation to community NGOs and has presented at numerous professional workshops, and conferences.

Rebecca Schiff is a faculty member in the Department of Health Sciences at Lakehead University in Thunder Bay, Ontario, Canada. Dr. Schiff has a long history of working closely with rural, remote, and Indigenous communities across Canada to investigate and research health issues and solutions, with a particular focus on determinants of community health and wellness, social justice, and sustainability.

Alina Turner is recognized as a leading homelessness researcher and is a Fellow at The School of Public Policy, University of Calgary. In her consulting work (Turner Research & Strategy), she supports with a variety of organizations to support human service system planning and integration. She engages in academic and applied research on issues including housing stress, poverty, domestic violence, migration and rural social issues.

Professionals Made in Germany: Employing a Turkish Migration Background in High-Status Positions

Ali Konyali * and Maurice Crul

Department of Public Administration and Sociology, Erasmus University, 3000 DR Rotterdam, The Netherlands; E-Mails: konyali@fsw.eur.nl (A.K.), crul@fsw.eur.nl (M.C.)

* Corresponding author

Abstract

This article emphasises the experiences of the prospective elite among the second generation in Germany by analysing empirical data collected through in-depth interviews across three occupational fields (law, education and corporate business). In spite of their disadvantaged background, some children of lower educated migrant parents from Turkey managed to occupy prestigious leadership positions. Many use their ethnic capital in creative and strategic ways to seek opportunities and obtain access to leading positions. They are now embracing new professional roles and have moved into new social circles due to their steep upward mobility. However, they still have to contend with the fact that their individual mobility stands in contrast to the low-status of the group to which they belong.

Keywords

ethnic capital; occupational achievement; professional identity; second generation; social disadvantage; social mobility

Issue

This article is part of the issue "International Migration and Ethnic Integration", edited by Yaojun Li (University of Manchester, UK) and Anthony Heath (University of Oxford, UK).

1. Introduction

Even though the Turkish presence has been part of everyday life in Germany's metropolitan areas for many decades, there is still a continuous public demand for their integration based on assumed cultural differences. Against the background of a negative discursive context and in spite of their disadvantageous Turkish migration background[1] (Crul, Schneider, & Lelie, 2012; Heath, Rothon, & Kilpi, 2008), some children of migrants from Turkey have made considerable achievements in Western European labour markets. Whereas extensive research focuses on the recurrent 'failed integration' thesis, professionally successful descendants have received less attention. However, the so-called second generation is entering 'the mainstream' as defined by Alba and Nee (2009). Climbing toward leading positions, they are embracing new roles and enter new social environments due to their steep upward mobility (Crul & Schneider, 2010, p. 1253).

Those very successful individuals are of course still so-called exceptions to the rule since their individual mobility stands in stark contrast to the overall group disadvantage of people whose background originates from Turkish migration into Germany. Therefore, this article aims to examine to what extent this contrast is mirrored in their self-conception; we want to examine the choices and reflections around making use of one's ethnic background as part of one's professional capital. The underlying assumption is that on the one hand, these professionals want to be evaluated only according to their merit. On the other hand, their professional selves are closely inter-

[1] The term 'Turkish migration background' should not be understood as an imposed homogenization of this group. It is used as a conceptual simplification identifying Turkey as the parental country of origin.

twined with their social selves, and the way others see them. This often results in situations that require them to reassert their professional legitimacy because they do not want to be pigeonholed within an ethnic niche or as 'the Turkish colleague'.

We will study this complicated process for the prospective elite among the second generation in Germany in three different occupational fields (law, education and corporate business). The two research questions of the article are: 1) What does it mean to acquire a high-status professional position in Germany by employing the fact that one belongs to a low-status group? and 2) How does this differ across occupational fields? Thereby, this article will provide an understanding of the patterns which emerge when individuals from a disadvantaged background attain privileged positions by examining the relationship between motivation, recognition and self-perception regarding their career. The data was collected through in-depth interviews with professionals who have lower educated migrant parents. In the following section, we will theorize the consequences of the exceptionally steep individual social mobility and its relationship with social status and group belonging. At the same time, we will discuss to what extent ethnic background resources can be instrumental for one's professional capital. This theoretical framework forms the basis for analysing the professionals' self-conceptions. In the conclusion, we will recapitulate the findings but also debate their implications for the theoretical debate on this issue.

2. Theoretical Framework

2.1. Ethnicity and Low-Status Group Belonging

Ethnicity is a concept that distinguishes groups of people from each other, whereas the significance and implications of ethnic identities varies across space and time. Social contexts shape ethnic groups as much as these groups shape them. Human interaction, assignment and assertion construct ethnic identities. They are not fixed and static but changeable, contingent, and diverse (Cornell & Hartmann, 2007). Barth (1969) defines ethnic groups as self-perpetuating, culture-bearing units that are distinguishable from others (p. 296). Thereby, ethnic identity becomes an imperative characteristic which defines peoples' identities and their societal positions (p. 304). Barth's definition emphasises the importance of circumstances by considering the persistent organizational relevance of ethnic identities, even if actual cultural differences might decrease over time (p. 318). This is in line with Brubaker's (2004) definition of ethnicity as a perspective on the world. Challenging the 'groupist' tone in most theorizations on ethnicity, he propagates a focus on processes that are triggered by the 'ethnic lens'. Our conception of ethnicity in this article will follow Brubaker's emphasis on process in relation to social mobility.

According to various studies, descendants of low-skilled migrant parents from Turkey can be seen as the most disadvantaged group when it comes to the educational achievement of children of migrants in Germany (cf. Crul, 2015; Schnell, 2014). Therefore, the German case provides a good illustration of how, for pupils from a migrant background, any disadvantages that may be caused by their parents' migration are combined with those which arise from social class affiliation. The first critical turning point having an effect on children's future in Germany is the transfer from primary school to one of the three levels of secondary education. Ample evidence shows that this decision does not solely depend on individual performance, but also on teachers' recommendations, parents' level of commitment and local education policy. Studies demonstrate that the proportion of *Hauptschule* recommendations for migrant children is disproportionately higher (Kristen, 2002).

Children of migrants from Turkey tend to have higher ambitions than their peers which seem to be stimulated by the desire to be socially mobile (Salikutluk, 2016; Schneider, Crul, & Van Praag 2014). This desire is also reflected by their parents' aspirations concerning their children's educational goals (Relikowski, Yilmaz, & Blossfeld, 2012). Notwithstanding, only a very small minority of this group attends a *Gymnasium* (high school) and has thereby the opportunity to receive access to higher education (Crul, Schnell, Herzog-Punzenberger, Wilmes, Slootman, & Aparicio Gómez, 2012).

The effect of a potential disadvantage for children of migrants from Turkey is also visible in terms of there being a longer transition phase from leaving school to entering the labour market, while they also receive lower returns from education concerning occupational attainment (Kalter & Granato, 2007). For several reasons, there are a number of sectors of the labour market which contain very few people with a background of Turkish migration in Germany (Sürig & Wilmes, 2015, pp. 82-86). Only a minority of this group enters highly skilled positions in the labour market. Thus, in spite of the fact that considerable intergenerational progress has been observed, this generation still experiences disadvantages in terms of employment and income (Kalter & Granato, 2007; Worbs, 2003). These overall findings make individuals who have experienced steep upward mobility an exception to the rule.

Institutional arrangements in Germany tend to favour social reproduction which endangers the social mobility of members of the second generation (Worbs, 2003). Even when controlling for formal educational qualifications, descendants of migrants from Turkey remain disadvantaged, which can be attributed to specific labour market discrimination (cf. Seibert & Solga, 2005; also see Waldring, Crul, & Ghorashi, 2015, for a study on the Netherlands). However, there might be other potential causes of the specific 'Turkish' disadvantage within Germany. First, descendants of migrants from Turkey lack resources, such as instrumental parental support, to a greater degree than other groups. In addition, the ethnic composition of their friendship networks and the fact that they commonly lack language proficiency only further weakens their position (Kalter, 2006). Second-generation Turkish men, in particular, experience higher unemployment, lower re-employment, and higher income-mobility risks at the beginning of their careers due to a lack of country-specific resources which tends to compound their initial disadvantage (Hartmann, 2016b).

The persistence of inequalities is a phenomenon that is not independent of contextual circumstances. Viewing ethnicity as irrelevant because of a statistical insignificance would ignore "the potential causality between ethnicity and social class" (Van de Werfhorst & Van Tubergen, 2007, p. 434). In our qualitative study, we selected professional success as the dependent variable. As it was indicated above, the institutional arrangements in Germany make individual success dependent upon the availability of family resources and personal circumstances (Hartmann, 2016a; Kalter, 2006). This is what makes our respondents a very select group with exceptional occupational achievements in spite of the double disadvantage of coming from a lower class social origin and having a low-status ethnic background (cf. Crul, Keskiner, & Lelie, 2017). That is to say, one could justifiably claim that professionally successful descendants of migrants from Turkey, almost by default, can be expected to come from families that were very supportive of their children's education (Crul, Schnell, et al., 2012; Schnell, 2014).

In order to overcome barriers towards attaining skilled positions, highly skilled members of the second generation in Germany have to overcome disadvantages associated with their status as being from a minority throughout their career trajectories (Schittenhelm, 2011). Achieving exceptional success with a devalued social identity might leave individuals with an "inordinate ambivalence and affective dissonance" (Fordham & Ogbu, 1986, p. 951) and what Ellis Cose (1993) called the "permanent vulnerability of one's status" (p. 41). In spite of professional success, individuals could still be perceived as belonging to the inferior societal out-group. However, paradoxically for the upwardly mobile, ethnicity can also act as a useful social resource in specific professional contexts. For those that have to deal with a restricted career entry, social and cultural capital coming from their Turkish background and Turkish language skills can become relevant as part of their compensatory strategies (Schittenhelm, 2011, p. 115).

2.2. Ethnicity and Steep Upward Mobility

In order to comprehend the professional success stories of descendants of migrants from Turkey in Germany, it is necessary to take into account the relativity of structural inequalities for individual cases. This is illustrated by the exceptionality of our respondents and their success, which came about *against all odds. But how can this success be explained?*

In a previous publication, we described the so-called multiplier effect. We concluded that successful children of immigrants have to make more effort by being more active in using opportunities and loopholes in the system to be as successful as their peers of native descent (Crul, Schneider, et al., 2017). The multiplier effect describes how with each consecutive step in their career they accumulate new cultural and social capital which opens up possibilities to take the next step on the ladder, thereby multiplying their chances of success. This helps them to move up and away from less successful co-ethnics. Although descendants of Turkish immigrants have to overcome their double disadvantage (of ethnic and social origin), their background can also act as a resource which some have used to advance their careers. The reflexivity about their upwardly mobile social identity is an important cornerstone of the multiplier effect. Their starting position within a lower class and background as being a descendant of migrants motivates them and helps them to succeed, although they are aware that they continue to be seen as a representative of a disadvantaged group.

The juxtaposition of ethnic belonging and individual labour market activities is documented in the discussion about migrant entrepreneurship (see Volery, 2007). This type of research, traditionally, has given a lot of importance to ethnic and group-specific resources, arguing that specific cultural properties can enable labour market success (cf. Bonacich, 1973). Recently, there has been increased attention towards highly skilled migrants, often referred to as expats. The emphasis in these studies often lies on temporary skilled migration, knowledge transfer, spatial mobility and networking issues (see e.g. Ackers, 2005; Castles, 2002; Khoo, McDonald, Voigt-Graf, & Hugo, 2007), as well as transnational ties and the way in which they negotiate multiple identities in the context of well-connected global cities (Favell, 2008). However, in contrast to migrant entrepreneurs and highly skilled migrants, second-generation professionals were either born or raised in the country of their parents' destination. The subjective experiences as belonging to a 'low-status' minority group (rather, being perceived as such) are likely to be more influential in shaping their ideas and their narratives about professionalism.

Individuals with an unfortunate social position have to adapt in order to navigate structural constraints (Merton, 1968). Exceptional cases of upward mobility contrast with the image of an unequal and underprivileged socio-economic situation of the migrant majority. Whereas social boundaries are (re-)created through everyday interactions (Elias & Scotson, 1965), Bourdieu argues that agents embody a deep understanding of appropriate behaviour and act within the structural limits of a field. Individual success depends on the convertibility of the different forms of capital an agent possesses (Bourdieu & Wacquant, 1992). In other words, ethnicity can be a social boundary that impedes social mobility as well as a social resource that individuals can mobilize in the context of upward mobility processes (Pott, 2001). Through the ethnic lens, in reference to Brubaker, the upwardly mobile professionals might be seen as 'Turkish' but they do not fit the stereotype of being poorly educated and doing low-level jobs.

The steep social mobility of the exceptional group we have studied in this article has led to its members being able to occupy professional positions in large (international) firms and organisations. Freidson (1999) views professionalism as specialized work that requires abstract, theoretical knowledge, which "cannot be performed mechanically because...the worker must exercise considerable discretion to adapt his knowledge and skill to each circumstance in order to work successfully" (p. 119). Schinkel and Noordegraaf (2011) additionally view professionalism as a form of symbolic capital. Accordingly, its substance is constantly at stake in power-driven internal and external contexts. People adjust to their new roles by trying out 'provisional selves' as possible professional identities, while individual and situational factors shape the repertory of possibilities (Ibarra, 1999). One could argue that professionalism necessitates the minimization of individual differences, but this does not mean that it is blind to individual differences. Especially in international companies, being able to deal with people from different nationalities is considered an important professional skill. Pécoud (2002) identifies the emergence of an economic dimension of multiculturalism, which views ethnic pluralism positively, as long as it contributes to the national economy.

The perception of ethnic difference is likely to be different across professional contexts, whereas it determines especially how 'newcomers' such as individuals with a disadvantageous, lower-status background perceive themselves as professionals. Accordingly, in the business sector, visible differences can be promoted as competitive assets. This can lead to achievement narratives of professionals who display their success as individuals who managed to turn their initial group disadvantage into an individual advantage (Konyali, 2014). Coming from a lower-class background and being of immigrant descent can also be a resource in the education and legal sectors because it can be employed in order to establish ties with a specific clientele (Rezai, 2017; Waldring, 2017).

Occupational fields offer distinct opportunity structures in terms of the employment of individual background resources (Crul, Schneider, et al., 2017). The fact that even the highly internationalized corporate business sector is not completely open to 'newcomers' is illustrated by various studies that provide further evidence to the existence of a so-called 'glass ceiling'. The education sector with its emphasis on meritocracy and emancipation is principally against making differentiations based on class and ethnicity, although it is undeniable that there is a middle-class bias among the professionals working in the field. The legal sector with its intrinsic emphasis on equality by law for all social and ethnic groups is at the same time a highly elitist profession, making it necessary for individuals to adapt to the dominant means of behaviour while conducting business. Thus, there are also different dynamics to be observed across sectors with either an emphasis on, for instance, differentiation (business) or equality (education), which can affect the role played by background characteristics.

3. Method

3.1. Data Collection

The data consists of interviews conducted within three occupational fields (see Table 1, for an overview of the sample). We have selected individuals working in a professional job who work in mid-level or higher managerial positions. Apart from very few exceptions, most respondents possessed a higher education diploma. As was noted in the theoretical framework, these criteria make them a very select group of respondents. Since we deliberately selected individuals from lower educated families, most of the respondent's parents had not been educated beyond primary school level. This meant that our respondents have usually shown a steep upward mobility. Moreover, individuals were only selected if they had been born in Europe or if they had been raised there and their parents had been born in Turkey. Data was collected through qualitative in-depth interviews in the German metropolitan area of Frankfurt am Main. The final selection of respondents in the *business* sector included professionals with organizational, managerial or employee responsibilities within a company, as well as professionals occupying a specialist or expert position. In the *legal* sector, we included lawyers who worked as associates or partners in corporate law firms, lawyers who worked independently or for smaller law firms. Finally, the respondents in the *education* field were drawn from various professional positions with educational responsibilities, including teaching, training as well as managerial positions.

3.2. Data Analysis

The semi-standardized interviews collected information about their educational and professional pathways. In addition, respondents could raise their own issues. The anonymity of all respondents was guaranteed beforehand and the authors changed the names displayed in this article. For the analysis, we made use of the qualitative data analysis software *Atlas.ti*. The software enabled us to identify dominant themes based on the initial coding of the material. Subsequently, the analysis clarified how the themes related to one another (cf. Bryman, 2015). Two contrasting themes emerged: the first being the importance the respondents attach to ethnic background resources in the respective professional contexts. This was mainly observable by examining the role of their Turkish migration background at work (cf. Section 4.1). The second theme was the importance others attach to this background which was analysed through their reflec-

Table 1. Overview of sample.

	Year and country of birth	Gender and Position
Business	1975 (Germany)	Male, Regional Head of Finance in a professional service company
	1976 (Germany)	Male, CEO in banking
	1971 (Germany)	Female, Senior specialist in banking
	1968 (Germany)	Male, Senior specialist in a professional service company
	1976 (Turkey); came to Germany before she went to primary school	Female, Head of Customer Service in banking
	1974 (Germany)	Male, Independent HR Consultant
	1968 (Germany)	Male, Partner in a professional service company
Education	1977 (Germany)	Male, Head of Public Relations of an educational association
	1967 (Turkey); came to Germany before she went to primary school	Female, Head of training for secondary school teachers at the teachers' academy of the federal state
	1970 (Turkey); in Germany since the age of seven	Female, Secondary school teacher/appointed to the delegation office in the Regional Ministry of Education
	1974 (Turkey); in Germany since the age of two	Female, Legal trainer at key qualifications office of university
	1982 (Germany)	Male, Chair of local educational umbrella association
	1982 (Germany)	Female, Project manager of a youth organization
	1965 (Turkey); in Germany since the age of twelve	Female, School psychologist
Law	1978 (Germany)	Female, Independent lawyer
	1972 (Turkey); came to Frankfurt before he went to primary school.	Male, Partner in a corporate law firm
	1979 (Germany)	Male, Associate in a corporate law firm
	1972 (Germany)	Male, Independent lawyer, sharing offices in a small law firm
	1981 (Germany)	Female, Associate in a corporate law firm
	1979 (Germany)	Male, Lawyer in a corporate law firm
	1971 (Germany)	Male, Independent lawyer/owner of a small law firm
	1962 (Germany)	Female, Independent lawyer in a small law firm

tions on crucial interactions with significant others such as clients or colleagues (cf. Section 4.2).

4. Analysis

4.1. Professionals Who Meet the Demands

Without exception, the interviewed respondents were aware of their disadvantaged starting position resulting from their belonging to a low-status group. Retrospectively, many managed to turn this disadvantage into their advantage by adapting themselves to the professional context in question. Their ability to convert their ethnic capital into a valuable professional resource is a key aspect of their upward mobility (cf. Bourdieu & Wacquant, 1992; Pott, 2001). This happens in different ways across the occupational fields. One way to do so is to carve out a niche by catering to a specific clientele or taking over responsibilities that relate to Turkey.

The *business* professionals operate in a predominantly internationalized corporate setting. Making use of background resources to build a professional profile was an important part of their narratives. In the following quote, a respondent working in the banking sector explains how he lobbied his own company to focus more on Turkish-speaking clients. Partly by making use of his 'ethnic capital' and corresponding vision of expansion, he was able to climb the ladder in his company:

> "It was my initiative. Before I ended up at this position, I was already quite successful within this company by focusing on the Turkish community.... I told the management that I have a concept in mind.... They found it very interesting. Because, I think when you are try-

ing to work with Turkish people, it is important to be able to conduct that work in their mother tongue in order to show them that you share common values. That makes working with them much easier. Because it is like that, I mean in the end people want to understand and they want to be understood. This is not different in the financial sector. I have told them this very well. I have said that this is why I am so successful here and that we can spread this around the country by multiplying this concept. Eventually, they agreed and a project team was built." (Male, CEO in banking)

In other cases, the use of ethnic resources was only important in a transitional period of careers. Nevertheless, the need to employ one's background of Turkish migration for a competitive advantage was often present. In general, business professionals assumed that having migrant parents equipped them with skills that helped them succeed in a professional context:

> "I think that my migration background has given me a lot of things. I mean it provided me with certain soft skills that enabled me to work towards this position. That for sure. However, nobody said, 'he is a Turk and that is why we will promote him'. Not at all." (Male, Regional Head of Finance)

The use of background resources seems to work slightly differently for professionals within the *education* sector. Many professionals we interviewed were intrinsically motivated, having idealistic reasons for working in the field. Most of them linked it to their own background and the felt need to make a difference. Their motivation to provide education is often linked to working for a clientele with a similar background to themselves. A belief in the necessity for change and their capability to contribute to this change drives them, no matter how small the subsequent changes might still be. These ideas also shape their career plans:

> "But when I applied, it seemed important to me that this post will be filled with someone who has an immigrant background and not necessarily that they take me, so it should be someone who is well qualified for this place and, uh, that was what was important to me. I just told myself that it would be a pity if I do not apply and no one else with a migration background applies." (Female, Secondary school teacher/appointed to the delegation office in the regional Ministry of Education)

The ability to recognize themselves as necessary newcomers in this field actually helped some of them to advance in their careers and to acquire their current position. But entering positions that were usually not occupied by persons with a migration background, they also have to cope with being the exception to the rule:

> "I find that just I am somehow already quite exotic in my area, in my professional field. And unfortunately, some colleagues who worked here for some time already, are not used to that. So, they look at you and test you. It is not a normality, to say the least." (Female, Head of training for secondary school teachers at the teachers' academy of the federal state)

In the field of *law*, we interviewed both independent and corporate lawyers. Whereas independent lawyers usually have individual clients, corporate lawyers often advise national and international companies. Similar to the respondents in the corporate business sector, many of the lawyers seized the opportunity to specifically take over responsibilities relating to the upcoming market in Turkey and Turkish-German business clients in Germany. These efforts included building active networks in the field. This is illustrated by the fact that next to being a member of the regular German Bar Association, most lawyers we interviewed were also a member of the German-Turkish lawyers' association. In particular, independent lawyers talked about how this gives them an inherent advantage when compared to other independent lawyers without a migration background:

> "Unfortunately, I have to say that I see colleagues who have severe difficulties. Because I can offer a range of services that others cannot. I mean especially German colleagues who have language deficiencies. I have to say that my potential clientele is larger, I get more mandates, and I have more possibilities. For instance, being able to do something like a German-Turkish law firm, that makes a difference." (Female, Independent lawyer)

Similarly, corporate lawyers have been able to move their career forward by actively forging ahead with the 'Turkish' agenda and more, in general, the international agenda of their company:

> "I think I made myself quite well known in the last three to four years. I am considered as one of the leading consultants overlooking Turkish transactions, both in Turkey and here in Germany. So, the work I am now performing has a quite strong connection to Turkey. Right now I am managing an acquisition in Turkey. But not only there, also in India, I am responsible as an international advisor." (Male, Partner in a corporate law firm)

Thereby they profit from the perception of others who think that they can bridge cultural barriers as trustworthy and competent professionals. Particularly for those in larger corporate firms, climbing the ladder is a crucial part of their identity as a professional, earning them respect in the company but it is also manifested in their self-perception.

The examples in this section show that 'professional selves' are not only highly affected by disadvantageous structural contexts that operate throughout their upwardly mobile career trajectory, but also by their individual background resources (cf. Ibarra, 1999). It provides them with an additional repertory for establishing themselves in a high-status position. The next section will show how our respondents cope with instances that remind them of the ambiguity that is involved when individuals experience a steep upward social mobility with the help of a background that is usually associated with low-status positions. This 'double-edged sword' is illustrated by situations and encounters that remind them of their disadvantageous background.

4.2. Better Than 'Others' but Still Inferior?

As we have argued in the theoretical framework of this article, having a Turkish background in Germany, means that one is considered as belonging to a low-status group with an inferior position in society (cf. Worbs, 2003). Most of our respondents already belong to a select group of individuals who have survived the stratified German school system that does not frequently provide the children of migrants from Turkey even the chance to reach higher education. However, as has been illustrated, the fact that there is a large population with a Turkish migration background in Germany and the intertwined business relations between Germany and Turkey can enable individuals to employ their background to their advantage. The tension caused by the usefulness of ethnic resources on the one hand, and the potential threat it poses to the equal treatment of individuals on the other, is present in our respondents' reflections. It is striking that the three different professional contexts we researched each offer different coping mechanisms to refute questions regarding their professionalism.

Respondents in the *business* sector stated that the stigma of being of Turkish descent was a motivating factor to 'do better', whereas they also encountered instances which challenged their professionalism by problematizing their ethnic background:

> "There were again and again cases of clients as well as colleagues where I would say that we were not a good match. This could have happened everywhere of course, but there were comments where I thought, 'did he now really mean to confront me with this? Was this really the person he does not like, or the Turk?'" (Male, Senior specialist in a professional service company)

Coping with the fact that they belong to a low-status group plays a continuous role in their professional self-conception. They do not want to victimize themselves, which is why they hesitate to label potentially discriminatory encounters as such. However, they also do not want to deny the relevance of their ethnic and social background. The following quote shows that this asks for a constant alertness and continuous effort to be accepted as a professional in the company:

> "I think that as a Turk in a German company, you have to make sure that you do not attract too much attention....Therefore, I think it is important that you are a little more eager to succeed. One at least always thinks about having to be better than the others are. There is some truth to that." (Male, Partner in a professional service company)

Their motivation to be successful, at least partly, also seems to have its origin in their lower-class background as respondents always refer to the hard manual labour their parents conducted; a clear motivating memory to do better. They tend to display a strong individual achievement narrative in which they present their story as one of a constant search for opportunities against the background of a huge group disadvantage (also see Konyali, 2014). Although this entrepreneurial mindset does not protect them from discriminatory encounters per se, it provides them with a work ethic that is in line with the dominant self-made paradigm in the field.

The *education* sector is organized very differently. Professionals in this sector were either motivated to educate students, conduct research or move into administrative positions. They can have a sizable impact on the development of the field as well as on the planning of the educational system.

On the one hand, respondents argued that their ethnic and social background should be secondary in their professional context. On the other hand, they were aware of their exceptional position as someone with a Turkish background and they acknowledged that they are filling an important gap:

> "What I am happy about is that children see, 'oh as a Turk you can also reach certain positions'. For instance, here we do not have a single Turkish school principal. In the neighbouring city, we had one....She told me that children would go to her office to see if she can really speak Turkish. They tested her. And then they were happy, saying 'I also want to become the head of the school'." (Female, School psychologist)

Most of all, they tried to avoid being cornered as a 'special expert' on migrant children only. There is a very explicit desire for acceptance as a professional:

> "Well, this certainly changed in comparison to the founding years of this association. For example, we organized a contest and then many parents of German children were also there of course—they were saying 'you have many Turks in your association, we did not expect this!'—so they could not derive from the professionalism involved that many people with a migration background were part of the organization." (Male, Head of Public Relations of an educational association)

It seems that, in the field of education, those individuals who wish to initiate change within the educational system want to downplay the perception that they work on something meant to exclusively benefit children with a migration background. The educational professionals are very aware of the dangers of being put in the 'ethnic niche', which could damage their image of being professional and competent.

Working in the field of *law* entails again other interactions with clients and superiors and other criteria for acceptance and professionalism. Lawyers are able to solve problems or represent interests but, above all, they are responsible for the compliance with rules by individuals, groups or institutions in all domains of society. In order to become a practicing lawyer, all respondents needed to follow a thoroughly institutionalized educational pathway, including completing undergraduate and graduate degrees, examinations and licensing procedures. Simply put, they had to be willing to commit several years to studying law in order to become a professional. This institutional set up can also become a legitimizing mechanism when their professionalism is contested:

> "Having a foreign sounding name means that one has to prove oneself again and again. This started with my job interview here at this company. I was told the following: 'please tell us something about yourself, so that I can hear if your German is really as good as you claim in your application'....There were of course others present during the job interview, and I said: 'I hope your colleague sitting next to you is an expert in employment law in order to enlighten you about the consequences of such a question'." (Female, Associate in a corporate law firm)

Consequently, there is also an observable difference among lawyers who work in corporate firms and those who are independent or work in smaller firms. Whereas the former group were motivated by their own success and individual motives, the latter often have the added ambition to provide help. However, what they have in common is their ambition to succeed in making a better living than their parents within a very prestigious professional position.

In general, we have shown that elements of individuals' ethnic background can help them move upwards in the labour market. This is not to say that they do not complicate their experiences on the 'way up' at the same time. Even individuals who are professionally successful cannot avoid the experience of discrimination and of being 'othered'. However, it seems that they are better equipped to reflect on their situation and thereby come up with coping mechanisms that help them avoid a further self-victimization (cf. Slootman, 2014).

5. Conclusion

In the German public discourse being 'Turkish', is a category that usually leads to the marginalization of individuals as being lower educated, doing lower level jobs and potentially forming a so-called *Parallelgesellschaft*. These generalizations are an almost daily experience for people of Turkish descent in Germany. This is not to victimize the respondents we discussed in this paper, but it is important to understand how their success was accomplished and seen by others with that societal perspective in mind. It truly happened 'against all odds', as they were not supposed to 'make it'. Their own background, being of lower educated parents from Turkey is constantly reflected in their success stories. They have all attained leading professional positions although there are important differences across occupational fields as these each offer distinct opportunity structures within the given context.

The experience in the three occupational fields is different, which has an observable effect on the respondents' claim of professionalism. To begin with, in spite of many recent developments towards internationalization of education, the nation-state continues to determine the arrangements in the educational sector. In contrast to the business professionals who act within an internationally standardized context where intercultural skills are perceived as a prerequisite, educational professionals face a much more ambiguous process of recognition by their colleagues and supervisors. Individual lawyers, in turn, can employ their migration background more straightforwardly in an entrepreneurial manner. Many have started independent law offices focusing on a clientele of Turkish origin. The corporate lawyers are very similar to the business professionals who work in an increasingly international context, which further legitimizes the position they acquired.

The findings indicate that the value of ethnicity as an individual resource across professional contexts is dependent on the organizational importance that is attached to individual difference. The risk of being pigeonholed by parents and other colleagues in the educational field stands in clear contrast to the way corporate companies perceive 'diversity' amongst their staff as an asset. This is not to say that business professionals are not confronted with instances that question their professionalism, as this is certainly the case. However, for corporate professionals, these confrontations occur more on a personal level, which is easier to cope with for individuals when they look at the issue from a professional point of view. Independent lawyers' claim to professionalism and its contestation is similar to the business professionals and their entrepreneurial attitude, they do however lack the strong organizational backing and subsequent acknowledged professionalism that corporate lawyers enjoy.

With this article, we also demonstrated the nuances of "ethnical capital" and its relation to being a member of a low-status group. The findings of this article point out that employing one's individual background is a 'double-edged' phenomenon. On the one hand, our respondents clearly benefitted from the employment of their Turkish migration background. On the other hand, they also experienced encounters and situations that highlighted the dividing line between themselves and others in spite of their professional success. This underlines the cognitive dimension of ethnicity as "a way of seeing and interpreting the world" (Brubaker, 2004, p. 184). Even if one can see interactions as those displayed in the empirical material as part of the process of 'normalization', one should keep in mind the enduring impact of stigmatization based on being a member of a particular ethnic group, which can have detrimental consequences for individuals who are not in a position to employ ethnic background resources to their advantage.

Being successful in balancing making use of ethnic capital on the one hand and avoiding being stigmatized or pigeonholed on the other hand is an important reflexive quality our respondents needed to develop to be able to position themselves successfully as professionals in their sectors. As such, the often-strategic social identity building efforts and work they needed to undertake provides a further crucial building block to understand how the theoretical concept of the multiplier effect works for this specific group that is successful against all odds (Crul et al., 2017). They often need to carve out alternative routes to leadership positions involving the use of ethnic capital resources. However, they can only do this successfully if they can simultaneously avoid, or actively counter, narratives of stigmatization. The form this takes is different across sectors, but in all cases, it is crucial for the acceptance of their professional identity among colleagues, supervisors and clients.

Acknowledgments

We would like to thank three anonymous reviewers for helpful comments on an earlier draft of this article. This work was supported by the European Research Council [284223].

Conflict of Interests

The authors declare no conflict of interests.

References

Ackers, L. (2005). Moving people and knowledge: scientific mobility in the European Union. *International migration, 43*(5), 99–131.

Alba, R., & Nee, V. (2009). *Remaking the American mainstream: Assimilation and contemporary immigration*. Harvard: Harvard University Press.

Barth, F. (1969). Ethnic groups and boundaries. In W. Sollors (Ed.) (1996), *Theories of Ethnicity: a classical reader* (pp. 294–324). New York: New York University Press.

Bonacich, E. (1973). A theory of middleman minorities. *American Sociological Review, 38*(5), 583–594.

Bourdieu, P., & Wacquant, L. J. (1992). *An invitation to reflexive sociology*. Chicago: University of Chicago Press.

Brubaker, R. (2004). *Ethnicity without groups*. Harvard: Harvard University Press.

Bryman, A. (2015). *Social research methods*. Oxford: Oxford University Press.

Castles, S. (2002). Migration and community formation under conditions of globalization. *International migration review, 36*(4), 1143–1168.

Cornell, S., & Hartmann, D. (2007). *Ethnicity and race: making identities in a changing World* (2nd ed.). London: Pine Forge Press.

Cose, E. (1993). *The rage of a privileged class*. New York: HarperCollins.

Crul, M. (2015). Is education the pathway to success? A comparison of second generation Turkish professionals in Sweden, France, Germany and the Netherlands. *European Journal of Education, 50*(3), 325–339.

Crul, M., Keskiner, E., & Lelie, F. (2017). The upcoming new elite among children of immigrants: a cross-country and cross-sector comparison. *Ethnic and Racial Studies, 40*(2), 209–229.

Crul, M., Schneider, J., Keskiner, E., & Lelie, F. (2017). The multiplier effect: how the accumulation of cultural and social capital explains steep upward social mobility of children of low-educated immigrants. *Ethnic and Racial Studies, 40*(2), 321-338.

Crul, M., Schnell, P., Herzog-Punzenberger, B., Wilmes, M., Slootman, M., & Aparicio Gómez, R. (2012). School Careers of Second-Generation Youth in Europe: Which Education Systems Provide the Best Chances for Success? In M. Crul, J. Schneider, & F. Lelie (Eds.), *The European Second Generation Compared: Does the Integration Context Matter?* (pp. 101–164). Amsterdam: Amsterdam University Press.

Crul, M., & Schneider, J. (2010). Comparative integration context theory: participation and belonging in new diverse European cities. *Ethnic and Racial Studies, 33*(7), 1249–1268.

Crul, M., Schneider, J., & Lelie, F. (2012). *The European second generation compared: does the integration context matter?* Amsterdam: Amsterdam University Press.

Elias, N., & Scotson, J. (1965). *The Established and the Outsiders*. London: Cass.

Favell, A. (2008). *Eurostars and Eurocities: free movement and mobility in an integrating Europe*. Oxford: Blackwell.

Fordham, S., & Ogbu, J. U. (1986). Black students' school success: coping with the "burden of 'acting white'". *The Urban Review, 18*(3), 176–206.

Freidson, E. (1999). Theory of professionalism: method and substance. *International Review of Sociology, 9*(1), 117–129.

Hartmann, J. (2016a). Do second-generation Turkish migrants in Germany assimilate into the middle class?. *Ethnicities, 16*(3), 368–392.

Hartmann, J. (2016b). Assimilation im Lebensverlauf? Die Karrieremobilität von türkischen Männern der zweiten Generation in Deutschland. *Zeitschrift für Soziologie, 45*(4), 281–297.

Heath, A. F., C. Rothon, & Kilpi, E. (2008). The second generation in Western Europe: education, unemployment, and occupational attainment. *Annual Review of Sociology*, *34*, 211–35.

Ibarra, H. (1999). Provisional selves: experimenting with image and identity in professional adaptation. *Administrative Science Quarterly*, *44*(4), 764–791.

Kalter, F., & Granato, N. (2007). Educational hurdles on the way to structural assimilation in Germany. In A. F. Heath, & S. Y. Cheung (Eds.), *Unequal chances: ethnic minorities in Western labour markets* (pp. 271–320). Oxford: Oxford University Press.

Kalter, F. (2006). Auf der Suche nach einer Erklärung für die spezifischen Arbeitsmarktnachteile von Jugendlichen türkischer Herkunft. *Zeitschrift für Soziologie*, *35*(2), 144–160.

Khoo, S. E., McDonald, P., Voigt-Graf, C. & Hugo, G. (2007). A global labor market: factors motivating the sponsorship and temporary migration of skilled workers to Australia. *International Migration Review*, *41*(2), 480–510.

Konyali, A. (2014). Turning disadvantage into advantage: achievement narratives of descendants of migrants from Turkey in the corporate business sector. *New Diversities*, *16*(1), 107–121.

Kristen, C. (2002). Hauptschule, Realschule oder Gymnasium?. *Kölner Zeitschrift für Soziologie und Sozialpsychologie*, *54*(3), 534–552.

Merton, R. K. (1968). *Social theory and social structure*. New York: Simon and Schuster.

Pécoud, A. (2002). 'Weltoffenheit schafft Jobs': Turkish entrepreneurship and multiculturalism in Berlin. *International Journal of Urban and Regional Research*, *26*(3), 494–507.

Pott, A. (2001). Ethnicity and social mobility: the case of Turks in Germany. *Journal of International Migration and Integration/Revue de l'integration et de la migration internationale*, *2*(2), 169–186.

Relikowski, I., Yilmaz, E., & Blossfeld, H. P. (2012). Wie lassen sich die hohen Bildungsaspirationen von Migranten erklären? Eine Mixed-Methods-Studie zur Rolle von strukturellen Aufstiegschancen und individueller. *Kölner Zeitschrift für Soziologie und Sozialpsychologie, Sonderheft*, *52*, 111–136.

Rezai, S. (2017). Self-made lawyers? Pathways of socially mobile descendants of migrants from Turkey in Europe. *Ethnic and Racial Studies*, *40*(2), 230–246.

Salikutluk, Z. (2016). Why Do Immigrant Students Aim High? Explaining the Aspiration–Achievement Paradox of Immigrants in Germany. *European Sociological Review*, *32*(5), 581–592.

Schinkel, W., & Noordegraaf, M. (2011). Professionalism as symbolic capital: materials for a Bourdieusian theory of professionalism. *Comparative Sociology*, *10*(1), 67–96.

Schittenhelm, K. (2011). Overcoming barriers. Career trajectories of highly skilled members of the German second generation. In M. Wingens, M. Windzio, H. D. Valk, & C. Aybek (Eds.), *A life-course perspective on migration and integration* (pp. 101–119). Dordrecht: Springer Science.

Schneider, J., Crul, M., & Van Praag, L. (2014). Upward mobility and questions of belonging in migrant families. *New Diversities*, *16*(1), 1–6.

Schnell, P. (2014). *Educational Mobility of Second-Generation Turks*. Amsterdam: Amsterdam University Press.

Seibert, H., & Solga, H. (2005). Gleiche Chancen dank einer abgeschlossenen Ausbildung? Zum Signalwert von Ausbildungsabschlüssen bei ausländischen und deutschen jungen Erwachsenen. *Zeitschrift für Soziologie*, *34*, 364–382.

Slootman, M. (2014). Reinvention of ethnic identification among second generation Moroccan and Turkish Dutch social climbers. *New Diversities*, *16*(1), 57–70.

Sürig, I., & Wilmes, M. (2015). *The integration of the second generation in Germany: results of the TIES survey on the descendants of Turkish and Yugoslavian immigrants*. Amsterdam: Amsterdam University Press.

Van de Werfhorst, H. G., & Van Tubergen, F. (2007). Ethnicity, schooling, and merit in the Netherlands. *Ethnicities*, *7*(3), 416–444.

Volery, T. (2007). Ethnic entrepreneurship: a theoretical framework. In L. P. Dana (Ed.), *Handbook of research on ethnic minority entrepreneurship. A co- evolutionary view on resource management* (pp. 30–41). Cheltenham; Northampton: Edward Elgar.

Waldring, I. (2017). Practices of change in the education sector: professionals dealing with ethnic school segregation. *Ethnic and Racial Studies*, *40*(2), 247–263.

Waldring, I., Crul, M., & Ghorashi, H. (2015). Discrimination of second-generation professionals in leadership positions. *Social Inclusion*, *3*(4), 38–49.

Worbs, S. (2003). The second generation in Germany: between school and labor market. *International Migration Review*, *37*(4), 1011–1038.

About the Authors

Ali Konyali is a PhD candidate within the framework of the ERC funded ELITES: Pathways to Success project at the Department of Public Administration and Sociology at Erasmus University Rotterdam, The Netherlands. He studied Arts and Culture and European Studies at Maastricht University, The Netherlands, as well as International Migration and Ethnic Relations at Malmö University, Sweden.

Maurice Crul (PhD) is a Professor at the Free University in Amsterdam and the Erasmus University in Rotterdam. He is co-director of IMISCOE, a network of European research institutes in the fields of migration and diversity. In the last twenty years, he mostly worked on the topic of education and children of immigrants, first within the Dutch context and then in a comparative European and transatlantic context. He is the coordinator of the ELITES: Pathways to Success project.

10

Jews, Muslims and the Ritual Male Circumcision Debate: Religious Diversity and Social Inclusion in Germany

Gökçe Yurdakul

Department of Diversity and Social Conflict, Humboldt University of Berlin, 10099 Berlin, Germany;
E-Mail: gokce.yurdakul@sowi.hu-berlin.de

Abstract

On 7 May 2012, the Cologne regional court ruled that circumcising young boys was a form of previous bodily harm (*körperverletzung*). Although both Muslims and Jews circumcise infant boys as a religious practice, the Cologne court found that the child's "fundamental right to bodily integrity" was more important than the parents' rights, leaving Muslim and Jewish parents under suspicion of causing bodily harm to their children. After heated public discussions and an expedited legal process, legal authorities permitted the ritual circumcision of male children under a new law. However, the German debates on religious diversity are not yet over. On the third anniversary of the Court decision in 2015, thirty-five civil society organisations organised a rally in Cologne for "genital autonomy", calling for a ban on ritual male circumcision. In this article, I will focus on religious diversity, which is undergoing changes through minority and immigrant claims for religious accommodation. Analysing the ongoing controversies of ritual male circumcision in Germany, I argue that this change is best observed with Muslim and Jewish claims for practicing their religion. By using political debates, news reports and information provided by lawyers and medical doctors who were involved in the public debate, I show that religious diversity debates are a litmus test for social inclusion: Muslims and Jews, in this context, are both passive subjects of social inclusion policies and active participants in creating a religiously diverse society in Germany.

Keywords

Germany; Jews; Muslims; religious diversity; ritual male circumcision; social inclusion

Issue

This article is part of the issue "Religious Diversity and Social Inclusion", edited by Gary Bouma (Monash University, Australia).

---

1. Introduction

On 7 May 2012, a German regional court in Cologne ruled that circumcising young boys was a form of bodily harm (*körperverletzung*). Although both Muslim and Jewish families circumcise infant boys as a religious practice, the Cologne court found that a child's "fundamental right to bodily integrity" superseded the religious rights of parents. This potentially rendered Muslim and Jewish parents under suspect of causing bodily harm to their children. After heated public discussions, international political pressure, and a speedy legal process, the regional court ruling was replaced by a new national German law that permitted the ritual circumcision of male children. Despite the national law, male circumcision continues to be a highly contested issue. On 7 May 2015, thirty-five civil society organisations organised a rally in Cologne for "genital autonomy", calling for a ban on ritual male circumcision, as this practice continues to be an integral part of Jewish and Muslim lives in Germany in the shadow of political and legal challenges.

In this article, I will focus on the role of the German debate on ritual male circumcision in shaping religious diversity. Although religious diversity has been defined in multiple ways, ranging from demographic description of a society to institutional recognition of religious minority groups, I will focus on the aspect of social inclusion of religiously diverse groups in institutional settings (Bouma, Ling, & Pratt, 2010; Vertovec & Wessendorf, 2006;). I aim to show relations between two religious minority groups who make claims to the German state authorities in order to practice ritual male circumcision—an act that challenges the norms of German society.

As a key aspect of social inclusion, religious diversity is undergoing contested changes through minority and immigrant claims for religious accommodation (Koopmans, 2013; Vertovec & Wessendorf, 2006). I argue that this change is best observed by analysing Muslim and Jewish claims for practicing their religion, and how these claims get taken up in public debates. Jews and Muslims in Germany have collaborated in bringing similar claims for religious practices in the past, such as in the case of pointing out to the parallel dynamics of anti-Semitism and anti-Muslim racism in Germany. This does not mean, however, that both communities collaborate on religious diversity claims. Jews and Muslims in Germany also have important fault lines, which divide both communities, which I have elaborated elsewhere (Yurdakul, 2010).

Using discourse analysis of political debates, newspaper reports, focus group interview with Muslim men as well as meetings[1] with key informants in the public debate, I show how religious diversity debates are a litmus test for social inclusion: How to socially include minority groups if their religious practices are conflicting with the norms of a majority society? The decisive point here is whether or not minority groups are considered as "full members" or "foreigners" in a given society. In this context, I suggest that Muslim and Jewish groups are both objects of social inclusion policies and active participants in negotiating religious diversity, thereby playing both passive and active roles in the shaping of a socially inclusive German society.

2. Who has the Right to Decide on the Limits of Religious Diversity?

Political and legal authorities make institutional arrangements in order to accommodate religious diversity (Bramadat & Koenig, 2009; Giordan, 2014). The regulation of religious diversity is often defined in a top-down manner, such as through government policies. European institutions, such as national and European-level Courts, act as authorities for playing important roles in shaping what kind of practices of religious diversity are permissible in the European public sphere (Greenfield, 2013; Koenig, 2007). However, religious groups, in this case Jews and Muslims in Germany, challenge these regulations in their everyday lives (Kastoryano, 2002; Laurence, 2001; Peck, 1998). Despite the top-down legal decision-making process, many Jewish and Muslim groups may continue practicing their religions and as a result they may be excluded from social institutions[2].

3. Stigmatisation of Jews and Muslims

Ritual male circumcision is the practice of removing the foreskin of a new born or prepubescent male child (Gollaher, 2000), and is a practice mainly associated with Jewish and Muslim religious traditions. The political significance of the ritual stems in part from the fact that it is irreversible, and as argued by some legal, political, and medical authorities and scholars, it is considered a major infringement of children's rights to bodily integrity (Schüklenk, 2012). While circumcision is a gendered practice that permeates across minority religious groups in many European countries, social service agencies, legal institutions, and other state-related institutions, such as hospitals, have a limited understanding of the practice itself. For these social actors, circumcision is often understood as a sign of cultural backwardness, and in some cases as an act of violence against male children. These understandings of circumcision as evidence of violence and backwardness—instead of as contested faith-based practices for example—are produced by reifying minority cultures as monolithic traditions marked by their inherent ignorance of children's well-being (Benatar, 2013; Lang, 2013).

Scholars have examined the body politics of Jewish histories in secular Europe. Sander Gilman discusses the stigmatisation of the Jewish body through medical constructions in his work on *The Jew's Body* (1991). He explains how the rhetoric of modern science marks the Jewish body as different. Gilman shows how modern medicine, as a discursive agent of secular authorities, stigmatises the Jewish body by disseminating it to its parts (such as the infamous Jewish nose) and describing it as deviant from "the norm". Law and medical sciences distill and embody non-Muslim and non-Jewish values i.e., those of Christian or, at least, liberal Christian values. Similarly, the Muslim body politics in Europe is about how Muslim bodies are marked as different and are excluded from the European public sphere (Korteweg & Yurdakul, 2014; Lettinga & Saharso, 2014). Drawing on such work on Jewish and Muslim bodies, I aim to show how discursive agents, such as legal authorities, newsmakers, and key political stakeholders try to shape minority bodies, those of Jews and Muslims, in Europe. I will focus on two major areas where secular discourse prevails (namely, science and

[1] These are meetings rather than interviews, because our conversations did not have traditional interview structure in a sociological sense. In addition, I had the chance to ask questions to some of them in public meetings.

[2] For Muslims, primarily from educational institutions and job market, such as in the case of Muslim women's headscarves (Korteweg & Yurdakul, 2014).

law) exceptionally present in Germany, which marks the limits of religious diversity and the borders of social inclusion into German society.

This study also contributes to ongoing scholarly discussions about ritual male circumcision among legal scholars, bioethicists and sociologists. I argue that many legal scholars fail to adequately look into the perspectives of minorities themselves, and instead simplify debates on rights and obligations (Merkel & Putzke, 2013). Criminalising religious practices through law enables governing authorities to gain greater control over minority religious practices. This focus on legal aspects presents us from understanding the performative effects of religious diversity. In other words, I suggest that we look at how the law affects people, rather than just *law in books*. In this article, I examine the German court decision in 2012, but also delve into how social actors discuss the outcomes of the legal debates. My analysis of the circumcision debate considers factors such as Jewish history in Germany as a potentially important contextual factor that affected the decision-making process in 2012[3].

By drawing on this contextual framework, as a sociologist, I focus on the majority-minority power relations and the interrelations between two minority religious groups in this debate. I do this by reconstructing how key stakeholders talk to each other in the public sphere by referring to their own political positions. In these discussions, we find how Muslims and Jews are both objects of German social inclusion policies, but also active participants of how to create a religiously diverse society in Germany. In the following, I will discuss the historical context of the circumcision debates and link them to current media and political controversies. My fieldwork in public discussions, focus group interview and meetings with key stakeholders shows how religious diversity is discussed within minority groups.

4. Historical Context

The 2012 circumcision debate in Germany was not the first debate on religious diversity within German context. It has persisted throughout history in relation to the particular traditions of Jews in Germany (Judd, 2007; Kokin, 2014; Lavi, 2009). With the incoming flux of immigrants from Muslim countries, most notably Turkish immigrants and their eventual settlement in Germany, this revived the debate on ritual slaughtering[4] (Lavi, 2009; 2010) and ritual male circumcision[5] (Yurdakul, 2013). As we shall see, the stigmatisation of minorities remains constant during these discussions, regardless of the outcome.

The history of debates around circumcision prior to the 2012 law has been detailed in a book, *Contested Rituals* by historian Robin Judd (2007). She describes the political and social circumstances of Jewish life in Germany and shows how exclusionary approaches can be found in the writings of German scholars since the turn of the century. These writings have been stigmatising Jewish ritual behaviours for centuries, from defaming their masculinities to pointing out ritual practices as barbarism (Judd, 2007; see also Heil & Kramer, 2013). Although this debate on circumcision took place in another socio-political period in the 19th century, it is interesting to see that some of the political actors (medical doctors, state attorneys and Jewish community leaders) and the theme (circumcision ban) similarly take front stage. In terms of stigmatisation, Judd quotes the example of a ritual male circumcision case in Baden in 1881. The state medical examiner, named E. Sausheim, argued that the mohel (circumciser) should be suspended and the oral suction (metistsah be'peh) should be outlawed (Judd, 2007, pp. 1-2).

The use of science and law to exclude Jewish religious practices have been exemplified in Sander Gilman's brilliant essay in *Haut Ab!,* the Jewish Museum's temporary exhibition catalogue on the ritual male circumcision (2014-15). He states that "No medical circumcision discussion had been independent from ideological perspective" (2014, p. 123, translated from German). He points to the unproven discussions on whether circumcision can be a cure for syphilis or cervical cancer, or even HIV. In some cases, newsmakers make blanket statements on sexual impotency of circumcised men (Stehr, 2012). In the context of these discussions, Sander Gilman concludes that at the end of all these debates the decisive factor is not science, but cultural acceptance (Gilman, 2014). In fact, in assimilatory efforts of Jews into German social and cultural life, in 1843 in Frankfurt, a liberal group of Jews, including Rabbi Abraham Geiger, who was the leading figure of Reform Judaism in Germany, wanted to abandon ritual male circumcision, arguing that it was barbaric (Gollaher, 2000).

Muslim immigrant integration and criminalisation of Muslims mark a shift in the current debates. Sander Gilman questions why the ritual circumcision debate came back onto the political agenda in Germany and even beyond, such as in Scandinavian countries or in Britain where it is still contested and performed under restricted conditions. He argues that this has a lot to do

[3] This contextual analysis of the circumcision debate, which brings social factors into the debate, is present in some recent legal scholarship (Fateh-Moghadam, 2012).

[4] Turkish butcher Rüstem Altinküpe brought the case of ritual slaughter to the court, and won his case in 2006 (*Jüdische Allgemeine* 1.10.2009). *Halal* slaughtering of meat is permitted in Germany under restricted conditions. For Jewish and Muslim ritual slaughtering in Germany (see Lavi, 2009).

[5] As I will discuss in the following pages, ritual male circumcision is permitted in Germany after a court case in 2012, but it is practiced under restricted conditions.

with the "fear of Islamisation" (Gilman, 2014, p. 125), as Islam is frequently regarded by newsmakers and politicians as a religion that is not compatible with German society, and Muslims have difficulties in being socially included into the German way of life.

5. Method

The data for this article has been collected from various media resources, legal documents, participant observations, meetings with key stake holders and focus groups. The legal data was collected from Court decisions and press releases of the Cologne local and regional courts (*Amtsgericht* and *Landgericht*) as well as the decisions and public statements of the German Ethics Council, which are available on their website.

The media data is from three German newspapers that spanned the political spectrum since the beginning of the legal circumcision debate on 26 June 2012 to 31 December 2014, when the circumcision debate was ongoing on a smaller scale. I collected all the articles that discussed "circumcision" from their online archives, sorting out those on female circumcision, or circumcision debates in non-Western countries to refine the sample[6]. The German newspaper data was collected from three major sources: *Süddeutsche Zeitung* (SZ), *tageszeitung* (taz) and *Frankfurter Allgemeine* (FAZ). I chose these three newspapers in order to cover the political spectrum in the German media. SZ appeals to a left-liberal readership, FAZ is a conservative newspaper, taz is a left-leaning newspaper, showing the perspectives of the Green Party[7]. For all these newspapers, I created a chronology of events, which documented what has been discussed in each newspaper on a weekly basis. In addition to the systematic data collection from these German daily newspapers, I also used newspaper articles from *Jüdische Allgemeine*[8], a weekly newspaper of the Central Council of Jews; *der Spiegel,* a popular weekly magazine, *die Zeit*, a high-brow weekly newspaper, as well as the European edition of the Turkish national newspaper, *Hürriyet*.

In addition to media data, the study also includes data from a focus group and four meetings with key stakeholders. The focus group participants were four Turkish Sunnite Muslim men, all of whom reside in Germany[9]. All of these men were circumcised as children either in Turkey or in Germany and they discussed how they are affected by the ongoing circumcision debate. I met with key informants who were active in the circumcision debate: Ilhan Ilkilic, MD, a member of the German Ethics Council who drafted the circumcision law; Mustafa Yeneroglu, lawyer and the previous head of the Islamic Community of Milli Görüs, who politically supported the legal case of male circumcision in Germany; and Zulfükar Çetin, co-author of the controversial book on circumcision, *Interventionen gegen die deutsche "Beschneidungsdebatte"* (*Interventions against the German "circumcision debates"*). This book was cited frequently in the German circumcision debates in order to exemplify minority men's perspective. A final informant for this research was Felicitas Heimann-Jelinek, the curator of the Jewish Museum exhibition on circumcision. I had the chance to directly ask her questions during a closed meeting within Jewish-Muslim Study Group at the Jewish Museum in December 2014.

6. Social Inclusion, Exclusion and Religious Diversity

The peak of the circumcision debate was the Cologne regional court's decision on 7 May 2012, which criminalised Jewish and Muslim parents for causing bodily harm to their children. The German public was divided into two groups: those who were pro-ban of circumcision argued that (1) the right of self-determination of the child is violated, (2) the circumcision is irreversible and irreparable. Without reason a child loses a healthy part of its body, (3) the surgery is dangerous to the human body like every other surgery, and (4) circumcision is only reasonable in those cases where it is medically indicated. Those who are against the ban argued that the exercise of parental care of § 1627 I BGB (German Civil Code), covers all of the parents' decisions as long as they benefit the well-being of the child. The main argument of those who are against the ban is that excluding a child from the religious group is against the child's well-being. This is justified as parents are prevented from passing on their values and beliefs to their children.

A major finding from my discourse analysis is that, "child's well-being" is vaguely defined, and is usually concealed under "child's right to bodily integrity" or "child's right to self-determination". For example, in its legal decision, the Cologne Regional Court concluded that:

> "Neither is the request of the parents capable of justifying the act, since the right of the parents to

---

[6] In this time period, hundreds of newspaper articles appeared in the newspapers, for example in the FAZ there are 352 mentionings of words Jewish and circumcision whereas 181 mentionings of Muslim and circumcision. In the SZ, such words appeared 370 to 186 and in the taz 248 and 160. These articles are only about male circumcision.

[7] SZ has the highest circulation at 1.1 million per day. FAZ has an estimated circulation of almost 400 thousand, taz has the lowest circulation among all, about 60 thousand.

[8] I thank Zülfukar Çetin for opening his newspaper archive for the missing resources.

[9] Due to the gender sensitivity of the subject, this focus group interview was solely conducted by my assistant Mr. Özgür Özvatan, at the Humboldt University of Berlin.

> raise their child in their religious faith does not take precedence over the right of the child to bodily integrity and self-determination. Consequently, the parental consent to the circumcision is considered to be inconsistent with the well-being of the child." (*Landgericht Köln*, 151 Ns 169/11)[10]

In this legal statement "children's well-being[11]" is constructed through an individualistic understanding of the child, isolated from their parental social context who are minorities. In fact, in a similar logic, medical doctor Matthias Franz, an opponent of circumcision, argues that "In this context, religious freedom cannot be a justification for (sexual) violence against young boys, who are unable to consent" (Franz, FAZ, 21.7.2012). In this case, German legal and medical authorities, rather than Jewish and Muslim parents, decide on behalf of the child who cannot give consent. In other words, children's well-being is best decided by the state authorities, as practices of religious diversity are not acceptable when it comes to minority parents.

One such argument along the same lines is that circumcision is a form of stigmatisation of children, because they cannot reverse the operation. The aforementioned court decision on the circumcision:

> "Moreover, the circumcision changes the child's body permanently and irreparably. This change runs contrary to the interests of the child in deciding his religious affiliation independently later in life. On the other hand, the parental right of education is not unacceptably diminished by requiring them to wait until their son is able to make the decision himself whether to have a circumcision as a visible sign of his affiliation to Islam." (Court decision from 7 May 2012; *Landgericht Köln*, 151 Ns. 169/11)

The marking of the body for a sign of belonging to Islam or Judaism is further interpreted as stigmatisation: "This is also a way to prevent a threatening stigmatisation of the child" (Court decision from 21 September 2011; *Amstgericht Köln*, 528 Ds 30/11). The discourse on stigmatisation of children has already been mentioned in criminal law scholar Holm Putzke's above mentioned statement, namely that the less parents circumcise their children, the less stigmatisation will take place. I argue that such an approach does work from a political point of view as it holds Muslim and Jewish parent responsible for the stigmatisation of their children and their exclusion from German society. In earlier works, Holm Putzke at the University of Passau, argued for the criminalisation of circumcision in Germany: "For the more frequently boys are not circumcised, the less this condition, this gives reason for stigmatisation" (2008, p. 21) in this way dividing Germany into circumcised and uncircumcised people.

Similarly, anti-circumcision debates were picked up by immigrant political actors even before 2012. Turkish-German sociologist and Islam-critic Necla Kelek brought up the issue in a German Islam Conference and also wrote about the possible harms of ritual male circumcision in her book Lost Sons (Kelek, 2006). Being a pro-ban advocate only for Muslim circumcision, Kelek differentiated between Jewish practices of circumcision, and the Muslim practice. According to her, Jewish practice is based on religion (therefore should be permitted), whereas the Muslim practice is merely a tradition (and therefore should be banned). In this way, Kelek argued that only religious acts have the potential to be legally permitted in Germany, disregarding other arguments such as a child's well-being.

The German media was divided in the debate. On the one hand, newsmakers gave public voice to medical authorities, religious clergy, legal authorities and scholars who are mostly pro-ban. German newspapers, such as *FAZ*, *die Welt* or weeklies, such as *der Spiegel*, were quick to publish photos of rabbis practicing circumcision ceremonies. They used provocative headlines, such as "*Ritual, Trauma, Kindeswohl*" (Ritual, trauma and well-being of the child), "*Auch die Seele leidet*" (The soul also suffers), "*Freiheit ist wichtiger als Tradition*" (Freedom is more important than tradition).

Those who are anti-ban were featured in mainstream newspapers but mostly writing editorial pieces for the minority newspapers, such as *Jüdische Allgemeine* or *Hürriyet*. Both Central Council of Jews and Islam Council reacted immediately grounding their arguments in different social and historical facts. Ali Kizilkaya, the executive director of Islam Council drew on to the integration debates and argued that Cologne Court's pro-ban decision is against Muslims efforts to integrate into Germany. Dieter Graumann, the previous Chairman of the Central Council of Jews in Germany argued that this decision makes Jewish life in Germany impossible. Although the Court decision was about the specific case of a Muslim boy, the politicians and newsmakers started focusing on Jewish circumci-

[10] This English-translation is available at the https://www.dur.ac.uk/resources/ilm/CircumcisionJudgmentLGCologne7May20121.pdf

[11] "Children's well-being" appears as a nebulous concept in policy-making and in legal discussions. According to the UN Convention on the Rights of the Child: "In all actions concerning children, whether undertaken by public or private social welfare institutions, courts of law, administrative authorities or legislative bodies, the best interests of the child shall be a primary consideration" (1990, Article 3). This statement may involve excessive statism (state authorities deciding on behalf of parents) but also discrimination against certain minorities (state authorities prohibiting Islamic rituals). However, it is noted that circumcision is irreversible and the child must decide later himself if he belongs to Islam. This statement of the Landgericht Köln brings Islamic practices under spotlight.

sion in Germany, with central figures of the Jewish community in Germany as well as the Chief Rabbi from Israel, commenting on the legal decision. Newsmakers in the European edition of *Hürriyet* were not so concerned about the decision, perhaps because Turkish communities in Germany have been confronted with such religious bans in the past, such as that of the headscarf debate. The circumcision issue carried second or third rate importance in their reporting. Some reporters mentioned travelling outside of Germany to carry out circumcisions, where families may take children to Turkey, if it were to be banned in Germany.

At this same time, there were those who were anti-ban, but were not represented in the media discussions. Social workers who are embedded within Muslim societies in Berlin claimed that they were excluded from the debates. Although they were coming from migrant families and had face-to-face contact with many Muslim families as part of their job, no journalist quoted their thoughts about the circumcision debate. Their voices went unheard, despite the fact that they were frontline social workers. In my meeting with Zülfukar Çetin, at that time a social worker at the anti-racist organisation *Reach Out*, he told me he felt excluded, he mentioned that no one asks the youth in the Berlin district of Kreuzberg about what they think, even though they are the subjects of the debate. In his book co-authored with Alexander Salih Wolter, Çetin pointed out that the debate polarised men as "circumcised" and "uncircumcised," therefore creating multiple forms of masculinities, which are in competition with each other. They argued that the so-called "Judeo-Christian tradition of the West" is paradoxically referring to Jewish traditions as crimes and therefore anti-Semitic in itself. This paradox reached its highest point in the circumcision debate, in which anti-Muslim racism accompanies anti-Semitism (Çetin & Wolter, 2012, p. 39). Both groups, they argued, were excluded from being members of German society due to their religious practices.

Another key actor in the debates was the German Ethics Council, a government agency which was responsible for making recommendations for drafting the 2012 circumcision law. The Ethics Council made an anti-ban decision and made suggestions to the legal authorities to draft the new circumcision law. In our meeting[12] with Ilhan Ilkilic, MD, a member of the German Ethics Council, he stated that the Ethics Council decided according to the presumption that religious freedom is seen as a more important liberal value than bodily integrity of children[13] (also see Ilkilic, 2014). According to the Ethics Council's suggestions for regulating male circumcision, a child's consent would still be important in conducting the circumcision; religious circumcisers can practice circumcision on children only until the 8th day, after this day medical personnel would be responsible for circumcision. The Ethics Council's draft law was passed to the *Bundestag*. With this law, Muslim and Jewish practices of religious diversity became lawful, implying that Muslims and Jews are socially included into the religious life in Germany.

However, a member of the *Ethikrat* (Ethics Council) was against the law altogether. Reinhard Merkel argued against the practice of circumcision on the grounds that there is no obligation under the law to take the consent of the child and no obligation for anaesthesia (*Die Zeit*, 1 October 2012). In fact, Merkel had previously pointed out the ethical, legal and historical problems of this decision earlier, by stating that: "No right to freedom permitted an interference with the body of a human. This is also true for circumcision in boys. And yet the case is difficult" (SZ, 30.8.12). He especially pointed to the fact that Jewish history in Germany has played an important role in passing this decision:

> "If an unknown religious group were to come to Germany today with the ritual of male circumcision, common in no other place of the world, it would be prohibited on the spot. And if it was solely Muslim religious practice, the Bundestag certainly would not have responded to the Cologne judgement with a resolution as on the 19 July. But circumcision is an ancient custom constitutive of Judaism. And that's the real problem of legal policy. Hiding this fact is useless; because only with this provenance its significance is clear. The terrible mass murder in history makes German Politics certainly most prominent and unique duty to show particular sensitivity to all Jewish matters. This cannot be shaken. Circumcision is obviously a matter of particular importance." (Merkel's commentary in the *Süddeutsche Zeitung*, 30.8.2012)

In fact, in this statement, Merkel says that Jewish and Muslim religious practices, such as circumcision, cannot be included into German social life. Due to the German responsibility towards Jews, the law was passed. This statement, I argue, shows how Jews and Muslim are still not considered as a part of German society, but as "foreigners". If Germans were not fulfilling their responsibility towards Jews in the frame of "*wiedergutmachen*" (to redress), the law would not be passed. Merkel implies that such religious practices would not belong to

---

[12] Yurdakul and Lavi meeting with Ilhan Ilkilic, 22.1. 2015, Berlin.

[13] Ilkilic mentions in an interview: "In my view religious freedom is more important than the violation of physical integrity, because the practice does not alter the function of the organ, if the operation is carried out safely and correctly. And in addition, a ban puts huge pressure on Muslims because circumcision represents an important ritual for them." (Ilkilic, 2013)

German society under normal circumstances. As Sander Gilman showed cultural acceptance of religious practices is the decisive factor in social inclusion (2014). In this case, Jewish and Muslim ritual of male circumcision is still a contested practice, despite the fact that it can be legally practiced in Germany.

The debate spread to international media, yet the importance given to the debate, especially in Israel and Turkey, varied. In the Israeli daily newspaper, Haaretz, the circumcision debate was a daily discussion. The European Rabbis Conference (*Europäische Rabbinerkonferenz)* was cited in the German newspapers: "The ruling is seen as the most serious attack on Judaism since the Holocaust." (SZ, 16.7.2012). The Chief Rabbi of Israel Yona Metzger came to Germany to discuss the issue with politicians and to hold a press conference in the hall of the Federal Press (*Bundespressekonferenz*), addressing the national and international media, and warning against anti-Semitism in Germany (taz, 21.8.2012). Similarly, President Shimon Peres sent a letter to the German President Joachim Gauck, asking him to intervene to safeguard the religious rights of Jews in Germany (SZ, 25.8.2012). In Turkey, the possible ban on circumcision did not find much political resonance. Turkish citizens carried out some independent campaigns to protest the legal decision (Tosun in Hürriyet, 29 June 2012).

During these discussions, Chancellor Angela Merkel has personally followed the circumcision debate. In fact, she infamously said: "I do not want Germany to be the only country in the world where Jews cannot practice their rituals. Otherwise, we turn into a laughing stock (*komiker nation*)"[14]. This shows her support to pass the circumcision law without causing more damage to Germany's international image (FAZ, 17.7.2012). Just before the passing of the law, she paid a political visit to the Central Council of Jews in Frankfurt, where she said that Germany shows tolerance to religions (FAZ, 25.11.2012). On 12 December 2012, approximately 6 months after the debate in Cologne, the *Bundestag* adopted the proposed law explicitly permitting male circumcision to be performed under certain conditions (§1631(d) part of the German Civil Code (BGB)), making ritual male circumcision a lawful religious practice in Germany.

7. A One Way Street: Inclusion into a Minority, but Exclusion from a Majority

As political scientist Kerem Öktem mentions in his study on "Signals from the Majority Society," in which he interviewed Jews, Muslims and Germans on the circumcision debate during these discussions in Germany, both Jewish and Muslim interviewees clearly stated that they felt that they are excluded from European societies as their religious practice and male bodies are criminalised and stigmatised (2013). In fact, in a focus group interview that we conducted with four religious Turkish and Sunnite Muslim men, we also heard many times that their circumcised male body is an integral part of their minority identity (see also Kokin, 2014). For example, in the focus group interview, Ali (pseudonym) said "being circumcised is a form of belonging. It is a part of being a man". Similarly, Tarik mentioned that he would find it shameful if a man is not circumcised. Our focus group participants discussed how being circumcised is an in-group identity marker for a minority group in Germany, that is striving to belong. In fact, this finding was also evident in other public testimonials by Turkish men, such as the co-leader of the Green Party and a prominent politician of Turkish background, Cem Özdemir, who wrote about how his relationship with his body gives him an in-group recognition and a feeling of belonging (2008, pp. 235-238).

A key finding in our focus group involved the shared identity markers among Muslim and Jewish groups that practices of circumcision engendered. One participant claimed that male circumcision is a bodily marker, which binds Jews and Muslims in Germany. Hasan said "In Judaism, in Torah it is definitely in it (in their religion). I mean...When we are all circumcised, then 'hey! You are also circumcised!'...I find it positive. Normal. You are also one of us[15]". Hasan is pointing to circumcision as an identity marker for both Jews and Muslims in Germany, a constitutive marker of their minority belonging.

Although some men, like the focus group participants, consider circumcision as a form of social inclusion, in the sense that it is belonging to a minority group in Germany, it is also regarded as a marker of social exclusion by many German legal, medical and political authorities. These groups express concern over whether granting freedom of religion to immigrants and minorities would cause social disintegration or not.

Reflecting on the minority perspectives on the debate, the Jewish Museum in Berlin organised an exhibition and a series of events. Focusing on the inclusion/exclusion dichotomy in a playful way, the title of the exhibition, called *Haut Ab!*, which was intended as a pun on the German term, "skin off!" or "get out!" Speaking to Felicitas Heimann-Jelinek, the curator of the exhibition[16], she aimed to contextualise the con-

[14] This is the translation in the National Post on 17 July 2012. The German original is cited as follows: "Ich will nicht, dass Deutschland das einzige Land auf der Welt ist, in dem Juden nicht ihre Riten ausüben können. Wir machen uns ja sonst zur Komiker-Nation." (Jones, 2012)

[15] In the framework on minority belongings, in our book on the headscarf debates, we focus on the ways in which Muslim women use the headscarf as a method of protest and asserting national belonging (2014).

[16] Meeting with Felicitas Heimann-Jelinek in the Jewish Muse-

troversial circumcision debate historically. At the same time, the exhibition showed the religious diversity of male circumcision practices, varying from photos of crying boys from Turkish immigrant families in order to reflect the contemporary history of ritual male circumcision in Germany, to videos on Jewish life in Germany.

A panel of scholars presented at an event on Jewish-Muslim relations, organised with the *Haut Ab!* exhibition on 4 December 2014. The panel included historian Alexander Hasgall, political scientists Mounir Azzaoui and Kerem Öktem, as well as Hannah C. Tzuberi, a scholar of Judaism and Islam. It was emphasised that the circumcision debate in Germany brought Jews and Muslims together as minorities who have been struggling for their practices of religious diversity to be socially included as minorities. Referring to a public poll that was conducted by a polling agency, Infratest, the academic director of the Jewish Academy Yasemin Shooman stated that 70% of German society was against the circumcision law (also see Heimann-Jelinek & Kugelmann, 2014). She questioned whether there is any protection of minorities in this context that their practices of religious diversity are clearly socially excluded.

With the introduction of the circumcision law, the debate on legal recognition and regulation of male circumcision in Germany seemed to be over. But German criminal lawyers have argued that section 1631 d BGB is against the constitution[17], and are preparing to continue the debate, with the support of some medical doctors. On 3 June 2015, the Elisabeth Hospital in Essen organised a conference on medical and legal perspectives on the circumcision debate. The conference included medical doctors who have been publicly active against circumcision. They argued that: "surgery in the genital area of a little boy means a painful and traumatic experience, which therefore should be considered independent of its implications" (Liedgens & Eckert, 2015). In short, the male circumcision debate is continuing to legalise and medicalise discourses in order to criminalise and pathologise Jewish and Muslim religious practices, leaving little opportunity to discuss religious diversity in a socially inclusive society.

8. Conclusion

Ritual male circumcision, a latent subject of discussion for many years, has returned to the Western secular political agenda (for a historical debate see Judd, 2007). The circumcision debate is, in fact, not a uniquely German debate, but it is a discussion on who has the authority to decide on body politics in Europe and in the rest of the Western countries, where Jews and Muslims are still considered strangers. Social inclusion, which is determined by legal authorities through court decisions, political actors and scholars, as well as media discussions, show how Jewish and Muslim religious practices are still discussed in the contexts of public threat and stigmatisation. The language that has been used in legal decisions and in the media have deeply stigmatised and criminalised Jewish and Muslim people in this context.

The purpose of this article is not to endorse ritual male circumcision, but rather to show how social inclusion and exclusion of minorities are decided in public debates through local courts, media debates, and scholars' press statements. Ritual male circumcision is one significant case, which shows different dynamics of what plays a role in determining religious diversity in order to socially include minorities. My suggestion for further analysis is to critically look at how social actors of minority groups challenge the existing socio-legal discourses through their religious practices and bodily performances. A systematic research agenda, which focuses on how legal decisions are interpreted and debated by minority groups, will enable us to see who belongs to Germany and Europe and what will shape German and European futures.

Acknowledgments

Earlier versions of this work were presented in the working group for " A Shared Perspective of Jews and Muslims for Europe Comparative Perspective on Issues of Cultural Practices and the Secular Public Sphere: The Example of "Male Circumcision" in Istanbul Policy Center (2014) and in the Jewish Museum in Berlin (2015). I am grateful to the members of working group, specifically Nilüfer Göle, Amnon Raz-Krakotzkin, Gabriel Motzkin, and Shai Lavi for their comments on earlier versions. I was invited to present this work with an invitation by Dr. Aviad Rubin at the University of Haifa, Department of Political Science (2013). I am grateful to his generosity and feedback from the departmental colleagues. I thank to my colleagues at the Council for European Studies Conference in Amsterdam (2012), especially Anna Korteweg, Liza Mügge and Leah Bassel, and to conference participants at the Sussex Migration Center's 2015 Annual Conference who discussed parts of this work with me. Last but not least, I am grateful to Birgit zur Nieden, Özgür Özvatan, Larissa Probst, Pauline Weller, Salina Abji and Jurek Wolter, who helped with the data collection and writing of this article. My thanks go to Shai Lavi, Esra Özyürek, David Abraham and Nadine Blumer who commented on the final version. The funds to publish this open-access article is

---

um on 20 January 2015 in the framework of the Jewish-Muslim Study Group, led by Nilüfer Göle and Amnon Raz-Krakotzkin.

[17] Bürgerliches Gesetzbuch (BGB) § 1631d Beschneidung des männlichen Kindes (German Civil Code, Circumcision of Male Children), http://www.gesetze-im-internet.de/bgb/__1631d.html (accessed on 15 April 2015)

generously provided by the German-Israeli Foundation Regular Grant (co-investigator with Shai Lavi).

Conflict of Interests

The author declares no conflict of interests.

References

Benatar, D. (2013). Evaluations of circumcision should be circumscribed by the evidence. *Journal of Medical Ethics*, *39*(7), 431-432.

Bouma, G. D., Ling, R., & Pratt, R. (2010). *Religious diversity in Southeast Asia and the Pacific.* Dordrecht: Springer.

Bramadat, P., & Koenig, M. (Eds.). (2009). *International migration and the governance of religious diversity.* Ontario: Metropolis.

Çetin, Z., & Wolter, S. A. (2012). Fortsetzung einer "Zivilisierungsmission: Zur deutschen Beschenidungsdebatten". In Z. Çetin, H. J. Voß, & S. A. Wolter (Eds.), *Interventionen gegen die deutsche "Beschneidungsdebatte"*. Münster: Edition Assemblage.

Fateh-Moghadam, B. (2012). Criminalizing male circumcision—Case Note: Landgericht Cologne Judgment of 7 May 2012- No. 151 Ns 169/11. *German Law Journal, 13,* 1131-1145.

Franz, M. (2012, July 21). Ritual, trauma, kindeswohl. *Frankfurter Allgemeine Zeitung (FAZ).* Retrieved from http://www.faz.net

Gilman, S. (1991) *The Jew's Body.* New York: Routledge.

Gilman, S. (2014). Gesundheit, Krankheit und Glaube: Der Streit um die Beschneidung. In F. Heimann-Jelinek & C. Kugelmann, (Eds.)*, Haut ab!: Haltungen zur rituellen Beschneidung, Jüdisches Museum Berlin* (pp. 119-129). Berlin: Wallstein.

Giordan, G. (2014). Introduction. In G. Giordan & E. Pace (Eds.), *Religious pluralism: Framing religious diversity in the contemporary world* (pp. 1-12). Cham, Heidelberg, New York, Dordrecht, London: Springer.

Gollaher, L. D. (2000). *Circumcision: A history of the world's most controversial surgery.* New York: Basic Books.

Greenfield, A. K. (2013). Cutting away religious freedom: The global and national debate surrounding male circumcision. *Rutgers Journal of Law and Religion, 15*(353), 361-363.

Heil, J., & Kramer, J. S. (Eds.). (2013). *Beschneidung: Das Zeichen des Bundes in der Kritik.* Berlin: Metropol Verlag.

Heimann-Jelinek, F., & Kugelmann, C. (2014). Haut ab!: Haltungen zur rituellen Beschneidung. In F. Heimann-Jelinek & C. Kugelmann (Eds.)*, Haut ab!: Haltungen zur rituellen Beschneidung, Jüdisches Museum Berlin* (pp. 19-26). Berlin: Wallstein.

Ilkilic, I. (2013, July 4). Inter-religious dialogue on matters of health. *Qantara.* Retrieved from https://en.qantara.de/content/interview-with-medical-ethicist-ilhan-ilkilic-inter-religious-dialogue-on-matters-of-health

Ilkilic, I. (2014). Islamische Aspekte der Beschneidung von minderjährigen Jungen. *Zeitschrift für medizisnche Ethik*, *60*, 63-72.

Jones, G. (2012, July 17). July German circumcision ban makes nation a 'laughing stock,' Angela Merkel says. *National Post.* Retrieved from http://news.nationalpost.com/news/german-circumcision-ban-makes-nation-a-laughing-stock-angela-merkel-says

Judd, R. (2007). *Contested rituals: Circumcision, kosher butchering, and Jewish political life in Germany.* Ithaca: Cornell University Press.

Kastoryano, R. (2002). *Negotiating identities: States and immigrants in France and Germany.* Princeton: Princeton University Press.

Kelek, N. (2006). Die verlorenen Söhne. *Plädoyer für die Befreiung des türkisch-muslimischen Mannes.* Köln: Kiepenheuer & Witsch.

Koenig, M. (2007). Europeanising the governance of religious diversity? An institutionalist account of Muslim struggles for public recognition. *Journal of Ethnic and Migration Studies*, *33*(6), 911-932.2

Kokin, D. S. (2014). "Der Bund, den Du an unserem Fleisch besiegelt hast:" Beschneidung in jüdischem Denken und jüdischer Praxis. In M. Langanke, A. Ruwe, & H. Theißen (Eds.), *Rituelle Beschneidung von Jungen: Interdisciplinäre Perspektiven* (pp. 99-112). Leipzig: Evangelische Verlagsanstalt.

Koopmans, R. (2013). Multiculturalism and immigration: A contested field in cross-national comparison. *Annual Review of Sociology*, *39*, 147-169.

Korteweg, A. C., & Yurdakul, G. (2014). *The headscarf debate: Conflict of belonging in national narratives.* Stanford: Stanford University Press.

Lang, D. P. (2013). Circumcision, sexual dysfunction and the child's best interests: Why the anatomical details matter. *Journal of Medical Ethics*, *39*(7), 429-431.

Laurence, J. (2001) (Re) constructing community in Berlin: Turks, Jews, and German responsibility. *German Politics & Society*, 22-61.

Lavi, S. (2009). Unequal rites: Jews, Muslims and the history of ritual slaughter in Germany. In J. Brunner & S. Lavi (Eds.), *Juden und Muslime in Deutschland.* Göttingen: Wallstein.

Lettinga, D., & Saharso, S. (2014). Outsiders within: Framing and regulation of headscarves in France, Germany and The Netherlands. *Social Inclusion*, *2*(3), 29-39.

Liedgens, P., & Eckert, K. (2015). Symposium zur Jungenbeschneidung, Hörsaalzentrum im Elisabeth-Krankenhaus Essen, 3 June.

Merkel, A. (2012, July 12). Umstrittene Rechtslage: Kanzlerin warnt vor Beschneidungsverbot. *Spiegel Online Politik.* Retrieved from http://www.spiegel.de/politik/deutschland/bundeskanzlerin-merkel-warnt-vor-beschneidungsverbot-a-844671.html

Merkel, A. (2012, July 17). Gesetzentwurf bis zum Herbst . *Frankfurter Allgemeine Zeitung (FAZ).* Retrieved from http://www.faz.net

Merkel, A. (2012, November 25). Merkel kritisiert Antisemitismus. *Frankfurter Allgemeine Zeitung (FAZ).* Retrieved from http://www.faz.net

Merkel, R. (2012, August 30). Die Haut eines Anderen. *Süddeutsche Zeitung (SZ).* Retrieved from http://www.sueddeutsche.de

Merkel, R., & Putzke, H. (2013). After Cologne: Male circumcision and the law. Parental right, religious liberty or criminal assault? *Journal of Medical Ethics, 39*(7), 444-449.

Münch, Peter. (2012, November 25). Streit um ein göttliches Gebot. *Süddeutsche Zeitung.* Retrieved from http://www.sueddeutsche.de

Öktem, K. (2013). *Signale aus der Mehrheitsgesellschaft. Auswirkungen der Beschneidungsdebatte und staatlicher Überwachung islamischer Organisationen auf Identitätsbildung und Integration in Deutschland.* Oxford: European Studies Centre, St. Antony's College. Retrieved from https://tezhamburg.files.wordpress.com/2013/09/signale-aus-der-mehrheitsgesellschaft.pdf

Özdemir, C. (2008). Kulturelle Unterschiede—Kleine Hindernisse. In C. Özdemir (Ed.), *Die Türkei: Politik, Religion, Kultur* (pp. 235-239), Weinheim, Basel: Beltz & Gelberg.

Peck, J. (1998). Turks and Jews: Comparing minorities in Germany after the Holocaust. In J. Peck (Ed.), *German cultures, foreign cultures: The politics of belonging* (pp. 1-16). Washington, DC: AICGS.

Putzke, H. (2008). *Criminal relevance of circumcising boys: A contribution to the limitation of consent in cases of care for the person of the child* (K. McLarren, Trans.). Retrieved from http://www.holmputzke.de/index.php/kontrovers/religioese-beschneidung

Schüklenk, U. (2012). Europe debates circumcision...but what about the child's best interests. *Bioethics, 26*(8), ii-iii.

Schwarze, T. (2012, October 1). Interview with R. Merkel: Ein kläglicher Gesetzentwurf. *Die Zeit*. Retrieved from http://www.zeit.de

Stehr, M. (2012, July 27). Unzumutbare Schmerzen. *Der Spiegel*. Retrieved from http://www.spiegel.de/spiegel/print/d-87482746.html

SZ. (2012, July 16). Schwerster Angriff auf jüdisches Leben seit dem Holocaust. *Süddeutsche Zeitung (SZ).* Retrieved from http://www.sueddeutsche.de

taz. (2012, August 21). Rabbiner will Medizinkurse. Retrieved from http://www.taz.de

Tosun, M. (2012, June 9). Sünnet Yapmayiz [We will not practice circumcision]. *Hürriyet*. Retrieved from http://www.hurriyet.com.tr/planet/20870182.asp

Vertovec, S., & Wessendorf, S. (2006). Cultural, religious and linguistic diversity in Europe: An overview of issues and trends. In R. Penninx (Ed.), *The dynamics of international migration and settlement in Europe* (pp. 171-199). Amsterdam: AUP.

Yurdakul, G. (2010). Juden und Türken in Deutschland: Integration von Immigranten, Politische Repräsentation und Minderheitenrechte. In G. Yurdakul & M. Bodemann, *Staatsbürgerschaft, Migration und Minderheiten: Inklusion und Ausgrenzungstragien im Vergleich* (pp. 127-160). Wiesbaden: Verlag Sozialwissenschaften.

Yurdakul, G. (2013). *Ritual Male Circumcision, Muslim women's headscarves, forced marriages: What are the limits of minority accommodation in Germany?* Paper presented at the Council for European Studies Conference, Amsterdam.

About the Author

Dr. Gökçe Yurdakul

Gökçe Yurdakul is Georg Simmel Professor of Diversity and Social Conflict at the Humboldt University in Berlin and the co-chair of the Department on Foundations of Migration at the Berlin Institute of Migration and Integration Research. Her most recent book is *The Headscarf debates: Conflict in national narratives* (2014, Stanford University Press, with Anna Korteweg). She is currently conducting research on *Contesting authorities over body politics: The religious/secular tension in Germany, Israel, and Turkey*, funded by the German-Israeli Foundation (2016–2018, co-investigators with Shai Lavi).

Perceived Accessibility of Public Transport as a Potential Indicator of Social Inclusion

Katrin Lättman *, Margareta Friman and Lars E. Olsson

SAMOT/CTF—Service Research Center & Department of Social and Psychological Studies, Karlstad University, 65188 Karlstad, Sweden; E-Mails: katrin.lattman@kau.se (K.L.), margareta.friman@kau.se (M.F.), lars.e.olsson@kau.se (L.E.O.)

* Corresponding author

Abstract

Perceived accessibility has been acknowledged as an important aspect of transport policy since the 70s. Nevertheless, very few empirical studies have been conducted in this field. When aiming to improve social inclusion, by making sustainable transport modes accessible to all, it is important to understand the factors driving perceived accessibility. Unlike conventional accessibility measures, perceived accessibility focuses on the perceived possibilities and ease of engaging in preferred activities using different transport modes. We define perceived accessibility in terms of how easy it is to live a satisfactory life with the help of the transport system, which is not necessarily the same thing as the objective standard of the system. According to previous research, perceived accessibility varies with the subjectively-rated quality of the mode of transport. Thus, improvements in quality (e.g. trip planning, comfort, or safety) increase the perceived accessibility and make life easier to live using the chosen mode of transport. This study (n=750) focuses on the perceived accessibility of public transport, captured using the *Perceived Accessibility Scale* PAC (Lättman, Olsson, & Friman, 2015). More specifically, this study aims to determine how level of quality affects the perceived accessibility in public transport. A Conditional Process Model shows that, in addition to quality, feeling safe and frequency of travel are important predictors of perceived accessibility. Furthermore, elderly and those in their thirties report a lower level of perceived accessibility to their day-to-day activities using public transport. The basic premise of this study is that subjective experiences may be as important as objective indicators when planning and designing for socially inclusive transport systems.

Keywords

perceived accessibility; public transport; social exclusion; social inclusion; subjective well-being; transport planning

Issue

This article is part of the issue "Transport Policy and Social Inclusion", edited by Miriam Ricci, Graham Parkhurst and Juliet Jain (University of the West of England, UK).

---

1. Introduction

Facing a future with ageing populations and an urging need for a sustainable development in transportation (Banister, 2008; United Nations, 2015), it now seems more important than ever to gather forces towards an inclusive sustainable transportation system that can offer high accessibility for all, including the disabled, those with physical or social impairments, or those who are not so young and able anymore.

It has been established that accessibility is positively connected to several travel outcomes, such as well-being (Parkhurst & Meek, 2014) and transport-related social inclusion (Farrington, 2007; Stanley, Stanley, Vella-Brodrick, & Currie, 2010) and that insufficient accessibility may cause social exclusion (Hui & Habib, 2014; Kenyon, 2011), proposing that accessibility is a key issue for research development on social inclusion and sustainable transport planning. Up until now however, measuring accessibility has been limited to objective measures such as travel time or distance, not capturing the perceived accessibility of individuals or certain groups of people, limiting the usefulness of the link between accessibility and social inclusion since the measured accessibility may not capture the reality (Curl, Nelson, & Anable, 2011). This gap in measuring accessibility has been pointed out by researchers for years, urging for the inclusion of subjective accessibility (Budd & Mumford, 2006; Curl et al., 2011; Farrington, 2007; Handy & Niemeier, 1997; Stanley & Vella-Brodrick, 2009; van Wee & Geurs, 2011), but up until now not much has been done. In 2015, we developed a quantifiable measurement for perceived accessibility in public transport, the Perceived Accessibility Scale (Lättman et al., 2015). Perceived accessibility is based on individual assessments of accessibility, rather than on objective estimates, and in the current study, the work is continued by further exploring perceived accessibility in relation to transport quality, safety, travel frequency, and age, looking for significant determinants.

1.1. Accessibility

A popular and well-used definition of accessibility is "the extent to which land-use and transport systems enable (groups of) individuals to reach activities or destinations by means of a (combination of) transport mode(s)." founded by Geurs and Ritsema van Eck (2001). As the definition implies, accessibility has conventionally been closely linked to the ability to move (e.g., mobility), and more specifically defined and operationalized through objective measurements such as travel time, distance to train station, or distance and travel time to a selection of destinations. This is risky, not only because of the lack of individual perspectives, but also as targeting increased mobility for certain groups of individuals in a society, may inadvertently decrease the mobility for other groups whose mobility-preferences we are not aware of (e.g. by moving bus-stops, changing time-tables) and they may experience social exclusion (Kenyon & Lyons, 2003). However, the focus in transport planning has of late shifted from mobility to accessibility (Halden, 2011; Preston & Rajé, 2007; Qviström, 2015) widening the scope of focus, but still not including individual or group perspectives. Individual characteristics are known to influence a person's level of access to transport modes in terms of needs, opportunities and abilities that set temporal-spatial constraints (e.g. age and physical condition) (Geurs & Van Wee, 2004). Budd and Mumford (2006) found several flaws in the common generalization that high (area) accessibility equals high individual accessibility; meaning that objective generalizations do not take into consideration awareness of opportunities, ability to use, personal relevance or interest.

Accessibility to important activities is influential for subjective wellbeing (De Vos, Schwanen, Van Acker, & Witlox, 2013; Olsson, Gärling, Ettema, Friman, & Fujii, 2013; Parkhurst & Meek, 2014). Not having full access to different travel modes may thus exclude people from various activities and lower their subjective wellbeing. Many researchers are aware of this link; however, looking past proposed solutions to reduce travel hardships with the aim of increasing accessibility in a cost-effective manner (Martens, 2012), or using objective determinants as the basis for accessibility evaluations (Bekiaris & Gaitanidou, 2012; Kryvobokov & Bouzouina, 2014; Lucas, 2012; van Wee & Geurs, 2011), we argue that, in order to improve social inclusion and wellbeing, we need to understand what drives perceived accessibility and use this knowledge to make it easier for people to be a part of society. Thus, perceived accessibility to social activities and friends cannot be evaluated using conventional accessibility measures, since these choices and routes are highly individual.

We define perceived accessibility in terms of *how easy it is to live a satisfactory life using the transport system* which includes accessibility while using the transport system per se, ease of getting to the transport system, and the perceived possibilities and ease to live the life one wants with help of the transport system. We argue that, what needs to be evaluated in order to improve accessibility is whether or not the travelers themselves (or potential travelers) perceive the transport system as accessible, and something they are able to benefit from, and also to explore what determines the perceived accessibility.

1.2. Social Inclusion and Accessibility

Preston and Rajé (2007), influenced by Sen (2000) established a conceptualization describing social exclusion as caused by an absence of access to social opportunities, rather than a lack of opportunities per se. In line with this work The Social Exclusion Unit (2004) has worked from the perspective that the main solution for transport-based social exclusion is accessibility planning. More specifically, they state that aiming for an increased accessibility to services and key locations by the transport services is essential in preventing social exclusion. Following this, work by Kenyon and Lyons (2003) and Currie and Stanley (2008) link social exclusion to a lack of access to social opportunities in the UK and Australia, respectively. Kenyon (2011, p. 764) more recently claims that "a lack of access to opportunities/social networks necessary for inclusion in the society can cause social exclusion". Research by Farrington and Farrington (2005), and Farrington (2007) conclude that greater accessibility is linked to greater social inclusion and social dimensions of sustainability. They also claim that by targeting accessibility we force transport planners in different areas to interact toward a common policy goal (Farrington & Farrington, 2005). More recently it has been established that people who experience the transport system as accessible also experience less social exclusion, and a key factor determining experienced accessibility is frequency of services (Hui & Habib, 2014). Another study has found positive links between public transport usage and social inclusion, "possibly suggesting that public transport is assisting people to be included" (Stanley et al., 2010, p. 283).

1.3. Quality

Since previous research has revealed relations between (some) public transport quality attributes and accessibility (Redman, Friman, Gärling, & Hartig, 2013) there is reason to believe that additional quality attributes also are important to accessibility. A large number of attributes have been proposed in attempting to define public transport quality, but most commonly used quality attributes in determining conventional accessibility are travel time (including waiting time and punctuality), distance and departures (Bates, Polak, Jones, & Cook, 2001; Friman, 2010; Hensher, Stopher, & Bullock, 2003). A recent literature review (Redman et al., 2013) revealed that reliability is a key quality attribute of public transport service, with frequency, fare prices, and speed also being important. Other studies have shown the importance of safety/security (de Oña, de Oña, Eboli, & Mazzulla, 2013; Friman & Gärling, 2001), the information given to travelers (de Oña et al., 2013), the system (with supply and reliability items) including comfort/design (dell'Olio, Ibeas, Cecín, & dell'Olio, 2011), and staff behavior (Friman & Fellesson, 2009) on transport quality.

More recently, researchers have begun to include safety aspects in their theories on individual accessibility, e.g. holistic safety-chains from origin to destination (Bekiaris & Gaitanidou, 2012) and women's fears while in the public transport environment (Loukaitou-Sideris, 2009). Safety refers to the emotional evaluations (feelings) of the individual (Redman et al., 2013), whereas most quality dimensions depend on cognitive evaluations.

It is generally held that we are able to affect up to 40 % of our own wellbeing, by participating in daily activities (Lyubomirsky, Sheldon, & Schkade, 2005). Unfortunately, not all of us have the ability to affect our own travel or our daily participation in activities due to insufficient accessibility, and this may lead to a form of seclusion that causes social exclusion. According to Currie and Stanley (2008) the mere risk of being socially excluded has a directly negative effect on subjective well-being. Social inclusion is dependent on the ability to use the transport system for social activities, as much as for getting to work. It is thus important to capture these aspects when measuring transport accessibility. Previous studies encompassing perceived accessibility have not been equipped with measures to quantify the results. The perceived accessibility scale (Lättman et al., 2015) was developed with the aim of capturing how easy it is to live a satisfactory life with the help of the chosen, or designated, travel mode. Without reliable measures of perceived accessibility, it is argued that evaluating and following up goals and visions regarding accessibility, from a user perspective, will be difficult, thus creating a broad and generalizable measure of perceived accessibility was needed in order to investigate or compare accessibility between different transport modes, between different groups of people, in different areas, for different purposes, or in different transport systems.

1.4. Aim and Hypotheses

In this study, we argue that the quality level of public transport creates prerequisites for possibilities and ease of engaging in preferred activities, and that the above-mentioned aspects—quality, safety, frequency of use, and age—affect perceived accessibility in public transport. By looking at transport service quality level in relation to perceived accessibility our hope is to reach an understanding of the driving factors of perceived accessibility. More specifically; we test the impact of perceived level of quality of the chosen transport mode, frequency of use, age and safety on perceived accessibility. We also propose that safety mediates (explains) some of the effect quality has on perceived accessibility, and that the effect of quality on perceived accessibility is moderated by (dependent on) frequency of use.

> **Hypothesis 1:** Perceived level of quality has a direct positive effect on perceived accessibility
> **Hypothesis 2a:** (Feelings of) safety has a direct positive effect on perceived accessibility
> **Hypothesis 2b:** The effect of quality on perceived accessibility is positively mediated by safety

The above hypotheses 1 and 2a are strengthened by a study (Lotfi & Koohsari, 2009) suggesting that a low level of perceived accessibility is due to people feeling unsafe and experiencing low quality in terms of comfort. We also believe that the effect of quality on perceived accessibility is positively mediated by the individual's feelings and perceptions of safety (2b). In other words we think that part of the relationship between perceived quality and perceived accessibility can be explained by safety.

It is furthermore hypothesized that frequency of use, as in how frequently the individual travels using the assessed transport mode, directly effects perceived accessibility (3a), but also moderates the effect of quality on perceived accessibility (3b). More specifically, it is suggested that more frequent travelers put more emphasis on aspects of quality, and the effect of quality on accessibility is higher for frequent travelers. This also implicitly indicates that the effect of quality on accessibility will be smaller in groups of less frequent travelers. Finally, we investigate whether age affects perceived accessibility proposing that age has a negative relationship with perceived accessibility, meaning that the older one gets, the lower the perceived accessibility, in line with previous research on age and accessibility (Sundling, Berglund, Nilsson, Emardson, & Pendrill, 2014).

Hypothesis 3a: Frequency of use has a direct positive effect on perceived accessibility
Hypothesis 3b: The effect of quality on perceived accessibility is moderated by (conditional on) frequency of use
Hypothesis 4: Age has a direct negative effect on perceived accessibility

In summary, this study will increase our knowledge of different aspects associated with perceived accessibility in public transport. Next section provides a description of the method and data used for analysis. The results of a conditional process model, applied in order to examine the proposed relations, will be discussed. Finally, we will draw some conclusions and discuss some avenues for future research.

2. Method

2.1. Participants

The data was collected in the City of Karlstad, a middle sized town in Sweden (90.000 inhabitants) on three occasions; June 2013, November 2013, and May 2014. Each data collection went on for three subsequent days, between 8.00 am and 5.00 pm approximately. The 750 participants were asked to complete a questionnaire while waiting for the bus, coming from the bus or sitting on the bus. People located in the town bus-transfer areas or on the bus at the time of the collection were asked to participate. The questionnaire was distributed on a clipboard and took approximately five minutes to complete. The participants were offered a lottery ticket with a chance of winning a 30 day bus pass. As this was the first approach to studying links between perceived quality occurring at different stages of travel (before, during), and perceived accessibility this initial data collection involved only bus-travelers. The participants were aged between 16 and 87, M = 27.60, SD = 13.47 (61 % women and 39 % men) the majority were on their way to or from work, school or social activities (visiting friends or family, shopping, sports etc.).

2.2. Survey and Instruments

The survey consisted of three sections. Part one included the quality attributes capturing the quality dimensions, part two included the perceived accessibility items, and part three included background data. The background data consisted of questions about frequency of travel by public transport (less than once a month, once a month, once a week, or daily), gender, and age.

2.2.1. The Perceived Accessibility Scale

The Perceived Accessibility Scale (PAC) is an aggregate measure of perceived accessibility (Lättman et al., 2015), developed for use in transportation. It is easy to use and distribute; due to its compactness and interpretable outcome, making it useful not only within research, but also as a tool on the policy and planning levels. The PAC consists of four items that measure the ease of travel ("It's easy to do [daily] activities with public transport"), the ability to live the life one wants ("If public transport was my only mode of travel, I'd be able to continue living the way I want"), and accessibility to activities ("It's possible to do the activities I prefer with public transport" and "Access to my preferred activities is satisfying with public transport"). These items capture the overall level of perceived accessibility on self-assessment scales, from 1–7 (1 = I disagree 7 = I completely agree) which are then indexed into an overall accessibility score, based on previous psychometric findings (Lättman et al., 2015). Cronbach's Alpha for this sample revealed a satisfying reliability of α = .88 (N=747).

2.2.2. Quality Dimensions

A set of items was devised to measure the perceived quality level of the public transport services (see Table 1). The items were intended to tap into different, but complementary, aspects of quality. For each item, the respondents checked a seven-point scale ranging from "very dissatisfied" (1) to "very satisfied" (7). They were asked to rate these items regarding trips with the local bus company (Karlstadbuss) in general, not just the ongoing trip. Given the relations between quality aspects, and when they occur during travel, we divided the items into four quality dimensions labeled; reliability/functionality, information, courtesy/simplicity (on board), and comfort. These sub-dimensions were established psychometrically sound by a confirmatory second-order factor analysis (χ^2= 149.69, df = 128, *p* = .092, NFI = .977, CFI = .996, RMSEA = .015) with quality as the main construct.

2.2.3. Safety

Safety represents the emotional evaluation the individual makes regarding aspects of safety connected to travel. Safety was measured using two reversed items, asking the participants to grade their level of security (I feel secure) on a 1–7 Likert-scale, and asking them to grade their usual level of distress or peace of mind (when traveling by public transport) on a continuum from 1–7 (I usually feel distressed–I usually feel calm). The correlation between the items was r = .31. We averaged the items to form a safety variable.

2.3. Conditional Process Modeling

In order to investigate the relation between overall quality level and perceived accessibility, with other predictor variables (age, frequency of use, and safety) that would also serve as a mediator (safety) and moderator (frequency of use) of the effect of quality, a conditional process model (Hayes, 2013) was deemed appropriate for the analyses. Conditional process modeling is used when the purpose is to estimate direct (X to Y) and indirect (intermediate through a mediator X-M-Y) pathways, and how the effect of one (or more) of these depend (is conditional) on another variable, the moderator (X-Y depends on W). For a more thorough description see Hayes (2013).

3. Results

As the aim of this study was to examine the relationships between level of quality and perceived accessibility, a quality index was initially created from the four quality dimensions described in section 2.2.2. A conditional process analysis (Hayes, 2013) was then run to determine the relations between quality index, frequency of travel, safety, age, and perceived accessibility, with safety as a proposed mediator of quality, and frequency as a proposed moderator of quality. As a final step, a cluster analysis was performed which looked more closely at the relationship between age and perceived accessibility. Table 2 provides descriptive statistics of all the included variables, while the results of the subsequent analyses follow below.

3.1. Quality-Index

In order to run a combined mediation and moderation analysis (see 2.3), a quality index had to be created from the four quality dimensions. A Principal Axis Factoring analysis (Warner, 2008) was used to determine whether the four quality dimensions described in section 2.2.2 are unidimensional (Byrne, 2010; Gorsuch, 1997). This analysis extracted one factor with an eigenvalue of 2.85, explaining 71.3 % of the variance in the factor. The Kaiser-Meyer-Olkin measure revealed a multiple KMO of .82, with all individual item KMO values above .80, putting the sampling adequacy well above the threshold of .5 (Field, 2013). The factor score coefficients were used to create the quality index in order to get a weighted relevance for the total score. A reliability analysis of the quality index revealed a satisfying Cronbach's alpha (α = .76), with no significant changes for item deletion. The factor loadings, factor score weights, and weighted relevance are presented in Table 3.

Table 1. Items measuring four dimensions of quality.

Reliability/Functionality	Information	Courtesy/Simplicity(on board)	Comfort
Travel time	Mobile app	Announcements	Air quality
(no. of) Departures	Info on homepage	Staff attitude/behavior	Cleanliness
Distance (to bus stop)	Info at bus-stop	Info on board	Lighting
Trip coordination		Boarding and exiting	Noise level
Payment options			(overall) Comfort
Punctuality			Seating

Table 2. Sample statistics, correlations, means (M) and standard deviation (SD) for each variable in the study.

Variable	1	2	3	4	5	6	7	M	SD
1. Age	---	---	---	---	---	---	---	27.60	13.47
2. Frequency	-.22*	---	---	---	---	---	---	2.61	0.68
3. Reliability/Functionality	.14*	-.04	---	---	---	---	---	26.52	5.26
4. Comfort	.17*	.04	.64*	---	---	---	---	26.83	5.99
5. Information	.05*	.00	.62*	.53*	---	---	---	12.30	2.77
6. Courtesy/ Simplicity (on board)	.21*	-.02	.66*	.67*	.59*	---	---	17.12	3.45
7. Safety	.03	.05	.56*	.61*	.46*	.54*	---	8.76	1.48
8. Perceived accessibility	-.07	.17*	.55*	.46*	.47*	.46*	.49*	5.12	1.34

Note: * p < .05.

3.2. Conditional Process Model

In order to examine the proposed relations, a conditional process model was used (described in 2.3). The analysis included proposed mediation of quality on perceived accessibility through safety and proposed moderation through frequency of use, using PROCESS model 5 (Hayes, 2013). The model proved significant (R^2= .377; $F^{(5,636)}$ = 79.93 $p < .001$) and showed that quality, age, and trip frequency predict perceived accessibility (PAC) (.050, -.012, and .273 respectively). The effect of quality on perceived accessibility is positively mediated by safety (the safer an individual feels—the higher their PAC score) (see Figure 1).

However, contrary to our hypothesis, the impact of quality on perceived accessibility is not moderated by frequency, suggesting that the importance of quality in predicting perceived accessibility is not conditional on frequency of use.

3.3. Cluster Analysis

The conditional process model confirmed age as a negative predictor of perceived accessibility; however, a plot of the result indicated a curvilinear relationship. A K-means cluster analysis was performed aimed at identifying potential subgroups in the data, looking at age and level of PAC. The clusters were calculated using an iterative process, searching for representative means in the data and assigning cases to the nearest mean.

Table 3. Factor loadings, factor score weights, and weighted relevance for the four quality dimensions* (N = 750).

Quality dimensions	Factor loadings	Factor score weights	Weighted relevance in %	α if item deleted
Reliability/Functionality	.825	.337	32 %	.61
Courtesy/Simplicity	.827	.337	32 %	.70
Comfort	.778	.242	21 %	.66
Information	.714	.180	15 %	.77

Note: * Factor loadings = The extent to which the item measurements are related to the latent construct. Factor score weights = How much each dimension affects the factor score.

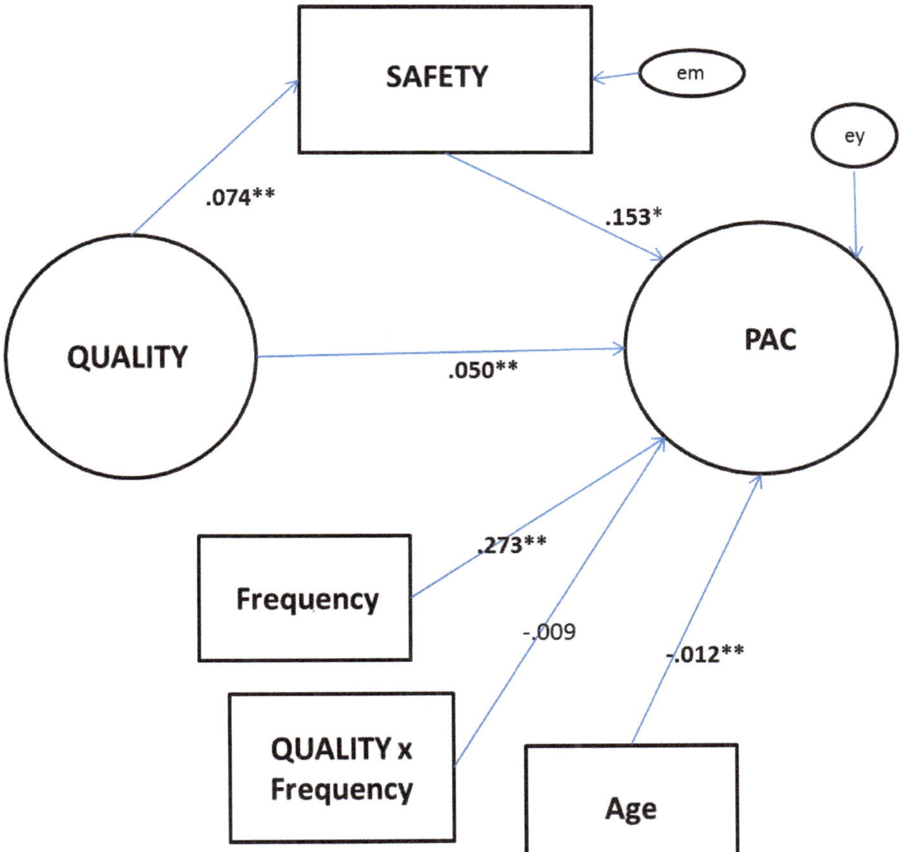

Figure 1. Conditional Process model of the effect of Quality, Safety, Frequency and Age on Perceived accessibility (PAC). (N=642). Note: *p <.005 **p <.001 (ey and em represent measurement error in the y (dependent) and m (mediating) variables, respectively).

Table 4. Classification of bus travelers by mean age and level of PAC (mean).

	Cluster 1 (n=473, 72%)	Cluster 2 (n=85, 13%)	Cluster 3 (n=73, 11%)	Cluster 4 (n=22, 3.5%)	ANOVA F	*p*
Age	21	34	52	68	2358.93	<.001
Perceived accessibility	5.21	4.77	5.09	4.82	2.95	.023

This process is repeated until only small differences occur when transferring cases between clusters, indicating a good fit. Several K-means analyses were run, in order to determine the preferred number of clusters, resulting in a model of 4 clusters, as displayed in Table 4. Individuals around the age of 34, and elderly (around 68), reported significantly lower levels of perceived accessibility than people in their twenties and fifties. No gender differences were observed when comparing the clusters.

4. Discussion

As hypothesized, our findings indicate that quality is important for perceived accessibility. Overall quality positively predicted perceived accessibility, which suggests that an increase in perceived quality will lead the users to perceive the transport mode as being more accessible, in turn making it easier for them to live the life they want, creating prerequisites for social inclusion. However, the results also show that some quality dimensions seem to contribute more than others. Specifically two quality dimensions appeared to be more important. Distance to bus stops, the availability of transport at convenient times, and flexibility and ease when buying tickets combine to make the first highly ranked dimension (Reliability/functionality) with staff attitudes and behavior, ease of getting on and off vehicles, announcements on board, and information available during travel being included in the second dimension (Courtesy/simplicity). These dimensions together make up for 64% of the weighted importance in the overall quality variable, and considering the close link between accessibility and social inclusion (Kenyon, 2011), these findings have implications for which service quality aspects that may be more important for building an inclusive sustainable transport system.

As expected, feeling safe is also important for perceived accessibility. Our findings show that perceived quality positively affects our feelings of safety, the higher the perceived quality the higher perceived safety, and that safety explains some of the effect perceived quality has on perceived accessibility. Safety also has a direct effect on perceived accessibility, not affected by perceived quality. These results imply that safety is an important predictor of perceived accessibility, both in its own right, but also as an intermediate mechanism for other accessibility determinants, such as quality dimension. This finding reminds us that it may be important not to confuse feelings of safety with other, cognitive evaluations, of the quality of the transport mode. The outcomes are in line with studies of perceived satisfaction which determine that an experience contains both emotional and cognitive evaluations (Friman, Fujii, Ettema, Gärling, & Olsson, 2013) and also a study by Lotfi and Koohsari (2009) successfully separating safety from quality and linking these to perceived accessibility.

The proposed conditional relationship was not supported in the analysis, suggesting that the importance of quality when predicting perceived accessibility is not conditional on frequency of travel. This may be good news, since an increase in quality would affect the levels of perceived accessibility for all passengers, not only those who travel frequently. However, frequency of use itself influences perceived accessibility, indicating that more frequent users perceive the chosen transport mode as more accessible than those who travel less often.

Our results further indicate that age is important for perceived accessibility. In line with previous research on accessibility and social exclusion, we had hypothesized that elderly would experience lower levels of perceived accessibility, However, two groups turned out to experience a lower level of accessibility, elderly and people in their thirties. Relying on our definition of perceived accessibility this outcome can be explained by different quantities, and types of, activities. A Swedish study shows that the elderly (aged 58–94) experience difficulties with long distances to bus stops, stairs and level-differences at interchanges, timetables that are not synchronized, and departure times that are not suitable for their daily activities (Berg & Levin, 2011). The other age group experiencing a low level of perceived accessibility belongs to a phase in life which is closely linked to parenting. Parenthood means a totally different activity pattern for most people, characterized by taking children to school and leisure activities. This group experiences the lowest level of perceived accessibility, an unexpected and important finding considering the ongoing development towards sustainable transport.

Another inference we draw is that the instrument for determining perceived accessibility, and how easy it is to live one's life with the help of public transport, also has the ability to differentiate between various groups in society. Conversely, the preconditions, as in the objective accessibility, are the same for all the participants in our study.

4.1. Conclusions

The main point emerging from our analyses is that perceived quality of the transport mode is an important driver of perceived accessibility along with safety, frequency of use, and age. Knowledge of the drivers of perceived accessibility will be useful when planning for the inclusive and sustainable transport system we will be dependent on in the near future.

Another conclusion is that the instrument for determining perceived accessibility also has the ability to differentiate between groups. This point out its usefulness compared to objective measurements of accessibility, where no consideration is given to individual differences within, for instance, a certain neighborhood. This also strengthens the given need of a complementary, subjective measure of accessibility not only for accessibility research per se, but it may also be useful for discovering groups of people in risk of social exclusion. For instance, our results suggest that it is not only the elderly that report lower levels of perceived accessibility, but rather, people in their thirties seem to be the group experiencing the lowest perceived accessibility in public transport, indicating that if public transport was the only alternative for this group they could be a target for social exclusion.

Our findings of the mediating role of safety in the relationship between perceived quality and perceived accessibility strengthens the role of emotional evaluations as intermediate mechanisms between input and outcome (as a part of an experience). In future studies on perceived accessibility, the emotional aspects ought to be highlighted in order for researchers to determine how important they are in this area.

4.2. Policy Implications

Usable and comparable methods are sought in order to boost policy progress. The quantifiable operationalization of perceived accessibility paves the way for social inclusion policy integration on multiple levels since it will not discriminate against certain groups if we use it for a representative or random sample of the population. The leap toward actually using knowledge of social research in transport planning becomes shorter when our ability to evaluate accessibility improves. We argue that, by means of listening to those who use the system, perceived accessibility can help us improve social inclusion and subjective well-being. However, we need to examine accessibility further in order to explain what drives it and how it differentiates between groups. Also, we need to compare the results of perceived accessibility with accessibility as measured by objective measures, to search for discrepancies and areas where accessibility needs improvements in order to minimize perceived social exclusion. There are a number of variables that were not measured in this study, but still have the potential to be important drivers of perceived accessibility, and thus indirectly also of social inclusion. Previous research mentions, for instance, costs (fares), socioeconomic status, and area of residence.

The findings of the present and other studies (Lotfi & Koohsari, 2009), e.g. that quality and feelings of safety have measurable effects on perceived accessibility, should be a reminder that subjective experiences may be as important as objective indicators when planning and designing socially inclusive transport systems. For many people, being able to live the life they want, e.g. experiencing ease of doing daily activities and having access to preferred activities, may be equally important for social inclusion. This insight is particularly significant to convey to the policy makers who are responsible for providing an attractive and accessible transport system.

4.3. Future Research

This research has investigated the role of perceived quality of a certain transport mode (bus) in the experience of actual travelers, on perceived accessibility. It is reasonable to assume that greater understanding will be reached when we can investigate perceived accessibility from the experience of non-travelers, and within other sustainable travel modes, or combinations of travel modes. An interesting approach would be comparative studies on perceived accessibility between different areas with different level of objective accessibility, between different groups of people or between cultures. Especially interesting is the unexpected findings that people in their thirties experience lower accessibility than other groups of users, even the elderly. Another approach with implications for social inclusion would be to compare our measure of perceived accessibility to (other) measures of social inclusion or social exclusion.

Acknowledgements

Financial support was obtained through grant 2014-05335 from the Swedish Governmental Agency for Innovation Systems.

Conflict of Interests

The authors declare no conflict of interests.

References

Banister, D. (2008). The sustainable mobility paradigm. *Transport Policy*, *15*(2), 73-80.

Bates, J., Polak, J., Jones, P., & Cook, A. (2001). The valuation of reliability for personal travel. *Transportation Research Part E: Logistics and Transportation Review*, *37*(2), 191-229.

Bekiaris, E., & Gaitanidou, E. (2012). Research roadmap towards an accessible public transport system for all. *Transport Research Arena 2012, 48,* 1274-1283. doi:10.1016/j.sbspro.2012.06.1103

Berg, J., & Levin, L. (2011). *Äldres vardagliga resor: Val av färdmedel och erfarenheter av kollektivtrafik*. Linköping, Sweden, VTI.

Budd, J. W., & Mumford, K. A. (2006). Family-friendly work practices in britain: Availability and perceived accessibility. *Human Resource Management, 45*(1), 23-42. doi:10.1002/hrm.20091

Byrne, B. M. (2010). *Structural equation modeling with AMOS* (2nd ed.). London: Routledge.

Curl, A., Nelson, J. D., & Anable, J. (2011). Does accessibility planning address what matters? A review of current practice and practitioner perspectives. *Research in Transportation Business & Management, 2,* 3-11.

Currie, G., & Stanley, J. (2008). Investigating links between social capital and public transport. *Transport Reviews, 28*(4), 529-547.

de Oña, J., de Oña, R., Eboli, L., & Mazzulla, G. (2013). Perceived service quality in bus transit service: A structural equation approach. *Transport Policy, 29,* 219-226. doi:http://dx.doi.org/10.1016/j.tranpol.2013.07.001

De Vos, J., Schwanen, T., Van Acker, V., & Witlox, F. (2013). Travel and subjective well-being: A focus on findings, methods and future research needs. *Transport Reviews, 33*(4), 421-442. doi:10.1080/01441647.2013.815665

dell'Olio, L., Ibeas, A., Cecín, P., & dell'Olio, F. (2011). Willingness to pay for improving service quality in a multimodal area. *Transportation Research Part C: Emerging Technologies, 19*(6), 1060-1070.

Farrington, J. (2007). The new narrative of accessibility: Its potential contribution to discourses in (transport) geography. *Journal of Transport Geography, 15*(5), 319-330. doi:10.1016/j.trangeo.2006.11.007

Farrington, J., & Farrington, C. (2005). Rural accessibility, social inclusion and social justice: Towards conceptualisation. *Journal of Transport Geography, 13*(1), 1-12. doi:10.1016/j.jtrangeo.2004.10.002

Field, A. (2013). *Discovering statistics using IBM SPSS statistics*. London: Sage Publications.

Friman, M. (2010). Affective dimensions of the waiting experience. *Transportation Research Part F: Traffic Psychology and Behaviour, 13*(3), 197-205. doi: http://dx.doi.org.bibproxy.kau.se:2048/10.1016/j.trf.2010.04.006

Friman, M., & Fellesson, M. (2009). Service supply and customer satisfaction in public transportation: The quality paradox. *Journal of Public Transportation, 12*(4), 4.

Friman, M., Fujii, S., Ettema, D., Gärling, T., & Olsson, L. E. (2013). Psychometric analysis of the satisfaction with travel scale. *Transportation Research Part A: Policy and Practice, 48,* 132-145.

Friman, M., & Gärling, T. (2001). Frequency of negative critical incidents and satisfaction with public transport services. II. *Journal of Retailing and Consumer Services, 8*(2), 105-114.

Geurs, K., & Ritsema van Eck, J. (2001). Accessibility measures: Review and applications. Evaluation of accessibility impacts of land-use transportation scenarios, and related social and economic impact. Utrecht, the Netherlands, RIVM.

Geurs, K., & Van Wee, B. (2004). Accessibility evaluation of land-use and transport strategies: Review and research directions. *Journal of Transport Geography, 12*(2), 127-140.

Gorsuch, R. L. (1997). Exploratory factor analysis: Its role in item analysis. *Journal of Personality Assessment, 68*(3), 532-560.

Halden, D. (2011). The use and abuse of accessibility measures in UK passenger transport planning. *Research in Transportation Business and Management, 2,* 12-19. doi:10.1016/j.rtbm.2011.05.001

Handy, S. L., & Niemeier, D. A. (1997). Measuring accessibility: An exploration of issues and alternatives. *Environment and Planning A, 29*(7), 1175-1194.

Hayes, A. F. (2013). *Introduction to mediation, moderation, and conditional process analysis: A regression-based approach.* New York, USA: Guilford Press.

Hensher, D. A., Stopher, P., & Bullock, P. (2003). Service quality: Developing a service quality index in the provision of commercial bus contracts. *Transportation Research Part A: Policy and Practice, 37*(6), 499-517.

Hui, V., & Habib, K. N. (2014). An investigation of transport-related social exclusion of the at-risk community (homeless people) in Toronto, Canada. Paper presented at the *Transportation Research Board 93rd Annual Meeting,* Washington DC.

Kenyon, S. (2011). Transport and social exclusion: Access to higher education in the UK policy context. *Journal of Transport Geography, 19*(4), 763-771.

Kenyon, S., & Lyons, G. (2003). The value of integrated multimodal traveller information and its potential contribution to modal change. *Transportation Research Part F: Traffic Psychology and Behaviour, 6*(1), 1-21. doi:http://dx.doi.org/10.1016/S1369-8478(02)00035-9

Kryvobokov, M., & Bouzouina, L. (2014). Willingness to pay for accessibility under the conditions of residential segregation. *International Journal of Strategic Property Management, 18*(2), 101-115.

Lättman, K., Olsson, L., E, & Friman, M. (2015). *Development and test of the perceived accessibility scale (PAC) in public transport.* Manuscript submitted for publication.

Lotfi, S., & Koohsari, M. J. (2009). Analyzing accessibility dimension of urban quality of life: Where urban designers face duality between subjective and objective reading of place. *Social Indicators Research, 94*(3), 417-435.

Loukaitou-Sideris, A. (2009). *How to ease women's fear of transportation environments: Case studies and best practices.* (No. FHWA-CA-MTI-09-2611).

Lucas, K. (2012). Transport and social exclusion: Where are we now? *Transport Policy, 20,* 105-113.

Lyubomirsky, S., Sheldon, K. M., & Schkade, D. (2005). Pursuing happiness: The architecture of sustainable change. *Review of General Psychology, 9*(2), 111-153.

Martens, K. (2012). *Priority setting for an inclusive transportation system.* Paper presented at the *92th Annual Meeting Transportation Research Board,* Washington DC.

Olsson, L. E., Gärling, T., Ettema, D., Friman, M., & Fujii, S. (2013). Happiness and satisfaction with work commute. *Social Indicators Research, 111*(1), 255-263. doi:10.1007/s11205-012-0003-2

Parkhurst, G., & Meek, S. (2014). The effectiveness of park-and-ride as a policy measure for more sustainable mobility. *Transport and sustainability, 5(5),* 185-211. doi:10.1108/S2044-994120140000005020

Preston, J., & Rajé, F. (2007). Accessibility, mobility and transport-related social exclusion. *Journal of Transport Geography, 15*(3), 151-160. doi:10.1016/j.jtrangeo.2006.05.002

Qviström, M. (2015). Putting accessibility in place: A relational reading of accessibility in policies for transit-oriented development. *Geoforum, 58,* 166-173.

Redman, L., Friman, M., Gärling, T., & Hartig, T. (2013). Quality attributes of public transport that attract car users: A research review. *Transport Policy, 25,* 119-127.

Sen, A. (2000). *Social exclusion: Concept, application, and scrutiny.* (Social Development Papers No. 1). Manila, Philippines: Asian Development Bank.

Stanley, J., Stanley, J., Vella-Brodrick, D., & Currie, G. (2010). The place of transport in facilitating social inclusion via the mediating influence of social capital. *Research in Transportation Economics, 29*(1), 280-286.

Stanley, J., & Vella-Brodrick, D. (2009). The usefulness of social exclusion to inform social policy in transport. *Transport Policy, 16*(3), 90-96. doi:10.1016/j.tranpol.2009.02.003

Sundling, C., Berglund, B., Nilsson, M. E., Emardson, R., & Pendrill, L. R. (2014). Overall accessibility to traveling by rail for the elderly with and without functional limitations: The whole-trip perspective. *International Journal of Environmental Research and Public Health, 11*(12), 12938-12968.

The Social Exclusion Unit. (2004). *Making the connections: transport and social exclusion.* (Final report). London: ODPM Publications.

United Nations. (2015). Adoption of the paris agreement (FCCC/CP/2015/L.9/rev. 1). Paris: United Nations.

van Wee, B., & Geurs, K. (2011). Discussing equity and social exclusion in accessibility evaluations. *European Journal of Transport and Infrastructure Research, 11*(4), 350-367.

Warner, R. M. (2008). *Applied statistics, from bivariate through multivariate techniques.* Los Angeles: Sage Publications Ltd.

About the Authors

Katrin Lättman is a PhD student in psychology at Karlstad University since 2014. She is a part of the Service and Market Oriented Transport Research Group (SAMOT) at the multidisciplinary Service Research Center (CTF) in Karlstad. Katrin's thesis focuses on introducing and exploring perceived accessibility and related social outcomes in sustainable transport.

Margareta Friman is professor in psychology and director of the Service and Market Oriented Transport Research Group (SAMOT), Karlstad University, Sweden. Her research focus on satisfaction with travel, service quality, soft transport policy measures, and wellbeing. Her articles have been published in international journals in psychology, environmental studies, economics, and transportation. She is associate editor for the Frontiers in Psychology´s section on environmental psychology.

Lars E. Olsson graduated in 2007 from Göteborg University with a Ph.D. in Psychology of decision making. He is now Associate Professor of Psychology at Karlstad University, Sweden. Lars has published research in the areas of sustainability, environmental behavior, consumer experiences, accessibility, travel behavior and well-being. His articles have been published in international journals in psychology, environmental studies, economics, and transportation.

12

The Design of Migrant Integration Policies in Spain: Discourses and Social Actors

Belén Fernández-Suárez

Department of Sociology, University of A Coruña, 15071 A Coruña, Spain; E-Mail: belenfernandez@udc.es

Abstract

Spain is one of the countries with the lowest social spending within the EU-15, and its welfare state has developed later and with less intensity. At the end of the 20th century, Spain became an immigration country, reaching 5.7 million immigrants in 2011. This article explores how the definition of migrant 'integration' is based more on a concept of universal rights and social cohesion by the main actors (political parties, trade unions, third sector organizations and immigrant associations) than on a notion of a cultural type. We will also analyze how the influence of European policies and restrictive liberalism have led to the implementation of programmes which aim to make civic integration compulsory for the renewal of residence and work permits. The empirical evidence for this article stems from 60 qualitative interviews with social actors in migrant integration policies during 2010 and 2011. The impact of the economic crisis on the foreign population, especially regarding its position in the labor market, will also be considered, explaining the reduction of specific and general policies targeting the migrant population. This cut in social spending has involved a deinstitutionalization of this particular policy field.

Keywords

actors; culture; discourse; immigration; institutionalization; integration; policies; political parties; Spain

Issue

This article is part of the issue "International Migration and Ethnic Integration", edited by Yaojun Li (University of Manchester, UK) and Anthony Heath (University of Oxford, UK).

---

1. Introduction

In this article, we will analyze how various actors, mainly political parties, have defined their vision for the *integration* of the foreign population. But we will also comment on the vision that the different actors involved have for the implementation of these specific immigrant integration policies. These policies directed at the foreign population in Spain are characterised by two factors: a) their strong decentralization, which assigns to various government levels (state, autonomies and municipalities) a degree of power in the implementation of such measures; and b) the substantial number of actors taking part in the implementation, deliberation and creation of such specific policies (political parties, governments, specialists in the various public administrations, trade unions, third sector organizations and the immigrant associations themselves). The analysis shows that there is a vaguely defined idea for the term 'integration' (Chari & Sandell, 2011, p. 146), which tends to be rooted in the social rights field rather than the cultural rights field.

At the end of the 20th century, Spain became an immigration country, reaching 5.7 million immigrants in 2011 (Arango, 2000, pp. 256–258; Fokkema & Haas, 2015, pp. 4–5; López-Sala, 2013, pp. 40–45). The economic growth that Spain experienced between 2000 and 2007 led to a widening of the labor market, along with a demand for intensive manpower in sectors such as construction and services with a low added value, and even in part-time jobs (Muñoz-Comet, 2016, p. 546). This need for manpower was largely satisfied by the arrival of immigrants (Mahía Casado, 2010, p. 10). The annual gross domestic product grew by an average of 3.4 points between the years 2000 and 2007, with immigration being responsible for 40% of that increase (Fundación Ideas, 2011, pp. 58–59, 83).

In Spain, at the onset of the 2008 economic crisis, there were 20.6 million people working. Of these, foreigner immigrant workers made up 13.8 percent of the total; almost 2.9 million workers. Following the reduction of the labor market in 2016, the working population rose to 18.3 million people, of whom 10.8 percent were of foreign nationality, amounting to nearly 2 million foreign workers (Labor Force Survey, 2016). Ultimately, this period saw the disappearance of 2.3 million employed people, of which 876.4 were foreign workers, that is, 37.3 percent of working people who lost their job in this period were foreigners (Labor Force Survey, 2016). Unemployment rates for the foreign active population are about 20.5 percent in 2016—based on data available for the second third of the year. The most significant change in this period was the unemployment rates among the Spanish population, which was at 18.8 percent in 2016. Understandably, differences between nationals and foreigners in the labor market are affected by variables such as gender, country of birth, educational level and social class, along with the tendency to prefer certain nationalities over others, for example, in the case of immigration from Latin American countries (Amuedo-Dorantes & De la Rica, 2007, pp. 263–267).

Prior to the crisis, immigration was perceived by nationals to be a temporary necessity, a labor need, but in the end, it came to be perceived as being a burden for an ungenerous Welfare State. Spaniards stratified their migration preferences according to cultural proximity and religion (Cook-Martín & Viladrich, 2009, pp. 155–161). Latin American migration became the most preferred, followed by migration from the EU-28 and, finally migration from Sub-Saharan nations, with Moroccan immigration being the least accepted of them all.

Spain is one of the countries with the lowest social spending within the EU-15 and its welfare state developed later and with less intensity (Arriba & Moreno, 2005, pp. 110–111; Rhodes, 1996, pp. 5–8; Sarasa & Moreno, 1995, pp. 26–28). In the case of Spain, joining the European Union in 1986 and the inclusion of immigrant rights in the political agenda of extreme left parties were the factors that led to the first aliens act. In 1994, the first state plan for the social integration of immigrants by the Ministry of Social Affairs was in the hands of a socialist government, a plan that established a set of administrative measures and proposals for the care of migrants.

The arrival of substantial flows of immigrants, starting from the year 2000, justified to a great extent the increase in measures specifically aimed at the immigrant population. In 2001, with a conservative government, the second immigration plan was approved, under the name Plan GRECO[1] and marked by a vision of immigration as border control and integration as assimilation (Gil Araujo, 2002, 2010, p. 106).

Since 2004, there has been an institutionalization process of this specific public policy. This has involved a consolidation of this area in the political agenda (in the state, autonomous communities and municipalities), its stable presence in the parliamentary political discourse, a specialization in the management and implementation of this type of sector policy and, eventually, an extension of the responsibility of the implementation of these policies to various social actors throughout virtually all public administrations. In the years preceding the crisis, at a time when economic prospects were good and the government was in the hands of the social democrats between 2004 and 2008, there was an increase in social policy expenditure typical of the Welfare State, along with the development of specific policies for gender equality, youth, and the integration of foreigners.

The debate over the integration model for immigrants in Spain started in the late nineties and the beginning of the first decade of this century, when Europe abandoned both the assimilationist and the multiculturalist models. At that time, our political class seemed to be seeking a middle way between these two choices or, at least that is how the notion of *interculturality* that got conservative and left-wing political forces to work together, was perceived. This proposal continued to evolve, and the variety of forces taking part gradually adopted more reactive stances, under the influence of European trends, which were not very keen recognising the rights of immigrant people, favouring instead a restrictive liberalism, which enforces *civic integration* programmes aimed at the learning of language and values (Goodman, 2010, pp. 757–763, 2014; Guiraudon, 2008; Jacobs & Rea, 2007, pp. 270–274; Triadafilopoulos, 2011, pp. 865–890).

The following sections describe the methodology of this research, the main results, and finally, some brief conclusions regarding the policies for immigrant integration in Spain.

2. Methodology

This publication is based on data collected using qualitative methodology, which included in-depth interviews with key informants, as well as the revision of documents from the various social and political actors (programmes, regulations, memorandums, websites, leaflets, press releases, published news stories, etc.).

The interview technique was based upon a method expounded by Lewis A. Dexter in his classic work *Elite and Specialized Interviewing* (1970) for four main reasons. Political and professional elites: 1) have busy schedules; 2) hold senior roles in their field, are considered experts, and as such, they like being the centre of attention. 3) Political and professional elites hold privileged, first-hand information and employing a technique which might compromise their treatment of such data might prevent them from publicly sharing it. Finally, 4) the interviewees were allowed to direct the course of the interview towards topics they considered more relevant. This made the inter-

[1] The Global Programme for the Regulation and Coordination of Aliens and Immigration, known as Plan GRECO, was passed on 17 April, 2001. Please see https://www.boe.es/boe/dias/2001/04/27/pdfs/A15323-15343.pdf

viewees more comfortable and lead to better empirical evidence being produced (Dexter, 1970, pp. 48–50).

The total number of in-depth interviews was 60: 22 of which were conducted with representatives of political parties; 14 of these interviews involved decision makers in the state and autonomous community governments; 4 interviews were with trade union decision makers; 10 were with the main third-sector organizations involved with foreigners; and another 10 were with immigrant associations with a wide presence in great part of the state territory. Of these, 23 interviews took place at the national level: 14 in Catalonia, 13 in Madrid and 9 in Andalucia. Fieldwork was conducted between 2010 and 2011 (see Table 1).

The following 3 characteristics led me to choose Catalonia, Madrid and Andalucia: a) they are 3 of the 4 regions in Spain with the highest concentration of foreign population; b) the three regional administrations have a substantial track record of addressing their needs; and c) their regional governments were in the hands of different political parties: Madrid was ruled by the conservative Popular Party, in Andalucia the progressive Spanish Socialist Workers' Party was in power, and finally Catalonia had a government made up of socialists, environmentalists and left-wing nationalists.

The interview sample was chosen to be representative, and so included political parties represented in the State government and in regional parliaments, majority trade unions or NGOs and immigration associations which were present in State and/or regional participation fórums. Also, in the case of immigrant associations, the key factor was that they were representative of the various national groups.

These interviews were transcribed in their entirety and subjected to a discourse analysis, which focused on the topics relevant for this study, namely: integration, policies, assimilation, rights, and cultural rights.

3. Discussion

3.1. The European Influence (and its Resistances) on the (Cultural) Integration Model of the Foreign Population

Criticism towards multiculturalism as an option for immigrant integration, based on its essentialist vision of culture and the risk of the fragmentation of society, has become a prevailing discourse among conservative political forces, also being adopted by traditional left-wing parties across Europe (Huntington, 1996; Joppke, 2004, pp. 242–247; Sartori, 2001). The fall of multiculturalism has made most member states of the European Union return to assimilationist stands and it has also led to the withdrawal of so-called multicultural policies (Faist, 2009, pp. 174–177; Joppke, 2004, pp. 243–248; Meer & Moddod, 2012, pp. 185–191).

When discussing multiculturalism, as it is linked to immigration, there are additional dimensions to consider: a) its philosophical proposal; and b) the actual *multicultural* policies that were implemented in the European states. These aspects are interrelated, but sometimes it appears that political discourses adopt the (diverse) 'philosophical' approach to multiculturalism—and, by association, to cultural relativism without distinctions—rather than addressing specific global 'policies' designed to foster the settlement of the foreign population.

The new assimilationist policies emerging towards the end of the 20th century are defined by the mandatory nature of civic integration for foreigners, where such integration can be measured as an effort to learn the language, the culture, the rules of social cohesion, in terms of the well-known *immigrant integration contracts* (Guiraudon, 2008; Jacobs & Rea, 2007, pp. 272–277; Triadafilopoulos, 2011, pp. 863–865; Wallace Goodman, 2010, pp. 760–764, 2014). Spain has not escaped this assimilationist twist, but its take on such contracts has remained in the category of 'willingness' to enrol in such courses when other criteria to renew residence and work permits are not met.

Such political measures call into question two paradigms within liberal democracies: the sovereignty of nation states over their interior politics; and the self-perception of liberal societies as institutions that can not only guarantee fundamental rights but also encourage the spreading of new rights to all citizens or to new sectors of the population (Freeman, 2003; Joppke, 2007, pp. 5–9; Loch, 2014, pp. 625–628; Triadafilopoulos, 2011, pp. 869–875).

The weakening of national sovereignty of states gives way to a greater geostrategic influence in the writing of policies and their design, resulting in a convergence

Table 1. Typological grid of qualitative interviews conducted in this research (2009–2010). Source: author's compilation.

	Spanish State	Catalonia	Madrid	Andalucia	Total
Political Parties	10	6	3	3	22
Immigration Decision Makers	4	4	5	1	14
Trade Union	1	1	1	1	4
NGOs	4	2	2	2	10
Immigrant Associations	4	2	2	2	10
Total	23	15	13	9	60

of discourses and in the type of similar responses in the various nation states (Freeman, 2003; Joppke, 2007, pp. 6–8; Loch, 2014, pp. 626–629). European policies for immigrant integration have been marked by the *modus operandi* of the *open method of coordination*, which respects the sovereignty of member states in their territory but tries to reach a consensus in discourses and policies for each particular area (Caviedes, 2004, pp. 290–294; Jacobs & Rea, 2007, pp. 268–272).

Liberal states are questioned for their role as institutions capable of expanding and granting rights, paving the way for a more restrictive liberalism that is ready to defend the values that they see as central to a society, reacting with coercive use of state power to the changes brought on by the rise of diversity in their societies (Triadafilopoulos, 2011, pp. 870–874). This shift involves an unprecedented attack on 'multiculturalist' policies. The reasons behind these new policies with such a strong assimilationist tendency are complex. We could talk about a loss of the economic and political hegemony of *western* societies which leads to breaching the political consensus (crises in the political party system with the emergence of populist far right forces), social factors (weakening of the Welfare State), and even cultural ones (diversity in our societies).

The alternative to multiculturalism in the field of cultural pluralism is the intercultural approach. This option seeks to counterbalance the rise of political xenophobia in Europe through the greater representation of parties that oppose immigration and assimilationism as the dominating model (Kymlicka, 2012, pp. 212–214). The accent on this policy lies in a further search for interaction and dialogue in the understanding that integration is a process experienced within each individual (Meer & Moddod, 2012, pp. 182–187).

The approval of the Common Basic Principles in 2005[2] was a turning point, giving rise to integration policies in the European Union countries which aimed to improve integration by stating that, for immigrants, "A basic knowledge of the language, the history and the institutions of the society is essential for integration". Such principles have been fully adopted in Spain, in the first Strategic Plan for Citizenship and Integration of 2007–2010 (Strategic Plan for Citizenship and Integration, 2007), and subsequently incorporated in the following Strategic Plan of 2011–2014 (Strategic Plan for Citizenship and Integration, 2011).

In the Spanish case, consensus to go this 'third way' was apparently quite strong among conservative and progressive forces, because this was perceived as being a middle ground between assimilationism and multiculturalism; an indication of the lack of consistency within certain political visions. The empirical evidence collected in our fieldwork shows the existing difficulties experienced by the political class in accurately defining the meaning of the intercultural option, and it also illustrates how multiculturalism and assimilationism are perceived as disposable options. Without going into too much detail about the development of intercultural policies, within specific programmes they had their place in regions ruled by various political groups. In 2008, this lukewarm approach was formally broken when the main conservative force in Spain, the *Partido Popular*, promoted an *integration contract* at the time of the general election in 2008. Since then, interculturality has begun to disappear from documents and agendas produced by conservative forces and, at the same time, it has diminished in progressive policies due to fears of a *welfare chauvinism* effect among natives. In the Spanish case, such a turning point and the turn towards assimilation occurred later in comparison to other European countries such as Holland, France or Germany, which incorporated such programmes prior to 2011 (Michalowski, 2007, pp. 71–75), when an 'effort for integration' was added to the Spanish immigration regulations. In Spain, the 'effort for integration' was an optional choice concerning the most vulnerable immigrants, as it compensated for the lack of compliance with a requirement to renew the residence and work permit, and thus it was only implemented after the law on foreigners was passed in 2009.

The official definition of integration at state level established in the first Strategic Plan for Citizenship and Integration (2007–2010), passed in the Council of Ministers on 16 February 2007, is as follows: "a bidirectional, dynamic process of mutual adjustment by all immigrants and all residents of member states", where "integration implies the respect for the core values of the European Union" (Strategic Plan for Citizenship and Integration, 2007). As we can see, there is a clear influence of basic common European principles passed in 2005.

This notion has three key ideas: firstly that integration is, rather than a state of affairs at a given time, a dynamic social process that takes place over time, having to be continuously reproduced and renewed; secondly, integration requires mutual or two-way efforts to adapt to the new reality, such efforts coming both from immigrants and from the society receiving them; and finally, that these mutual efforts must be carried out within the framework of the core values of the European Union (Strategic Plan for Citizenship and Integration, 2007).

3.2. The Discourse of Political and Social Actors on the Integration of Immigrants in Spain

For a start, it should be acknowledged that multiculturalism as a critical approach is more easily linked to left-wing parties (Jupp, 2003), at least from the point of view of the most conservative parties. On the other hand, we find that left-wing parties perceive conservative parties as assimilationist forces, whose take on immigration involves the fear of the loss of the national identity. The left fears being defined as 'woolly liberal' and

---

[2] This communication [COM (2005) 289 final] of the Commission is part of the Common Agenda for Integration, within the Framework for the Integration of Third-Country Nationals in the European Union (http://eur-lex.europa.eu/legal-content/ES/TXT/?uri=uriserv:l14502)

the right dreads being labelled 'racist'. A good example of such perceptions can be seen in the following statements made by some members of parliament coming from various parties in the Spanish parliament:

> "I believe that 'Izquierda Unida' [a left-wing party] defends multiculturalism. It does" (An MP of the Popular Party)

> "The Popular Party is in the assimilationist model" (An MP of the Spanish Socialist Workers' Party)

> "The right, the Popular Party and Convergència [a conservative regionalist party can be said to be assimilationist in the sense that they want to impose an autochthonous culture—be it Catalonian or the Spanish—, with each person renouncing to their origins. I believe that is the path they would follow." (Decision-maker for Migration and Citizenship in Iniciativa per Catalunya Verds, Catalonian Green Party)

The political discourse tends to classify and stratify foreigners, according to their proximity to the Spanish culture(s) perceived as static, and for this purpose, some ethnic markers are taken into account, such as phenotypic features, language or religion. In Spain, this aspect of political and social discourses means that some policies have more impact on certain communities, for example: religious diversity measures, hiring intercultural mediators specialised in a certain national community, or the teaching of Spanish and other co-official languages in Spain. We can see traces of such discourses in the following quotes:

> "I think that people who come to a country such as ours have to adopt our values, our law and our Constitution, as well as all that we have done to construct our cultural heritage over time....That's why I believe that what the people who arrive to a country such as ours must do is to accept and respect all the progress that we have made; there are some nationalities that find that easier because of their culture to adapt to it and there are others that find it more complicated, more complex, because of their culture, because of what they have received and even, on many occasions, because of their lack of education, huh." (A member of the parliament from the Popular Party)

> "Spain has always historically prioritised, and the Spanish laws have alway prioritised, Latin America and the Philippines; former colonies. It sounds a bit outdated since Spain lost its colonies and so on. We believe we indeed should not break those ties with them, we have to further strengthen such ties. But, indeed, it's basically Latin American countries [meaning those with the right to vote in the municipal election], and some other country nowadays for reasons of relationships, security, for fishing even, or commercial relations and so on—Spain is starting to open up to them, to deploy those options traditionally reserved for Ibero-American countries." (Coordinator of the parliamentary group Izquierda Unida-Iniciativa per Catalunya-Esquerra Republicana de Cataluña in the 9th parliamentary term)

> "The good one is the one which is culturally or religiously closer to us. And the bad one is the other one." (Decision-maker for the Immigration Area of Partido Iniciativa per Catalunya Verds, an environmentalist-socialist party)

A characteristic of the discourse on the integration of immigrants in Spain which runs through the various Public Administrations and territories is a difficulty to integrate those foreigners who from a cultural point of view are the farthest away, more specifically, the Muslim population concentrated in Catalonia. The cultural debates that have the greatest impact with regard to religious diversity centre around the building of mosques and the use of the hijab or the burqa in public spaces. Islamophobia as a type of xenophobia has an oblivious echo on many public discourses, this concept being understood as viewing Islam as a compact, monolithic block opposing social change; isolated and sharing no common values with other cultures it coexists with. It is viewed as being inferior to Western culture and perceived as sexist, irrational or primitive; it is seen as being linked to international terrorism and engaged in a clash of civilizations (Martín Muñoz, 2012).

The political and social discourse in Spain usually links immigration to employment; therefore, this is seen as the initial point of integration. Such a discourse is stronger among conservative stances, leaving arguments such as cultural enrichment to progressive forces. The economic recession experienced in Spain could have been one of the main motives for changing the positive acceptance of immigration, yet the downturn encouraged stereotypes linked to the traditional xenophobic discourses related to labor competitiveness (Cea D´Ancona & Valles Martínez, 2015, pp. 136–137)

In the discourse of left-wing political parties in Spain, we find a vision of integration that highlights egalitarianism regarding access to rights, the defence of the extension of political rights—voting in local elections—to foreigners being the most extensive proposal from far-left parties. Such discourses include standardising access of foreigners to the Welfare State, defending the need to implement policies of immigrant integration and, finally, a certain lukewarm position of interculturality (directed more specifically towards migrant and specialised audiences). Interculturality is incorporated as a technical term directed at experts, and as a halfway point for political positions but with a little practical development. The comments of a member of parliament from a peripheral, conservative regionalist party of Catalonia illustrates this point:

"We are located within interculturality, as everyone else in Spain. Now the discussion is what we mean by interculturality....I think everybody is formally into interculturality and nobody would nowadays defend a position which is purely multiculturalist or purely assimilationist. But neither do I think there is a particularly well-developed doctrine from political parties, and I believe that the practices in government tend to be misunderstood multiculturalism. Differences tend to be trivially emphasised, there's a tendency to pigeon hole people under their origins and, from this, to promote associationism or integration policies. This ethnic approach to sorting types of immigrants is used to garner votes. My feeling is that this is pretty generalised and that's why I say the rhetoric is always intercultural, but practice is a bad version of multicultural." (An MP from Convergència i Unió in the Spanish parliament)

Basically, if we cross the axes of ideology and national sentiment we will be able to find four ideal types (see Table 2):

a) the assimilationist model associated with forces that adopt a strong Spanish nationalist sentiment, and can be defined as conservative, as is the case of the *Partido Popular*. This will be the first force to enact in Spain the 'integration contract' which demands that immigrants make an effort to get to know the Spanish language and culture. In exchange for this 'duty', it's understood that they will be entitled to Welfare State rights;
b) the model of defence of standardization of access to the Welfare State and integration, based on 'constitutional patriotism', or legislative patriotism, which defends interculturality in education and cultural areas as an enhancement of diversity. This is characteristic of political forces that define Spain as a nation-state and are ideologically located on the left, such as the Spanish Socialist Workers' Party and Izquierda Unida. The more left-wing the party is, the greater its defence of the rights of foreigners, particularly of their right to vote.
c) the model of assimilationism for the immigrant population situated in regions perceived as 'peripheral nations' with a culture and language of their own. This includes a defence of interculturality for specific matters (education, social cohesion and community involvement) which derives from the a positive view of 'cultural diversity' and is characteristic of peripheral regionalist parties that identify themselves as progressive, such as *Bloque Nacionalista Galego* (in Galicia) or *Esquerra Republicana de Catalunya* (Catalonia). These forces also defend the provision of greater access to the Welfare State for the foreign population and the extension of political rights for immigrants.
d) The assimilationist model for immigrants which advocates multiculturalism in the centre-periphery relationships, which is characteristic of conservative regionalist stances such as *Convergència i Unió* (Catalonia) and the *Partido Nacionalista Vasco* (Basque Country). It is important to keep in mind that the conservative Convergència i Unió advocated for there to be an 'effort for integration' from immigrants, in the 2011 regulations for aliens in the State, in exchange for parliamentary support to back those regulations.

Rhetoric on integration produced by trade unions, nonprofit organizations and immigrant associations plays a role in mediation or symbolic approximation between foreigners and those responsible for governmental discourses on immigration. Trade unions in Spain characteristically have a low membership, those with a greater representation in trade union elections are *Comisiones Obreras* and *Unión General de Trabajadores*. Foreign members in the various territories still do not get close to representing foreign workers among the whole of the labor force, accounting for about ten percent of the total in 2016. At the national level, the percentage of foreign members in *Comisiones Obreras* is between 5 and 7 percent of the total, while these account for 3 percent of the total members of the *Unión General de Trabajadores*.

The view of trade unions on integration is mainly social, civic and political. Both organizations highlight that immigrants must be assured access to the Welfare State,

Table 2. Stances regarding political recognition of the identity of each migrant community (2008–2011). Source: Author's compilation based on empirical data.

Ideological Axis (Left–Right)	**Centralism–Peripheral Nationalism Axis**	
	Centralism	**Peripheral Nationalism**
Left–Progressives	Defence of normalization and civic integration. Interculturality.	Assimilationism for immigrants at the cultural level. Defence of interculturality in specific areas.
Right–Conservatives	Assimilationism	Assimilationism for immigrants—Interculturality in the relationships of stateless nations (ie. autonomous communities of Spain).

which needs to be resized due to population growth. They also stress that the equality criterion must be central and advocate the normalization of services to foreigners. There is also a defence of increased political rights for the foreign population, and argument that is especially strong on the part of *Comisiones Obreras*. In terms of their cultural model, they advocate interculturality as a way to live together in a culture of diversity, rather than in a diversity of cultures.

Organizations that support immigrants, which are entities in charge of implementing integration policies, are the ones with the greatest level of development and influence on governments where immigrant integration is concerned. Such entities dominate discourses for the defence of human rights, they are key defenders of interculturality, are partially responsible for these kinds of programmes, and they fight for a standardised access to the Welfare State for foreigners. The standardization principle is present in the vast majority of discourses of all social actors, in terms of promoting foreigner's access to the general public services instead of establishing services and specific benefits which specifically respond to the needs of the foreign population; nevertheless, it is also true that this approach needs support in order to achieve integration and social cohesion in the host society.

Immigrant associations have less influence on governments than trade unions and immigrant supporting entities. These former groups depend on public aid to a greater extent than the latter, making their discourse more critical, albeit mitigated by their status as implementers of assistance programmes. Immigrant entities that represent more discriminated groups speak in terms more closely approaching the defence of positions favourable to positive discrimination, because their members suffer more intensely from the consequences of racism and xenophobia. They are the ones who embrace most vigorously the discourse of interculturality because it is in their everyday practices, while support entities are the ones who best know the theory supporting such claims.

Quantitative data show how the hegemonic picture that linked immigration to the need for manual laborers has collapsed in Spain. Academic literature shows that the perception of Spaniards has changed and that the positive side of the presence of foreigners is linked to cultural wealth. To this, we must add the emergence of identity policies challenging the serious redistributive crisis that is having an impact on social equity. This means that the debates on diversity management must be considered as core debates. In the absence of 'means' to implement policies, resulting from the failure to redistribute wealth, 'symbolic' policies emerge. The best example of this is discourse as a policy itself.

4. Conclusions

Discourses are a prelude to policies; they precede and predict future actions. Restrictions start by being verbalised and subsequently solidified. A good example of this was the exclusion from access to public health of immigrants in an irregular administrative situation that was made on the grounds of austerity policies and which took place under the conservative government of *Partido Popular* in 2012. Prior to this, there had been declarations defending different rights for immigration in a regular situation and foreigners in an irregular administrative situation (Royal Decree-Act 16/2012, 2012).

Just as austerity cut this social right from some of the most vulnerable foreigners, the logic of universal rights, access standardization, the fight for public health access and, finally, an organised and sensitised group of social actors was able to reverse this situation in 2015. The conservative government was pressured to reinstate foreigner's access in an irregular administrative situation to the primary health system. This may be the best demonstration of the existence of an egalitarian force in the vision of foreign integration.

At the cultural level, it is worth noting that differences are hard to accept in Spain, so talking about a shared identity is not easy given the considerable internal plurality of the Spanish state. Applying this ongoing debate to the arrival of immigrants allows for a certain *de facto* diversity, but it does not support it, at least on a national scale. Interculturality only takes a centre role when we talk about educational programs or when we consider immigrant communities that are culturally distant, such as Moroccans; where intercultural mediation does seem necessary to mediate. In this sense, much remains to be done if we wish to develop the kind of approach that is respectful of difference that forms the basis of any social cohesion project.

Acknowledgments

This publication draws upon data from the research of my PhD thesis 'The (Weak) Institutionalization of Integration Policies for Immigrants: A Comparative Analysis of Andalucia, Catalonia and Madrid', defended in the Department of Sociology and Political and Administrative Science of the University of A Coruña in December, 2015. This thesis was financed by the Ministry of Science and Education through an educational grant for research staff training (BES-2006-12706) linked to the research project (SEJ2005-06762). This publication had the economic support of Xunta de Galicia [Galician government] through the aid programme for the consolidation and structuring of research units (GRC2014/048). I would like to thank the Universidade da Coruña professors Renée DePalma Ungaro and Antía Pérez Caramés their help regarding language issues. I would also like to express my appreciation for the contributions I have received from the anonymous assessors of the text, who have been a great help for me to improve it.

Conflict of Interests

The author declares no conflict of interests.

References

Amuedo-Dorantes, C., & De la Rica, S. (2007). Labor market assimilation of recent immigrants in Spain. *British Journal of Industrial Relations*, *45*(2), 257–284. doi:10.1111/j.1467-8543.2007.00614.x

Arango, J. (2000). Becoming a country of immigration at the end of the twentieth century: The case of Spain. In R. King, G. Lazaridis, & C. Tsardanidis (Eds.), *Eldorado or fortress? Migration in Southern Europe* (pp. 253–276). London: Palgrave Macmillan. doi:10.1057/9780333982525_12

Arriba, A., & Moreno, L. (2005). *Spain: Poverty, social exclusion and "safety nets"*. London: Routledge.

Caviedes, A. (2004). The open method of co-ordination in immigration policy: A tool for prying open Fortress Europe. *Journal of European Public Policy*, *11*(2), 289–310, 2004. doi:10.1080/1350176042000194449

Cea D´Ancona, M. Á., & Valles Martínez, M. S. (2015). Changes in the perception of Latin American Inmigrants in host countries during the Great Recession. In M. Aysa-Lastra & L. Cachón (Eds.), *Immigrant vulnerability and resilience. Comparative perspectives on Latin American Immigrants during the Great Recession* (pp. 129–146). New York: Springer. doi:10.1007/978-3-319-14797-0_7

Chari, R., & Sandell, R. (2011). Los "nuevos Españoles": Un reto con sabor político. *Panorama Social*, *13*, 134–150.

Cook-Martín, D., & Viladrich, A. (2009). The problem with similarity: Ethnic-affinity migrants in Spain. *Journal of Ethnic and Migration Studies*, *35*(1), 151–170. doi:10.1080/13691830802489309

Dexter, L. A. (1970). *Elite and specialized interviewing*. Evanston: Northwestern University Press.

Faist, T. (2009). Diversity: A new mode of incorporation?. *Ethnic and Racial Studies*, *32*(1), 171–190. doi:10.1080/01419870802483650

Freeman, G. P. (2003). *Incorporting immigrants in liberal democracies* (CMD Working Papers). Princeton: Center for Migration and Development, Princeton University.

Fokkema, T., & Haas, H. (2015). Pre-and post-migration determinants of socio-cultural integration of African immigrants in Italy and Spain. *International Migration*, *53*(6), 3–26. doi:10.1111/j.1468-2435.2011.00687.x

Fundación Ideas. (2011). *La contribución de la inmigración a la economía española. Evidencias y perspectivas de futuro*. Madrid: Fundación Ideas.

Gil Araujo, S. (2002). Políticas públicas como tecnologías de gobierno: Las políticas de inmigrantes y las figuras de la inmigración. In C. Clavijo & M. Aguirre (Eds.), *Políticas sociales y Estado de Bienestar en España: Las migraciones. Informe 2002* (pp. 147–200). Madrid: Fundación Hogar del Empleado.

Gil Araujo, S. (2010). *Las argucias de la integración. Políticas migratorias, construcción nacional y cuestión social*. Madrid: Iepala Editorial.

Goodman, S. W. (2010). Integration requirements for integration´s sake? Identifying, categorising and comparing civic integration policies. *Journal of Ethnic and Migration Studies*, *36*(5), 753–772. doi:10.1080/13691831003764300

Goodman, S. W. (2014). *Immigration and membership politics in Western Europe*. Cambridge, UK: Cambridge University Press.

Guiraudon, V. (2008). Contratos de integración para inmigrantes: Tendencias comunes y diferencias en la experiencia europea. *Elcano Newsletter*, *45*, 7.

Huntington, S. P. (1996). *The clash of civilizations and the remaking of world order*. New York: Simon & Schuster.

Jacobs, D., & Rea, A. (2007). The end of national models? Integration courses and citizenship trajectories in Europe. *International Journal on Multicultural Societies*, *9*(2), 264–283.

Joppke, C. (2004). The retreat of multiculturalism in the Liberal State: Theory and policy. *The British Journal of Sociology*, *55*(2), 237–257. doi:10.1111/j.1468-4446.2004.00017.x

Joppke, C. (2007). Beyond national models: Civic integration policies for immigrants in Westerrn Europe. *West European Politics*, *30*(1), 1–22. doi:10.1080/01402380601019613

Jupp, J. (2003). *Immigration, asylum and extremist politics*. Paper presented at The Challenges of Immigration and Integration in the European Union and Australia Conference, 18–20 February, University of Sydney, Australia.

Kymlicka, W. (2012). Comment on Meer and Modood. *Journal of Intercultural Studies*, *33*(2), 211–216. doi:10.1080/07256868.2012.649528

Labor Force Survey. (2016). *Labor force survey 2016*. Madrid: Spanish National Statistics Institute (INE).

Loch, D. (2014). Integration as a sociological concept and national model for immigrants: scope and limits. *Identities: Global Studies in Culture and Power*, *21*(6), 623–632. doi:10.1080/1070289X.2014.908776

López-Sala, A. M. (2013). Managing uncertainty: Immigration policies in Spain during economic recession (2008–2011). *Migraciones Internacionales*, *7*(2), 39–69.

Mahía Casado, R. (2010). La irrupción de España en el panorama de las migraciones internacionales: Por qué llegaron, por qué siguen llegando y por qué lo seguirán haciendo. *ICE: Revista de economía*, *854*, 5–22.

Martín Muñoz, G. (2012). La islamofobia inconsciente. In G. Martín Muñoz & R. Grosfoguel (Eds.), La islamofobia a debate. *La genealogía del miedo al islam y la construcción de los discursos antiislámicos* (pp. 35–46). Madrid: Casa Árabe.

Meer, N., & Moddod, T. (2012). How does interculturalism contrast with multiculturalism? *Journal of Intercultural Studies*, *33*(2), 175–196. doi:10.1080/07256868.2011.618266

Michalowski, I. (2007). Modelos de acogida en Alemania, Francia y los Países Bajos: Diseño y efectividad de los programas de acogida e integración. In J. Biles, I. Michalowski, & L. Winnemore (Eds.), *Políticas y modelos de acogida. Una mirada transatlántica: Canadá, Alemania, Francia y los Países Bajos* (pp. 67–92). Barcelona: Fundación CIDOB.

Muñoz-Comet, J. (2016). Potential work experience as protection against unemployment: Does it bring equal benefit to immigrants and native workers? *European Sociological Review*, *32*(5), 537–551.

Royal Decree-Act 16/2012. (2012). Royal Decree-Act 16/2012 of 20 April, of urgent measures to guarantee the sustainability of the National Health System. Retrieved from https://www.boe.es/diario_boe/txt.php?id=BOE-A-2012-5403

Rhodes, M. (1996). Southern European welfare states: Identity, problems and prospects for reform. *South European Society and Politics*, *1*(3), 1–22. doi: 10.1080/13608749608539480

Sarasa, S., & Moreno, L. (1995). *El Estado del Bienestar en la Europa del Sur*. Madrid: CSIC.

Sartori, G. (2001). *La sociedad multiétnica. Pluralismo, multiculturalismo y extranjeros*. Madrid: Editorial Taurus.

Strategic Plan for Citizenship and Integration. (2007). 2007–2010. Retrieved from http://extranjeros.empleo.gob.es/es/IntegracionRetorno/Plan_estrategico/pdf/PECIDEF180407.pdf

Strategic Plan for Citizenship and Integration. (2011). 2011–2014. Retrieved from http://extranjeros.empleo.gob.es/es/Programas_Integracion/Plan_estrategico2011/pdf/PECI-2011-2014.pdf

Triadafilopoulos, T. (2011). Iliberal means to liberal ends? Understanding recent immigrant integration policies in Europe. *Journal of Ethnic and Migration Studies*, *37*(6), 861–880. doi:10.1080/1369183X.2011.576189

Wallace Goodman, S. (2010). Integration requirements for integration´s sake? Identifying, categorising and comparing civic integration policies. *Journal of Ethnic and Migration Studies*, *36*(5), 753–772. doi: 10.1080/13691831003764300

Wallace Goodman, S. (2014). *Immigration and membership politics in Western Europe*. Cambridge: Cambridge University Press.

About the Author

Belén Fernández Suárez is a Sociology professor in the University of A Coruña, Spain. She holds a PhD degree in Sociology from the University of A Coruña. She is part of the International Migrations Sociology Group (ESOMI) of the University of A Coruña, which is a member of the international network IMISCOE (International Migration, Integration and Social Cohesion). Her main lines of research are migration policies and, specifically, those policies for the integration of immigrants, as well as the study of political discourses on migrations.

Supporting a Design Driven Approach to Social Inclusion and Accessibility in Transport

Russell Marshall [1,*], Steve Summerskill [1], Keith Case [2], Amjad Hussain [3], Diane Gyi [1], Ruth Sims [4], Andrew Morris [1] and Jo Barnes [1]

[1] Loughborough Design School, Loughborough University, Loughborough, LE11 3TU, UK; E-Mails: r.marshall@lboro.ac.uk (R.M), s.summerskill2@lboro.ac.uk (S.S.), d.e.gyi@lboro.ac.uk (D.G.), a.p.morris@lboro.ac.uk (A.M.), j.barnes@lboro.ac.uk (J.B.)
[2] Mechanical and Manufacturing Engineering, Loughborough University, Loughborough, LE11 3TU, UK; E-Mail: k.case@lboro.ac.uk
[3] Department of Industrial and Manufacturing Engineering, University of Engineering and Technology, 54890 Lahore, Pakistan; E-Mail: chamjad@gmail.com
[4] Department of Psychology, University of Derby, Derby, DE22 1GB, UK; E-Mail: r.sims3@derby.ac.uk

* Corresponding author

Abstract
This paper presents research into the area of public transport and accessibility, addressing the support of practitioners in achieving socially inclusive solutions to the mobility issues of diverse populations. For decades, social policy has been underpinned by a stereotyping of populations into simplified sub groups: old, young, disabled, etc. and thus solutions often fail to properly address the richness of human variability. These shortcomings are often 'managed' through the ability for people to adapt, however, this is not a sustainable way in which to build a socially inclusive transport infrastructure. A software design tool called HADRIAN is presented. This tool provides a means to evaluate designs for their physical inclusiveness through the use of a virtual user group. This virtual user group is the embodiment of over 100 people that can be used to assess an existing or proposed design and to gain an understanding of what may be done to improve its accommodation. A case study exploring the use of the tool is described together with work in exploring the correlation of the individuals within the HADRIAN system with data on the UK population as a whole and how the inclusion or exclusion of individuals with specific characteristics can be used to inform a more representative view of the inclusiveness of a design.

Keywords
accessibility; design change; digital human modelling; HADRIAN; mobility issues; SAMMIE; simulation; social inclusion; transport

Issue
This article is part of the issue "Transport Policy and Social Inclusion", edited by Miriam Ricci, Graham Parkhurst and Juliet Jain (University of the West of England, UK).

1. Introduction

It is often stated that transport can have a direct positive impact on social inclusion by providing people with access to services such a healthcare and shopping, to help them get to a place of work, and to increase their interaction with others both on the transport itself and at their destination (Mackett, Achuthan, & Titheridge, 2008). Transport also appears to be of particular importance to older users and the ageing population has the potential to significantly affect public transport planning in future years (Barnes et al., 2015; Green, Jones, & Roberta, 2014). The inverse is also true in that social exclusion as a result of transport exclusion is a major concern, particularly as people age and potentially lose access to personal transport as they have to give up driving, as their mobility decreases, as they retire and potentially have reduced income, these factors are also prevalent in those that have disabilities (Green et al., 2014; Mackett & Thoreau, in press). In a survey by the Department for Transport (2001) that considered the needs of older travellers over a third of respondents aged 60 or over said they would like to travel more and also identified both transport related and health related barriers to this occurring. Successive governments in the UK have explicitly recognised these links and have put in place policies intended to improve the lives of older people through access to transport. For example concessionary travel on buses has been offered to children, older people and people with disabilities for many years. Currently referred to as the concessionary travel pass (CTP), free bus travel appears to have resulted in an increase in the bus usage of older people and to have provided an increase to services. However, the success of the aims of the policy to provide free travel are not necessarily clear. For example, for many of those who are eligible for free travel, the availability of the CTP would have coincided with retirement and thus may have increased their bus usage regardless of free travel (Mackett, 2014). Another issue concerns safety, whilst public transport is generally considered to be safe, more than 5000 people are injured on buses and more than 300 killed or seriously injured in the UK each year and older people are over represented as bus/coach casualties (Department for Transport, 2013).

These issues highlight one of the core difficulties in policy generation, in that it is often very difficult to predict the outcome of a policy change or to investigate the detailed causal factors behind some of the observed population trends. In the case of concessionary travel there is much evidence to suggest it has addressed its aims, however there is also evidence to suggest that such policies have other unforeseen effects and potentially do little to address social inclusion due to the presence of other barriers not associated with cost (Musselwhite & Haddad, 2010; Rye & Mykura, 2009). For some considerable time it has been well recognised that the journey from public policy to a design solution is problematic and ideally should include causation, evaluation and instrumentation (Linder & Peters, 1984). Furthermore it appears that policy makers, particularly in the case of local authorities involved in transport planning, do not tend to innovate, but rather rely on pre-conceived solutions that focus on supply rather than demand (May, Kelly, Shepherd, & Jopson, 2012).

One means of aiding policy makers, planners and designers to gain a greater understanding of any planned change on social inclusion, or to retrospectively evaluate a situation to inform change, is to utilise modelling and simulation tools. There have been a number of modelling and simulation approaches that have been explored that utilise mapping tools such as GIS (geographic information systems) for example, CAPITAL (Church, Frost, & Sullivan, 2000), LUPTAI (Yigitcanlar et al., 2007) and AMELIA (Mackett et al., 2008) amongst others (Ford, Barr, Dawson, & James, 2015; Karou & Hull, 2012). However the majority of these approaches have limited capability to address individual user needs within a broader population based approach. As such, the richness of end user requirements can be lost in the generalisation and homogenisation of groups within the population.

This paper presents ongoing research into 3D modelling and simulation and the use of digital human modelling (DHM) tools to explore and inform accessibility and inclusion. Through the use of a unique database on older and disabled people that forms a virtual user group, together with an existing DHM tool called SAMMIE (Porter, Marshall, Freer, & Case, 2004), a prototype tool called HADRIAN has been developed. A case study of the use of the tool is presented together with research into exploring how inclusivity explorations with individuals can be used to inform a broader understanding about accessibility for populations.

2. HADRIAN

HADRIAN is an inclusive design tool aimed at supporting practitioners in inclusive design practice, be they designers, architects, town planners etc., through the exploration of the accessibility of their ideas prior to implementation. The tool is the output of iterative research and development initially funded by the Engineering and Physical Sciences Research Council (EPSRC) as part of their Extending Quality Life (EQUAL) Programme. This process began with a stakeholder review of requirements (Gyi, Porter, & Case, 2000; Oliver, Gyi, Porter, Marshall, & Case, 2001), followed by a pilot study exploring data collection methods (Marshall, Case, Oliver, Gyi, & Porter, 2002), and then progressed into the structural development of a software task analysis tool and the creation of a user database through the collection of a wealth of data on 102 individuals, the majority of whom are older and/or disabled (Marshall, Case, Porter, Sims, & Gyi, 2004; Porter et al., 2004). The resulting prototype tool (Marshall et al., 2010) addressed two main concerns: 1. the applicability of the data used to inform designers and simulation tools in inclusive design practice, notably data on human variability, joint range of motion, behaviour and coping strategies; and 2. a means of accessing simulation functionality that is more attuned to the working methods of designers.

Figure 1 shows a prototype of the database of individuals. A significant amount of data is available including: age, gender, occupation, any registered disabilities, anthropometry (body measurements), joint range of motion, task capability and behaviour video's, reach range, and a selection of questionnaire responses regarding views on transport use. The data themselves form a potentially useful resource for practitioners, particularly in fostering an understanding and empathy with users and providing insights into the effects of ageing and the significant variability in disability.

The data in the database can also be used to support DHM application. HADRIAN works together with the SAMMIE DHM system by providing data on the creation of human models for simulation purposes. In this manner HADRIAN provides a virtual user group for user trials conducted in the digital environment. Interaction points, workplaces, and environments can all be 3D modelled and then evaluated with the virtual users as shown in Figure 2. Using a task-based methodology tasks can be defined and assessed for each individual as a virtual analogue of the real-world equivalent.

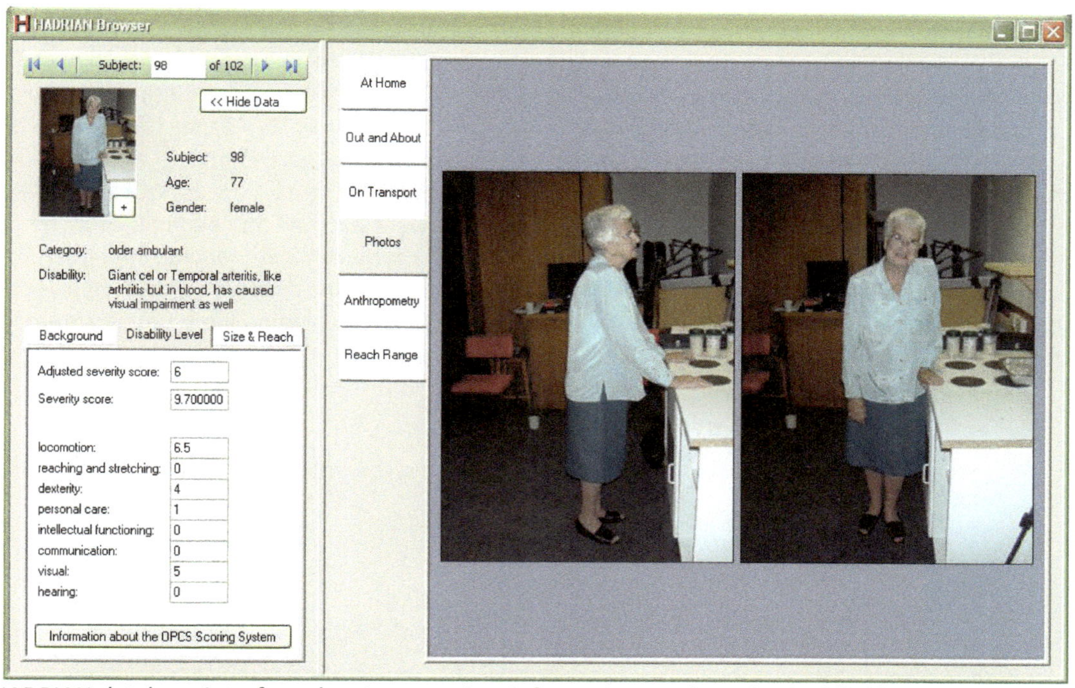

Figure 1. HADRIAN database interface showing overview information on the individual (left) and a range of detailed information in this instance photos for empathy (right).

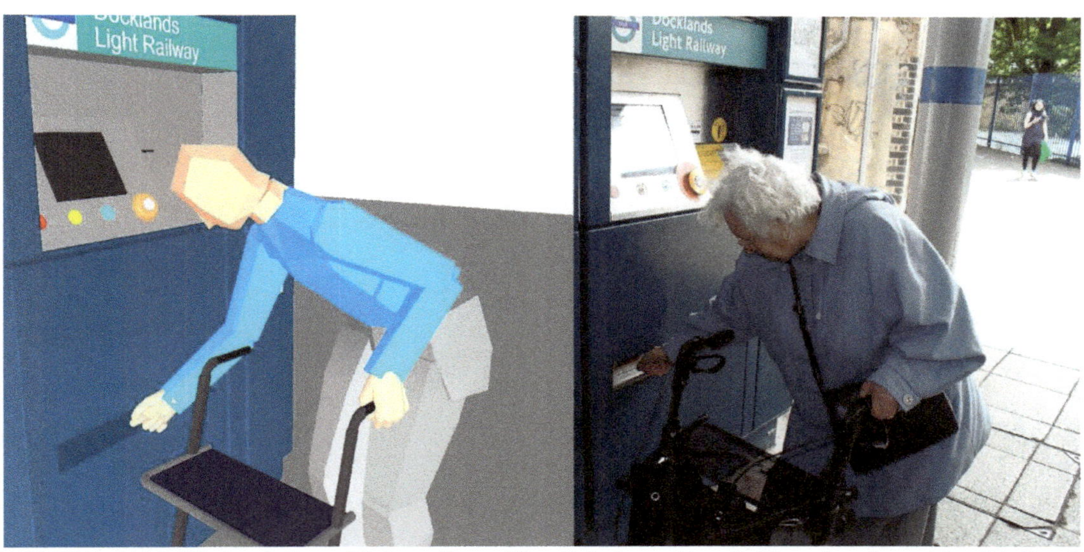

Figure 2. HADRIAN–SAMMIE simulation of interacting with a ticket machine (left) and real-world validation (right) during trials at the DLR station in Greenwich, London.

3. The Use of HADRIAN Data in a Public Transport Inclusion Case Study

Informed by concerns regarding the prevalence of bus travel with older users and the number of injuries and fatalities that occur each year, feasibility research has been conducted aimed at improving safety for older public transport users (OPTU). Funded by the Medical Research Council under their Lifelong Health and Wellbeing programme, part of the OPTU project focused on the use of a human modelling approach as a means of exploring issues and evaluating design interventions. Based upon an analysis of the police accident database STATS_19 exemplar case studies were identified (Barnes et al., 2015). To illustrate the process, one of those case studies is outlined here. This case study focused on the use of a typical bus design operated in the UK and any causal factors associated with accidents to standing passengers that represent 41% of older casualties (Barnes et al., 2013).

To perform the evaluation a representative bus model was required. A typical example of a large bus was identified from a local operator and permission sought to access the vehicle whilst not in service. To capture the vehicle geometry in an expedient manner a FARO LS 3D Scene scanning system (FARO, 2015) was used to digitally capture the interior of the bus. The system utilises a 360-degree laser scanner mounted on a tripod that digitally encodes everything in the line of sight. The tripod was positioned in three locations along the length of the bus and scans were captured. Each scan takes approximately 60 seconds however with associated set-up time and planning of the data capture the complete scan time on site was approximately one hour. The scans initially take the form of a point cloud consisting of hundreds of thousands of data points. Using specialist software in the form of Geomagic (3D Systems, 2015) the three scans were merged into a single dataset, noise and unwanted scan geometry were removed to produce a coherent point cloud.

The point cloud was then decimated to reduce the complexity down to a manageable level and finally tessellated to turn the points into a triangular mesh of surfaces as shown in Figure 3. Further work was required to break the complete bus model down into functional elements such as seats, handles, rails etc. Holes were patched and geometry missed due to line-of-sight occlusion was modelled manually. To complete the process the geometry was imported into the SAMMIE DHM system where simple external geometry was added and textures applied. The original bus and the resulting models are shown in Figure 4.

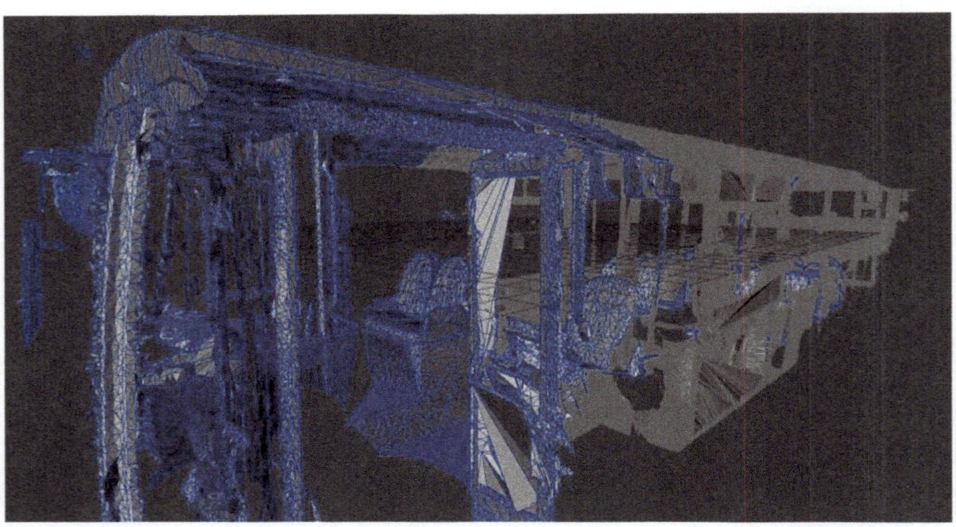

Figure 3. Tessellated 'point cloud' resulting from three scans combined to create the bus geometry.

Figure 4. Bus used for the modelling activity, a 42 seat Kinchbus No 12 (left) and the resulting model in SAMMIE (right).

The use of a digital modelling process to evaluate this type of scenario has many advantages including the ability to model a broad range of users, to explore representative scenarios in a manner that does not face the real world issues of participant recruitment, ethics and safety and problems associated with taking a bus out of service for an extended period. However the DHM approach is not without its limitations. DHM tools typically support static evaluations of key-frame postures and tasks. However, accidents are invariably dynamic events and so there is a requirement for some hypothesis in the recreation of the accident event. Dynamic modelling technology is available but was deemed beyond the remit of this research. Taking a static approach still provides the potential to evaluate key design parameters that may prove to be causal factors in accidents and identify potential design countermeasures.

Figure 5 shows the resulting setup of the model within the SAMMIE DHM system. The bus has been populated to provide a realistic case study environment and to provide the potential to explore the impact of passengers on accessibility, particularly to hand holds that may be obstructed by passengers seated or standing.

The methodology for the case study focuses on the ability for a standing passenger to be able to hold on to the vehicle whilst traversing along the vehicle. Standing passengers are at greatest risk when the vehicle moves off or comes to a stop e.g. whilst passengers are making their way to a seat, or whilst they are stood with a view to making their way to the front to alight. Whilst causation of any particular accident in these conditions has many contributing factors, the approach taken was to assume that passengers should be able to hold on and brace themselves against any acceleration or deceleration at all times whilst on the vehicle.

Using HADRIAN in its intended manner all 102 participants in the virtual user group would be evaluated. However, for expediency a single participant was used to demonstrate the principle. The analysis explored the scenario using participant number 13 (P13) in the HADRIAN database. P13 is a 69 year old female with good mobility who lives independently. A female participant was selected as STATS_19 showed that 78% of accidents occurred to female passengers, in addition P13 had a relatively small stature (1537mm = 10th %ile UK Female) with average joint range of motion (mobility), see Figure 6. P13 provides a relatively extreme case in their ability to traverse along the vehicle whilst maintaining a hand hold due to having short arms. Other participants in the HADRIAN user group would provide alternative challenges such as limited mobility and/or the need to use a stick or a frame.

The analysis involved positioning and posturing of the digital human model to explore the opportunity to hold onto at least one of the hand holds throughout the length of the vehicle. Where hand holds were out of reach the analysis would identify the failure of the task and highlight the possible need to explore design interventions. Wherever possible a constant grip of a hand hold was maintained such that the human model would essentially always be holding on with at least one hand hold to give themselves some chance of bracing if required (Figure 7).

The analysis highlighted a number of potential issues that would be faced by someone such as P13. Figure 8 and Figure 9 show that when a passenger has to move beyond the forward facing seating area to the transverse seating area, the ability to maintain a hand hold becomes problematic. Once the passenger commits to holding onto the left hand curved handle and steps forward there is no convenient handle on the right hand side. The next handle on the right is out of reach for P13.

Figure 5. Bus interior modelled and populated in the SAMMIE DHM system.

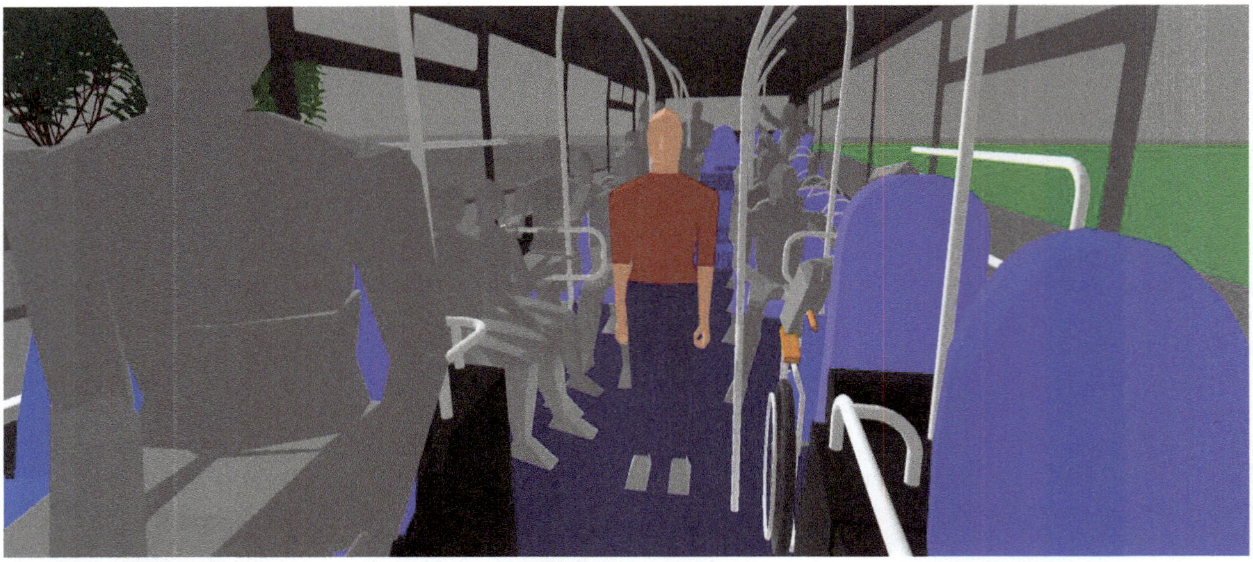

Figure 6. HADRIAN P13, UK Female digital human model within the bus.

Figure 7. Human models would hold on to at least one hand hold within the vehicle whilst traversing.

Figure 8. P13 moves forwards maintaining grip of the left hand handle but finds there is no conveniently placed right hand handle.

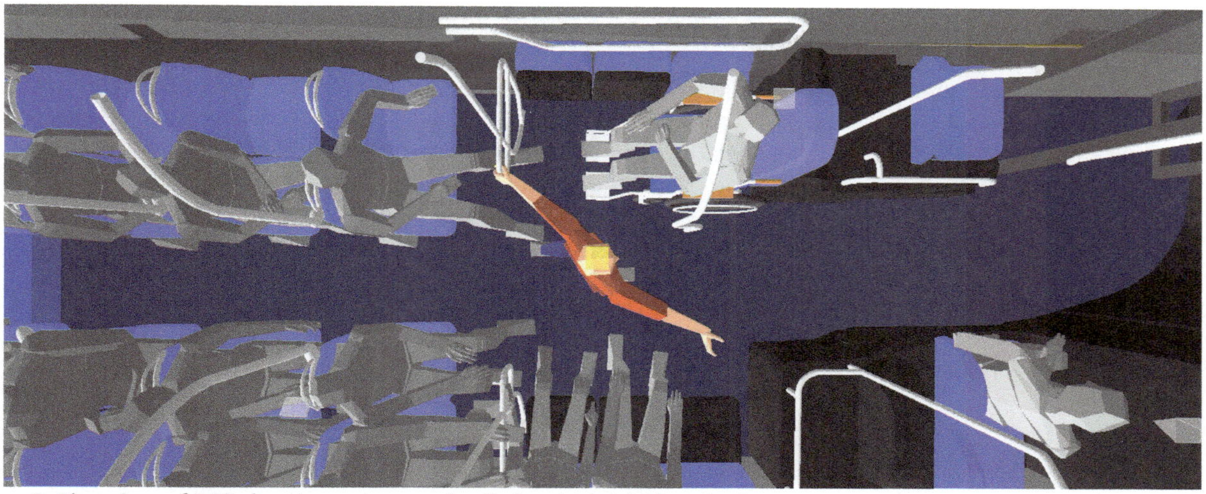

Figure 9. Plan view of P13 showing no conveniently located right hand grip.

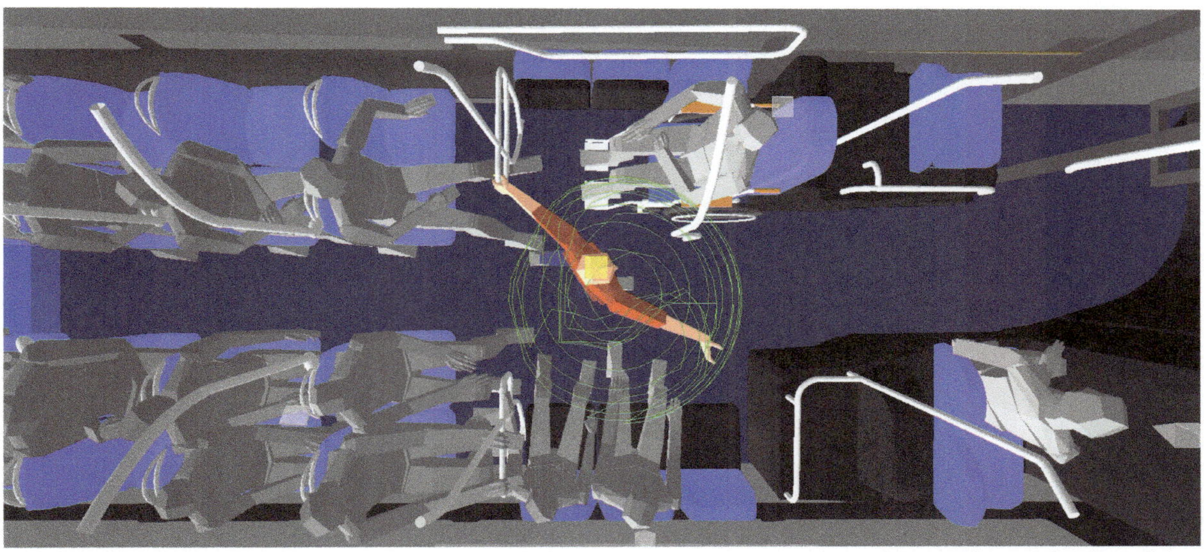

Figure 10. Reach contour for P13 confirming the lack of right hand handle, but also indicating the availability of the next left hand upright.

Figure 11. P13 moves forwards gripping the next left hand upright with the right hand.

Figure 10 shows 'reach contours' for the right hand with a palm grip. This reach evaluation tool gives an idea of the reachable volume of space afforded to the human model in the posture shown. This highlights what hand holds may be within reach. In this case no handholds to the right are within reach, however P13 could potentially reach for the hand hold to their left.

Figure 11 and Figure 12 show the posture required to move forward through this area, maintaining grip. Due to the lack of a suitable handhold to the right, the left hand upright could be gripped with the right hand. Beyond this point the passenger would need to bring their left hand forward to join the right hand, both holding onto the left hand upright as shown in Figure 13. Moving further forward an alternate right-left grip could be resumed.

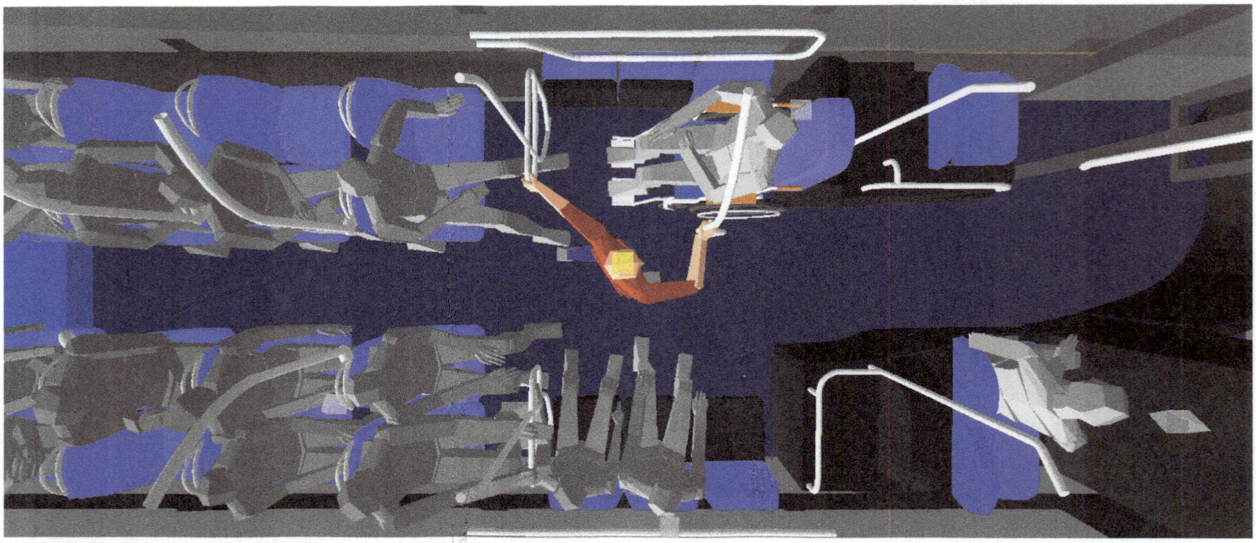

Figure 12. Plan view of the P13 showing the grip of the two left hand handles.

Figure 13. P13 moves forwards resulting a double handed grip of the left hand upright.

The results of the analysis with one exemplar task and user described here, shows how the use of human modelling can be used to explore issues with transport designs and infrastructure. Whilst beyond the scope of this paper the research also explored other scenarios such as seated passengers and also possible design interventions. In brief, there were three main findings:

- The transverse seating area has a reduced availability of hand holds for passengers standing or traversing through this area. The use of digital modelling and simulation could be used to explore the addition of more upright handholds to improve the situation for standing passengers but also to explore any effect on wheelchair and pushchair user needs in an attempt to provide a universal solution

- The assessment performed has highlighted that the current configuration may need a two handed grip at certain points during the traversal through the vehicle. In many instances this would be impractical or impossible due to the number of potential travelers who would be holding a personal items such as a bag, stick, umbrella or other encumbrance (see Barnes et al., 2013, for further detail of this scenario)
- The seat back handholds are important in the forward facing seating area but are probably secondary for most passengers as the uprights provide improved, unobstructed access. The use of digital modelling and simulation could be used to explore the implication of providing redesigned seat back mounted handles to allow access that is unobstructed by other seated passengers

More broadly the use of digital human modelling technologies combined with improved data on a broader range of the population has the ability to support a more inclusive approach to transport design and planning. Designers, engineers, and planners are often faced with data on accessibility issues but do not always have the ability to explore the nature of the barrier to accessibility nor to simulate potential improvements. The case study example described here provides a brief insight into how such tools can offer benefits in this area. However, the simulation shown is for one individual and yet most inclusivity issues concern the needs of populations, public transport must be designed to meet the needs of the majority of users and not reflect individual user needs.

4. Exploring the Representativeness of the HADRIAN Database

From its inception the sampling strategy of the HADRIAN database attempted to capture data from participants with an even distribution across each of the measures recorded. For example the database has participants with an age in every decile between the 10's (18yrs) to the 80's (89yrs), in every decile for percentile stature for both males (1st–99th) and females (1st–98th) etc. However, it was always understood that even with careful sampling the 102 individuals would never be representative of a whole population. It is therefore important to discuss the value of any results gained from the exploration of accessibility issues with members of the HADRIAN virtual user group in the context of their ability to inform decisions that affect whole populations.

In the previous section a single individual is used in an assessment. With a single participant, insights into usability can still be obtained. However, drawing broader conclusions regarding the needs of a design aimed at the broadest range of users is not straightforward. The insights gained cannot necessarily be used to support a design intervention without further understanding of the implications of the intervention on other users. If the case study in the previous section were repeated with the whole HADRIAN user group the results would be much broader in scope. More insights would be generated and there is a greater likelihood that conflicting requirements would be highlighted and subsequently support an opportunity to evaluate any necessary trade-offs if an intervention were to be made. Validation work with the database does support this claim with many of the insights generated by the use of HADRIAN reflecting those observed in real-world evaluations (Marshall et al., 2013; Summerskill et al., 2009). Yet the issue of representativeness is still a potential concern. As a counterpoint to these concerns, real world testing of physical products tends to utilise relatively modest numbers of people. For example research has shown that the majority of issues can be identified with as few as four or five participants (McClelland, 1995). As such a user group of 102 might be considered to be of a good size to explore the majority of requirements. Indeed it is not uncommon for designers to use so-called personas to aid in the development of products and services (Saffer, 2007). These personas are research based archetypal users, employed by a design team to maintain focus on user needs. Typically between one and seven personas would be employed on a project (Marshall et al., 2013). In research by Goodman-Deane, Langdon, and Clarkson (2010) personas are highlighted as one of a number of methods that are engaging for designers suiting their informal and flexible ways of working. Whilst the HADRIAN database and its virtual user group are not personas in the traditional sense, they do offer similar characteristics particularly in the ability to foster engagement with end users (Högberg, Lundström, Hanson, & Wårell, 2009).

5. Disability Follow Up Survey of Great Britain

To explore these issues further, recent work on the HADRIAN database has investigated the ability to inform practitioners on the representativeness of the individuals in the HADRIAN user group. The approach taken has been to compare the capabilities of the individuals in the database to the data in the Office of National Statistics' (ONS) Disability Follow-up Survey (DFS) conducted in 1996/1997. This survey aimed to collect information about the prevalence of disability in Great Britain and the characteristics of those who were disabled (Grundy, Ahlburg, Ali, Breeze, & Sloggett, 1999).

The DFS survey was established to understand and

measure the ability to perform certain tasks that were divided into ability categories. Individuals were selected on the basis of certain criteria, for example, the receipt of benefits and an age greater than 16 years. To measure the level of disability, approximately three hundred questions were asked of 7300 participants, covering a variety of ability categories. A total of ten categories are defined including: Locomotion; Reaching and Stretching; Dexterity; Seeing; Hearing; Personal Care; Continence; Communication; Behaviour and Intellectual functioning. The questions largely concerned a self-assessment requiring participants to identify their ability to perform tasks, and the relative ability in that task, associated with each category, such as:

- Cannot walk at all
- Can only walk up and down a flight of stairs if goes sideways or one step at a time

or

- Cannot see well enough to recognise a friend across a room
- Cannot see well enough to recognise a friend across a road

The resulting responses were then evaluated by an expert panel so that an overall consensus on a disability scale might be achieved (Martin & Elliot, 1992). These scales were arranged in such a manner that the higher the value of severity score, the greater the severity of a particular disability. For example, a person with a reaching and stretching severity score of 9.5 (RS1-Reach and stretch level 1) has a more severe disability as compared with a person with a 5.5 (RS6) severity score. In this way, the data were used to measure the level of disability and estimate disability prevalence in the overall UK population at that time.

6. The Disability Follow Up Survey Severity Scales

One of the significant characteristics of the DFS is the view taken of disability and its categorisation focusing on practical abilities rather than medical definition. Thus the severity of a disability is defined as the extent to which an individual's performance of activities is limited by impairments (Martin, Meltzer, & Elliot, 1988). After developing scales for each category, there was a need to assess the overall impact of these impairments on an individual's ability/disability. The overall severity scale was constructed according to the formula:

Worst (score in any category) + 0.4 (second worst) + 0.3 (third worst)

The above formula was applied to everyone in the survey to calculate an overall severity score for each person. Finally, these overall severity scores were grouped into the ten severity categories; their levels and ranges are shown in the table 1.

During the data collection for the HADRIAN database, relevant scales from the DFS were used for the assessment of level and severity of disability from all 102 participants. Because of this similarity in severity scales used in the HADRIAN database and the DFS, it might be said that the individuals presented in the database, are similar in some specific ability categories with the population represented by the ONS data.

The common severity scales used for different areas of disability in the disability survey and the HADRIAN database; are presented in tables 2 to 5. Only four of the ten categories were used due to practical constraints in data collection and the focus being primarily on physical rather than cognitive abilities.

Similar scales were developed for the other categories by the DFS however discussion here is limited to those which HADRIAN and the disability survey have in common.

Table 1. Levels of disability severity in accordance with overall severity scores Sources: Grundy et al. (1999) and Martin et al. (1988).

Severity category	Overall severity score
10 (most severe)	19 or higher
9	17–18.95
8	15–16.95
7	13–14.95
6	11–12.95
5	9–10.95
4	7–8.95
3	5–6.95
2	3–4.95
1 (least severe)	0.5–2.95

6.1. Locomotion

Table 2. Different levels of locomotion ability and respective severity scores. Sources: Grundy et al. (1999) and Martin et al. (1988).

Level	Question	Severity Score
L1	Cannot walk at all	11.5
L2	Can only walk a few steps without stopping or severe discomfort/cannot walk up and down one step	9.5
L3	Has fallen 12 or more times in the last year	7.5
L4	Always needs to hold on to something to keep balance	7.0
L5	Cannot walk up and down a flight of 12 stairs	6.5
L6	Cannot walk 50 yards without stopping or severe discomfort	5.5
L7	Cannot bend down far enough to touch knees and straighten up again	4.5
L8	Cannot bend down and pick something up from the floor and straighten up again	4.0
L9	Cannot walk 200 yards without stopping or severe discomfort/Can only walk up and down a flight of 12 stairs if holds on and takes a rest/Often needs to hold on to something to keep balance/Has fallen 3 or more times in the last year	3.0
L10	Can only walk up and down a flight of 12 stairs if holds on (doesn't need a rest)	2.5
L11	Cannot bend down to sweep up something from the floor and straighten up again	2.0
L12	Can only walk up and down a flight of stairs if goes sideways or one step at a time	1.5
L13	Cannot walk 400 yards without stopping or severe discomfort	0.5

6.2. Reaching and Stretching

Table 3. Different levels of reaching and stretching ability, and respective severity scores. Sources: Grundy et al. (1999) and Martin et al. (1988).

Level	Question	Severity Score
RS1	Cannot hold out either arm in front to shake hands	9.5
RS2	Cannot put either arms up to head to put a hat on	9.0
RS3	Cannot put either hand behind back to put jacket on or tuck shirt in	8.0
RS4	Cannot raise either arm above head to reach for something	7.0
RS5	Has difficulty holding either arm in front to shake hands with someone	6.5
RS6	Has difficulty putting either arm up to head to put a hat on	5.5
RS7	Has difficulty putting either hand behind back to put jacket on or tuck shirt in	4.5
RS8	Has difficulty raising either arm above head to reach for something	3.5
RS9	Cannot hold one arm out in front or up to head (but can with other arm)	2.5
RS10	Cannot put one arm behind back to put on jacket or tuck shirt in (but can with other arm)/Has difficulty putting one arm behind back to put jacket on or tuck shirt in, or putting one arm out in front or up to head (but no difficulty with other arm)	1.0

6.3. Dexterity

Table 4. Different levels of dexterity and respective severity scores. Sources: Grundy et al. (1999) and Martin et al. (1988).

Level	Question	Severity Score
D1	Cannot pick up and hold a mug of coffee with either hand	10.5
D2	Cannot turn a tap or control knobs on a cooker with either hand	9.5
D3	Cannot pick up and carry a pint of milk or squeeze the water from a sponge with either hand	8.0
D4	Cannot pick up a small object such as safety pin with either hand	7.0
D5	Has difficulty picking up and pouring from a full kettle or serving food from a pan using a spoon or ladle	6.5
D6	Has difficulty unscrewing the lid of a coffee jar or using a pen or pencil	5.5
D7	Cannot pick up and carry a 5lb bag of potatoes with either hand	4.0
D8	Has difficulty wringing out light washing or using a pair of scissors	3.0
D9	Can pick up and hold a mug of tea or coffee with one hand but not with the other	2.0
D10	Can turn a tap or control knob with one hand but not with the other/Can squeeze the water from a sponge with one hand but not the other	1.5
D11	Can pick up a small object such as a safety pin with one hand but not with the other/Can pick up and carry a pint of milk with one hand but not the other/Has difficulty tying a bow in laces or strings	0.5

6.4. Personal Care

Table 5. Different levels of personal care ability and respective severity scores. Sources: Grundy et al. (1999) and Martin et al. (1988).

Level	Question	Severity Score
PC1	Cannot feed self without help/Cannot go to and use the toilet without help	**11.0**
PC2	Cannot get into and out of bed without help/Cannot get into and out of chair without help	**9.5**
PC3	Cannot wash hands and face without help/Cannot dress and undress without help	**7.0**
PC4	Cannot wash all over without help	**4.5**
PC5	Has difficulty feeding self/Has difficulty getting to and using the toilet	**2.5**
PC6	Has difficulty getting in and out of bed/Has difficulty getting in and out of a chair	**1.0**

7. Population Estimation for the DFS

The DFS aimed to produce national estimates about the number of people with different levels of severity of disability in Great Britain. The sample of 7300 people was statistically treated to estimate the number of people in the country with a similar level of disability. In this way, the proportions of the UK adult population (+16 years) with the listed levels of disabilities were estimated. The results of this survey were first published in 'Disability in Great Britain' by the Department of Social Security in their research report number 94 (Grundy et al., 1999; Martin et al., 1988).

Figure 14 provides the percentage of the UK adult population (16+ years of age) in each disability severity level for two different disability categories. For example, in both of these categories level 9 (L9 and R9) are the most common. The locomotion ability level associated with L9 (Table 2) is exhibited by just over 3 percent of the overall UK population. Similarly, reach and stretch level R9 (Table 3) occurs in just under 1 percent of the UK adult population.

From these percentages, it is possible to estimate the total number of persons in the UK population with a given ability level. By multiplying the percentage associated with a level (e.g. L9, approx. 3.1%) with the total adult population (45.6M at the time of the survey), the total number is estimated at about 1.41M persons in the UK adult population with this level of locomotion ability. In the same way, estimations against different areas of disability and levels of disability can be easily made.

8. HADRIAN Database Correlation with DFS

As described earlier HADRIAN has a database of 102 individuals which represents a variety of people on the basis of their abilities, shapes, sizes and behaviours. The database also contains a disability severity score for each individual in line with the DFS. This provides a means to provide an indication of how prevalent the ability level of a single individual in the HADRIAN database is within the UK population. Or alternatively, and more usefully in the context of design, if an individual in the HADRIAN database is excluded during the evaluation of a design, it is possible to provide a broad indication of the proportion of the UK population that would be similarly excluded.

Being able or unable to do some task under a specific capability category, describes an individual's ability to comfortably interact with products, services or environments. The DFS disability data were intended for the purpose of indicating the capability of individuals to perform certain tasks. Some of the questions also inquire about specific product, service and environment interactions. A number of the same questions were also put to the HADRIAN participants so that self-reported abilities, together with, their recorded task behaviours, coping strategies and comfortable postures could be coded into the digital human modelling system. In this manner the difficulties identified through the use of the HADRIAN virtual user group are in some way able to provide a broader view of issues likely to be faced by the population.

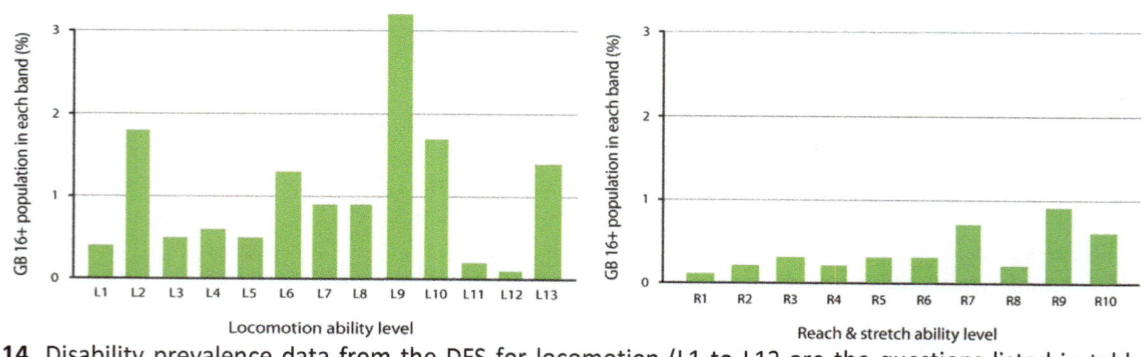

Figure 14. Disability prevalence data from the DFS for locomotion (L1 to L13 are the questions listed in table 2) and reach & stretch (R1 to R10 are the questions listed in table 3). From the Inclusive design toolkit: user capabilities. Source: Clarkson, Coleman, Hosking, and Waller (2015).

As an example Table 6 and Table 7 show the locomotion and reaching and stretching ability levels of the HADRIAN participants, their prevalence within the database and the estimation of their prevalence in the UK population through the DFS. The final column also provides an indication of the number of the population who may be excluded if a participant with a given severity score in the database were excluded.

The data shown in the tables above provide an example of how the capabilities of the individuals in the HADRIAN user group could be used as indicators of the capabilities of the population. They also provide an example of how simulation tools more broadly could be used to support population level decisions and policies. Table 6 shows that there are 102 individuals in the database of which 63 have no impairment to their locomotion that registers on the DFS scales. As we know that the HADRIAN database has used the same method for severity level assessment as used in the DFS, it can be said that there are 63 individuals in this database whose locomotion ability is representative of about 39.5 million of the UK adult population. Exploring further there are 6 individuals in the database with a locomotion severity score 6.5 (L5). It can be estimated that there are about 226,000 people in the population with a similar level of locomotion capability. In terms of application, these correlations allow analyses performed with individuals from the HADRIAN database to be place in a broader context. As an example, a task may require a user to climb a flight of 20 steps to access a

Table 6. HADRIAN severity scores and DFS-based population estimation for locomotion.

Locomotion severity score (L)	Number of persons in the HADRIAN database	Population estimation from the DFS (Thousands)	Population estimation from the DFS (%)	Cumulative population estimation from the DFS (Thousands)	Cumulative population estimation from the DFS (%)
No disability	63	39,455	86.5%	45,600	100.0%
L13 (0.5)	0	626	1.4%	6,145	13.5%
L12 (1.5)	0	41	0.1%	5,518	12.1%
L11 (2.0)	0	110	0.2%	5,477	12.0%
L10 (2.5)	6	784	1.7%	5,367	11.8%
L9 (3.0)	11	1,438	3.2%	4,583	10.1%
L8 (4.0)	0	414	0.9%	3,145	6.9%
L7 (4.5)	1	398	0.9%	2,730	6.0%
L6 (5.5)	1	598	1.3%	2,332	5.1%
L5 (6.5)	6	226	0.5%	1,735	3.8%
L4 (7.0)	5	256	0.6%	1,508	3.3%
L3 (7.5)	3	221	0.5%	1,253	2.7%
L2 (9.5)	1	833	1.8%	1,031	2.2%
L1 (11.5)	5	198	0.4%	198	0.4%
Total	**102**	**45600**			

Table 7. HADRIAN severity scores and DFS-based population estimation for reach and stretch.

Reach and Stretch severity score (L)	Number of persons in the HADRIAN database	Population estimation from the DFS (Thousands)	Population estimation from the DFS (%)	Cumulative population estimation from the DFS (Thousands)	Cumulative population estimation from the DFS (%)
No disability	81	43,859	96.2%	45,600	100.0%
RS10 (1.0)	5	279	0.6%	1,741	3.8%
RS9 (2.5)	15	390	0.9%	1,462	3.2%
RS8 (3.5)	0	113	0.3%	1,072	2.4%
RS7 (4.5)	1	306	0.7%	959	2.1%
RS6 (5.5)	0	159	0.4%	653	1.4%
RS5 (6.5)	0	130	0.3%	494	1.1%
RS4 (7.0)	0	90	0.2%	364	0.8%
RS3 (8.0)	0	159	0.4%	274	0.6%
RS2 (9.0)	0	69	0.2%	116	0.3%
RS1 (9.5)	0	47	0.1%	47	0.1%
Total	**102**	**45600**			

train station platform. This platform has no lift or ramp and thus the steps are the only means of access. A locomotion severity score of 6.5 (L5) is defined as "cannot walk up and down a flight of 12 stairs" and thus individuals categorised as L5 would not be able to complete the task and would be excluded from catching trains at the station. From the population estimations, it would also be possible to conclude that up to 226,000 adults in the UK would also be excluded. However, it is also possible to assume that, if those categorised as L5 are excluded, anyone with a greater level of disability e.g. L1-L4 would also be excluded. The right hand column in Table 6 and Table 7 is estimated by cumulatively summing the numbers of the population in the current level of severity with all levels of greater severity. Thus for the train station example, a flight of 20 steps actually has the potential to exclude 1.7M adults in the UK based on locomotion alone.

Returning to the bus simulations described earlier. The perception may be that there are some modest issues with traversing a bus for older passengers. If we place the results in context and evaluate the impact with more of the HADRIAN sample a clearer result can be obtained that may support the need for an intervention. For example if the assessment was repeated with participant 92, an 83 year old female, who has a reaching and stretching severity score of 2.5 (RS9), defined as "cannot hold one arm out in front or up to head (but can with other arm)" it is likely that this individual could not complete the task. As shown earlier, it is likely that two hands would be required to provide an older passenger with the ability to brace themselves against movement of the vehicle. The implication on P92 not being able to complete the task is that up to 1.5M people in the UK adult population would also be unable to complete the task. Thus, the conclusion might be drawn that the UK has buses in general service that are potentially dangerous for more than a million people within the current adult population if standing whilst the bus is moving. This conclusion is not particularly unexpected as it is well understood that passengers and particularly those who are older should not stand on a moving bus. Equally from discussion with bus operators and drivers, training suggests that drivers should not move off until older passengers are seated. However, these situations do occur and the accident data shows that older people continue to be injured and killed in these situations. Simulations such as those shown above, together with the ability to extrapolate the results to provide an indication of the magnitude of an issue at a population level, provide a means to obtain objective data to inform whether an intervention should be made.

9. Discussion

The potential of simulation tools such as HADRIAN that combine rich and applicable data on people together with the ability to assess existing or future designs provide an opportunity to evaluate accessibility in a proactive manner. This simulation capability can then be used to further explore issues that may be identified through a range of other sources from focus groups through to accident data. This understanding can focus on the detail such as causation, or can take a broader look at the potential impact of the issue through the potential to quantify the magnitude of the problem. As discussed, identifying a number of individuals who have a problem with a given design or environment is useful, however being able to gain in insight into the broader representation of these problems within the population has the potential to support decision making on possible interventions or design decisions in a much clearer manner.

However, this approach is not without its complexities. The correlation of individuals in the HADRIAN database with population estimations has to be considered with care. In the first instance the DFS survey was of 7300 people from which they have statistically extrapolated the representativeness to the whole UK adult population. So in many ways the concept is extrapolating one individual's capabilities to a proportion of 7300 people to a proportion of the UK population. This includes many assumptions and this requires the totals to be taken in an advisory context. Furthermore the DFS survey is now nearly 20 years old. The data within it are likely to be less representative of the population than they were particularly with an ageing population. It can be seen that in the 20 years since the survey was conducted the proportion of the UK population that is 65 years and over has increased from 15.8% to 17.7%. In addition the population itself has increased from 45.6M adults to 52.25M (Office for National Statistics, 2015). The implications of these changes is unknown and it may be possible to assume that an increasing older population would increase the prevalence of disability and increase the numbers in each of the DFS categories, making current estimations conservative. However our ageing population is also due to people living longer, thus our ageing population may be more able, making current estimations pessimistic.

The DFS survey itself is also somewhat problematic for this kind of application. As discussed by Waller, Langdon and Clarkson (2010) the DFS survey was never intended to support this kind of analysis and has its own limitations in sampling, interpretation of the responses and in the questions/categories it defines. For example the categories mix broad abilities. As described earlier, L5 is defined as "cannot walk up and down a flight of 12 stairs" whereas L7 is defined at "cannot bend down far enough to touch knees and straighten up again". The categories assume that someone at level L5 is more disabled than someone at L7, however being unable to walk up 12 stairs does not necessarily mean you cannot bend down to touch your knees. Whilst the categories have a broader scope than might be considered ideal, they can be largely described as univariate, dealing with one type of disability in each case. However, most tasks are multivariate. Requiring a combination of locomotion, reaching and stretching, dexterity etc. These combinations are not accounted for in this approach. If a HADRIAN participant has a combination of ability levels of which a number are relevant to a particular task, the exact reason they may be excluded may be difficult to filter out from the combined ability of that individual. For example, Participant 96 in the database is a wheelchair-using older woman, can only walk a few steps/cannot walk up or down one step (score 9.5 for Locomotion), cannot get in/out of bed without help (score 9.5 for Personal Care), has difficulty using a pen or pencil (score 5.5 for Dexterity), cannot hold one arm out in front or up to head (but can with other arm) (score 2.5 for Reaching and Stretching) may be excluded from a task for any combination of those factors. HADRIAN does provide some insight into a task failure and where this has a clear mapping to the DFS categories the population estimation may be clearly defined. Research such as that performed by Clarkson et al. (2015) has attempted to unpack some of the interrelated nature of these data in their inclusive design toolkit. However, further research is still required to address the limitations with the DFS data to make them ideally suited to this form of application. At present, for situations in which a task failure is attributed to an ability that crosses DFS categories the population estimation would be down to the practitioner using the system to decide the most relevant category to estimate the percentage of the population potentially affected.

10. Conclusions

In order to support practitioners in the development and implementation of socially inclusive policy and design changes, a software simulation tool called HADRIAN has been developed. HADRIAN works with a digital human modelling system called SAMMIE to allow virtual users to assess the accommodation of existing or planned designs. The use of the simulation tool, through a case study exploring the safety of standing passengers on UK buses, has highlighted the ability to identify accessibility issues for individuals within a virtual user group. Such an approach has the potential to provide an understanding for practitioners on the issues that might be faced by real people. Whilst only one virtual user has been shown in this paper, digital evaluations combined with automated analysis of virtual user-groups has the ability to evaluate the experiences of up to 102 virtual humans in the case of HADRIAN in a manner that is expedient, and avoids the ethical issues with real-world user trials. The experiences of the individuals are further explored through their correlation with the disability follow-up survey of Great Britain. Using the survey's findings, it is possible to make broad estimates of the potential population impact of an individual virtual user being excluded through poor design. The correlation process does have its own concerns as the original data were never intended to support his form of application and so the data must be treated with care. However, even with the acknowledged limitations, a further understanding of the potential representativeness of any simulation results would be beneficial. Together the approaches provide a possible means of exploring social inclusion and accessibility issues that consider individual user needs, whilst also providing a means to quantify the impact on the population of a policy or design change.

Acknowledgements

The authors gratefully acknowledge the support of the Engineering and Physical Sciences Research Council (EPSRC) and their Extending Quality Life (EQUAL) and Sustainable Urban Environments (SUE) programmes as well as the Medical Research Council (MRC) and their Lifelong Health and Wellbeing Programme (LLHW).

Conflict of Interests

The authors declare no conflict of interests.

References

3D Systems. (2015). 3D digital design and fabrication solutions. *3D Systems*. Retrieved from http://www.3dsystems.com

Barnes, J., Lawton, C., Morris, A., Marshall, R., Summerskill, S., Kendrick, D. . . . Conroy, S. (2013). Improving safety for older public transport users (OPTU): A feasibility study (MRC Research Final Report). Loughborough, UK: Loughborough University.

Barnes, J., Morris, A., Welsh, R., Summerskill, S., Marshall, R., Kendrick, D. . . . Bell, J. (2015). Injuries to older users of buses in the UK. *Public Transport*, *8*(1), 25-38. doi:10.1007/s12469-015-0113-8

Church, A., Frost, M., & Sullivan, K. (2000). Transport and social exclusion in London. *Transport Policy*, *7*, 195-205.

Clarkson, P.J., Coleman, R., Hosking, I., & Waller, S. (2015). Inclusive design toolkit. *Inclusive design toolkit*. Retrieved from: http://www.inclusivedesigntoolkit.com

Department for Transport. (2001). *Older people: Their transport needs and requirements* (Technical Report). London: Department for Transport.

Department for Transport (2013). *Reported road casualties Great Britain: 2012* (Annual Report). London: Department for Transport.

FARO. (2015). Measurement Technologies. *FARO*. Retrieved from http://www.faro.com/home

Ford, A. C., Barr, S. L., Dawson, R. J., & James, P. (2015). Transport accessibility analysis using GIS: Assessing sustainable transport in London. *ISPRS International Journal of Geo Information*, *4*, 124-149. doi:10.3390/ijgi4010124

Goodman-Deane, J., Langdon, P., & Clarkson, J. (2010). Key influences on the user-centred design process. *Journal of Engineering Design*, *21*(2-3), 345-373.

Green, J., Jones, A., & Roberta H. (2014). More than A to B: The role of free bus travel for the mobility and wellbeing of older citizens in London. *Ageing Society*, *34*, 472-494.

Grundy, E., Ahlburg, D., Ali, M., Breeze, E., & Sloggett, A. (1999). *Disability in Great Britain* (Research Report 94). London: Corporate Document Services.

Gyi, D. E., Porter, J. M., & Case, K. (2000). Design practice and "design for all". *Proceedings of the IEA 2000/HFES 2000 Congress* (pp. 913-916). San Diego, CA: Human Factors and Ergonomics Society.

Högberg, D., Lundström, D., Hanson, L., & Wårell, M. (2009). *Increasing functionality of DHM software by industry specific program features* (SAE Technical Paper 2009-01-2288). Warrendale, PA: SAE International.

Karou, S., & Hull, A. (2012). Accessibility measures and instruments. In A. Hull, C. Silva, & L. Bertolini (Eds.), *COST Action TU1002—Accessibility instruments for planning practice* (pp. 1-19). Brussels: COST Office.

Linder, S. H., & Peters, B. G (1984). From social theory to policy design. *Journal of Public Policy*, *4*(3), 237-259. doi:10.1017/S0143814X0000221X

Mackett, R. (2014). Has the policy of concessionary bus travel for older people in Britain been successful? *Case Studies on Transport Policy*, *2*, 81-88. doi:10.1016/j.cstp.2014.05.001

Mackett, R., Achuthan, K., & Titheridge, H. (2008). AMELIA: A tool to make transport policies more socially inclusive. *Transport Policy*, *15*(6), 372-378. doi:10.1016/j.tranpol.2008.12.007

Mackett., R., & Thoreau, R. (in press). Transport, social exclusion and health. *Journal of Transport & Health*. doi:10.1016/j.jth.2015.07.006

Marshall, R., Case, K., Oliver, R. E., Gyi, D. E., & Porter, J. M. (2002). A task based 'design for all' support tool. *Robotics and Computer-Integrated Manufacturing*, *18*(3-4), 297-303.

Marshall, R., Case, K., Porter, J. M., Sims, R. E., & Gyi, D. E. (2004). Using HADRIAN for eliciting virtual user feedback in 'design for all'. *Journal of Engineering Manufacture*, *218*(9), 1203-1210.

Marshall, R., Case, K., Porter, J. M., Summerskill, S. J., Gyi, D. E., Davis, D., & Sims, R. E. (2010). HADRIAN: A virtual approach to design for all. *Journal of Engineering Design*, *21*, 253-273.

Marshall, R., Cook, S., Mitchell, V., Summerskill, S., Haines, V., Maguire, M., & Case, K. (2013). Design and evaluation: End users, user datasets and personas. *Applied Ergonomics*, *46*(B), 311-317. doi:10.1016/j.apergo.2013.03.008

Martin, J., & Elliot, D. (1992). Creating an overall measure of severity of disability for the office of population and census and surveys disability survey. *Journal of Royal Statistical Society*, *155*(1), 121-140.

Martin, J., Meltzer, H., & Elliot, D. (1988). The prevalence of disability among adults. London: Her Majesty's Stationary Office.

May, A. D., Kelly, C., Shepherd, S., & Jopson, A. (2012). An option generation tool for potential urban transport policy packages. *Transport Policy*, *20*, 162-173.

McClelland, I. (1995). Product assessment and user trials. In E. N. Corlett & J. R. Wilson (Eds.), *Evaluation of human work* (pp. 249-284). London: Taylor & Francis.

Musselwhite, C., & Haddad, H. (2010). Mobility, accessibility and quality of later life. *Quality in Ageing and Older Adults*, *11*(1), 25-37.

Oliver, R., Gyi, D., Porter, J. M., Marshall, R., & Case, K. (2001). A survey of the design needs of older and disabled people. In P. T. McCabe, M. A. Hanson, & S.A Robertson (Eds.), *Contemporary ergonomics* (pp. 365-370). London: Taylor and Francis.

Office for National Statistics. (2015). Overview of the UK Population. *Office for National Statistics*. Retrieved from: http://www.ons.gov.uk/ons/dcp171776_422383.pdf

Porter, J. M., Marshall, R., Freer, M., & Case, K. (2004). SAMMIE: A computer aided ergonomics design tool. In N. J. Delleman, C. M. Haslegrave, & D. B. Chaffin, D.B. (Eds.), *Working postures and movements, tools for evaluation and engineering* (pp. 454-470). Boca Raton, FL: CRC Press.

Rye, T., & Mykura, W. (2009). Concessionary bus fares for older people in Scotland: Are they achieving their objectives? *Journal of Transport Geography*, *17*(6), 451-456. doi:10.1016/j.jtrangeo.2008.08.003

Saffer, D. (2007). *Designing for interaction: Creating smart applications and clever devices*. New York: AIGA Design Press.

Summerskill, S. J., Marshall, R., Case, K., Gyi, D. E., Sims, R. E., & Davis, P. (2009). Validation of the HADRIAN system using an ATM evaluation case study. *Lecture notes in computer science: Proceedings of the second international conference* (pp. 727-736). San Diego, CA: HCI International

Waller, S. D., Langdon, P. M., & Clarkson, P. J. (2010). Using disability data to estimate design exclusion. *Universal Access in the Information Society*, *9*(3), 195-207.

Yigitcanlar, T., Sipe, N., Evans R., & Pitot, M. (2007). A GIS-based land use and public transport accessibility indexing model. *Australian Planner*, *44*(3), 30-37. doi:10.1080/07293682.2007.9982586

About the Authors

Russell Marshall is a senior lecturer and head of the Design Ergonomics Group in the Design School at Loughborough University. His research interests cover a broad range of topics within Product, Industrial and Engineering Design including: Digital Human Modelling and tools and techniques for facilitating and empowering designers in human-centred and inclusive design practice; Ergonomics and Human Factors in design, Modular product design, and drawing and visualisation. Russell is also principal developer of SAMMIE the digital human modelling system.

Steve Summerskill is a Senior Lecturer at Loughborough University. His research and enterprise activity exploit the combination of industrial design and ergonomics skill sets. Digital Human Modelling is a key tool in the research activities performed. A recent example of Steve's research is a project performed for the UK Department for Transport (DfT) which involved identifying a key blind spot associated with collisions between trucks and vulnerable road users, which led to revisions of European standards.

Keith Case is Professor of Computer Aided Engineering in Mechanical, Electrical and Manufacturing Engineering at Loughborough University and is a Chartered Engineer, Fellow of the Chartered Institute of Ergonomics & Human Factors and a Fellow of the British Computer Society. In 1994 he received the Ergonomics Society Otto Edholm Award in recognition of his significant contribution to the development and application of ergonomics, primarily in the area of digital human modelling.

Amjad Hussain is an Associate Professor at the Department of Industrial & Manufacturing Engineering, University of Engineering and Technology, Lahore, Pakistan. He gained his PhD in Human Factors/Ergonomics from Loughborough University, UK. His main focus research areas are: Engineering Design; Inclusive Design; Human Factors/Ergonomics; Digital Human Modelling; Socio-technical System Design; Automation; Corporate Social Responsibility (CSR); Ageing and Industrial Workplace Design.

Diane Gyi is a Reader in Health Ergonomics and Design at Loughborough University. Her health background and knowledge of theory and practice has allowed her to integrate ergonomics into design, involving collaborations with over 50 organisations in grants to the value of over £3 million. Applications of her work have covered topics as diverse as vehicle seating, inclusive design and healthy ageing. Diane is a member of the Editorial Boards for both the Journal of Industrial Ergonomics and Applied Ergonomics.

Ruth Sims is a senior lecturer in psychology and ergonomics at the University of Derby. Her background is predominantly in the area of inclusive design/design for all, particularly considering physical design issues for older and/or disabled people, but also including social and psychological aspects of inclusion both in the physical world and online. She teaches undergraduate social and developmental psychology, as well as on Masters level ergonomics and behaviour change programmes.

Andrew Morris has 27 years' experience in the field of road transportation safety, vehicle safety, accident investigation, crash-injury and driver behaviour research. Recently, he has worked as project leader within large European consortiums on behalf of the European Commission on a number of major road safety initiatives including the SafetyNet, PENDANT, TeleFOT and DaCoTA projects. He has published over 180 refereed technical publications, reports and conference papers in the subject of accident research, road crash injury, accident causation and driver behaviour.

Jo Barnes is a Lecturer in the Design School having worked at Loughborough since 2005 initially as a researcher. She has a healthcare background in the area of traumatic injury and has spent over 15 years undertaking research in the area of road safety and injury prevention. Prior to coming to Loughborough University Jo held the position of Research Fellow in the Accident Research Centre at Monash University in Australia.

Does a Rise in Income Inequality Lead to Rises in Transportation Inequality and Mobility Practice Inequality?

Joko Purwanto

Transport & Mobility Leuven, 3010 Leuven, Belgium; E-Mail: joko@tmleuven.be

Abstract

Social and economic inequalities have sharpened in the late 20th century. During this period, Europe has witnessed a rising unemployment rate, a declining wages for the least qualified workers, a slowing of income growth, and an increasing gap between the richest and the poorest. Based on the hypothesis of the relation between socio-economic condition and mobility behaviour, it is necessary to ask how these socio-economic inequalities manifest themselves in transportation: does a rise in income inequality lead to a rise in transportation inequality and mobility practice inequality? This question is particularly relevant today as some European countries are facing high socio-economic inequalities following the financial crisis that started in 2008. Using results from transport, car ownership and mobility surveys as well as household surveys from the Paris (Île-de-France) region between eighties and late nineties, this paper tries to answer this question. The results show how inequalities in transportation and mobility practice have decreased during the period in spite of an increase in income inequalities. We find that the evolution of socio-economic inequality, most specifically income inequality was simply one of the determining factors of the evolution of inequalities in transportation and mobility practice. In fact, the most important role in that evolution is not played by the evolution of income inequality but by the evolution of elasticity between transportation and income. Reducing the effects of this elasticity should be the main target of transport policies to diminish inequality in transportation and mobility practice.

Keywords

car ownership; income inequality; mobility practice; Paris region; social inequality; transportation; travel budget; travel costs; travel time; trips frequency

Issue

This article is part of the issue "Transport Policy and Social Inclusion", edited by Miriam Ricci, Graham Parkhurst and Juliet Jain (University of the West of England, UK).

---

1. Introduction

In the last 30 year period, Europe has witnessed an increase in economic and social inequality. These problems take several forms, for example, the growth of unemployment especially within the poorest population categories, the fall in real wages of the least qualified workers, the general deceleration in income growth, and the increasing income gap between the richest and the poorest. Piketty (2002) has found that inequality in the distribution of income per consumption unit in France has been constant since the eighties after having undergone a strong decrease during the previous decade. A weak trend of increasing inequality can, however be detected since the nineties. Based on this phenomenon, one can now ask if these inequalities in social and economic sectors have an impact on mobility. Can a relationship between them be explored?

In order to answer this question, this paper presents an analysis of the dynamic of inequality by using the method of concentration index decomposition developed by Podder (1993) and by Wagstaff, Van Doorlaer and Watanabe (2003). This method allows us, first, to analyse the contribution of each socio-economic and demographic factor to the inequalities in mobility in static terms: at a given point in time and, second, in dynamic terms: between two points in time. Finally, this method helps analyse the impact of policies by separating out the effects on inequality of various changes.

This paper will first present three sources of data that concern the Paris region (L'Île-de-France) of France to support this work. Subsequently, using the above three types of data we present an analysis of the economic inequalities of the Paris region followed by an exploration of the demographic and socio-professional characteristics of the households. Finally, it will introduce the concentration index decomposition previously mentioned as the main method. This method application allows us to come to some conclusions as answers to the main question of this research.

The phenomenon of inequalities in mobility in its various forms, among others, the mobility characteristics of people coming from different socio-economic classes is in fact closely related to spatial segregation issues such as socio-spatial exclusion. In the context of the relationship between spatial segregation and inequalities in mobility, this paper helps prepare a framework of analysis for social exclusion from the starting point of mobility. More specifically, this paper shows the potential of using an econometrical methodology to describe the role of the different socio-economic factors that contribute to inequalities in mobility and its evolution.

2. Data

Having chosen the Paris region of France as a case study, the analysis was based on the results of three kinds of survey as explained in the following three subsections.

2.1. Global Survey of Transport

The first type of survey was the *Enquêtes Globales de Transport* or Global Survey of Transport of the years 1983, 1991 and 1997 (Direction Régionale et Interdépartementale de l'Équipement et de l'Aménagement, 1983, 1991, 1997). Abbreviated as EGT, it is a background survey on trips of people living in the Paris region (Île-de-France) which includes most of the basic themes of a mobility survey: number of trips, choice of mode, types of connections, patterns, lengths, travelling speed, and time budget. 10027 households (23601 individuals and 80181 trips) were surveyed in 1983, 11291 households (26009 individuals and 91243 trips) in 1991, and 4285 households (9681 individuals and 35907 trips) in 1997. The survey questionnaire focuses on three types of information concerning the interviewee's trips during one particular working day, the day prior to the interview, outside the holiday season: the general characteristics of the household, the characteristics of people aged more than 5 years old, and the trips of persons.

In this survey, each household was required to indicate their total annual household income, including: bonuses, the "13th month" salary, all other secondary activity income, all income related to movable and non-movable property, social benefits and so on. The definition of income in this survey is not elaborated upon, i.e. interviewees had the liberty to interpret it. No deduction due to direct taxes is taken into account in this income definition. Each household interviewed was required to answer this question by selecting one of the annual household income classes. 1983 survey consists of 13 income classes while that of 1991 and 1997 consist of 10 classes.

Two problems have been detected in relation to income information of EGT.

The first problem concerns the use of per household income as the living standard indicator.

Income per household information might give some idea of how much a household disposes in term of financial resource; however this information is a poor indicator of living standards. For example the standard of living in a household composed by a single person earning a monthly wage of €3,000 is not equal to the living standard of a household with three or four children whose parents earn the same monthly income as the previous household. To obtain a better living standard indicator, we need to take into account at least two additional aspects, household size and composition, for example by calculating the household average income per consumption unit. Unfortunately the information available in EGT does not allow us to calculate the consumption unit value per household as in this survey we cannot distinguish the age of each household's member. The best that we could do in this case was to calculate the average income per capita of the household.

For this work the average per capita income of the household is calculated by assigning the average per household income value of each class to every household belonging to that class and then dividing this value by the household size. Once the income data has been reordered in function of per capita income classes it is possible to see that this distribution had too many biases, for example through checking on the per household and per capita car ownership level in function of their income. The Appendix 1 shows an example of these biases based on 1997 EGT result.

In spite of some fluctuations, Appendix 1 shows that per household and per capita car ownership levels have increased in general with the household income level. This relationship becomes erroneous when trying to represent these car ownership levels in function of per capita income. In Appendix 1 it can be seen that the per household and per capita car ownership level of the 6th decile households are lower than those of the other deciles. This has to do with the high percentage of single person households that belong to the 6th decile.

To cope with this problem, the method used in Claisse et al. (2000) has been adopted and assigned to each household a theoretical and random value of income within the concerned income class. First, it is necessary to determine the percentage of households found theoretically below and above of the central (income) value of the concerned income class. This percentage is calculated in function of the slope of the cumulated distribution curve of the household population according to their income. An example of the estimated percentages for 1997 EGT is given in the Appendix 2.

The second problem detected was that of non-response.

The non-response percentages on the income question were respectively 11.7%, 11.4% and 9.8% for 1983, 1991 and 1997 EGT. These non-response households did not fundamentally correspond to any category representing homogenous characteristics. However, it was found that the majority of these households (52%) were families whose heads were older than 50 years old (against 39% of the households that have answered the income question). 30% of these non-response households had retired heads (against the average of 22%) and 45% of these non-response households had non-active heads (against the average of 34%).

To deal with this non-response problem, we used one of imputation of missing-data methods proposed by Richardson & Loeis (1997) and Armoogum & Madre (1997). Imputation of missing-data are methods of dealing with item non-response by imputing (estimating) values for the missing data based on some other source of information. Among these imputation methods is the "class mean imputation". Based on this method we first divided the sample population into strata based on other variables in the dataset, and then calculated the mean of the variable to be imputed within each strata. More precisely, we divided the households having replied the income question based on their car ownership level. In each car ownership level class, we calculated the average per capita income by distinguishing the households composed by only one person. The objective was to take into account the household structure effect in order to get a better homogeneity between the households found in the same class of car ownership. We finally imputed the average income per person for the non-response households as a function of their car ownership level.

2.2. INSEE Household Budget Survey (BDF)

The second type of survey was the *Enquêtes Budget de Famille* or the Household Budget Survey of the French National Institute of Statistics and Economic Studies (INSEE). Abbreviated as BDF, INSEE conducts this survey every 5 years and covers households living in France. For the purpose of this research it has only taken an extract of data consisting of households living in the Paris region or *francilien* household. The amount of these *franciliens* households covered in the survey are 1999, 2180, 1455 and 1706 respectively for the survey years of 1979, 1984, 1989 and 1994.

The main objective of this survey is to analyse the expense and the income resources of the observed households in order to allow comparisons between the different living standards and consumption choices of the different household categories. The main information gathered in the BDF is the nature and totality of households' expenditure, consumption and income resources. In this research, only some descriptive information of the households such as family composition, education level, type of employment of each family member as well as their mobility characteristics and budget have been used.

BDF has income information in terms of total annual household income. As opposed to EGT, BDF interviewees are asked to give their income information precisely instead of selecting a class of income. The interviewed households provide this information for each of the 73 household income types. These 73 types are grouped into three main categories: activity income, social benefits and capital income. Activity income is the sum of all salary including those of independent (liberal profession) income and income coming from secondary activities. Social benefits include retirement benefits, unemployment benefits, scholarships, familial social benefits, housing subsidies, subsidies or financial support in relation to invalidity, to specific family composition, other social benefits and the RMI or the *Revenu minimum d'insertion* which is a French form of social benefits aimed at people without any income who are of working age but do not have any other rights to unemployment benefits. Capital income is the sum of all income coming from tradable financial assets or securities and all income coming from real-estate assets. The sum of these three main income categories is the total annual household income. It is possible to consider this total yearly household income the household net income after obligatory tax deduction at source. However, direct taxes such as income, property and housing taxes are not yet excluded. The definition of household income in BDF is relatively comparable then to the one of the EGT.

Having income information declared specifically (rather than in income classes) allows us to proceed directly to living standard measures. In this work we present data from BDF not only in its original unit (per household income) but also in more living standard related measures, namely per person income and per consumption unit income. The latter is possible as we find household information in BDF not only in terms of size but also in terms of structure, such as the age of each household member.

We used the Eurostat consumption unit scale to

calculate per consumption unit income. This scale gives weight of 1 (one) to the household head (or the first adult member of the household), weight of 0.5 to each of the remaining adult members and 0.3 to each of the child members. Adult members are all persons of 14 year-old and older living in the household. This choice of scale is made solely on the base of comparability. INSEE and Organisation for Economic Co-operation and Development or OECD also use the Eurostat scale for their work.

2.3. INSEE Parc Auto Surveys

The last type of survey was the *Enquête INSEE de conjoncture auprès des ménages* or INSEE's households situation survey between 1972 and 1994 followed by the *Panel Parc-Auto* or Car Fleet Panel Survey conducted between 1994 and 1998 by three French institutes INRETS, ADEME and SOFRES.

In this survey and panel, household income is declared in 12 classes. We have implemented an imputation method upon these 12 classes in order to obtain 4 quartiles of household income and per consumption unit income. This particular imputation method consists of interpolating the distribution of a variable of interest, i.e. car ownership level per household, in order to define the limit between each income quartile and calculating the average car ownership level in each quartile. Here we made the rather strong assumption that within each income quartile, the household car ownership level did not vary in function of income.

The use of this simple method which is based on the interpolation of income class distribution can be generalized without problem to all orders of quantiles (tertile, quintiles, decile, etc.) under the condition that the number of original classes always be higher than the number of quantiles. Madre & Purwanto (2003) show the application and validation of this method by using as a case study a sample of households that have declared their total income (in number) in the INSEE-INRETS National Survey of Transport and Communication (*l'Enquête Nationale INSEE-INRETS Transports et Communications de*) 1993-1994.

3. Economic Inequalities in Paris Region

The *Île-de France* or Paris region is the region with the highest living standard in comparison to the other French regions. According to the *Institut National de la Statistique et des Études Économiques* (1998), the living standard level of Paris region is on average twice that of French overseas departments and 1.4 times of that of the other French departments' altogether.

However, in the interior of the region that can be divided into three concentric geographical zones, i.e. municipality of Paris or *Intramural Paris*, *Petite Couronne* (the Inner Circle) and *Grande Couronne* (the Outer Circle), the inequality in income distribution is quite strong. Appendix 3 shows how, between its three concentric geographical zones, Paris is the zone with the lowest average per household income. However as Intramural Paris households are composed by strong proportion of single person families, the living standard of the zone, calculated in term of per-unit consumption income, is the highest in the region. Households living in the Outer Circle, the zone with the weakest urbanization level in the region, have the lowest living standard.

The *Institut National de la Statistique et des Études Économiques* (1998) also remarks that the average per consumption unit income in France increased by an average of 4% per year during the seventies followed by a growth deceleration during the eighties when annual growth was merely 0.85%. The living standard growth remained constant between 1990 and 1996.

During the same period, the Paris region had a different evolutionary curve: based on calculations using BDF data as shown in the Appendix 3 the region underwent a period of stagnation or slight drop of per consumption unit between 1979 and 1989 followed by a rise between 1989 and 1994. It can also be observed that the per-household income grew less than the per person income during the whole observed period. This phenomenon was caused by a significant drop of the household size in all zones during the same period as shown in the Appendix 4.

Observing imputation method calculation results of EGT (Appendix 5), we see an increase in both levels of income, i.e. per household and per person income in Paris region between 1983 and 1991 followed by a weak drop or stagnation between 1991 and 1997.

At first sight, income data shown by two different data sources appears to have different evolution curves. In order to understand this one should remember that the income structures in the two surveys are not the same. The average incomes calculated from BDF are generally lower than those calculated from EGT. It is not easy to track down the evolution of the household income between 1979 and 1997, for example, using these two sources.

3.1. Income Distribution Analysis Based on Three Sources of Data

According to Piketty (2002) inequality of income per consumption unit in France was in stagnation in the eighties, after undergoing a sharp drop in the seventies. Still according to him, a slight rising trend can be detected since the beginning of nineties and this dynamic evolution of income distribution inequality in France was consistent with the trends experienced by all Western countries: income inequality especially in wage stopped falling in the eighties and nineties.

Moreover, the *Institut National de la Statistique et des Études Économiques* (1998) finds that income inequality today between 1990 and 1996 increasingly affected young families. Income continued to rise for older age groups while it stopped growing for younger age groups: households with a family head age between 25-35 years had the same income per consumption unit (in constant currency) as the same category ten or twenty years earlier.

Are these phenomena seen over the same period in the Île-de-France (Paris region)?

In the following paragraphs we will see an analysis of the Paris region using three different sources of information: EGT, BDF, and INSEE Parc Auto.

First, the analysis based on three comprehensive surveys of transport (EGT) shows that there was a significant increase in inequality of household income distribution between 1983 and the nineties (1991 and 1997).

The increase in household total income distribution and per person income distribution inequality was confirmed by calculating Gini coefficients. We see that changes in Gini coefficients (Appendix 6) and 10th/1st decile ratios (Appendix 7) between 1983 and 1991 in the Paris region as well as in its three geographical subregions were more significant compared to those coefficients and ratios from the 1991–1997 period. Inequalities of household income distribution increased more during the 1983-1991 period than during the following period. The same evolutionary trends are found in inequalities in terms of per person income distribution as shown in the Appendix 8 and the Appendix 9.

It is noticeable that income distribution inequalities among Parisian households were always higher than those between peri-urban households, i.e. households within the Inner and Outer Circle of the region.

The analysis from the four BDF surveys confirmed how inequalities in household income distribution among Parisians are greater than those that occur among peri-urban households. The results of these surveys also confirm that inequalities among the Outer Circle households are the lowest in the region (see Appendix 10 to Appendix 15).

There is no observable singular and clear trend of inequality evolution in Paris region between 1979 and 1994 from Gini coefficient and $10^{th}/1^{st}$ decile ratio appendix above, that has been calculated using BDF results. It is also possible to see a slight inversing trend on per-person and per-consumption unit income distribution: while Gini coefficients of the total household income distribution (Appendix 12) and the per-unit consumption income distribution (Appendix 14) in the whole Paris region (see Île-de-France columns) and in the Inner Circle were decreasing between 1979 and 1984, the $10^{th}/1^{st}$ ratios were increasing, as shown in the Appendix 13 for per person income distribution and the Appendix 15 for per-unit consumption income distribution. This shows how the inequality in general might decrease at the same time as the disparity between the richest and the poorest grows larger.

One significant finding from those Appendices is the trend that inequality in income distribution at all levels (namely, household, per capita and per consumption unit) in Intramural Paris increased between 1989 and 1994 as shown by the two inequality indicators, i.e. Gini coefficients and 10th /1st ratios. In the two other regions, the inequality indicators show rather stagnation and even slight decrease of income inequalities.

Finally, analysis of inequalities in household income distribution by applying the interquartile ratio ($4^{th}/1^{st}$) based on the *Parc Auto* Survey data shows three things. First, the $4^{th}/1^{st}$ ratios were in general lower for the 1980's relative to the 1970's, second, that the ratios were stagnant between the second half of the 1980's and the first half of the 1990's, and third, that starting from 1995, the magnitude of the ratios returned to the levels seen at the end of the 1970's (see the Appendix 16).

A calculation done using the same ratio based on household surveys (BDF) confirms these results and reconfirms that inequalities in household income distribution were the strongest among central Parisian households and the weakest among the households living in the outer circle area (Appendix 17).

In general, we can confirm a trend of reducing inequalities in income distribution among households in the Paris region from the seventies to the eighties, stagnation during the eighties, followed by an increase from the eighties to the nineties especially in Intramural Paris.

3.2. Demographical and Socio-Professional Characteristics of the Households

Elderly households, namely households with head of the family being 66 years old or more, composed the majority of the first decile in the distribution of income per consumption unit. The Appendix 18 however, shows a significant drop in the share percentage of these elderly households in the 1st decile from the first survey in 1979 (44%) to the forth survey in 1994 (13%). During the same period, we see an increasing percentage of younger households in this lowest income group, particularly those with heads under 25. This rejuvenation of the poorest households can imply the existence of two factors: employment or wage inequality that touches mostly younger people and the extension the study period. The *Institut National de la Statistique et des Études Économiques* (1998) shows this: the age at which more than 50% of young people had stable employment is 25 years (23.5 years in 1970), while the median age of school leavers was 21 years (20.5 years in 1990).

Regarding inequality in employment, Chauvel (1998) finds that during the 1990's in France, when the unemployment rate reached 13% of the working population, 25% of active people under 24 years old were unemployed. Wage inequality in France has worsened since 1975: while wages for older people continued to increase, wages of hiring younger people steadily declined. In 1995 the average living standard of households with heads aged between 50 and 59 years old was 40% higher than those with heads of 30 years old while in 1975 it was only 10-15% (Baudelot & Establet, 2000).

Younger families, in particular those whose head was aged younger than 31, were very poorly represented among the wealthiest households (10th decile). An increase in the proportion of very elderly households (≥66) in this decile was visible between 1979 and 1994.

We conclude that in Île-de-France there was a rejuvenation of the poorest households and an aging of the wealthiest households. The *Institut national de la statistique et des études économiques* (1998), moreover, finds that this aging was due to two factors: the increase in the average income of all pensioners and progression of capital income or heritage towards end-of-life.

The increase in average income for all pensioners' resulted solely from generational replacement, for example, a household with a 60 year-old head at a given date, had an average per consumption unit income higher than a household with the head of family of the same age at an earlier date. From one period in time to another, we are no longer in the presence of the same people. In 1996, people reaching retirement age may have benefited from more favourable retirement regulations, and often belonged to couples receiving two pensions.

Regarding socio-professional category, Appendix 19 shows a significant decrease in the percentage of retired households among households of the 1st decile 1984 (37%) to 1994 (15%) which was consistent with the results of Appendix 18. In 1984, 37% of households in the 1st decile were households with retired heads, whereas in 1994, 47% were households of with employees and/or workers at their heads. What can be seen is that these last two categories of actives were the most disadvantaged professional categories. Yet the total percentage of workers in the Ile-de-France experienced a real decline since the early 1980's.

Despite the 30% increase of the minimum wage in 1968, according to Piketty (2002), France was the country with the highest wage inequality in the western world in 1970, this inequality decreased rapidly during the seventies and then stabilized during the eighties and nineties, with a very small increase from 1983 to 1984. Piketty suggests, this stability was due primarily to the ongoing differences in the level of education and qualifications which explains the permanence of wage gaps. While the least skilled wage passed the certificate of study in brevet, the most qualified employees also lengthened the duration of their studies, attaining diplomas of higher education. The whole hierarchy of qualifications and wages moved up without notable change in difference. Secondly, this stability seems due to social perceptions that likely play a role in wage hierarchies. What a society considers a "fair" inequality probably contributes to the inertia of this wage inequality (see Jardin, 2003).

Over half of households in the 10th decile belonged to executives and liberal professions. The percentage of retired person households was rather important among this richest group that increased from 19% in 1984 to 23% in 1994. On the other hand, the proportion of retired households in the 1st decile of households experienced a significant drop from 37% in 1984 to 15% in 1994. Fournier (2003) finds that these retirees were mostly those people who have received the best share of the cake at the end of their working life. Although strong inequalities existed within this category, the revaluation of pensions made in the 1980's led to a revenue increase of senior citizens at the same time when the active youth incomes stalled.

Finally, Appendix 20 shows that the 1st decile of per consumption unit income were composed of households consisting of first singles, then unemployed, large and single parent households. Between 1979 and 1994, we find that the share of single households among first decile households decreased while it also increased in the 10th decile. In contrary, the share of 'unemployed' households among the poorest households doubled during the same period which is consistent with the phenomenon of inequality in employment.

4. Concentration Index Decomposition

The basis of the method is linked to the need to incorporate the analysis of mobility distribution to the econometrical framework through a simplified model of mobility. In principle, this analytical work requires a twofold approach.

First, the identification of sources of mobility inequalities is based on a formulation of concentration index as an indicator of its determinants. Assuming that during a given period, the relation between a mobility indicator *y* of a person *i* and a set of *k* individual factors x_k is represented by the following linear equation:

$$y_i = \alpha + \sum_k \beta_k x_{ki} + \varepsilon_i \tag{1}$$

where β_k are the coefficients and ε_i is the random term. When equation (1) has significant relationship, it can be used to decompose the socio-economic cause of inequality in mobility.

Wagstaff, et al. (2003) show that based on the relationship estimated in equation (1), the concentration index *C* of the variable *y* can be written as

$$C = \sum_k (\beta_k \bar{x}_k / \mu) C_k + GC_\varepsilon / \mu \tag{2}$$

where μ is the average of y, x_k is the average of x_k, and C_k is the concentration index of x_k. Residual or GC_ε (generalized concentration index for the error term) is defined in the last part of equation (2) as:

$$GC_\varepsilon = \frac{2}{n}\sum_{i=1}^{n} \varepsilon_i R_i \quad (3)$$

with n being the total number of population segments and R_i being fractional rank of the ith person in the income distribution. Equations (1) and (2) show how the concentration index C is in fact composed of two elements, the deterministic and the residual. The first element is the deterministic element, equal to the weighted sum of the concentration index relative to regressors k. The weight is simply the elasticity of y with respect to x_k, calculated at the sample average. The second element is the residual element that represents the mobility inequalities not captured by the factors x_k.

Secondly, where data allows, it is important to understand the causes of changes in mobility inequalities over time. Several approaches can be used for this purpose. The simplest option consists of evaluating the discrepancy between inequalities in two different points in time assuming that all components of social, economic and demographic inequalities are changing.

$$\Delta C = \sum_k (\beta_{kt}\bar{x}_{kt} / \mu_t) C_{kt} - \sum_k (\beta_{kt-1}\bar{x}_{kt-1} / \mu_{t-1}) C_{kt-1} + \Delta(GC_{\varepsilon t} / \mu_t) \quad (4)$$

However, this approach does not allow one to specify if variation in the inequality of mobility ΔC is due to change in inequalities (concentration index) of its determining factors, C_k, or if it is due to change of other influences—β_k and x_k. For this reason, a decomposition of mobility inequality using the method developed by Oaxaca (1973) appears to be slightly more fruitful. Assuming η_{kt} as the elasticity of y with respect to x at time t, the decomposition structure of Oaxaca can be written as follows:

$$\Delta C = \sum_k \eta_{kt}(C_{kt} - C_{kt-1}) + \sum_k C_{kt-1}(\eta_{kt} - \eta_{kt-1}) + \Delta(GC_{\varepsilon t} / \mu_t) \quad (5)$$

or

$$\Delta C = \sum_k \eta_{kt-1}(C_{kt} - C_{kt-1}) + \sum_k C_{kt}(\eta_{kt} - \eta_{kt-1}) + \Delta(GC_{\varepsilon t} / \mu_t) \quad (6)$$

or according to Lachaud (2003):

$$\Delta C = \sum_k 0{,}5(\eta_{kt} + \eta_{kt-1})(C_{kt} - C_{kt-1}) + \sum_k 0{,}5(C_{kt} + C_{kt-1})(\eta_{kt} - \eta_{kt-1}) + \Delta(GC_{\varepsilon t} / \mu_t) \quad (7)$$

Equations (5) to (7) allow tracing the double sources of variation in mobility inequality: (i) variations of inequality of the determining factors of mobility and (ii) variations of elasticity of the determining factors. It is worth noting that the method of decomposition proposed by these equations weights the variation of inequalities by the average of elasticities and the variation of elasticities by the average of inequalities (concentration indexes).

5. Inequalities in Transport and Mobility

In equation (1), y_i, the dependent variable measures of mobility. Ten indicators of mobility are considered:

- Number of trips per day per person (all modes)
- Number of trips by car per day per person
- Number of trips by public transit per day per person
- Number of trips on foot per day per person
- Distance travelled (km) per day per person (all modes)
- Distance travelled (km) by car per day per person
- Distance travelled (km) by public transit per day per person
- Average speed (km/h) per day per person (all modes)
- Average speed (km/h) by car per day per person
- Average speed (km/h) by public transit per day per person

To explain variations of these mobility variables, we adopt a classic model of trip generation. This model explains the number of trips produced per household by using several explanatory variables. According to McNally (2000), these variables are: the car ownership level of the household, household income, household size, the number of actives per household, etc. We have generalized this model by converting it to the "individual" level and by using it to estimate other indicators of mobility.

We retain several explanatory variables as follows:

- age and the square of age
- average income per person in the household
- social professional category of each individual: active (worker), retired, unemployed, student, and staying at home (inactive) where male and female are distinguished in each type
- dwelling zones in Paris region: Intramural Paris or Paris Inner circle and Outer circle

The independent variable of "age" does not enter the equation linearly. This allows one to incorporate the effect that mobility increase with age up to a certain point and then gradually drops.

The average income per person represents the living standard of the household in which the person belongs to. We used the inactive individual ("F-at home") as the referenced social professional category and the

Outer Circle ("F-Outer Circle") as the referenced dwelling zone.

These independent variables do not fully explain the variation in mobility as given in Appendix 21 to Appendix 23. The coefficients of determination R^2 were relatively low, especially for the frequency of trips and walking. The regression results are summarized in the following paragraph.

First, mobility indicators depended directly on the age of individuals. Coefficients on age are almost all positive. In fact, except for walking related indicators, the age squared was significantly involved in a negative way. Secondly, contrary to popular belief, per capita income played a small role. This was indicated by the values of estimated coefficients that were low compared to other coefficients of variables. However, these coefficients were generally positive. Third, the coefficients of the number of cars per person are generally highest in absolute terms compared to those of other variables. Except in frequency and distance in public transport and in frequency of walking, these values were always positive. Fourth, being a professionally active man actually promotes mobility by car. This was indicated by the high positive values of the coefficients in this category for frequency, distance and travel speed by car. Being a professionally active woman or a student promoted mobility by public transit. Housewives and other non-active categories show positive strong coefficients in walking frequency. Fifth, living in the Outer Circle seemed to be a factor that boosted mobility, in particular in terms of distance and speed. We find the opposite characteristics of living in Intramural Paris, which boosted trip frequency in public transit and walking. Living in the Inner Circle was always found between these two extremes.

Before analysing the decomposition of inequalities of the different mobility indicators, it is important to look at the indicator of inequalities that we used. In this analysis, it is the concentration index or concentration coefficient of mobility in comparison to individual income distribution. Inequality is then measured by a variable, in this case the mobility indicators, which is distributed between the different persons ranked according to their individual income. We observe then for example, if this variable of mobility is more concentrated among individuals with low income or among individuals with high income or if it is distributed proportionally according to the individual income.

Appendix 24 shows the concentration index of several mobility indicators. The positive values of these indexes suggests in most of the indicators that these variables were more concentrated among the individuals with high income. The higher the index value, the more concentrated this variable was among "rich" people and the inequality was more pronounced. On the contrary, negative values, which is found in the indicator of the "number of trips on foot per day per person" means that this variable was concentrated more among the individuals with low incomes.

In observing the fluctuation of these coefficients in time, it can be seen that most of these values were decreasing inversely to the trend of increasing inequality in the distribution of income per capita. The latter has been calculated in term of Gini index of the income per person distribution which grew from 0.315 in 1983 to 0.359 in 1991 and finally to 0.360 in 1997.

Does the fact that mobility indicators become in general less concentrated amongst wealthier people, necessarily mean that inequality of mobility has decreased during the observed period?

The answer to this question is rather difficult. For example, the decreasing concentration of trip frequency per day, by any modes, amongst the rich means that low income people have been moving with increasing frequency. On one hand, this might mean reduction in mobility inequality as we can interpret this as an increase in the mobility capacity of low income people but on the other hand, it might mean that low income people are "obliged" to make more frequent trips per day in order to fulfil their needs. The same also applies to other variables such as the distance travelled, by any mode, i.e. long distance travel might suggest freedom for some people but at the same time this might mean burden as low income people which are forced to live in the outskirts, far from their places of work or study. Finally the average speed might be the only indicator where a reduction of concentration among the rich people is always positive.

The aim of this research is, however, not to make a normative judgment on which level a concentration index of particular mobility indicators is fair or unfair. The aim is to discover how the different determining factors influence the final value of the concentration index.

6. The Role of the Evolution of Socio-Economic Inequalities on Transportation and Mobility Practice Inequalities

Detailed results of the decomposition method application, in relation to the equations (1) to (4) are given in Appendix 25 to Appendix 27. The Appendices show that inequality in the distribution of per capita income and per capita car ownership were the two main factors that explained the cause of inequalities in mobility at a particular point in time. For example, as shown in the Appendix 26, the inequalities of the income per person distribution explained 44%, 29%, and 38% of the cause of inequalities in travelled distance distribution of all modes respectively for the year 1983, 1991, and 1997. Inequality in the distribution per capita of car ownership was in fact the factor that explained most the causes of inequalities in the distribution of three variables, namely, travelling speed (Appendix

27), trip frequency by car (Appendix 25) and travelled distance by car (Appendix 26). It is interesting to note that this factor explained most of the causes of inequalities in the distribution of trip frequency on foot (57%, 48%, and 48% for the three observed years) as shown in Appendix 25, in other words, the more private cars were concentrated among the high income people, the more low-income people walk.

In Appendix 26 we see how in the previous example inequalities in per capita income, per capita car ownership and socio-professional category, reinforced the concentration of the travelled distance by private cars among high income people. Inequalities in car ownership show negative values of contribution to the distribution of trip frequency (Appendix 25) and distance travelled (Appendix 26) in public transport. This means the more concentrated among rich people car ownership was, the less rich people used public transit.

Inequality in age distribution contributed positively to mobility inequalities, meaning that the tendency that older people were richer than younger people contributed to the concentration of more mobility towards the rich (or, in case of frequency of travelling on foot, towards the low income people).

Finally, except for the trip frequency in all modes and in public transit, inequality in the distribution of geographical area of the household contributed negatively to the mobility inequalities. This means that the trend where rich people lived more in Intramural Paris than in the Inner and Outer Circles weakened the concentration of mobility among the rich.

One problem has been found in relation to the residuals that for some mobility indicators were high, such as in the case of trip frequency per day by public transit (1991 and 1997), travelled distance per day by public transit (1991, 1997) and average travel speed by car and public transit (all observed years). These high residuals mean that the independent variables used were not sufficient to explain the concerned dependent mobility indicator variables.

Transversal analysis above reveals elements that constitute inequalities of mobility at a given point in time. In fact, the main objective of the use of this decomposition method is found in its dynamic analysis between two points in time. Results of this dynamic analysis are given in the following Appendices.

Between 1983 and 1991, it can be seen that inequalities decreased for all mobility indicators as shown by the Appendix 24. An explanation for this decrease can be found again in the evolution of two factors: income and car ownership level.

First, it was noticed that the evolution of inequality in the distribution of car ownership during this period largely determined the evolution of inequalities in the distribution of travel speed and trip frequency by car. The evolution of this factor was responsible also for 105% of the reduction in inequalities in the trip frequency by car (Appendix 28). A percentage higher than 100% means that there were other factors whose evolutions in time contributed negatively to the inequalities of the corresponding mobility indicator.

Second, the evolution of inequality in per capita income distribution played a very important role in the evolution of inequalities in mobility on foot and on public transit. For example, it was responsible for 85% of the reduction of inequalities in trip frequency by public transit (Appendix 28) and for 104% of the reduction of inequalities in the travel distance (all motorized modes) during the same period (Appendix 29). Apart from that, it was responsible for 105% of the increase of inequalities in trip frequency on foot (Appendix 28).

During the following period (1991–1997), it was discovered that the role of the evolution of per capita income distribution inequality decreased significantly. Noticeably this evolution contributed negatively to changes in the inequality of many mobility indicators: on the one hand, it counterbalanced the reduction of inequalities in particular as regards those of travelled distance of all motorized modes, by car and trip frequency by public transport but, on the other hand, it offset the rising inequality in the average speed distribution of all motorized modes and car.

Inequality in the distribution of car ownership continued to play an important role in the evolution of inequality in mobility. The dynamic variations of this factor were responsible for reduction of inequalities for the number of trips of all modes, in public transport and on foot and the travelled distance in public transport. In addition, it contributed significantly to the rising inequality of the average speed of all motorized modes and car.

The evolution of the inequality in the distribution of different socio-professional categories contributed to reducing inequalities in the number of trips and distance by car. But it counteracted the reduction of inequalities in the distance and trip frequency by public transport.

The evolution of the inequality in the distribution of age contributed significantly to reducing inequalities in the total distance of travel (all motorized modes) and to offset the rising inequality in the trip frequency on foot.

Finally, the evolution of the inequality in residential location distribution, unlike the previous period, was in most cases, consistent with the overall trends in inequalities of mobility. In other words, changes in the distribution of people living in three areas (Intramural Paris, Inner and Outer Circles) between 1991 and 1997, generally contributed to reducing inequalities of mobility.

As in the previous discussion on the static contribution, there is found a problem that concerns the residuals. High residual values are found in some mobility indicators such as trip frequency per day on foot (1991–1997), travelled distance per day by public transit (1991–1997), and the average travel speed by public transit (both periods). Other dependent variables are needed to explain the concentration index evolution of those mobility variables.

Although the analysis of the total variation of the factors contributing to the dynamics of the concentration index is interesting, it does not itself differentiate changes due to the effects of elasticities and inequalities.

Concerning income per capita, we found that the effect of elasticities determined the contribution of this factor to the equalities of mobility indicators. According to the Oaxaca-type decomposition results, this contribution reduced inequality in all indicators, except the average speed for all motorized modes. In other words, instead of rising inequality in per capita income distribution between 1983 and 1991, income factor actually helped reduce inequalities in the travel distance by decreasing the elasticity of trip distance with respect to income. The same was also found in almost all indicators of mobility: neutralizing or reducing the effects of the elasticity of mobility with respect to income appeared to be one of the reasons for the reduction of inequalities in mobility between 1983 and 1991. Exceptions might occur when it comes to the number of walking trips: a decrease in the effects of elasticity contributed to the reduction of the concentration index of the frequency of walking trips which means more concentration of walking trips among low income people and more inequality.

Reductions in the effects of elasticity of mobility compared to the number of cars per capita also contributed in reducing inequalities in mobility, especially in car trips. Neutralizing or reducing the effects of the elasticity of mobility, especially by private car, with respect to the number of cars per capita, appeared to lead to the reduction of inequalities in mobility.

Finally, as raised in the previous section, changes in residential location altogether offset in most cases, changes in inequality. The change in the proportion and distribution of people living in Intramural Paris between 1983 and 1991 contributed in general to increasing inequalities in mobility during the same period. For the Oaxaca method, it is revealed that this increase was due firstly to the increase of the effects of the elasticity of mobility with respect to the fact of living in Intramural Paris between 1983 and 1991.

During the following period, between 1991 and 1997, the overall trend continued. In general, the effect of elasticity was higher than that of inequality. However, in cases of conflict which were somewhat more frequent, sometimes it was the effect of inequality that prevails, especially for the distance travelled by public transport.

7. Conclusions

Inequalities in mobility are determined by different socio-economic and geographic factors and income distribution inequality is only one of the important determining factors.

This study found that on any given date, inequality in the distributions of income per capita and car ownership per capita were the two primary factors that help explain most of the inequalities in mobility. Dynamically, the evolution of the inequality of these two factors was also the most important element in reducing inequalities in mobility between 1983 and 1997. The evolution of inequality in the distribution of car ownership during this period greatly affected the evolution of mobility inequality, speed and mobility by private car in particular, while evolution in the inequality of per capita income distribution during the same period determined the evolution of inequality in mobility on foot or by public transport in particular. During the following period (1991 - 1997), the role of the evolution of inequality in the per capita income distribution decreased while that of the per capita car ownership remained important.

It was also noticeable that the contribution of the evolution of determining factors to the evolution of inequality in mobility was driven mostly by the evolution of the effects of cross-elasticities of the indicators of mobility with respect to their determinants. This was especially true for income and car ownership. Between two dates, reducing the effects of cross-elasticities of mobility with respect to income and/or the rate of car ownership seemed to be a means for lowering the concentration indices of mobility and reducing inequality. Lowering the effects of the cross-elasticities can be done, for example, by reducing the regression coefficient of the different mobility indicators with regard to their determining factors, namely income and car ownership. In the real world, policies such as subsidizing public transport tickets with regard to the different income or socio-professional groups should lead to reducing mobility inequality directly and also that of spatial segregation, such as the socio-spatial exclusion phenomenon, indirectly.

The method of decomposition of inequality developed by Oaxaca (1973) and Wagstaff et al. (2003) is valid to decompose the causes of inequality of an object or a variable that is normally distributed or can be expressed by explanatory variables through a model of ordinary least square (OLS). The indicator of mobility as the frequency of travel, or indicator of car ownership level as the number of cars in a household is distributed following multinomial law. A modification of the model of decomposition of inequality for variables whose distributions are abnormal is a subject for future research. This change will allow a better understanding of the contribution of each explanatory variable whose distribution is abnormal.

The use of a better data source is also a point of improvement. The information recorded in the Global Survey of Transport (EGT) is the description of mobility on one particular weekday. The reliability can be expected from its sample size: the number of households, individuals, and trips being recorded. However, it might not be a stable representation of mobility behaviour, because mobility can vary from one day to another, from one week to another and from one season to another during the same year. The use of averaged information over a longer time period might improve this aspect.

Finally, there is a difficulty that can be quite disturbing in implementing this approach with regard to the level of mobility itself. Firstly, mobility can be considered as a dependent variable, determined by factors such as income. However, mobility can also be considered as one of the explanatory variables that affects income. In fact the two-way-relationships are valid but in this paper, only the first one has been given attention. Furthermore, this study has presented a set of mobility indicators as dependent variables which have been explained by the same independent variables. The low determination coefficients and the high residual values for some mobility indicators show the consequence of this choice. Future study focusing on fewer mobility indicators explained by more carefully selected independent variables should give more meaningful results. Despite this drawback, our study has shown the potential of the decomposition method used to analyse mobility inequality.

Secondly, mobility level is ambiguous. It is not easy to determine whether a very low trip frequency is the result of some constraining situation suffered by an individual. It is also difficult to determine whether low-mileage travel means the mobility coercion of an individual. Similarly, it is also difficult to say if high mileage undertaken by an individual signifies constraint or freedom for that individual. It is likely that high mileage is the phenomenon of over-mobility (Gibout and Toupin,(2002)). Indicators of mobility remain fairly trivial for this approach. Paulo (2007) states that it is impossible to elaborate precise quantitative criteria or indicators that allow us to order the mobility situation in terms of inequality but we can at least use the most frequently observed trends in individual practice of mobility as references. While Purwanto (2009) gives some preliminary hints on how to set a framework for these criteria, Jouffe, Caubel, Fol and Motte-Baumvol (2015) indicate that mobility inequalities are often interpreted normatively in terms of "lack" which is simply based on the assumption of lower mobility capacity of the poor in one hand and on the other hand, the domination of the rich in terms of movement. This interpretation, according to them, risks reducing the complexity of the phenomenon.

Acknowledgments

The author would like to thank Jean-Loup Madre and the *Institut français des sciences et technologies des transports, de l'aménagement et des réseaux* (IFSTTAR, formerly INRETS), Marne-la-Vallée, France for supervising and hosting the author's research activities as a doctoral candidate between 2000 and 2004 where materials, analysis and findings in this paper are among the obtained results. The author would also like to thank Université Louis Lumière Lyon2, Lyon, France, for financing the author's doctoral study and Transport & Mobility Leuven, Belgium, for technically and financially supporting the writing of this article.

Conflict of Interests

The author presented an earlier version of this paper in the International Transport Economic Conference in Minneapolis, June 15th 2009 under the title "Decomposing the causes of inequalities of people mobility".

References

Armoogum, J., & Madre, J.-L. (1997). *Item sampling, weighting and non-response*. Paper presented at the International Conference on Transport Survey Quality and Innovation. Grainau, Germany.

Baudelot, C., & Establet, R. (2000). *Avoir trente ans: En 1968 et en 1998.* Paris: Seuil

Chauvel, L. (1998). *Le destin des générations: Structure sociale et cohortes en France au XXe siècle.* Paris: Presses Universitaires de France.

Claisse, G., Diaz Olvera, L., Dille, B., Klein, O., Mignot, D., Paulo, C., Plat, D., Pochet, P., (2000). *Inégalités de déplacement et équité sociale revenus, indices, et inégalités d'accès à la VP. Résultats provisoires du projet IDEES* (Rapport Intermédiaire no. 2). Paris, France: Ministère de l'Equipement, des Transport et du Logement.

Direction Régionale et Interdépartementale de l'Équipement et de l'Aménagement. (1983). *Enquêtes globales transports*. Paris, France: Préfet de la région d'Île-de-France.

Direction Régionale et Interdépartementale de l'Équipement et de l'Aménagement. (1991). *Enquêtes globales transports*. Paris, France: Préfet de la région d'Île-de-France.

Direction Régionale et Interdépartementale de l'Équipement et de l'Aménagement. (2001). *Enquêtes globales transports*. Paris, France: Préfet de la région d'Île-de-France.

Fournier, M. (2003). Inégalités: De quoi parle-t-on? *Sciences humaines*, *136*, 22-22.

Institut National de la Statistique et des Études Économiques. (1998). *Revenus et patrimoine des ménages* (INSEE Synthèse 19). Paris, France: Insee.

Jardin, E. (2003). La disparition des rentiers: Entretien avec Thomas Piketty. *Sciences humaines*, *136*, 34-35.

Jouffe, Y., Caubel, D., Fol, S., & Motte-Baumvol, B. (2015). Faire face aux inégalités de mobilité (document 708). *Cybergeo: European Journal of Geography Espace, Société, Territoire*. Retrieved from http://cybergeo.revues.org/26697. doi:10.4000/cybergeo.26697

Lachaud, J.-P. (2003). *La dynamique de l'inégalité de la malnutrition des enfants en Afrique. Une analyse comparative fondée sur une décomposition de régression.* Bordeaux, France: Centre d'économie du développement, Université Montesquieu-Bordeaux.

Madre, J.-L., & Purwanto, A. J. (2003). Des quantiles interpolés pour suivre l'évolution des inégalités. Paper presented at the 39th Colloque de l'Association de Science Régionale De Langue Française, École nationale des travaux publics de l'État,Lyon.

McNally, M. G. (2000). The activity-based approach. In D. A. Hensher & K. J. Button (Eds.), *Handbook of transport modelling* (pp. 55-73). Oxford, UK: Pergamon.

Oaxaca, R. (1973). Male-female wages differences in urban labour markets. *International Economic Review, 14*, 693-709.

Paulo, C. (2007). Une mesure des inégalités de mobilité et d'accès au volant. *EspacesTemps.net*. Retrieved from http://www.espacestemps.net/articles/une-mesure-des-inegalites-de-mobilite-et-acces-au-volant

Piketty, T. (2002). *L'économie des inégalités*. Paris: Editions La Découverte.

Podder, N. (1993). The disaggregation of the Gini coefficient by factor components and its applications to Australia. *Review of Income and Wealth, 39*(1), 51-61.

Purwanto, A. J. (2009). Which equality for mobility. *Paper presented at the BIVEC-GIBET transport research day 2009*. Vrij Universiteit Brussel (VUB), Brussels, Belgium.

Richardson, A., & Loeis, M. (1997). Estimation of missing income in household travel surveys. *Proceedings of the 21st Australasian transport research forum. (pp.249-266)* Victoria, Australia: ARRB Group Limited.

Gibout, C., & Toupin, F., (2002). *Mobilité subie, déplacements choisis: Le cas de la sur-mobilité en région tourangelle. Research synthesis on mobility and inequality.* Tours, France: Agence d'Urbanisme de l'Agglomération de Tours.

Wagstaff, A., Van Doorlaer, E., & Watanabe. (2003). On decomposing the causes of health sector inequalities with an application to malnutrition inequality in Vietnam. *Journal of Econometrics, 112*, 207-202.

About the Author

Joko Purwanto obtained his Degree in Civil Engineering in 1997 and is experienced in transport infrastructure project feasibility studies in Indonesia. He pursued Masters (2000) and Doctoral (2004) degrees in transport economics in France. Between 2005 and 2008 he worked as a research fellow in transport and energy sectors modelling at the DG Joint Research Centre of the European Commission in Seville, Spain. In 2008 he joined Transport & Mobility Leuven in Belgium and works as senior researcher.

Appendix 1. Incoherencies due to transforming household income class to per capita income decile. Source: 1997 EGT result based calculation*.

Household income class	Car ownership level	Car ownership level per capita	Household income per capita in decile	Car ownership level	Car ownership level per capita
Less than €5700	0.21	0.18	D1 (1st decil)	0,57	0,17
€5700-€11400	0.27	0.17	D2	1,01	0,30
€11400–€17100	0.43	0.26	D3	0,71	0,26
€17100–€22800	0.74	0.40	D4	1,14	0,39
€22800–€28500	0.92	0.46	D5	1,14	0,45
€28500–€34200	1.17	0.50	D6	0,78	0,34
€34200–€45600	1.27	0.51	D7	1,27	0,55
€45600–€68400	1.54	0.58	D8	0,93	0,55
€68400–€114000	1.64	0.59	D9	1,12	0,65
More than €114000	1.89	0.63	D10	1,03	0,67
Average	0.97	0.43	Average	0,97	0,43

Note: * The original currency used in the data processing was 1998 French Franc. We perform a conversion into 2015 € (Euro) to be used as currency in this paper using methodology given by the *Institut national de la statistique et des études économiques* (Insee) website: http://www.insee.fr/fr/service/reviser/calcul-pouvoir-achat.asp?sommeDepart =1&deviseDepart=Franc&anneeDepart=1998&deviseArrivee=Euro&anneeArrivee=2015 (as retrieved on 13 May 2016). Given the currency depreciation due to inflation, the purchasing power of 1 (one) French Franc in 1998 is the same as that of 0.19 Euros in 2015.

Appendix 2. Theoretical estimation of household income distribution for each household income class of 1997 EGT. Source: EGT result based calculation.

Household income class	Theoretical percentage of household with income below the class central value	Theoretical percentage of household with income above the class central value
Less than €5700	Not available (NA*)	NA
€5700-€11400	0.39	0.61
€11400–€17100	0.48	0.52
€17100–€22800	0.51	0.49
€22800–€28500	0.57	0.43
€28500F–€34200	0.51	0.49
€34200–€45600	0.70	0.30
€45600–€68400	0.81	0.19
€68400–€114000	0.88	0.12
More than €114000	NA	NA

Note: * We need upper and lower values for each class in order to estimate the theoretical percentage. For the lowest and highest class we then assign arbitrary values.

Appendix 3. Average income in Paris region in 2015 Euros. Source: BDF 1979, 1984, 1989, 1994 results based calculation.

	1979	1984	1989	1994
	per-household income			
Paris	33693	36888	38055	44699
Inner Circle	41900	37602	39715	39782
Outer Circle	42434	39535	40912	40320
Île-de-France	39736	38188	39704	41127
	per-person income			
Paris	18511	20842	21569	25574
Inner Circle	17472	17332	18165	18576
Outer Circle	15430	15549	17383	17533
Île-de-France	17041	17485	18020	20770
	per-consumption unit income			
Paris	22950	25550	26324	31195
Inner Circle	24443	23247	24320	24524
Outer Circle	22838	22198	23857	24023
Île-de-France	23441	23395	24690	27018

Appendix 4. Average Eurostat scale consumption unit. Source: BDF 1979, 1984, 1989, 1994 results based calculation.

	1979	1984	1989	1994
Paris	1.46	1.45	1.42	1.41
Inner Circle	1.74	1.64	1.65	1.64
Outer Circle	1.88	1.81	1.75	1.72
Île-de-France	1.71	1.66	1.62	1.62

Appendix 5. Average income in Paris region in 2015 Euros. Source: calculation results of EGT 1983, 1991, 1997 results based calculation.

	1983	1991	1997
	per-household income		
Paris	28613	32212	31148
Inner Circle	30438	32944	31377
Outer Circle	32298	34743	34850
Île-de-France	30576	33430	32674
	per-person income		
Paris	17131	19326	19132
Inner Circle	14221	15833	15028
Outer Circle	12928	14296	14577
Île-de-France	14579	16143	15952

Appendix 6. Per household income distribution: Gini coefficients. Source: EGT result based calculation.

	Île-de-France	Paris	Inner circle	Outer circle
1983	0,30	0,34	0,29	0,28
1991	0,35	0,40	0,34	0,32
1997	0,36	0,40	0,33	0,35

Appendix 7. Per household income distribution: 10th/1st decile ratios. Source: EGT result based calculation.

	Île-de-France	Paris	Inner circle	Outer circle
1983	8,00	10,39	7,37	6,83
1991	11,21	17,90	9,74	9,00
1997	11,73	17,94	9,77	10,19

Appendix 8. Per person income distribution: Gini coefficients. Source: EGT result based calculation.

	Île-de-France	Paris	Inner circle	Outer circle
1983	0,32	0,33	0,31	0,29
1991	0,36	0,38	0,35	0,33
1997	0,35	0,38	0,33	0,34

Appendix 9. Per person income distribution: 10th /1st decile ratios. Source: EGT result based calculation.

	Île-de-France	Paris	Inner circle	Outer circle
1983	9,05	10,79	8,59	7,54
1991	12,01	16,89	10,83	9,55
1997	12,24	16,19	10,26	10,81

Appendix 10. Per household income distribution: Gini coefficients. Source: BDF result based calculation.

Year	Île-de-France	Paris	Inner circle	Outer circle
1979	0.37	0.38	0.39	0.34
1984	0.36	0.43	0.35	0.32
1989	0.37	0.42	0.37	0.32
1994	0.38	0.50	0.36	0.30

Appendix 11. Per household total income distribution: 10th/1st decile ratios. Source: BDF result based calculation.

Year	Île-de-France	Paris	Inner circle	Outer circle
1979	13.63	14.65	13.04	11.35
1984	13.60	23.04	13.49	9.64
1989	13.96	16.88	15.91	9.49
1994	14.40	50.11	11.59	7.81

Appendix 12 Per person income distribution: Gini coefficients. Source: BDF result based calculation.

Year	Île-de-France	Paris	Inner circle	Outer circle
1979	0.37	0.36	0.40	0.33
1983	0.36	0.41	0.35	0.32
1989	0.35	0.37	0.35	0.33
1994	0.38	0.48	0.35	0.31

Appendix 13. Per person income distribution: 10th/1st decile ratios. Source: BDF result based calculation.

Year	Île-de-France	Paris	Inner circle	Outer circle
1979	10.15	11.07	10.84	8.77
1984	11.91	18.68	11.51	8.61
1989	11.27	12.66	12.22	9.12
1994	13.40	37.33	10.89	7.76

Appendix 14. Per consumption unit income distribution: Gini coefficients. Source: BDF result based calculation.

Year	Île-de-France	Paris	Inner circle	Outer circle
1979	0.34	0.34	0.38	0.31
1983	0.33	0.39	0.32	0.29
1989	0.33	0.36	0.33	0.29
1994	0.35	0.47	0.33	0.27

Appendix 15. Per consumption income unit distribution: 10th/1st decile ratios. Source: BDF result based calculation.

Year	Île-de-France	Paris	Inner circle	Outer circle
1979	9.25	10.67	9.46	7.87
1984	10.24	17.35	10.25	7.23
1989	9.78	11.80	10.85	7.09
1994	10.94	36.16	8.91	6.19

Appendix 16. Per household income distribution: 4th/1st quartile ratios. Source: INSEE Parc Auto result based calculation.

Year	4th/1st	Year	4th/1st	Year	4th/1st
1974	5.77	1984	5.05	1994	4.91
1975	5.48	1985	4.50	1995	5.67
1976	4.90	1986	4.37	1996	5.05
1977	5.75	1987	4.83	1997	5.71
1978	5.62	1988	4.63	1998	5.52
1979	5.42	1989	4.66		
1980	5.34	1990	4.73		
1981	5.57	1991	4.56		
1982	5.65	1992	4.58		
1983	4.79	1993	4.78		

Appendix 17. Per household income distribution: 4th/1st quartile ratios. Source: BDF result based calculation.

Year	Île-de-France	Paris	Inner circle	Outer circle
1979	5.82	6.60	5.73	5.04
1984	5.62	7.69	5.49	4.71
1989	5.88	7.49	6.19	4.76
1994	6.12	12.58	5.72	4.25

Appendix 18. Distribution (%) of the different head of family age groups in per consumption unit income classes. Source: BDF 1979, 1984, 1989, 1994 result based calculation.

	1979		1984		1989		1994	
Age of the head of family	**1er**	**10th**	**1er**	**10th**	**1er**	**10th**	**1er**	**10th**
age<=20 years	1.9	0.0	2.6	0.0	3.7	0.0	5.0	0.0
21–25 years	7.0	1.3	7.8	1.0	10.6	0.9	17.2	0.0
26–30 years	0.9	5.7	8.9	9.7	6.9	5.7	8.1	5.0
31–35 years	9.2	14.5	7.4	11.1	9.5	11.2	11.6	7.1
36–40 years	6.7	10.5	8.1	11.8	10.2	9.4	7.8	7.3
41–45 years	9.4	10.8	4.3	9.6	7.1	14.3	10.5	10.5
46–50 years	4.3	7.4	7.4	7.1	5.0	10.4	9.4	16.3
51–55 years	5.2	16.0	5.4	14.6	7.2	11.4	8.4	11.8
56–60 years	6.7	13.0	7.1	11.0	8.4	12.7	4.7	13.7
61–65 years	4.8	7.5	8.0	11.1	5.6	9.3	4.5	8.1
66 years<=age	44.1	13.3	33.1	12.9	25.7	14.7	12.7	20.3
Total	100.0	100.0	100.0	100.0	100.0	100.0	100.0	100.0

Appendix 19. Distribution (%) of the different socio-professional categories in per consumption unit income classes. Source: BDF result based calculation.

	1984		1989		1994	
Socio-professional category	**1st**	**10th**	**1st**	**10th**	**1st**	**10th**
active: farmers	1.0	0.0	0.0	0.0	0.0	0.0
active : craftsmen, retail traders, liberal professions	5.6	3.2	8.3	6.9	5.5	8.8
active : executives, liberal professions	5.9	51.1	7.7	53.9	4.9	57.6
active : intermediate occupations	5.8	18.7	5.6	13.0	4.4	4.1
active : employees	11.8	4.7	13.5	1.4	24.9	2.7
active : labourers	13.6	1.4	15.3	0.9	22.2	1.2
inactive : retired persons	37.3	19.1	23.9	23.0	14.9	23.1
Other inactive	19.1	1.7	25.8	0.9	23.3	2.6
Total	100.0	100.0	100.0	100.0	100.0	100.0

Appendix 20. Distribution (%) of the different household types in per consumption unit income classes. Source: BDF result based calculation.

	1979			1984			1989			1994		
Household type	**1st**	**10th**	**all**	**1st**	**10th**	**all**	**1st**	**10th**	**all**	**1st**	**10th**	**all**
Single person household	50.3	18.3	24.5	46.7	24.3	28.0	46.0	26.2	31.2	45.5	29.2	32.2
Mono-parental household	4.0	0.6	2.2	3.1	0.0	2.3	1.9	1.8	1.9	6.8	0.0	2.7
Large family household	6.9	2.1	4.8	6.9	2.8	4.6	3.9	1.5	3.4	6.3	3.1	4.2
Household with at least one unemployed	12.0	2.6	6.7	20.0	2.6	8.0	17.8	1.5	8.2	30.4	6.2	11.0

Appendix 21. Estimation results of trip frequencies. Source: EGT result based calculation.

	number of total trips/day			number of car trips/day			number of transit trips/day			number of on foot trips/day		
	1983	1991	1997	1983	1991	1997	1983	1991	1997	1983	1991	1997
Constant	3,0E+03***	3,2E+03***	3,1E+03***	9,7E-01***	1,4E+03***	1,5E+03***	-4,0E-01***	-7,4E-01***	-5,9E-01***	2,4E+03***	2,5E+03***	2,2E+03***
Age	1,4E-02**	3,5E-02***	6,1E-02***	5,0E-03*	1,2E-02**	1,8E-02**	2,9E-02***	5,0E-02***	4,7E-02***	-2,0E-02***	-2,8E-02***	-4,0E-03*
Age^2	-4,0E-04***	-6,0E-04***	-9,0E-04***	-1,7E-04***	-2,6E-04***	-3,1E-04***	-3,4E-04***	-5,5E-04***	-5,4E-04***	1,1E-04**	2,1E-04***	-5,6E-05*
Income	4,2E-06***	8,0E-07**	8,5E-07*	-2,3E-07*	-3,9E-07*	-6,1E-07*	3,4E-06***	1,5E-06***	1,8E-06***	9,9E-07**	-2,8E-07*	-3,6E-07*
M-active	-5,5E-02*	-2,3E-01***	-7,0E-01***	5,7E-01***	4,5E-01***	-2,5E-02*	4,1E-01***	4,3E-01***	3,8E-01***	-1,0E+03***	-1,1E+03***	-1,0E+03***
M-retired	5,1E-02*	-6,0E-03*	-1,6E-01*	-6,5E-02*	-1,5E-01*	-2,8E-01**	2,0E-01***	2,8E-01***	3,2E-01***	-8,0E-02*	-1,4E-01**	-2,0E-01*
M-unemployed	-2,7E-01**	-4,3E-01***	-4,0E-01**	-8,3E-02*	-3,4E-01**	-2,9E-01*	3,6E-01***	3,7E-01***	5,1E-01***	-5,4E-01***	-4,6E-01***	-6,2E-01***
M-student	-5,8E-01***	-7,3E-01***	-7,8E-01***	-7,3E-01***	-9,7E-01***	-9,9E-01***	5,7E-01***	9,2E-01***	5,9E-01***	-4,2E-01***	-6,8E-01***	-3,8E-01**
M-at home	-1,1E+03***	-1,3E+03***	-1,4E+03***	-1,3E-01*	-9,3E-01**	-8,6E-01**	1,4E-01*	7,9E-01***	5,2E-02*	-1,1E+03***	-1,2E+03***	-5,7E-01**
F-active	-3,2E-02*	-1,5E-01**	-3,3E-01**	5,0E-03*	-4,6E-02*	-1,6E-01*	6,0E-01***	6,1E-01***	5,2E-01***	-6,4E-01***	-7,2E-01***	-6,8E-01***
F-retired	-3,5E-01***	-4,3E-01***	-3,7E-01**	-1,3E-01*	-3,8E-01***	-5,0E-01***	9,9E-02**	2,9E-01***	3,0E-01***	-3,2E-01***	-3,4E-01***	-1,7E-01*
F-unemployed	-2,6E-01**	-2,5E-01**	-2,5E-01*	-2,9E-01**	-4,9E-01***	-2,3E-01*	3,9E-01***	4,2E-01***	2,9E-01**	-3,6E-01**	-1,7E-01**	-3,1E-01**
F-student	-5,3E-01***	-5,5E-01***	-8,0E-01***	-6,9E-01***	-9,4E-01***	-1,0E+03***	5,4E-01***	9,9E-01***	7,1E-01***	-3,8E-01***	-6,0E-01***	-4,8E-01***
F-at home	Category of reference											
Paris	4,23E-01***	3,14E-01***	3,23E-01***	-6,79E-01***	-8,98E-01***	-9,88E-01***	5,26E-01***	5,29E-01***	6,08E-01***	5,76E-01***	6,83E-01***	7,03E-01***
Inner circle	1,39E-01***	-4,70E-02*	1,17E-01**	-3,43E-01***	-4,81E-01***	-3,18E-01***	2,21E-01***	1,47E-01***	2,31E-01***	2,60E-01***	2,87E-01***	2,04E-01***
Outer circle	Category of reference											
Car ownership	3,86E-01***	4,17E-01***	2,46E-01**	1,94E+03***	1,75E+03***	1,80E+03***	-7,44E-01***	-6,73E-01***	-8,00E-01***	-8,04E-01***	-6,61E-01***	-7,54E-01***

Note: *t-student statistics ***p<0,0001 ** 0,0001<=p<0,05 * p>=0,05.*

Appendix 22. Estimation result of travel speed. Source: EGT result based calculation.

	average travel speed			**average car travel speed**			**average transit travel speed**		
	1983	**1991**	**1997**	**1983**	**1991**	**1997**	**1983**	**1991**	**1997**
Constant	4,9E+03 ***	5,3E+03 ***	4,9E+03 ***	1,2E+04 ***	1,5E+04 ***	1,1E+04 ***	1,1E+04 ***	1,1E+04 ***	9,0E+03 ***
Age	1,8E-01 ***	3,9E-01 ***	2,6E-01 ***	1,5E-01 **	3,0E-01 ***	2,7E-01 ***	1,4E-01 ***	3,9E-01 ***	2,4E-01 ***
Age^2	-2,0E-03 ***	-4,8E-03 ***	-3,2E-03 ***	-1,6E-03 **	-4,0E-03 ***	-3,4E-03 ***	-1,6E-03 ***	-4,5E-03 ***	-2,8E-03 ***
Income	2,4E-06 *	5,2E-06 **	1,1E-06 *	1,7E-06 *	3,8E-07 **	-9,8E-07 *	3,8E-06 *	3,4E-06 *	4,4E-07 *
M-active	5,9E+03 ***	9,4E+03 ***	6,2E+03 ***	3,3E+03 ***	5,7E+03 ***	4,6E+03 ***	2,6E+03 ***	5,2E+03 ***	3,2E+03 ***
M-retired	8,6E-01 *	3,7E+03 ***	2,1E+03 **	1,1E+03 *	4,0E+03 *	2,9E+03 **	9,3E-01 *	3,8E+03 **	1,3E+03 *
M-unemployed	2,4E+03 **	3,0E+03 **	1,9E+03 **	1,7E+03 *	2,7E+03 **	3,6E-01 *	1,2E+03 *	1,2E+03 *	1,0E+03 *
M-student	1,0E+00 **	2,7E+03 ***	6,4E-01 *	8,0E-01 *	1,0E+03 **	1,3E-01 *	5,1E-01 *	1,7E+03 *	2,3E-01 *
M-at home	3,8E+03 **	4,4E+03 *	8,6E-01 *	3,9E+03 *	2,2E+03 **	2,1E+03 *	1,1E+03 *	4,7E+03 *	1,4E+03 *
F-active	2,9E+03 ***	4,9E+03 ***	3,3E+03 ***	9,4E-01 *	1,7E+03 *	2,0E+03 **	1,5E+03 **	2,9E+03 **	1,5E+03 **
F-retired	7,1E-01 *	2,7E+03 ***	1,8E+03 **	1,1E+03 *	2,9E+03 *	3,4E+03 **	5,2E-01 *	1,9E+03 *	5,7E-01 *
F-unemployed	2,8E+03 ***	1,8E+03 **	9,2E-01 *	2,8E+03 **	2,1E+03 *	6,8E-01 *	8,0E-01 *	-3,9E-02 *	-2,9E-01 *
F-student	1,2E+03 **	2,4E+03 **	9,7E-01 *	1,1E+03 *	-3,3E-01 **	4,2E-01 *	-3,8E-01 *	1,8E+03 *	5,5E-01 *
F-at home	Category of reference								
Paris	-6,0E+03 ***	-8,4E+03 ***	-7,0E+03 ***	-6,5E+03 ***	-8,3E+03 ***	-7,4E+03 ***	-7,3E+03 ***	-1,0E+04 ***	-7,5E+03 ***
Inner circle	-4,3E+03 ***	-5,9E+03 ***	-5,2E+03 ***	-5,3E+03 ***	-6,3E+03 ***	-6,1E+03 ***	-5,6E+03 ***	-6,6E+03 ***	-6,2E+03 ***
Outer circle	Category of reference								
Car ownership	5,4E+03 ***	4,8E+03 ***	5,6E+03 ***	2,6E+03 ***	2,0E+03 *	2,6E+03 ***	2,2E+03 ***	1,8E+03 **	2,0E+03 ***

Note: *t-student statistics ***p<0,0001 ** 0,0001<=p<0,05 * p>=0,05.*

Appendix 23. Estimation results of travel distance. Source: EGT result based calculation.

	total km/day			total transit km/day		
	1983	1991	1997	1983	1991	1997
Constant	6,1E-01 *	-4,5E+03 **	-1,1E+03 *	-1,8E+03 *	-8,5E+03 **	-4,3E+03 *
Age	3,4E-01 ***	9,3E-01 ***	6,4E-01 ***	2,4E-01 ***	7,2E-01 ***	4,4E-01 **
Age^2	-4,1E-03 ***	-1,1E-02 ***	-7,5E-03 ***	-2,7E-03 ***	-7,8E-03 ***	-4,8E-03 ***
Income	3,3E-05 ***	2,3E-05 ***	2,1E-05 ***	2,7E-05 **	2,1E-05 *	1,6E-05 *
M-active	1,3E+04 ***	2,2E+04 ***	1,4E+04 ***	5,5E+03 ***	9,3E+03 ***	6,3E+03 ***
M-retired	2,2E+03 **	6,0E+03 ***	3,8E+03 **	1,8E+03 *	4,0E+03 **	2,5E+03 *
M-unemployed	5,5E+03 ***	8,4E+03 ***	7,4E+03 ***	3,7E+03 **	5,7E+03 **	4,7E+03 **
M-student	3,0E+03 ***	9,3E+03 ***	3,3E+03 **	4,4E+03 **	1,2E+04 **	5,5E+03 **
M-at home	3,2E+03 *	8,1E+03 **	1,5E+03 *	1,8E+03 *	1,0E+04 *	1,6E+03 *
F-active	7,0E+03 ***	1,2E+04 ***	8,4E+03 ***	6,0E+03 **	1,0E+04 ***	6,4E+03 **
F-retired	1,8E+03 **	4,6E+03 ***	3,0E+03 **	1,3E+03 *	3,7E+03 *	2,4E+03 *
F-unemployed	3,9E+03 **	4,1E+03 **	3,1E+03 **	2,9E+03 *	4,5E+03 *	2,2E+03 *
F-student	2,9E+03 ***	9,9E+03 ***	4,8E+03 ***	4,0E+03 **	1,2E+04 **	6,9E+03 *
F-at home	Category of reference					
Paris	-7,0E+03 ***	-1,1E+04 ***	-1,0E+04 ***	-2,2E+03 ***	-3,9E+03 ***	-2,7E+03 ***
Inner circle	-5,1E+03 ***	-8,4E+03 ***	-6,9E+03 ***	-1,5E+03 ***	-2,9E+03 ***	-2,2E+03 ***
Outer circle	Category of reference					
Car ownership	5,6E+03 ***	5,2E+03 ***	4,5E+03 ***	-5,1E+03 ***	-8,2E+03 ***	-6,8E+03 ***

Note: *t-student statistics ***p<0,0001 ** 0,0001<=p<0,05 * p>=0,05.*

Appendix 24. Concentration index of mobility indicators in comparison to income per person distribution. Source: EGT result based calculation.

Indicators of mobility	1983	1991	1997
Number of trips per day per person (all modes)	0.035	0.020	0.005
Number of trips by car per day per person	0.126	0.111	0.097
Number of trips by public transit per day per person	0.093	0.028	0.008
Number of trips by foot per day per person	-0.079	-0.100	-0.110
Distance travelled (km) per day per person (all modes)	0.125	0.096	0.092
Distance travelled (km) by car per day per person	0.168	0.155	0.155
Distance travelled (km) by public transit per day per person	0.102	0.041	0.013
Average speed (km/h) per day per person (all modes)	0.090	0.066	0.077
Average speed (km/h) by car per day per person	0.119	0.109	0.115
Average speed (km/h) by public transit per day per person	0.111	0.041	0.032

Appendix 25. Static contribution of factors to the concentration index of trip frequency per day. Source: EGT result based calculation.

Variable	All modes			Private car			Public transit			On foot		
	1983	1991	1997	1983	1991	1997	1983	1991	1997	1983	1991	1997
Age	31%	145%	1269%	8%	21%	43%	129%	714%	3600%	51%	66%	11%
Age2	-66%	-185%	-1481%	-20%	-32%	-60%	-105%	-571%	-3333%	-19%	-37%	12%
Income	77%	31%	123%	-3%	-6%	-10%	118%	196%	987%	-20%	6%	7%
M-active	-1%	-10%	-115%	11%	8%	0%	22%	68%	240%	30%	28%	23%
M-retired	0%	0%	-14%	0%	-1%	-3%	2%	13%	109%	0%	1%	2%
M-unemployed	2%	4%	23%	0%	1%	2%	-5%	-12%	-115%	-4%	-3%	-5%
M-student	16%	33%	148%	14%	18%	22%	-30%	-146%	-413%	-13%	-18%	-9%
M-at home	0%	0%	7%	0%	0%	0%	0%	0%	-1%	0%	0%	0%
F-active	-1%	-8%	-62%	0%	-1%	-4%	39%	111%	360%	23%	22%	17%
F-retired	-3%	-7%	-38%	-1%	-2%	-6%	1%	16%	117%	3%	3%	2%
F-unemployed	1%	2%	12%	1%	1%	1%	-3%	-10%	-52%	-2%	-1%	-2%
F-student	12%	25%	165%	11%	17%	25%	-23%	-154%	-547%	-9%	-15%	-13%
Paris	12%	13%	54%	-14%	-15%	-20%	29%	75%	373%	-18%	-16%	-15%
Inner circle	-1%	0%	-6%	1%	1%	2%	-2%	-3%	-45%	1%	1%	1%
Car ownership	26%	55%	121%	92%	90%	103%	-94%	-296%	-1467%	57%	48%	48%
Residual	8%	0.5%	-98%	2%	1 %	3%	23%	100%	200%	19%	18%	23%
Total	100%	100%	100%	100%	100%	100%	100%	100%	100%	100%	100%	100%

Appendix 26. Static contribution of factors to the concentration index of travelled distance per day. Source: EGT result based calculation.

Variable	All modes			Private car			Public transit		
	1983	1991	1997	1983	1991	1997	1983	1991	1997
Age	58%	125%	163%	25%	35%	51%	120%	537%	2231%
Age2	-49%	-104%	-152%	-23%	-35%	-54%	-97%	-439%	-1923%
Income	44%	29%	38%	10%	3%	9%	110%	146%	562%
M-active	25%	32%	29%	20%	24%	18%	32%	73%	254%
M-retired	1%	3%	4%	0%	1%	1%	2%	10%	55%
M-unemployed	-3%	-3%	-6%	-1%	-1%	-2%	-6%	-10%	-68%
M-student	-6%	-14%	-8%	4%	4%	5%	-26%	-95%	-254%
M-at home	0%	0%	0%	0%	0%	0%	0%	0%	-2%
F-active	17%	21%	20%	4%	5%	6%	43%	95%	292%
F-retired	1%	3%	4%	0%	1%	1%	2%	11%	61%
F-unemployed	-1%	-1%	-2%	0%	0%	-1%	-3%	-5%	-25%
F-student	-5%	-15%	-12%	3%	4%	6%	-20%	-100%	-346%
Paris	-14%	-16%	-21%	-14%	-13%	-16%	-13%	-29%	-108%
Inner circle	1%	2%	5%	1%	1%	3%	1%	3%	28%
Car ownership	27%	22%	27%	71%	73%	73%	-73%	-188%	-769%
Residual	8%	17%	8%	-3%	3%	2%	32%	78%	147%
Total	100%	100%	100%	100%	100%	100%	100%	100%	100%

Appendix 27. Static contribution of factors to the concentration index of the average travel speed. Source: EGT result based calculation.

Variable	All modes			Private car			Public transit		
	1983	1991	1997	1983	1991	1997	1983	1991	1997
Age	52%	115%	116%	22%	37%	55%	30%	163%	269%
Age2	-42%	-105%	-109%	-16%	-37%	-55%	-25%	-139%	-244%
Income	6%	14%	3%	2%	0%	-1%	7%	13%	3%
M-active	20%	29%	22%	5%	8%	7%	7%	23%	28%
M-retired	1%	4%	4%	0%	2%	3%	0%	5%	6%
M-unemployed	-2%	-2%	-2%	-1%	-1%	0%	-1%	-1%	-3%
M-student	-4%	-9%	-3%	-1%	-1%	0%	-1%	-8%	-2%
M-at home	0%	0%	0%	0%	0%	0%	0%	0%	0%
F-active	12%	18%	13%	2%	3%	4%	5%	16%	14%
F-retired	1%	3%	4%	1%	1%	3%	0%	3%	3%
F-unemployed	-1%	-1%	-1%	-1%	0%	0%	0%	0%	1%
F-student	-3%	-8%	-4%	-1%	0%	-1%	1%	-8%	-6%
Paris	-21%	-24%	-25%	-11%	-10%	-12%	-20%	-41%	-66%
Inner circle	2%	3%	6%	1%	1%	3%	2%	4%	18%
Car ownership	44%	42%	57%	11%	8%	13%	14%	23%	50%
Residual	36%	20%	20%	83%	88%	86%	82%	49%	30%
Total	100%	100%	100%	100%	100%	100%	100%	100%	100%

Appendix 28. Dynamic contribution of factors to the concentration index of trip frequency per day. Source: EGT result based calculation.

	All modes		Private cars		Public transit		On foot	
	1983-1991	1991–1997	1983-1991	1991–1997	1983-1991	1991–1997	1983-1991	1991–1997
Age	-120,0%	-250,0%	-60,0%	-146,2%	-123,1%	-341,5%	123,8%	-540,0%
Age2	93,3%	270,3%	45,0%	176,9%	95,4%	439,0%	-104,8%	500,0%
Income	138,7%	-1,4%	13,5%	25,4%	84,6%	-92,7%	105,7%	14,0%
M-active	9,9%	27,0%	26,5%	70,6%	1,5%	4,9%	19,0%	-30,0%
M-retired	0,8%	5,0%	2,8%	15,6%	-2,8%	-22,0%	3,4%	15,0%
M-unemployed	-0,9%	-2,6%	-4,4%	-4,6%	-1,5%	25,4%	3,8%	-28,0%
M-student	-6,0%	-7,4%	-10,0%	-7,7%	20,0%	-48,8%	-38,1%	80,0%
M-at home	0,0%	-2,4%	0,0%	-3,7%	0,0%	0,3%	0,0%	-4,0%
F-active	8,1%	10,8%	6,3%	17,7%	7,7%	19,5%	19,0%	-30,0%
F-retired	3,3%	4,1%	9,1%	25,4%	-4,8%	-21,5%	5,2%	-5,0%
F-unemployed	0,4%	-2,0%	-1,5%	0,8%	-0,2%	5,9%	2,6%	-14,5%
F-student	-4,7%	-25,0%	-25,0%	-38,5%	33,8%	-9,8%	-36,7%	10,0%
Paris	11,3%	-1,4%	-5,0%	15,4%	9,2%	-34,1%	-9,5%	-10,0%
Inner circle	-1,6%	2,6%	-1,5%	-3,8%	-0,8%	12,1%	1,0%	6,0%
Car ownership	-13,3%	31,8%	105,0%	-7,7%	-6,2%	131,7%	14,3%	50,0%
Residual	-19,2%	40,7%	-0,7%	-35,6%	-13,1%	31,4%	-8,9%	86,5%
Total	100,0%	100,0%	100,0%	100,0%	100,0%	100,0%	100,0%	100,0%

Appendix 29. Dynamic contribution of factors to the concentration index of travelled distance per day. Source: EGT result based calculation.

	All modes		Private cars		Public transit	
	1983-1991	1991–1997	1983-1991	1991–1997*	1983-1991	1991–1997
Age	-212,5%	-750,0%	-55,0%		-169,5%	-250,0%
Age2	170,8%	1000,0%	70,0%		140,7%	250,0%
Income	104,2%	-175,0%	60,0%		84,7%	-46,4%
M-active	-4,2%	100,0%	-10,0%		3,4%	-10,7%
M-retired	-6,3%	-32,5%	-5,6%		-3,2%	-11,4%
M-unemployed	-3,8%	65,0%	-4,0%		-2,7%	17,5%
M-student	23,3%	-140,0%	4,0%		22,0%	-21,4%
M-at home	0,0%	2,1%	0,0%		0,0%	0,9%
F-active	0,0%	50,0%	-9,0%		6,8%	3,6%
F-retired	-5,0%	-30,0%	-1,6%		-4,1%	-12,5%
F-unemployed	-2,3%	21,3%	-3,2%		-0,7%	3,9%
F-student	35,0%	-75,0%	-6,0%		35,6%	14,3%
Paris	-8,3%	100,0%	-20,0%		-1,7%	7,1%
Inner circle	-0,4%	-65,0%	1,0%		-0,3%	-8,2%
Car ownership	45,8%	-100,0%	50,0%		6,8%	82,1%
Residual	-36,5%	129,2%	29,4%		-17,8%	81,3%
Total	100,0%	100,0%	100,0%		100,0%	100,0%

Note: *concentration index of the corresponding variable does not change during this period.

Appendix 30. Dynamic contribution of factors to the concentration index of the average travel speed. Source: EGT result based calculation.

	All modes		Private cars		Public transit	
	1983-1991	1991–1997	1983-1991	1991–1997*	1983-1991	1991–1997
Age	-120,8%	118,2%	-150,0%		-49,3%	-211,1%
Age2	129,2%	-136,4%	220,0%		42,0%	233,3%
Income	-18,3%	-63,6%	17,1%		3,0%	47,8%
M-active	-4,2%	-18,2%	-20,0%		-2,9%	7,8%
M-retired	-7,8%	6,4%	-13,6%		-2,4%	2,2%
M-unemployed	-2,5%	-5,5%	0,0%		-0,6%	7,1%
M-student	10,8%	34,5%	0,0%		2,6%	-28,4%
M-at home	0,0%	-0,6%	0,0%		0,0%	1,3%
F-active	-4,2%	-18,2%	-7,0%		-1,7%	20,0%
F-retired	-5,9%	9,1%	-8,9%		-1,3%	3,4%
F-unemployed	-3,1%	-1,5%	-3,7%		-0,5%	-2,4%
F-student	8,3%	16,4%	-21,8%		6,2%	-16,7%
Paris	-12,5%	-27,3%	-20,0%		-7,2%	44,4%
Inner circle	0,4%	25,5%	1,0%		0,7%	-43,3%
Car ownership	50,0%	145,5%	47,0%		8,1%	-73,3%
Residual	80,5%	15,7%	59,9%		103,2%	107,9%
Total	100,0%	100,0%	100,0%		100,0%	100,0%

Note: *concentration index of the corresponding variable does not change during this period.

The Role of Human Values and Relations in the Employment of People with Work-Relevant Disabilities

Lieke Kuiper [1,*], Minne Bakker [2] and Jac van der Klink [3]

[1] Health Sciences, VU University, 1081 HV Amsterdam, The Netherlands; E-Mail: l.m2.kuiper@student.vu.nl
[2] Department of Medical Humanities, VU University Medical Center, 1081 HV Amsterdam, The Netherlands; E-Mail: mi.bakker@vumc.nl
[3] Tranzo Scientific Center for Care and Welfare, Department of Social and Behavioral Sciences, Tilburg University, The Netherlands; E-Mail: j.j.l.vdrklink@uvt.nl

* Corresponding author

Abstract
The aim of this study is to discuss the role of human values and relations in the employment of people with work-relevant disabilities. *Purpose:* Finding and maintaining a paid job is known to be more difficult for people with a disability. The aim of the study is to explore the use which people with a disability make of their private and professional network in finding and maintaining a paid job and the role values play in these relations. This was placed in the context of three complementary perspectives: a perspective that stresses the importance of other than merely rationalistic values, a perspective that stresses the importance of values in work and an interpersonal perspective in which 'the Other' is central. *Methods:* Semi-structured interviews were held with 8 people with a working disability. As well, 4 interviews were held with people from their private network (family and partner) and 4 interviews with people from their professional network (colleagues and employers). All interviews were audio-taped and transcribed verbatim. A framework analysis was used to identify the different values in the interviews. This was done with use of MAXqda. *Results:* The interviews showed that both romantic and rational values and arguments were mentioned by the employers in the context of hiring people with a work-relevant disability; they need to be willing to adjust. The importance of human relations was emphasised in the values mentioned by the respondents when talking about having a paid job. Moreover, 'the Other' played an important role in the employment process of people with a work-relevant disability. People with such a disability asked their private network to help them and to provide emotional support. *Conclusion:* Enabling values and relations had more chance if they were in line with the mission and central value of the organisation. This was one of the first studies on the role that human values and relations play in maintaining a paid job for people with a work-relevant disability. The study gives a first impression of how human values and relations play a role, but more research is needed to provide more detailed insights, for example in different groups (e.g. non-employed people with a disability).

Keywords
disability; employment; human relations; values; work

Issue
This article is part of the issue "Humanity as a Contested Concept: Relations between Disability and 'Being Human'", edited by Paul van Trigt (Leiden University, The Netherlands), Alice Schippers (Disability Studies in Nederland, The Netherlands) and Jacqueline Kool (Disability Studies in Nederland, The Netherlands).

---

1. Introduction

In December 2006, a new rights based disability paradigm was set with the declaration of The United Nations Convention on the Rights of Persons with Disabilities. Within this paradigm, values such as dignity and human rights of people with disabilities have become more important. This paradigm presupposes a broader perspective on quality of life of people with disabilities; a perspective that goes beyond meeting the basic (care) needs, and focuses on social participation. This social participation could be enhanced via improved access to health, education or employment (Mahar, Cobigo, & Stuart, 2013). Paradigms are important and presumably necessary, but certainly not sufficient for values, and subsequently behaviours, to be implemented in daily practice and (working) life. In the study reported in this article, we investigated values and value perspectives that people with a disability encounter in the workplace, facilitating or hindering their participation.

Maintaining a paid job can be difficult, especially for people with a work-relevant disability. In this article, we consider a disability to be work-relevant if it is a chronic disease, illness or disability, which may or may not be caused by work itself, but in all cases will impact the individual's functioning at work, indicating its relevance considering labour (Borst-Eilers, 1999). Employers generally expect more absenteeism and lower productivity from people with a work-relevant disability (Van Petersen, Vonk, & Bouwmeester, 2004), which can make them reluctant to hire people with a disability (Winsemius & van Houten, 2010). Insight is growing, though sporadically, that, on the other hand, hiring people with a work-relevant disability is one of the aspects of increasing workplace diversity (Ball, Monaco, Schmeling, Schartz, & Blanck, 2005; Muyia Nafukho, Roessler, & Kacirek, 2010). This diversity, in its turn, increases the creativity of the company by having different kinds of people in the organisation. A more diverse workforce attracts new customers and improves the company's or its brand's image (Vries et al., 2005).

Although the importance of work is widely acknowledged, the value of work is often described in terms of practical issues, such as income or daily structure. However, other values than income, such as building and maintaining meaningful relations and contributing to something valuable, play an increasingly important role for present day workers (Gheaus & Herzog, 2016; Van der Klink et al., 2016), and this may count even more for people with a work-relevant disability. Indeed, the disability itself often leads towards a re-orientation on values, in which other values than income and career become important. There is often a need for more resources (like job control) too (Koolhaas, 2014; Koolhaas, Brouwer, Groothoff, Sorgdrager, & Van der Klink, 2009), because people with a disability not only need to cope with their job demands but also with the demands of their condition.

Values of work can be regarded as governing interpersonal behaviour (Bardi & Schwartz, 2003; Maio & Olson, 1995; Taylor, 1989, 1992). Although issues related to the employment or not of people with a work-relevant disability have been largely researched, the role of values and their governing of interpersonal behaviour in the employment of people with a work-relevant disability have not been studied so far. Even so, to the best of our knowledge, there has been no research that inquires the role of the professional and private network of people with a work-relevant disability in their employment. Both perspectives, however, provide interesting insights in aspects playing a role in finding and maintaining a job for people with a work-relevant disability. Therefore, the aim of this study is to gain insight into how human values and relations play a role in the employment of people with work-relevant disabilities.

To achieve this aim we used three complementary but not mutually exclusive theoretical perspectives to approach our empirical data in a framework analysis: a perspective that stresses the importance of other than merely rationalistic economic values; a perspective that stresses the importance of values in work and an interpersonal perspective in which 'the Other' is central.

The first perspective is an overarching perspective that finds its roots in two contrasting societal views from different historical periods: rationalism and romanticism (Berlin, 1999; Van der Wilt, Deinum, & Van Engelen, 2016). This perspective is inspired by the theoretical framework of Berlin. As he saw it, the Romantic revolution involved a rejection of the Rationalistic idea that (1) "all genuine questions can be answered," (2) "all these answers are knowable," and (3) "all these answers must be compatible with one another" (Berlin, 1999, pp. 21-22). This rationalism contrasts with the 'romantic' vision that the world is not organised by geometry but by poetry. Important values and goals cannot be 'discovered'; they have to be created. Romanticism asserts that also other values (driven by what is 'right' in a more moral way) are important and that values can be mutually conflicting (Berlin, 1999). Berlin states: "The notion that there are many values, and that they are incompatible; the whole notion of plurality, of inexhaustibility, of the imperfection of all human answers and arrangements; the notion that no single answer which claims to be perfect and true, whether in art or in life, can in principle be perfect or true—all this we owe to the romantics" (Berlin, 1999 p. 146). In our society, and especially in the economy and the labour market, values have predominantly been derived from a rationalistic point of view (efficiency, cost-effectiveness, etc.). The position of example is apt, because there are recent developments in economy and management that use a broader, 'romantic', value perspective than exclusively rationalistic values (corporate responsibility). Thus, in this broader perspective, the orientation on and the achievement of values that are outside the dominant (mainstream) rationalistic and economic values are central.

The second perspective can be seen as an elaboration of this: it is based on the values that people should be able to realise with their work and in their work. Throughout the history of philosophy from 'Aristotle to Arendt' people have thought about the value of human action and work. Mostly, at least three aspects are recognised: livelihood (making a living), creativity (creating something) and participation (being part of a community). In this tradition Gheaus and Herzog (2016) recently identified four values people should be able to realise with work, besides income: (1) excellence, (2) social contribution, (3) community and (4) social recognition (Gheaus & Herzog, 2016). Another modern value based framework is the capability approach developed by Amartya Sen (1980, 1993, 2009). In this approach, people should be enabled to realise 'beings and doings people have reason to value'. According to Sen these values are group and context dependent and should not be formulated by experts but 'collected' in the target group in a democratic procedure. In this line, Van der Klink et al. (2016) identified and validated (Abma et al., 2016) seven work values in a population of Dutch workers: (1) the use of knowledge and skills, (2) the development of knowledge and skills; (3) involvement in important decisions; (4) building and maintaining meaningful contacts at work; (5) setting own goals; (6) having a good income; and (7) contributing to something valuable. Values are 'transformed to capabilities if they are important for a worker in his/her work situation and if s/he is enabled and able to achieve the value in their work'. Thus, the context is essential. Within this perspective, in which the value people should realise with and in their work is central, the values Gheaus and Herzog identify are focused on what values should be achieved *with* work (work itself as a capability), while Van der Klink et al stress which values people should be able and enabled to achieve within their work (work capabilities).

The third perspective stresses the interpersonal perspective and is based on the theory of Levinas. After 2500 years of philosophy wherein either the self (egology) or 'being' (ontology) is central, Levinas introduces a totally different point of departure: the Other. A person is not determined by his or her self or by destiny, but by 'the Other'. Levinas' point of view may be elucidated by contrasting it with Sartre's view on the other. For Sartre, the discovery of the identity depends on others because 'I can never see myself as others see me' (Sartre, 1943). The gaze of the other attributes characteristics to me that I cannot determine from myself, but it also 'objectifies' me and with that, I am reduced to a thing that is not subject to change. By that, the other denies me my freedom to act differently, to be different.

As Sartre relates the other to the self, Levinas takes a diametrically opposite starting point by placing 'The Other' in the central position and stating that human behaviour is determined by the responsibility towards 'the Other' (Levinas, 1961). For Levinas, 'the Other' is not knowable and should not be made into an object of the self, as is done by traditional philosophy that puts the self in the central position (from which either other people and the world can be objectified, or the other is considered as threatening the integrity of the self—as in Sartrian philsosophy). For Levinas, the responsibility for 'the Other' as a person is central and unconditional.

From this asymmetric relationship originates an ethical appeal. Ethics thus sprouts from my concern for 'The Other'. Levinas outlines that freedom is predominantly a responsibility: my natural freedom becomes a moral freedom because I am invited to responsibility by the Other.

These three perspectives will be used in order to get insight into the motives for people with a work-relevant disability to work and the motives of employers to hire people with a work-relevant disability (or, in a broader context; the motives of the network to "invest" in people with a work-relevant disability).

2. Methods

2.1. Study Design

An exploratory qualitative network study was executed. This design was used to explore the views, opinions and attitudes of people with a work-relevant disability and their professional and private network, about their roles in the employment of people with a work-relevant disability and their motives and underlying values to do so.

2.2. Recruitment

Eight qualitative, semi-structured interviews with people with a work-relevant disability were conducted. Five people with a work-relevant disability gave permission to interview their private and professional related network as well, which led to another eight interviews. So, in total 16 interviews were conducted.

The eight people with a work-relevant disability were recruited from the networks of Emma at Work (employment agency for people with a work-relevant disability), Disability Studies in the Netherlands, Bartiméus (organization delivering services to visually impaired people) and the FNV (Federatie Nederlandse Vakbeweging), the largest trade union in the Netherlands. Participants were purposefully recruited. Inclusion criteria were: having a work-relevant disability and (experience with) a paid job. The people from the private and professional network were recruited by the primary interviewees (the persons with the work-relevant disability).

All participants were contacted via an e-mail in which the study objective was explained and their permission to be interviewed was formally requested. If they replied to the e-mail, they were subsequently called by phone. All optional participants who were contacted by phone enrolled in the study. During this phone conversation, both the study's objective and their permission to be interviewed were repeated, and an appointment was made for the interview.

2.3. Data Collection

Semi-structured, in-depth interviews were conducted with people with a work-relevant disability and the people from their private and professional networks. Interviews were conducted with the help of a topic list to increase the homogeneity between the topics spoken about in the interviews (Frambach, Van der Vleuten, & Durning, 2013). The topic list was based on intuition and relevant themes suggested in the literature (Leufstadius, Eklund, & Erlandsson, 2009). After each interview, the researcher evaluated the topic list to see if changes were necessary. The information collected from the initial interviews was used in the successive interviews. This led to new questions for the next interview(s), resulting in additional data generation (Van IJzendoorn, 1988). Important themes on the topic list were 'change as a result of getting a paid job', 'benefits a paid job can offer people with a work-relevant disability' and 'getting hired with a work-relevant disability'. The interviews were conducted either at the participants' home, at the office, or another quiet place to prevent disturbance.

2.4. Data Analysis

Based on the three complementary perspectives, a framework was formed to analyse the data. The key elements of each perspective were coded and these codes were assigned to text fragments in the transcripts. This was done with the use of a code book. The codes were noted as a priori codes in the codebook, provided with a separate label, definition and description for each code. The code book was designed by the researchers involved in the analysis, based on relevant literature considering the theories concerned. This led to a framework to structure and analyse the data in the transcripts in a meaningful way (Gale, Heath, Cameron, Rashid, & Redwood, 2013). The interpersonal perspective, based on Levinas, with responsibility for 'the Other' as central theme was covered by three a priori codes: feeling responsible, showing responsibility and claiming responsibility. The society perspective based on Berlin was put into operation by eight a priori codes: being aware of, feeling and acting according to a 'rationalistic' value (cost-effectiveness); the same triptych for 'not-rationalistic' or 'romantic', broader values and separate codes for incompatibility and incommensurability of these different viewpoints. The value perspective, as based on Gheaus and Sen/Van der Klink et al., was covered by 22 codes: the four values of Gheaus and the seven of Van der Klink et al were covered by two codes each: the importance of the value and the achievement of the value.

Each of the sixteen transcripts was analysed by two members of the research team. If a piece of text matched the description of one of the codes in the codebook, that piece of text was assigned to that code. For the analysis of the data, qualitative analysis software program MAXqda was used. In the phase of mapping and interpretation, the relationships between the concepts, typologies and associations with these concepts were explored (Green & Thorogood, 2014). The differences and similarities between the views of the respondents were investigated. Finally, all findings were interpreted.

3. Results

3.1. Participants

The group of people with a work-relevant disability, who joined the study, consisted of six women and two men. They all were in the age range from 23 to 65 years old. They had different kinds of disabilities, illnesses or diseases, but all of them defined their disability as having impact on their work. One person currently did not have a paid job, but had experience with having a paid job (see Table 1). The interviews lasted on average 43 minutes with a range between 26 and 83 minutes.

The people from the private and professional networks of those with a work-relevant disability consisted of six females and two males. They were between 28 and 66 years old (see Table 2).

Hereunder, various aspects of human values and relations in the context of employment are described. Three different theoretical perspectives were used to analyse the data, based on Levinas, Berlin and Gheaus/Sen as elaborated in the introduction. The reporting is structured based on these three perspectives. First, the results of the framework analysis of Levinas will be discussed, followed by Berlin and then Sen. All the results focus on the role of human relations as guided by values, in the employment of people with a work-relevant disability. Representative quotes are given in the text. Clues are added to indicate the source of the quotation (R refers to a person with a work-relevant disability. C refers to people from the private or professional network. See Tables 1 and 2 for more details about the respondents).

Table 1. Demographic information about the participants with a work-relevant disability.

	Sex	Age	Type of disability	Paid job
R1	Female	26	Chronic disease	Administrative assistant
R2	Female	26	Psychiatric disability	Administrative job during the summer
R3	Female	43	Chronic disease	None
R4	Female	48	Sensory disability	Freelancer, CEO, member of several Supervisory Boards
R5	Female	28	Physical and mental disability	Sheltered work
R6	Male	38	Psychiatric disability	Sheltered work
R7	Female	65	Sensory and mental disability	Sheltered work
R8	Male	52	Sensory disability	Psychosocial supporter at the county

Table 2. Demographic information about the participants who were part of the private and professional network of the interviewees with a work-relevant disability.

	Sex	Age	Connection	Paid job
C1.1	Female	46	Supervisor R1	Manager
C1.2	Female	25	Colleague R1	Project coordinator
C1.3	Female	56	Mother R1	Nurse
C1.4	Male	28	Brother R1	Social media agent
C2.1	Female	59	Commissioner R2	Director
C2.2	Male	63	Partner R2	Program manager, strategic adviser
C6.1	Female	36	Head of the HRM department of R6	Head of the HRM department
C6.2	Female	66	Friend R6	None

3.2. Moral Perspective

In this perspective, inspired by the work of Berlin, the central viewpoint is that people in an organisation often cherish a broader set of values than those that are strictly in line with the 'rationalistic' organisational goals (maximise profit and (cost-)effectiveness).

Employers use both rational and non-rational 'romantic' arguments when discussing the employment of a person with a work–relevant disability. This shows that—although both types of arguments seem contrary—they do not necessarily exclude one another. All three employers mentioned the importance of accessibility and inclusiveness. The importance of accessibility is the most expressed 'romantic' value by the employers interviewed. As people with a work-relevant disability have trouble finding and maintaining a job, the employers feel an urge to help them. They feel responsible for the people with a work-relevant disability as well as feeling responsible for society as a whole.

The employers emphasize that people with a work-relevant disability are part of society, a society with a labour market that is not accessible and inclusive for people with a disability. The employers want to contribute to the solution, to change society and make it more inclusive for people with a disability. They acknowledge that a better world starts at home and, therefore. they want to be part of the solution, not of the problem.

> "We have an important role in society in general and want to set an example for society. This means giving people who have fewer chances in life opportunities as well." (C1.1)

Another important value, which played a role in employing people with a work-relevant disability, is the importance of a pleasant working atmosphere. This is not necessarily related to the disability as such, but to the attitude of the employee with the disability. Working hard, being a good colleague and being willing to contribute to the company and its working atmosphere are important reasons to hire and employ someone with a work-relevant disability.

A positive attitude, sometimes rooted in gratitude for getting opportunities and a job, can improve the working atmosphere and working culture, resulting that people from the professional network experience the providing of help to the people with a work-relevant disability less as a burden than as a commitment towards a respected colleague.

> "I think she delivers a positive contribution to the working culture by the way she is standing in life." (C1.1)

However, in some cases the rational argument of cost-effectiveness outweighed the broader 'romantic' values. This implies a hierarchy in which 'romantic' values are restricted to a certain limit value. They can be used to argue for a certain investment in the employee, but this investment is not infinite, neither in time, nor in money. The employers in our sample drew a line under to what extent they could invest in people with a disability. They found it hard to make this explicit, as there is not a strict criterion for the worth of romantic values. However, all the employers stated that there is such an imaginary line, which can change over time and from case to case. Nevertheless, there is a limit.

> "Look, if we needed to invest in a 10.000-euro computer for a task of three months, we would have solved it differently [and not have employed her]." (C4.2)

On the other hand, romantic and rational values can reinforce each other. Sometimes the romantic value of creating a pleasant working atmosphere results in more cost-effectiveness. Supervisors use these kinds of rational arguments to convince their superiors of the importance of 'romantic' values.

> "I think the working culture is determining the way you approach the people you meet, so by setting R1 as an example and learning from her positive attitude we will probably change the way we approach our clients for the better, which will be beneficial for the company." (C1.1)

3.3. Value Driven Perspective

In this perspective, the value people should realise with and in their work is central. The work values as according to the capability approach and the values formulated by Gheaus and Herzog may represent values from an *individual* or personal perspective. For people with a work-relevant disability, several of these values are overtly related to human relations. Not all values will be discussed; hereunder, the focus will be on values which were most frequently mentioned and/or had a striking, different meaning in the group of people with a work-relevant disability. Four of the 'capabilities' (the development of knowledge and skills; building and maintaining meaningful contacts at work; having a good income; and contributing to something valuable), and three of the values of Gheaus will be presented (being part of a community, excellence and social recognition) (Gheaus & Herzog, 2016) .

3.3.1. The Development of Knowledge and Skills

This value not only represents the development or growth in itself, but rather the respondents express that they feel that they were given a chance by their employer or colleague to grow and evolve in their jobs. In general, the respondents express gratitude for the opportunities given by their professional network. To some respondents, getting this opportunity is more important than the actual personal growth or development. This reflects the essence of the concept of capability in which the opportunity to achieve is central and not the actual performance (that can depend on—restricted—choice).

> "My self-esteem has grown, because I got the chance to learn and got some education in the meantime. They do not see me as a hopeless case. That is really valuable to me." (R1)

3.3.2. Building and Maintaining Meaningful Contacts at Work

Being surrounded by other people is described as an important aspect of work by almost all people with a work-relevant disability. Having a paid job gives them the opportunity to meet new people. Making connections gives them the feeling that they are (still) valuable. People who have been unemployed for a certain amount of time, who are living in an institution and/or have a small group of friends or social contacts describe even more benefits of having a paid job than people who had a large private network. They have been feeling lonely for a certain amount of time and the gain of not being on their own but being able to connect on a regular basis was tremendous for this group.

People who have had a paid job for quite some time make use of the connections made. They use their professional network to create new chances. Moreover, they mention that some people from their professional network became part of their personal network as well. Some people were still friends with people who had been their colleagues years before.

> "I: What has having a job given you—what would you not get if you didn't have a job?
> R: Friends" (R2)

The social part of work was recognised as important by the professional and private network of the people with a work-relevant disability as well.

> "You are actually doing something that you like, also aimed at socializing, for example, which sounds very much like getting through the day." (C1.3)

This value seems to be particularly important for people with a work-relevant disability; because of their diminished energy, it is very difficult to maintain a social network beside their work.

3.3.3. Having a Good Income

Remarkably, income was not mentioned by all respondents as a value of work (where this is one of the explicitly mentioned values in work for non-disabled (Abma et al., 2016; Jahoda, 1982)). For these respondents, other values such as social contact, structure or social contribution are the reasons to work. For some respondents, however, their income is of great value. Not so much because of the possibilities it gives them to buy material things, but rather because it gives them freedom and independence. Not relying on the government or partner/parents gives them a feeling of freedom.

> "When I had enough financial security and a cell phone and a credit card, I was able to manage every situation. I did not need my eyes that badly anymore." (R4)

> "To keep that independency, because there were times when I was really depending on my parents, I was not working because of my disease, and that didn't feel well." (R2)

This is in line with how the ancient Greek looked at the relation between work and income. Work performed to earn a living was very low esteemed, not much higher than slavery, but work that served a higher goal like independency or freedom or a societal goal, was highly esteemed (Van der Klink, 2015).

3.3.4. Contributing to Something Valuable

When people with a disability are not able to work, they receive social benefits in The Netherlands. This means a basic income is guaranteed for them. However, earning their own money gives most respondents the opportunity to repay society. Society gave them an income when they were not able to earn it themselves; now they want to contribute to society, by earning their own money and repay it by paying taxes. Besides paying taxes, a contribution is made by producing goods or providing services which are beneficial to others, as pointed out by some respondents. Being able to contribute strengthens their identity and their role in society.

> "[Work means] really doing something for society to get money" (C6.1)

> "[About making sockets] I am really useful for someone else. Socket, well, if you don't have power you can't do a lot of things. Take a kettle, you need a socket. A stove needs power as well. So many things need power. Think about a vacuum cleaner, a fridge, a freezer, a washing machine, you can go on and on and on. If there is no power, if there are no sockets, all those things are not useful anymore." (R6)

The notion that work is more than an economic transaction and should add (other) values for the worker and for society is a reflection of the ancient Greek perception mentioned above and of the broader 'romantic' perspective.

3.3.5. Being Part of a Community

Having someone with a work-relevant disability in the workforce is only possible in a community that is willing to adjust. People with a work-relevant disability do sometimes need some special care. This can imply going on sick leave more often than people without a work-relevant disability, but can also imply taking the elevator instead of the stairs or making sure the hallway is empty to prevent someone with a visual disability from hitting boxes which stand in the way and falling. This need for adjustments means that the other people in the company need to take the person with a work-relevant disability into account. Adaptation has to be reciprocal.

It is normal in a company that people have to take their colleagues into account; however, the people with a work-impacting disability, their colleagues and employers, when interviewed, declare this happens on a more regular basis for people with a work-relevant disability. The willingness to change your behaviour to help someone in the community was seen as an obligation and not as a choice, because you are helping the wider community and not only the person who receives help. Admitting someone into the community means reaching goals as a group.

> "I am not worried about being absent, my colleagues know about it [having a work-relevant disability], if the work that needs to be done is urgent they will work it out. It gives me a safe feeling, them knowing that [needing to adjust]." (R1)

The respondents are, in general, well aware of their dependence on others, also considering their job. Some try to prevent difficulties, by putting extra effort into building a network that could forestall problems. They are conscious about their sometimes fragile position and building a network or safety net can partly overcome this fragility.

> "I: How does such a network arise?
> R: By building it reeeeeeally carefully, investing lots and lots of time, attention, being seriously interested, being careful. Keeping in touch with all those people, remembering birthdays, asking about their wives, that kind of simple stuff, letting them know you exist, on Facebook, on Twitter, on Instagram, whatever, LinkedIn of course." (C.1)

This value shows a divergence of perceptions. From the perspective of the 'community', having a person with a work-related disability as a member can contribute to the diversity and development of the group. From the perspective of the person with the work-relevant disability, however, it appears to be a value on the 'safety level' with the function of a life vest or safety net.

3.3.6. Excellence

Having a work-relevant disability means people have to overcome all kinds of boundaries, every single day. These boundaries imply that working is more of a challenge for them than for their colleagues who do not have a disability. By not giving up hope and keeping their heads up, people with a disability are set as an example for and by their colleagues and employers. Their positive attitude to face every challenge is seen as a contribution to the work in which they excel and that is sometimes deliberately used to change the working climate.

Feeling appreciated for their hard work and being able to influence the company is giving a boost to the self-esteem of people with a work-relevant disability. It makes them more loyal to their colleagues, their employer and their company as well. It therefore strengthens their will to keep working despite all the challenges.

> "It's wonderful to hear colleagues say: 'Gosh, you know, I think about the things I do' or 'I complain less about aches, because you suffer every day.' Wow, those are the things that make me realise one's personality can make a tremendous difference in a department or a company." (R1)

The downside of the fact that being able to keep up, to act 'normal' and not complain, is that some people with a disability have the feeling that in order to be accepted they are not allowed to complain or at least not too much. This can be troubling for some of them. Besides, the type of recognition based on their positive attitude is experienced as difficult and frustrating by some respondents.

They do not want recognition based on their disability, but rather based on their (professional) capacities and work. In their attempt to be 'normal', they sometimes feel uncomfortable to accept this type of recognition.

> "Every time I had to overcome boundaries, because I was young, because I was not able to see well, that made me think: 'Fuck you, I will not play the part you want me to'. I do not like to carry a stigma with me....I did not come this far by pointing at my disability. If I have a problem, I need to solve it." (R4)

For this target group, the value of excellence is not so much applicable to the 'output' of work, the product, but rather to the 'throughput', the mode of carrying it out.

3.3.7. Social Recognition

The fact that people with a work-relevant disability perform in a paid job, leads to different kinds of appreciation by the people surrounding them. First of all, there is the recognition of the boundaries people with a disability have to face by the people from their professional network, as discussed above. Secondly, having a paid job changes the way society feels about people with a work-relevant disability as well. People with a disability often feel less valued based on experiences through their lives of having been bullied or denied a job because of their disability. Paid work changes, for some of them, their role in society. It is important for these people to be acknowledged in their capacities, to be valued as a 'normal' human being, to be part of society.

> "Her bullies are all stay-at-home mums at this point and she is travelling the world, she outranked them all in some way. She did not go to her school reunion. First she did, wanted to go and show them: 'Look here I am, I am having a life of my own'. But they are not worth it." (C4.1)

The interviews show that being recognised as 'having a life of their own', acting and performing like everybody else is an important recognition for people with a work-relevant disability.

3.4. Interpersonal Perspective

In this perspective, being responsible for 'the Other' is central. The definition of 'the Other' is based on Levinas: the Other as a subject that cannot be objectified nor controlled.

Having a paid job can be exhausting for people with a work-relevant disability. This means they explicitly or implicitly demand their private network to take this into consideration. They expect their private network not to exclude them when they do not have the energy to join them or the energy to be cheerful when they get home. Moreover, people with a work-relevant disability ask their private network to spare them and dismiss them from household tasks. They need the support and collaboration of the people from their private network to hold their job. Besides that, the emotional support, the willingness to adjust and the pride expressed by people from their private network gives the people with a disability firmness and a feeling of having a safety net and being able to take a risk and try to excel.

People with a work-relevant disability appeal to their private and professional network to take responsibility and to see their colleague not merely as instrumental but as a source.

This reflects the categorical imperative by Kant but is specifically concordant with the conception of 'the Other' according to Levinas. The interviews show that this conception plays a very important role in the employment process of people with a disability.

> "My mum is a big support, she will always back me up, she is really proud of me. [It influences my work] It makes me feel positive to know there are always people [like mum] happy with my being." (R1)

The professional network needs to accept the person with a work-relevant disability, who in most cases differs from the general workforce, as 'the Other' and take responsibility for him/her. This means the workforce needs to be open-minded to change itself and to accept and adapt to the person with a work-relevant disability. It is therefore necessary that there is a focus on the need to adapt and adjust the work environment to make it possible for the person with a work-relevant disability to become—and stay—part of the professional network. Therefore, it is necessary to focus not solely on the Otherness but ask about the needs of the person with a work-relevant disability and the need to adjust. The focus should be on the need to change the working atmosphere. By being willing to adjust, the person with a work-relevant disability is not only Another but becomes part of the professional network as an 'Other'.

> "Everyone has to take that [R1 being frequently absent] into account, the tasks assigned to her have to be tuned on that [R1 being absent sometimes]....This means her colleagues have to know about it, accept and adjust." (C1.1)

4. Discussion

4.1. Summary of the Results

The results give insight into how human values and relations play a role in the jobs of people with work-relevant disabilities. Both romantic and rational values and arguments were mentioned by both employees and employers in the context of employing people with a work-relevant disability. These values can reinforce each other but can also be incompatible. With regard to specific work values, there seem to be some differences in the appreciation of these values compared with people without a work-relevant disability. Because this was not a comparative study, this observation must be considered with caution. The importance of human relations was emphasised in the values mentioned by the respondents, when talking about having a paid job. The interviews showed that 'the Other' plays a very important role in the employment process of people with a work-relevant disability. People with such a disability, appeal to their professional network for consideration and practical support and to their private network to help them and to provide emotional support. Both networks need to be willing to adjust.

In this article, three different perspectives were used to gain a deeper insight into the value of human relations in work for people with a work-relevant disability. The three perspectives have in common that they all stress the importance of a broader value perspective than a just self-centred economic perspective. They differ in how the individual level interacts with the context. The moral perspective focuses on the morality, on the basis of the acts of the individual in a societal context, the value driven perspective focuses on the values of work for the individual in his or her micro-, meso- and macro context (Van der Klink et al., 2016) and the interpersonal perspective focuses on the responsibility of the individual from and to the individual 'Other'.

We chose these three perspectives because of their complementary characteristics. For the moral, societal perspective, we chose Berlin because he devoted his professional work to 'a strikingly audacious project: to define Western philosophy as a single coherent tradition based upon a faith in rationality, to convince us that such faith is unwarranted—even dangerous—and to advance his own ideas to take its place.' (Sylva, 1999). Our choice for Sen's capability approach was motivated by the increasing importance and influence of this value driven approach in many fields and because of the recent operationalization for work (Abma et al., 2016; van der Klink et al., 2016). The recently formulated values of Gheaus and Herzog were added because of their complementarity. Levinas was chosen because he was undoubtedly the thinker with the most extreme position regarding our responsibility towards the Other, a beacon that is probably unreachable but can show us the direction.

Sen and Levinas both underline the importance of responsibility. For Levinas, this is predominantly an appeal to the individual: your responsibility for 'the Other' is a personal responsibility. For Sen the responsibility is both individual and societal: people have a societal claim to be enabled to achieve their capabilities. Levinas and Berlin also have a common focus on responsibility as a 'romantic' value. For Levinas, this responsibility is a very specific appeal of the individual 'Other'. The employers in our sample stressed that they felt, besides their responsibility towards the individual employee with a work-relevant disability, a responsibility to society too. This is more in line with Berlin. Sen's capabilities might be seen as a translation to a specific context of Berlin's broad scope on values that should not be merely rational. However, Sen would object to the distinction rationalistic versus not rationalistic. In one of his most influential essays, he analyses the economic literature from Smith to Edgeworth and notes that the precise formalising of self-interest as an economic principle is an irrational misconception (Sen, 1977). Sen argues that the 'rationalistic' economic man is significantly worse off because of a failure to recognise the distinction between actual individual preferences and our ethical ideals:

> "A person thus described may be 'rational' in the limited sense of revealing no inconsistencies in his choice behaviour, but if he has no use for these distinctions between quite different concepts, he must be a bit of a fool. The purely economic man is indeed close to being a social moron." (Sen, 1977)

For people with a work-relevant disability, the context seems even more important and relevant. The relationships with their private and professional network play an important role in the meaning that the values of work become relational values. This was found in every perspective.

The relationship between the individual and the concept of 'the Other' is a reciprocal one. People with and without a work-relevant disability feel, answer and ask responsibility of each other. 'The Other', as Levinas describes, is not allowed to be objectified and integrated in the self; you have to leave him or her 'the Other', in the sense that you owe him/her responsibility and respect as a person, a separate identity on its own (Levinas, 1961). The interviews show that the private and professional networks are demanded—and willing—to change and act out of responsibility towards the person with a work-relevant disability, designated as 'the Other'. Our results showed that this 'Other' tries to make a change too, feeling responsible to 'return' or 'repay' by being 'a model employee'. By that, it is meant that being responsible for 'the Other' is conditional. There has to be a reciprocal relationship with 'the Other' to feel responsible for 'the Other'. Here, practice as reflected in our interviews does not meet one of the cornerstones of Levinas' theory: that the responsibility for 'The Other' is unconditional. By imposing conditions on the responsibility for 'the Other', that 'Other' loses its role as the centre of attention. Even the good practices we investigated could not meet the high ethical standards of Levinas. Notwithstanding, the data are in line with seeing 'the Other' as a separate identity and not merely instrumental as contributor to rational goals. As such, the data are in line with Kant's categorical imperative. This imperative was meant as a moral guideline, a practical philosophically based rule. Levinas does not make the claim of a moral imperative. He designates his point of view as 'first philosophy', prior to practical ethics. This leaves the possibility to consider Levinas' description of the Other as a regulative ideal, a beacon, something to strive for with as highest achievable operationalization as Kant's categorical imperative.

According to our material, romantic and rational values can be sometimes incompatible or hierarchical. When the cost to fulfil a romantic non-rational value exceeded a certain limit, the romantic value went down. This confirms the presumption that there is a certain limit to which the romantic value is seen as achievable and that, in the present work, rational values must in the end prevail. Romantic values can have a place but that place is limited by rationalistic borders.

Values such as 'Having a good income' or 'Contributing to something valuable' seem, for people with a work-relevant disability, especially meaningful in the context of the relationships with their private and professional networks. In the case of people with a work-relevant disability, there is a strong interaction between, on the one hand, the private and professional network and society as a whole and, on the other hand, these personal values. The values that guided the relations and, vice versa, were almost all values that were affected by the way other people conceived people with a disability. This seems specific for people with a work-relevant disability.

Besides that, values can have a different meaning for the people with and without a work-relevant disability. Earning an income, for instance, is one of the values identified by people without a disability to work (Abma et al., 2016; Van der Klink et al., 2011). People with a work-relevant disability valued an income more because of the independency it gave, than because of getting an income as value in itself. This may relate to the fact that they would receive a benefit if they did not work, but the independence from others and the pride in being self-sufficient were strong (interpersonal) values in themselves.

The product of their labour is, in contrast to people without a work-impacting disability, not the main indication of the excellence of people with a work-relevant disability. Being able to contribute to the working process, to a company and to society by having a paid job and acting 'normal' and, despite the disability, not being inferior to colleagues without a work-relevant disability is a way of being excellent when you have a disability. Some interviewees with a disability even managed to be excellent at setting an example of how to cope with problems. In general, considering the capability perspective of which '"being" people and "doing" people have reason to be valued' is an important aspect. For people with a work-related disability, it seems the 'being' aspect is more important than the 'doing' identity. Being a 'normal', valuable and valued person is even more important than doing all the things you value.

4.2. Methodological Strengths and Limitations

Semi-structured, in-depth interviews as data gathering method combined with a framework analysis fitted the aim of this study and the research question but, as in every qualitative research, the results are not meant to be generalised. The research population consisted of an appropriate sample of people with a work-relevant disability, which led to a diverse group of people. There were relatively large proportions of females, people with a sensory disability and people with a mental disability. Although the ages of the study population varied, there were three people in their forties, three people in their twenties, but none in their early thirties. Around the age of thirty, people are making decisions about having children or not, therefore important insights may have been missed. Two of the respondents (R3 and R4) spoke about the difficulty of combining a paid job and having a disability. They both derived a different conclusion from this dilemma: R3 decided to stop working and R4 decided not to have children to be able to hold on to her job. It could have been interesting to interview someone who was in his or her early thirties and was deciding if he or she wanted to have children or not.

The COREQ-checklist was used to ensure all important aspects of this research were reported (Tong, Sainsbury, & Craig, 2007). The research fell short in two of the 32 criteria of this checklist; namely, data saturation and participant checking. Although data saturation was accomplished within the respondents group of people with a work-relevant disability, data saturation was not accomplished within the respondents group from the professional networks nor in the group of respondents from the personal networks of the primary respondents. This could mean that there might be additional values relevant. However, all values included in the framework were mentioned in the interviews, which implies that we gained a broad insight into the meaning of these values and their differences.

Neither the transcripts nor the results were sent to the participants meaning that there might have been an unrectified mistake in the transcripts. Input from the participants might have given some extra information that could have enriched the results found.

To the best of our knowledge, this is the first research on values and relations with respect to people with a work-relevant disability. This makes this research innovative, but also a proper comparison with other studies is more or less impossible.

4.3. Implications and Conclusion

People with a work-relevant disability need adjustments in order to work. The paradigm mentioned at the beginning of this article, secures the rights of people with a disability on these adjustments and on participation. This study investigated which value systems exist in daily working situations that could serve as a matrix for the implementation of these rights. The perspectives we used showed to be useful in structuring and interpreting our data. Employers who valued the romantic value of accessibility, inclusiveness and creating a better working atmosphere as a rational value were willing to take the needs of the people with a disability into account. They felt responsible for the fact that employees with a work-relevant disability could achieve the value of having work and important values in that work. We found that 'enabling values and relations' had more chance if they were in line with the mission and central value of the organisation.

A practical application of this study might use the help it provides us to select the right arguments if we want to introduce a person with a work-relevant disability for employment. With employers that are receptive for only 'rationalistic' arguments, we should choose Sen's strategy of an alternative rationality: it is rational to strive for diversity and a fit of values of the company and its employees and to meet societal standards of responsibility. When dealing with employers that have a broader value perspective, a more direct appeal to the responsibility can be made.

This was one of the first studies on the role that human values and relations play in maintaining a paid job for people with a work-relevant disability. The study gives a first impression of how human values and relations play a role, but more research is needed to provide more detailed insights, for example in different groups (e.g. non-employed people with a disability). Further research can provide more insights that policy makers and the government can use to improve the work participation of people with a work-relevant disability.

Acknowledgements

Thanks are due to Paul van Trigt, Jacqueline Kool and Alice Schippers, for early discussions on this topic and the chance to take part in this special issue. Also thanks to the two anonymous reviewers for their comments on an earlier draft of this paper.

Conflict of Interests

The authors declare no conflict of interests.

References

Abma, F. I., Brouwer, S., De Vries, H. J., Arends, I., Robroek, S. J. W., Cuijpers, M. P., ... Van der Klink, J. J. (2016). The capability set for work: Development and validation of a new questionnaire. *Scandinavian Journal of Work, Environment and Health*, *42*(1), 34–42.

Ball, P., Monaco, G., Schmeling, J., Schartz, H., & Blanck, P. (2005). Disability as diversity in Fortune 100 companies. *Behavioral Sciences and the Law*, *23*(1), 97–121. doi:10.1002/bsl.629

Bardi, A., & Schwartz, S. H. (2003). Values and behavior: Strength and structure of relations. *Personality and Social Psychology Bulletin*, *29*, 1207–1220.

Berlin, I. (1999). *The roots of romanticism*. Princeton, NJ: Princeton University Press.

Borst-Eilers, E. (1999). Beleidsvisie inzake kenniscentra voor arbeidsrelevante aandoeningen, (48), 19.

Frambach, J., Van der Vleuten, C., & Durning, S. (2013). Quality criteria in qualitative and quantitative research. *Academic Medicine*, *88*(4), 552.

Gale, N. K., Heath, G., Cameron, E., Rashid, S., & Redwood, S. (2013). Using the framework method for the analysis of qualitative data in multi-disciplinary health research. *BMC Medical Research Methodolog*, *13*(117), 1–8.

Gheaus, A., & Herzog, L. (2016). The goods of work (other than money!). *Journal of Social Philosophy*, *47*(1), 70–89. doi:10.1111/josp.12140

Green, J., & Thorogood, N. (2014). *Qualitative methods for health research* (3rd ed.). London: SAGE Publications.

Jahoda, M. (1982). *Employment and unemployment: A social-psychological analysis*. London: Cambridge University Press.

Koolhaas, W. (2014). *Sustainable employability of ageing workers—The development of an intervention*. Rijksuniversiteit Groningen.

Koolhaas, W., Brouwer, S., Groothoff, J., Sorgdrager, B., & Van der Klink, J. J. L. (2009). Bevorderen van de duurzame inzetbaarheid van de oudere werknemer. Langer doorwerken gaat niet vanzelf. *Tijdschrift Voor Bedrijfs- En Verzekeringsgeneeskunde*, *17*(7), 286–291.

Leufstadius, C., Eklund, M., & Erlandsson, L. K. (2009). Meaningfulness in work—Experiences among employed individuals with persistent mental illness. *Work*, *34*(1), 21–32. doi:10.3233/WOR-2009-0899

Levinas, E. (1961). *Totalité et Infini: Essai sur l'extériorité*. La Haye: Nijhoff.

Mahar, A. L., Cobigo, V., & Stuart, H. (2013). Conceptualizing belonging. *Disability and Rehabilitation*, *35*(12), 1026–1032. doi:10.3109/09638288.2012.717584

Maio, G. R., & Olson, J. W. (1995). Relations between values, attitudes, and behavioral intentions: The moderating role of attitude function. *Journal of Experimental Social Psychology*, *31*(3), 266–285.

Muyia Nafukho, F., Roessler, R. T., & Kacirek, K. (2010). Disability as a diversity factor: Implications for human resource practices. *Advances in Developing Human Resources*, *12*(4), 395–406. doi:10.1177/1523422310379209

Sartre, J. P. (1943). *L'être et le néant*. Paris: Editions Gallimard.

Sen, A. (1977). A critique of the behavioral foundations of economic theory. *Philosophy & Public Affairs*, *6*(4), 317–344.

Sen, A. (1980). Equality of what? In S. McMurrin (Ed.), *The Tanner lectures on human values*. Salt Lake City: University of Utah Press.

Sen, A. (1993). Capability and well-being. In M. Nusbaum & A. Sen (Eds.), *The quality of life*. Oxford: Oxford University Press.

Sen, A. (2009). *The idea of justice*. London: Allen Lane.

Sylva, D. A. (1999). Book review "The roots of romanticism." *New York Times*.

Taylor, C. (1989). *Sources of the self*. New York: Cambridge University Press.

Taylor, C. (1992). *The ethics of authenticity*. Cambridge: Harvard University Press.

Tong, A., Sainsbury, P., & Craig, J. (2007). Consolidated criteria for reporting qualitative research (COREQ): A 32-item checklist for interviews and focus groups, *19*(6), 349–357.

Van der Klink, J. J. L. (2015). *Value at work: Sustainable employability as capability; a multidisciplinary perspective. Inaugural lecture*. Tilburg University.

Van der Klink, J. J. L., Bültmann, U., Burdorf, A., Schaufeli, W. B., Zijlstra, F. R. H., Abma, F. I., ... Van der Wilt, G. J. (2016). Sustainable employability—Definition, conceptualization, and implications: A perspective based on the capability approach. *Scandinavian Journal of Work, Environment and Health*, *42*(1), 71–79. doi:10.5271/sjweh.3531

Van der Klink, J. J. L. Van Der, Bültmann, U., Brouwer, S., Burdorf, A., Schaufeli, W. B., Zijlstra, F. R. H., & Wilt, G. J. Van Der. (2011). Werk als waarde. *Gedrag & Organisatie*, *2011*(24), 342–356.

Van der Wilt, G. J., Deinum, J., & Van Engelen, B. (2016). The value of life [De waarde van het leven]. In T. Wobbes & M. den Muijsenbergh (Eds.), *The Euro in the consulting room. Money does play a role* [De euro in de spreekkamer. Geld speelt wel een rol] (3rd ed.). Annalen van het Thijmgenootschap.

Van IJzendoorn, M. H. (1988). De navolgbaarheid van kwalitatief onderzoek I: methodologische uitgangspunten. *Nederlands Tijdschrift voor Opvoeding, Vorming en Onderwijs*, *4*(5), 280–288. Retrieved from http://openaccess.leidenuniv.nl/bitstream/handle/1887/1417/168_082.pdf?sequence=1

Van Petersen, A., Vonk, M., & Bouwmeester, J. (2004). *Onbekend maakt onbemind: Attitude onderzoek naar de positie van arbeidsgehandicapten op de arbeidsmarkt. 09-01-2004*. Leiden. Retrieved from http://www.uitgeverijbetelgeuze.eu/pdf/Onbekend_maakt_onbemind.pdf

Vries, S. De, Ven, C. Van De, Nuyens, M., Stark, K., Van Schie, J., & Van Sloten, G. C. (2005). *Diversiteit op de werkvloer: hoe werkt dat?* Hoofddorp. Retrieved from http://www.studentcontent.nl/documenten/Arbeidsmarktdynamiek/diversiteit_op_de_werkvloer_hoe_werkt_dat.pdf

Winsemius, A., & van Houten, M. (2010). *Participatie ontward*. Utrecht. Retrieved from https://www.movisie.nl/sites/default/files/alfresco_files/Participatie ontward%5BMOV-222582-0.3%5D.pdf

About the Authors

Lieke Kuiper is a student of Health Sciences and Philosophy at the Vrije Universiteit Amsterdam. She holds a bachelor's degree in Health Sciences and a bachelor's degree in Philosophy. She likes to combine both research fields to get a broader perspective on the subject of study. As well as this, she likes to use the views of different 'stakeholders' to get a clearer view on the research subject.

Minne Bakker is a researcher at the Department of Medical Humanities, VU Medical Centre in Amsterdam. In her research, Minne is interested in the participation of people with disabilities. She has a PhD degree in Medical Sociology. The patient perspective is very important in all her studies. Besides being a researcher, Minne is a teacher in Medical Sociology, qualitative research methods and medical ethics.

Jac van der Klink is professor of mental health at work and sustainable employability at Tranzo, the scientific centre for care and welfare at the Tilburg School of Social and Behavioural Sciences, Tilburg University. He was professor of Occupational Health at UMC Groningen from 2006 until 2014. He is a strategic advisor at the Netherlands School of Public and Occupational Health (NSPOH) and Ascender, a provider of work-related consultancy and care in the mental health and sustainable employability field.

16

Social Exclusion of Australian Childless Women in Their Reproductive Years

Beth Turnbull *, Melissa L. Graham and Ann R. Taket

Centre for Health through Action on Social Exclusion (CHASE), School of Health and Social Development, Deakin University, Burwood, VIC 3125, Australia; E-Mails: b.turnbull@deakin.edu.au (B.T.), melissa.graham@deakin.edu.au (M.L.G.), ann.taket@deakin.edu.au (A.R.T.)

* Corresponding author

Abstract

Research suggests Australian childless women are at risk of pronatalism-driven social exclusion. This exploratory, mixed methods, cross-sectional study described and explored the social exclusion of Australian childless women aged 25 to 44 years, and asked: what are the nature and extent of social exclusion of childless women; and do the nature and extent of exclusion vary for different types of childless women? A total of 776 childless female Australian residents aged 25 to 44 years completed a self-administered questionnaire. Quantitative data were collected on childlessness types, indicators of exclusion and perceived stigmatisation and exclusion due to being childless. Data were analysed using descriptive statistics, One Way ANOVAs and Kruskal Wallis Analysis of Ranks. Qualitative data on childless women's experiences were inductively thematically analysed. Findings suggest societal-level pronatalism drives exclusion of Australian childless women. While exclusion occurs in all domains of life, childless women experience more exclusion, and perceive more exclusion due to being childless, in the social and civic domains than the service and economic domains. Circumstantially and involuntarily childless women, followed by voluntarily childless women, perceive more exclusion due to being childless than undecided and future childed women. Experiences are influenced by the nature of women's 'deviance' from pronatalism.

Keywords

childlessness; demography; fertility; pronatalism; social exclusion; stereotypes; stigma

Issue

This article is part of a regular issue of Social Inclusion, edited by Professor Ulf R. Hedetoft (University of Copenhagen, Denmark).

---

1. Introduction

Increasing numbers of Australian women aged between 25 and 44 years have no biological children, rising from 33 per cent in 2006 to 35.5 per cent in 2011 (Australian Bureau of Statistics [ABS], 2007, 2012a). Research suggests pronatalism in Australian society places childless women at risk of social exclusion (see for example Graham & Rich, 2012a; Sawer, 2013).

Social exclusion is a multidimensional process driven by unequal power relationships interacting between the societal, community, relationship and individual levels, and manifesting in a continuum of inclusion and exclusion characterised by constraints upon the extent and quality of resources and opportunities for participation in the social, civic, service and economic domains of life (Levitas et al., 2007; Popay et al., 2008). Research suggests societal-level pronatalism drives stigmatisation and exclusion of childless women. Pronatalism constructs women as mothers, manifesting at a societal level in policies, discourses and ideologies designed to promote fertility by representing motherhood as a moral, patriotic and economic duty, and at community, relationship and individual levels in cultures, beliefs, attitudes and behaviours that assume motherhood is natural, innate and inevitable (Gillespie, 2000; Graham & Rich, 2012a; Veevers, 1979). By constructing motherhood as central to being a woman, pronatalism perpetuates patriarchal power by disempowering women as resource-less mothers, and marginalising 'deviant' childless women (Gillespie, 2000; Park, 2002).

Political and media analyses have revealed hegemonic pronatalist discourses in Australian society constructing childed women as idealised 'insiders' and childless women as stigmatised 'outsiders' (Graham & Rich, 2012a, 2012b; Sawer, 2013). Canadian and United States studies found most adults believed motherhood was innate and natural (Miall, 1994), and more adults had negative or neutral than positive attitudes towards being childless (Koropeckyj-Cox & Pendell, 2007). Research from Australia, the United Kingdom and United States found women experienced being childless as discrediting, and believed others perceived childless women as unnatural, deficient, unfulfilled and incomplete (Letherby, 1999; Rich, Taket, Graham, & Shelley, 2011; Sternke & Abrahamson, 2015). Some involuntarily childless women internalised pronatalism, perceiving themselves as failures and incomplete (Bell, 2013; Sternke & Abrahamson, 2015). There is, however, limited research investigating the exclusion of childless women in their reproductive years from the social domain, which encompasses social networks, support and interaction, and social and leisure participation (see for example, Albertini & Mencarini, 2014; Bell, 2013; Debest & Mazuy, 2014; Doyle, Pooley, & Breen, 2013; McNamee & James, 2012; Sternke & Abrahamson, 2015), the service domain, which incorporates availability, accessibility, affordability, appropriateness and adequacy of services (see for example Baker, 2003; Hammarberg, Astbury, & Baker, 2001; Mollen, 2006; Onat & Beji, 2012; Parry, 2004) and the economic domain, including participation in employment, the nature and quality of working lives, and material and financial resources (see for example Doyle et al., 2013; Fieder, Huber, & Bookstein, 2011; Huber, Bookstein, & Fieder, 2010; Malik & Coulson, 2013; Rich et al., 2011). There is no existing research in the civic domain, which includes participation in community and political activities, groups and organisations.

While the extant evidence reveals the complexity and diversity of childless women's experiences, it emerges from disparate studies investigating distinct domains of life and undifferentiated or particular types of childless women. There is no Australian research investigating social exclusion of different types of childless women in their reproductive years from multiple domains of life. This exploratory study aimed to describe and explore the social exclusion of Australian childless women aged 25 to 44 years, and asked: (1) what are the nature and extent of social exclusion of childless women; and (2) do the nature and extent of social exclusion vary for different types of childless women?

While acknowledging the negative connotations associated with terms used to describe women with no children, 'childless' and 'childed' are used to describe women without and with children respectively in this paper.

2. Methods

The study was conducted in Australia during 2014. Ethics approval was obtained from Deakin University's Human Ethics Advisory Group (HEAG-H 175_2013). The cross-sectional, mixed-methods study employed a fully mixed concurrent equal status design (Leech & Onwuegbuzie, 2009).

2.1. Sampling

The target population was childless female Australian residents aged 25 to 44 years who were not pregnant and identified as never having assumed the role or identity of a biological or social mother, for example, of adopted, step or fostered-children. The age range encompassed Australian women's mean age of first birth of 28 years, peak reproductive age of 30 to 34 years, and usual completion of fertility between 40 and 44 years (ABS, 2008, 2010a; Australian Institute of Health and Welfare, 2010).

The formula for a binomial distributions k-sample for the chi-square test (Brown et al., 2010) yielded a minimum sample size of 427, including 171 voluntarily childless women, who freely chose not to have children (Veevers, 1979), 64 involuntarily childless women, who wished to have biological children but were unable to achieve a viable pregnancy (Daniluk, 2001), 64 circumstantially childless women, who were unable to have children due to other circumstances such as having no partner, partner infertility, or health issues other than those preventing a viable pregnancy (Cannold, 2005), 64 undecided women, who were unsure about whether to have children, and 64 future childed women, who intended to have biological or social children in future.

In the absence of a sampling frame, participants were recruited by promoting the study through 38 women's health services, 13 blogs and Facebook pages, professional networks and snowball sampling. Of the 1,411 respondents, 631 women who did not click the 'submit' button at the end of the questionnaire were excluded pursuant to the ethics approval as deemed withdrawals; and four whose dates of birth fell outside the target age range were excluded. The total sample size was 776 women, a completion rate of fifty-five per cent.

2.2. Data Collection and Measures

A self-administered online questionnaire collected quantitative data on socio-demographic variables, types of childlessness and social exclusion. Indicators of exclusion were measured using the social interaction subscale of the Duke Social Support Index (George, Blazer, Hughes, & Fowler, 1989) and the MOS social support index (Chronbach's $\alpha = 0.97$; one-year stability $\alpha = 0.78$) (Sherbourne & Stewart, 1991) in the social domain, participation in community groups, activities and events (ABS, 2010b) in the civic domain, degree of problems accessing and using services (Dermott et al., 2012) in the service domain, and employment status (Melbourne Institute of Applied Economic and Social Research, 2012) and personal income (ABS, 2011) in the economic domain. Data were also collected on stigma consciousness (Chronbach's $\alpha = 0.72 - 0.74$) (Pinel, 1999) and degree of perceived exclusion from domains of life due to being childless. Open-ended questions employing the critical incident technique, which seeks to obtain detailed accounts of participants' experiences of past incidents (Butterfield, Borgen, Amundson, & Maglio, 2005), gathered qualitative data on each domain (see Appendix).

2.3. Data Analysis

Aggregate scores were computed for social interaction, social networks, social support, community participation, problems accessing and using services and stigma consciousness (Hughes, Blazer, & Hybels, 1990; Sherbourne & Stewart, 1991). Employment status was computed from items on paid work status, underemployment and unemployment. Personal income ranges were recoded into income levels (ABS, 2012c). Five-point scales measuring degree of perceived exclusion due to being childless were collapsed into binary ordinal variables consisting of no perceived exclusion or at least a slight degree of perceived exclusion.

Descriptive statistics examined socio-demographic characteristics, indicators of exclusion and stigmatisation and exclusion due to being childless. One Way ANOVAs and Scheffe's post-hoc tests analysed differences between types of childless women's stigma consciousness. Kruskal Wallis H and Dunn's post-hoc tests analysed differences in social interaction, social support, community participation, problems accessing or using services, employment status, personal income and perceived exclusion due to being childless.

Qualitative data were inductively thematically analysed through data immersion by reading and re-reading all qualitative data, coding and recoding, and identification of categories and underlying themes. A framework of experiences across all domains was generated, illustrated by participant quotations from all types of childless women in all domains of life. De-identified quotations were attributed using identification numbers (denoted as ID), childlessness type and age. No more than one quotation from any participant was used.

3. Results

3.1. Demographic Characteristics

Table 1 shows participants' demographic characteristics and comparable Australian data. Compared with Australian females aged 25 to 44 years (89.4%) (ABS, 2012b), 39.5 per cent fewer participants were married, in a civil union or de facto relationship (49.9%; n=386; 95% CI for difference -43.0 – -35.9). A higher percentage (10.8%) of participants identified as lesbian or bisexual (13.0%; n=97) than Australian women aged 16 to 59 years (2.2%; 95% CI for difference 8.5 – 13.4) (Smith, Rissel, Richters, Grulich, & Visser, 2003). Compared with Australian women aged 15 years or over (19.9%) (ABS, 2012b), 58.1 per cent more participants possessed a bachelor degree or higher (78.0%; n=605; 95% CI for difference 55.0 – 60.9). Almost half the participants (48.5%; n=361) were in the high-income bracket, compared with 20 per cent of Australian adults (95% CI for difference 24.9 – 32.1) (ABS, 2013). Close to three-quarters of participants (73.2%; n=554) identified as having no religion or being unsure, compared with 22.4 per cent of Australian females (ABS, 2012b). In contrast, only 21.0 per cent of participants identified as Christian, compared with 69.2 per cent of Australian females (ABS, 2012b).

Table 2 shows types of childless women and differences in demographic characteristics. There were differences between types of childless women's age ($F = 51.8$; df = 4; $p < 0.001$), relationship status ($\chi = 97.6$; df = 4; $p < 0.001$), sexual orientation ($\chi = 13.1$; df = 4; $p = 0.01$), religious status ($\chi = 16.1$; df = 4; $p = 0.003$), area of geographic residence ($\chi = 11.8$; df = 4; $p = 0.02$) and educational attainment ($H = 20.1$; df = 4; $p < 0.001$).

3.2. Indicators of Exclusion

Table 3 shows indicators of exclusion in the social, civic, service and economic domains. Circumstantially childless women had lower social support scores than the undecided (Dunn's Test = -97.0; $p = 0.001$), involuntarily childless (Dunn's Test = 114.1; $p = 0.004$), voluntarily childless (Dunn's Test = -115.6; $p < 0.001$) and future childed (Dunn's Test = -171.3; $p < 0.001$). While there was an overall difference in social interaction scores ($H = 11.3$; df = 4; $p = 0.02$), post hoc testing identified no differences between types of childless women.

Table 1. Demographic characteristics of participants and comparable Australian data.

	Participants per cent (n)	Australian per cent	Percentage difference (95% CI)
Age (n=775)			
25-29	25.4 (197)	24.8	0.6 (-2.4 – 3.8)
30-34	30.3 (235)	24.0	6.3 (3.2 – 9.6)
35-39	22.7 (176)	25.3	-2.6 (-5.44 – 0.5)
40-44	21.5 (167)	25.8[1]	-4.3 (-7.0 – -1.3)
Relationship status (n=773)			
Single	33.4 (258)	Not available	
Relationship (not living together)	9.3 (71)	Not available	
De facto relationship	26.4 (204)	35.7	-9.3 (-12.3 – -6.1)
Engaged	5.4 (42)	Not available	
Married/civil union	23.5 (182)	53.7[2]	-30.2 (-33.1 – -27.1)
Separated/divorced	1.3 (10)	10.1	-8.8 (-9.4 – -7.8)
Widowed	0.8 (6)	0.5[1]	0.3 (-0.2 – 1.1)
Sexual orientation (n=745)			
Lesbian or bisexual	13.0 (97)	2.2[3]	10.8 (8.5 – 13.4)
Heterosexual	87.0 (648)	97.8	-10.8 (-13.4 – -8.5)
Educational attainment (n=776)			
Year 12 or below	5.0 (39)	58.6	-53.6 (-55.0 – -51.9)
Certificate/diploma	17.0 (132)	21.5	-4.5 (-7.0 – -1.8)
Bachelor degree	41.0 (318)	14.8	26.2 (22.8 – 29.7)
Graduate/postgraduate qualification	37.0 (287)	5.1[4]	31.9 (28.5 – 35.3)
Employment status (n=773)			
Employed/self-employed	93.0 (719)	71.6	21.4 (19.5 – 23.1)
Unemployed	6.3 (49)	3.9	2.4 (0.9 – 4.3)
Not in labour force	0.6 (5)	24.5[4]	-23.9 (-24.3 – -23.1)
Personal income level (n=744)			
Low (first three deciles)	9.3 (69)	30.0	-20.7 (-22.7 – -18.5)
Lower middle (fourth decile)	7.3 (54)	10.0	-2.7 (-4.5 – -0.7)
Middle (third quintile)	7.4 (55)	20.0	-12.6 (-14.3 – -10.6)
Upper middle (fourth quintile)	27.6 (205)	20.0	7.6 (4.4 – 10.9)
High (fifth quintile)	48.5 (361)	20.0[5]	28.5 (24.9 – 32.1)
Aboriginal or Torres Strait Islander status (n=771)			
Aboriginal or Torres Strait Islander	1.4 (11)	2.5	-1.1 (-1.7 – -0.03)
Non-Aboriginal or Torres Strait Islander	98.6 (760)	97.5[1]	1.1 (0.03 – 1.8)
Country of birth (n=771)			
Born overseas	14.1 (109)	26.2	-12.1 (-14.4 – -9.5)
Born in Australia	85.9 (662)	73.8[6]	12.1 (9.5 – 14.4)
Language spoken at home (n=772)			
Language other than English	6.2 (48)	19.5	-13.3 (-14.8 – -11.4)
English only	93.8 (724)	80.5[6]	13.3 (11.4 – 14.8)
Religion (n=757)			
Christian	21.0 (159)	69.2	-48.2 (-51.0 – -45.2)
Judaism	0.4 (3)	0.5	-0.1 (-0.4 – 0.6)
Islam	0.1 (1)	2.3	-2.2 (-2.29 – -1.7)
Indian religions	1.8 (14)	4.2	-2.4 (-3.1 – -1.2)
Folk, new and other religions	3.4 (26)	1.5	1.9 (0.8 – 3.4)
No religion or unsure	73.2 (554)	22.4[6]	50.8 (47.5 – 53.9)
Geographic residence (n=776)			
Major city	77.4 (601)	68.4	9.0 (6.0 – 11.9)
Inner regional	15.2 (118)	19.7	-4.5 (-6.9 – -1.8)
Outer regional	6.4 (50)	9.5	-3.1 (-4.6 – -1.2)
Remote	0.3 (2)	1.5	-1.2 (-1.5 – -0.7)
Very remote	0.6 (5)	0.8[7]	-0.2 (-0.6 – 0.6)

Notes: 1 Australian females aged 25 to 44 years (ABS, 2012b); 2 Registered marriages only (ABS, 2012b); 3 Australian females aged 16 to 59 years (Smith et al., 2003); 4 Australian females aged 15 years and over (ABS, 2012b); 5 Income deciles of Australian adults (ABS, 2013); 6 Australian females (ABS, 2012b); 7 Australian residents (ABS, 2008).

Table 2. Demographic characteristics of types of childless women.

	Involuntary	Circumstantial	Voluntary	Undecided	Future childed	F^1/ χ^2/ H^3	df	p value
Type of childless women (n=768)	n=161	n=161	n=281	n=139	n=123			
Per cent	8.3%	21.0%	36.6%	18.1%	16.0%			
Age in years (n=767)	n=64	n=161	n=280	n=139	n=123			
Mean	36.9 (SD=4.9)	36.5 (SD=5.3)	36.0 (SD=5.6)	31.7 (SD=4.1)	30.1 (SD=3.4)	51.8[1]	4	<0.001
Relationship status (n=765)	n=64	n=160	n=281	n=138	n=122			
Single	17.2%	64.4%	31.0%	13.1%	13.1%	97.6[2]	4	<0.001
Partnered	82.2%	35.6%	69.0%	86.9%	86.9%			
Sexual orientation (n=738)	n=62	n=156	n=272	n=132	n=116			
Heterosexual	90.3%	91.0%	81.3%	88.6%	91.4%	13.1[2]	4	0.01
Lesbian or bisexual	9.7%	9.0%	18.8%	11.4%	8.6%			
Religion (n=765)	n=63	n=152	n=277	n=136	n=122			
Religious	41.3%	32.9%	20.9%	22.1%	27.9%	16.2[2]	4	0.003
Not religious/unsure	58.7%	67.1%	79.1%	77.9%	72.1%			
Geographic residence (n=786)	n=64	n=161	n=281	n=139	n=123			
Major city	70.3%	84.5%	72.2%	79.9%	80.5%	11.8[2]	4	0.02
Regional/ remote	29.7%	15.5%	27.8%	20.1%	19.5%			
Educational attainment (n=768)	n=64	n=161	n=281	n=139	n=123			
Year 11 or below	0.0%	1.2%	2.1%	1.4%	0.0%			
Year 12 or equivalent	1.6%	2.5%	4.6%	3.6%	4.1%			
Certificate or diploma	20.3%	14.9%	23.8%	12.2%	8.9%			
Bachelor or above	78.1%	81.4%	69.4%	82.7%	87.0%			
Mean rank	388.4	398.3	352.0	402.2	418.8	20.1[3]	4	<0.001

Notes: 1 One Way ANOVA; 2 Chi Square Test for Independence; 3 Kruskal Wallis Analysis of Ranks.

Table 3. Indicators of exclusion in the social, civic, service and economic domains.

	All participants	Involuntary	Circumstantial	Voluntary	Undecided	Future childed	H^1	df	P value
Social interaction score[2]	n=765	n=63	n=159	n=276	n=138	n=121			
Median	7.0	7.0	7.0	7.0	8.0	8.0			
Mean rank		335.7	372.5	361.0	404.5	422.2	11.3	4	0.02
Social support score[3]	n=739	n=60	n=150	n=273	n=130	n=119			
Mean	55.4 (SD = 17.5)	54.2 (SD =22.2)	46.1 (SD = 18.2)	56.6 (SD = 17.3)	56.3 (SD= 16.1)	63.0 (SD = 12.3)			
Mean rank		383.1	269.0	384.5	366.0	440.3	49.0	4	<0.001
Community participation score[4]	n=771	n=64	n=160	n=278	n=138	n=123			
Mean	3.2 (SD = 2.3)	3.3 (SD = 2.8)	3.3 (SD = 2.4)	3.2 (SD = 2.3)	3.3 (SD = 2.5)	3.1 (SD = 2.0)			
Mean rank		373.7	386.1	386.0	379.0	375.3	0.4	4	0.98
Problems accessing/using services score[5]	n=776	n=64	n=161	n=261	n=139	n=123			
Mean	70.7 (SD = 6.1)	70.4 (SD = 6.6)	70.3 (SD = 6.5)	70.8 (SD = 6.3)	69.9 (SD = 5.6)	71.4 (SD = 5.1)			
Mean rank		363.2	372.6	394.4	382.2	391.2	1.8	4	0.77
Employment status	n=773	n=64	n=159	n=280	n=139	n=123			
Employed	83.3%	87.5%	82.4%	81.8%	82.0%	87.8%			
Underemployed	9.7%	6.3%	9.4%	10.4%	10.1%	8.9%			
Unemployed	6.3%	4.7%	8.2%	6.8%	7.2%	3.3%			
Not in labour force	0.6%	1.6%	0.0%	1.1%	0.7%	0.0%			
Mean rank		398.4	378.5	376.9	377.5	401.0	3.6	4	0.5
Personal income levels	n=744	n=60	n=158	n=267	n=134	n=117			
Low	9.3%	5.0%	9.5%	9.4%	11.9%	8.5%			
Lower middle	7.3%	5.0%	7.6%	8.2%	7.5%	4.3%			

	All participants	Involuntary	Circumstantial	Voluntary	Undecided	Future childed	H[1]	df	P value
Middle	7.4%	10.0%	6.3%	7.5%	8.2%	6.0%			
Upper middle	27.6%	26.7%	22.2%	28.5%	25.4%	35.9%			
High	48.5%	53.3%	54.4%	46.4%	47.0%	45.3%			
Mean rank		392.6	384.8	360.0	355.9%	367.9%	3.0	4	0.6

Notes: 1 Kruskal Wallis Analysis of Ranks; 2 Ordinal scale from 0 to 13. Higher scores indicate more social interaction; 3 Interval scale from 0 to 76. Higher scores indicate greater levels of instrumental and affective social support; 4 Interval scale from 0 to 14. Higher scores indicating participation in more community groups/events and activities; 5 Aggregate score from 5 to 75. Lower scores indicating a greater degree of problems accessing or using service.

Table 4. Perceived stereotyping, stigmatisation and exclusion due to being childless.

	All participants (n=764)[3]	Involuntary (n=64)[4]	Circumstantial (n=160)[5]	Voluntary (n=279)[6]	Undecided (n=138)[7]	Future childed (n=123)[8]	F[1]/H[2]	df	P value
Stigma consciousness score[9]									
Mean	36.6 (SD = 9.4)	33.3 (SD = 8.6)	34.1 (SD = 8.1)	36.2 (SD = 9.0)	37.9 (SD = 9.9)	41.2 (SD = 9.5)	13.3[1]	4	<0.001
Exclusion from social interaction[10]									
Median	5.0	4.0	4.0	5.0	5.0	5.0			
Mean rank		330.2	303.1	383.0	422.7	460.7	53.5[2]	4	<0.001
Exclusion from social support[10]									
Median	5.0	4.0	4.0	5.0	5.0	5.0			
Mean rank		355.5	305.1	382.7	424.0	450.2	46.7[2]	4	<0.001
Exclusion from community life[10]									
Median	5.0	4.0	4.0	5.0	5.0	5.0			
Mean rank		303.9	310.6	407.9	402.7	433.0	49.3[2]	4	<0.001
Exclusion from services[10]									
Median	5.0	5.0	5.0	5.0	5.0	5.0			
Mean rank		349.2	358.5	382.1	414.3	402.4	14.5[2]	4	<0.001
Exclusion from material and financial resources[10]									
Median	5.0	5.0	5.0	5.0	5.0	5.0			
Mean rank		367.8	365.4	372.9	401.3	413.3	11.7[2]	4	0.02
Exclusion from employment[10]									
Median	5.0	5.0	5.0	5.0	5.0	5.0			
Mean rank		392.9	370.7	377.0	392.7	387.3	3.4[2]	4	0.5

Notes: 1 One Way ANOVA; 2 Kruskal Wallis Analysis of Ranks; 3 n=730 for stigma consciousness and 763 for community life; 4 n=150 for stigma consciousness; 5 n=150 for stigma consciousness, 159 for community life and 161 for education; 6 n=263 for stigma consciousness, 278 for social interaction and employment, 281 for services and education, and 280 for material and financial resources; 7 n=132 for stigma consciousness, 137 for social interaction and 139 for education; 8 n=117 for stigma consciousness and 122 for employment and material and financial resources; 9 Aggregate index from 10 to 70, with lower scores indicating greater stigma consciousness ; 10 Ordinal scale from 1 to 5, with scores of 4 or below indicating at least a slight degree of exclusion due to being childless.

3.3. Stigmatisation and Exclusion Due to Being Childless

Table 4 shows stigmatisation and exclusion due to being childless. Future childed women's mean stigma consciousness score was higher than voluntarily, circumstantially and involuntarily childless women's scores ($p < 0.001$). Undecided women's mean stigma consciousness score was higher than circumstantially ($p = 0.02$) and involuntarily ($p = 0.03$) childless women's scores. The results suggested future childed women perceived less stigmatisation due to being childless than voluntarily childless women, and future childed and undecided women perceived less stigmatisation than circumstantially and involuntarily childless women.

Participants perceived at least a slight degree of exclusion due to being childless from social interaction (47.3%), social support (42.5%), community life (36.8%), services (20.5%), material and financial resources (17.7%) and employment (12.2%). In relation to social interaction, circumstantially childless women perceived more exclusion than voluntarily childless (Dunn's test = -79.9; $p = 0.001$), undecided (Dunn's test = -119.6; $p < 0.001$) and future childed women (Dunn's test = -157.6; $p < 0.001$), involuntarily childless women perceived more exclusion than undecided (Dunn's test = -92.6; $p = 0.02$) and future childed women (Dunn's test = -130.6; $p < 0.001$), and voluntarily childless women perceived more exclusion than future childed women (Dunn's test = -77.7; $p = 0.004$). In relation to social support, circumstantially childless women perceived more exclusion than voluntarily childless (Dunn's test = -77.6; $p = 0.001$), undecided (Dunn's test = -118.9; $p < 0.001$) and future childed women (Dunn's test = -145.1; $p < 0.001$), while involuntarily childless (Dunn's test = -94.8; $p = 0.02$) and voluntarily childless women (Dunn's test = -67.5; $p = 0.02$) perceived more exclusion than future childed women. Involuntarily and circumstantially childless women perceived more exclusion from community life than undecided (Dunn's test = -98.7; $p = 0.006$ and Dunn's test = -92.1; $p < 0.001$), voluntarily childless (Dunn's test = -104.0; $p = 0.001$ and Dunn's test = -97.3; $p < 0.001$) and future childed women (Dunn's test = -129.1 and -122.4; $p < 0.001$). Circumstantially childless women perceived more exclusion from services than undecided women (Dunn's test = -55.8; $p = 0.02$).

3.4. Experiences of Inclusion and Exclusion

Childless women described pronatalism-driven experiences on a continuum of connection and inclusion within, exclusion within, and exclusion from, all domains of life. Each theme or element of a theme was experienced by all types of childless women in all domains of life, unless types of childless women and domains of life are specified. Some women described only connection and inclusion or exclusion, some reported connection and inclusion in some domains and exclusion in others, and some reported inclusion and exclusion in the same domain. Substantially more women reported exclusionary experiences within, than connection and inclusion within or exclusion from, the domains.

3.4.1. Experiences of Inclusion and Connection

Many women described experiences of inclusion and connection arising from their 'deviance' from pronatalism. Experiences of inclusion and connection are subtly different. 'Inclusion' refers to experiences in which childless women feel included by childed people and within childed domains of life. 'Connection' refers to experiences in which childless women have the resources and opportunities to connect and participate, despite the potential for exclusion by childed people or from childed domains of life.

Some women described experiences of inclusion. For example, some involuntarily childless, circumstantially childless and future childed women received emotional and instrumental support, while some women valued being included in children's lives.

> I am fortunate to have some friends around me who invite me to share in their families. I am a godmother and have regularly held nannying roles – it's a privilege to be entrusted with the responsibility of caring for people's kids and for them to tell me they know I'd treat them as if they were my own. (ID 224; undecided; age 32 years)

Furthermore, some voluntarily childless, undecided and future childed women reported others' understanding of their priorities and decisions.

> My mother had a talk with me when I was in my early twenties. She said that she completely understood and agreed with my stance about being childfree and gave her full support. She told me that knowing me as well as she did, having children would be a mistake for me and I would probably always regret having them. (ID 125; voluntarily childless; age 40 years)

Other women described experiences of connection. For example, some women experienced affirmation of being childless through observations of or interactions with childed people.

> Seeing overburdened mothers on public transport makes me grateful I don't have children. (ID 477; circumstantially childless; age 37 years)

Furthermore, many women valued their freedom to participate and contribute in all domains of life, and others actively built lives in which being childless was valued and affirmed.

> I work full-time, but my husband works part-time in an unskilled job while he is studying for a more skilled job. I don't think we could have this arrangement if we had children. (ID 299; voluntarily childless; age 44 years)

> I have a great group of friends and family who are like-minded....Even if I had children I would not go to mother's groups ... because that wouldn't be my 'cuppa tea'. I like people who live outside of the box. (ID 117; circumstantially childless; age 42 years)

3.4.2. Exclusionary Experiences within the Domains of Life

Many women experienced being childless as a stigmatising attribute, which resulted in exclusionary interpersonal interactions within domains of life, with friends, family, community members, service providers, clients and colleagues. For example, many women described others' assumptions and expectations they had children or would have children. When such expectations were not met, they experienced others' disappointment, invalidation of their worth and pressure to become childed. For example, some involuntarily childless women received unhelpful encouragement to become childed. Some circumstantially childless women felt pressured to settle for 'any man', and many circumstantially childless, undecided and future childed women were pressured to 'hurry up'. In addition, many voluntarily childless and undecided women described others' arguments they would feel different once they met the 'right man' or had children, were 'missing out', or were unqualified to decide not to have children. Voluntarily childless and undecided women also felt others pathologised their choices.

Many women also described being stereotyped and judged by others. Women who were perceived as making choices that contributed to being childless felt stereotyped as child-hating, career-focused, materialistic and selfish.

> There is a perception you are selfish (so what if you are?!), a baby-hater, have something wrong with you or are ruthless. Your personality is judged by a decision you make about one aspect of your life. (ID 139; undecided; age 33 years)

All types of childless women felt judged as incomplete and unfulfilled. Involuntarily, circumstantially and voluntarily childless women who would not or could not ever become childed, felt further judged as defective and failed women. Some involuntarily and circumstantially childless women internalised such judgements.

> The pressure to find a man and have a baby [as soon as possible] is huge. I feel it every single day of my life. There is no relief from feeling abnormal, shamed and like a failure. (ID 751; circumstantially childless; age 35 years)

Some involuntarily and circumstantially childless women who wanted children felt judged as unhappy and desperate. In contrast, some voluntarily childless, undecided and future childed women felt judged as abnormal and unnatural for not wanting, or not yet having, children. All except involuntarily childless women felt judged as culpable for not having or delaying children.

> [W]hen I was 27 I was diagnosed with [polycystic ovarian syndrome] and was then informed by an older female [general practitioner] that I should have considered such diseases before I decided to be single and without a child. (ID 115; future childed; age 31 years)

Many women described others' beliefs they lacked knowledge, emotions, abilities and attributes that women acquired only upon becoming childed, including not understanding children and parenting, and being incapable of maturity, happiness, love, empathy and selflessness. Many women experienced invalidation of their views, contributions and expertise as a result of such beliefs.

> We live in [an area] for private schools so there's always chatter about whose child goes where. I feel excluded from these discussions because I have no children but I also feel private schools suck money from public schools. Expressing that opinion is unpopular and is normally met with 'well you would think differently if you had kids'. No, I wouldn't. I find that assumption offensive. (ID 556; circumstantially childless; age 38 years)

Furthermore, many women felt others perceived their feelings, experiences and needs as less important than those of childed people, and accordingly prioritised the needs of childed people.

> Not being granted leave during holiday periods to allow parents to take leave. Not having access to any flexible working arrangements (part time, work from home etc.), which are only granted to parents. Having to work back late to cover people leaving early to pick up kids from school. (ID 011; circumstantially childless; age 33 years)

In addition, many women experienced public questioning about their personal reasons for having no children, in response to which they felt required to justify, defend or conceal being childless. Finally, many women felt marginalised, invisible and irrelevant in interactions, activities and spaces dominated by childed people and children.

> When I get together with my friends, they always talk about their children, and I sit there and have very minimal to say/input. I then tune out and feel lonely and very depressed. (ID 333; involuntarily childless; age 36 years)

3.4.3. Exclusion from Childed Domains of Life

Some women experienced exclusion from domains of life idealising, prioritising, dominated by or catering exclusively to childed people, or stigmatising childless women. In the social domain, some women experienced exclusion from financial and emotional support from family who prioritised childed relations, and many women experienced exclusion from childed social networks.

> Losing several very good friends to the world of 'mummyhood', even when you make all sorts of efforts to keep the relationship close it dies ... I feel these relationships would probably have survived and grown if I too had chosen to have children. (ID 119; voluntarily childless; age 36 years)

In the service domain, some circumstantially and voluntarily childless women were denied access to contraception and sterilisation procedures because medical practitioners believed they should become childed or would change their minds. Other women experienced exclusion from services that catered exclusively to childed people, or did not understand childless women's needs.

> Gynaecological services for women not wishing to get pregnant are hard to access and [obstetric gynaecologists] seem uninterested in childfree woman and have a lack of knowledge about gynaecological problems outside of those relating to childbirth. (ID 017; voluntarily childless; age 35 years)

In the economic domain, some women experienced exclusion from employment and promotion opportunities by employers who assumed they would become childed, invalidated their expertise in working with children, or prioritised childed people's employment needs. Further, some involuntarily and circumstantially childless women described financial hardship arising from attempts to become childed, or following divorces from husbands who wanted to become childed.

> Due to marital separation with husband after the stress of not having children my material and financial resources have suffered enormously. No longer have a home, struggle to make ends meet. (ID 218; involuntarily childless; age 32 years)

Finally, some women engaged in self-regulated exclusion from childed people, activities, groups, events and spaces, in order to avoid stigmatising experiences.

> Went to appointment at [a hospital miscarriage clinic]. Same rooms and waiting rooms as pregnant women going for their check-ups. Indicated to sit at chairs facing wall and not towards the pregnant women ... I would have gone back to that clinic but it was too difficult due to so many other pregnant women around. (ID 087; involuntarily childless; age 33 years)

4. Discussion

This exploratory, mixed-methods study was the first to investigate the social exclusion of different types of childless women in their reproductive years, across multiple domains of life in Australian society. This discussion explores the nature and extent of social exclusion of childless women, differences in the social exclusion of types of childless women, and the study's strengths and limitations.

4.1. The Nature and Extent of Social Exclusion of Childless Women

The findings revealed a complex picture of the social exclusion of childless women. The qualitative and quantitative findings suggested childless women experienced pronatalism-driven stigmatisation, congruent with studies finding other people stereotyped and stigmatised childless women (Çopur & Koropeckyj-Cox, 2010; Koropeckyj-Cox & Pendell, 2007; LaMastro, 2001). The qualitative findings further suggested pronatalism manifested in a continuum of connection and inclusion within, exclusionary experiences within, and exclusion from, all domains of life. Some women felt being childless resulted in experiences of connection and the freedom to contribute and participate. However, many women experienced exclusion within the domains of life. For example, reflecting previous research that voluntarily childless women experienced pressure from family and friends to become childed (Rich et al., 2011), all types of childless women experienced such pressure in all domains of life. Many women were expected to justify being childless, supporting earlier findings that being childless was a discrediting attribute that women were required to justify or conceal in order to maintain credibility (Bell, 2013; Rich et al., 2011). In addition, confirming and expanding upon research finding childless women felt workplaces prioritised childed people's needs for annual and carers leave, flexible work and work-life balance, and that others doubted their professional credibility (Doyle et al., 2013; Rich et al., 2011), many women experienced subordination of their needs to those of childed people, assumptions they lacked qualities only childed women could possess, and discrediting of their views and expertise, in all domains of life. At the other end of the continuum, some childless women experienced exclusion from resources and participation in domains of life dominated by, prioritising or catering exclusively to childed people. This finding augments existing research revealing involuntarily childless women's exclusion from a childed social world (Loke, Yu, & Hayter, 2012; Malik & Coulson, 2013).

Supporting the qualitative findings, the quantitative findings revealed exclusion varied within and between the domains of life. In the social domain, childless women had moderate levels of social interaction and high levels of social support. While Italian research found that childless women were less likely to receive social support than childed women (Albertini & Mencarini, 2014), it compared childless with childed women. In the civic domain, a new area of research for childless women in their reproductive years, childless women had low levels of participation in community groups, events and activities. In the service domain, childless women had a low degree of problems accessing or using services. However, in the context of qualitative findings that some women felt excluded from mental and reproductive health services, and a United States study finding 22 per cent of childless women had difficulty obtaining healthcare (Bernstein, 2001), the aggregate score may have disguised problems with particular services. In the economic domain, most women were employed and in the upper middle or high personal income brackets, in accordance with the weight of Australian and international research (Debest & Mazuy, 2014; Miranti, McNamara, Tanton, & Yap, 2009; Waren & Pals, 2013).

In relation to perceived exclusion due to being childless, childless women perceived more exclusion in the social and civic domains than the service and economic domains. This may be explained by the implications of pronatalism in different domains. For example, stigmatising experiences may be more salient in the social and civic domains, while freedom to participate may be more pertinent to the service and economic domains. In addition, when considering the continuum of connection and inclusion within, exclusionary experiences within, and exclusion from, domains of life, the qualitative findings revealed substantially more women described exclusionary experiences within domains of life, than experiences of connection and inclusion within, or exclusion from, domains of life. This facilitates an understanding of why the quantitative findings did not consistently reveal exclusion from, or connection and inclusion within, domains of life, by suggesting exclusionary experiences within domains of life are more relevant to childless women.

4.2. Differences in Social Exclusion of Types of Childless Women

The findings revealed an equally complex picture of exclusion of types of childless women. In relation to the indicators of exclusion, circumstantially childless women reported lower levels of social support than other types of childless women. There were no statistically significant differences in other indicators of exclusion, suggesting different types of childless women had similar levels of resources and participation. Australia's divergent cultural, social, political and economic context from other countries may explain inconsistencies with United States and French studies, which found voluntarily childless women had higher workforce participation rates and incomes than other childless women (Abma & Martinez, 2006; Waren & Pals, 2013). In relation to perceived exclusion due to being childless, circumstantially and involuntarily childless women, followed by voluntarily childless women, perceived more exclusion than undecided and future childed women. These differences corresponded with findings that involuntarily, circumstantially and voluntarily childless women perceived more stigmatisation due to being childless than future childed women, and involuntarily and circumstantially childless women perceived more stigmatisation than undecided women.

The qualitative findings provided additional evidence of nuanced differences in childless women's experiences of inclusion and exclusion. Such differences were influenced by whether women's 'deviance' from pronatalism was non-volitional (innocent), volitional (guilty), and temporary or permanent. For example, some involuntarily and circumstantially childless women, for whom being childless was non-volitional, received sympathy and support. However, others felt stereotyped as unhappy and desperate, consistent with previous research with involuntarily childless women (McCarthy, 2008). In contrast, women whom others perceived as culpable for choices that 'contributed' to being childless, felt stereotyped as selfish, materialistic and child-hating. Furthermore, women who were permanently childless felt judged as failures. In addition, some circumstantially childless and voluntarily childless women who were permanently childless, and undecided women who were considering becoming permanently childless, experienced divorce or separation from partners who wanted to become childed, building upon earlier research with involuntarily childless women (Bell, 2013).

The findings also supported earlier studies revealing childless women's agency (Doyle et al., 2013; Park, 2002), by suggesting childless women are not simply passive receivers of social exclusion. Rather, their internalised, disempowered or empowered responses influenced experiences of social exclusion. Expanding upon research with involuntarily childless women (Bell, 2013), some involuntarily and circumstantially childless women who perceived themselves as failures, incomplete and unfulfilled, were deeply cognisant of being excluded. Furthermore, while some women inadvertently exacerbated exclusion by avoiding stigmatising experiences, others made empowered choices to build lives in which being childless was valued and affirmed.

The influence of the nature of women's 'deviance' from pronatalism facilitates an understanding of differences in types of childless women's degree of perceived exclusion. Some involuntarily and circumstantially childless women's greater degree of exclusion may have been influenced by permanent, internalised and disempowered non-conformance, despite involuntarily childless women's 'innocent' deviance. In contrast, some voluntarily childless women may have been protected from their volitional ('culpable') and permanent deviance by empowered choices. Finally, some undecided and future childed women may have been protected by temporary non-conformance with pronatalism, whereby they were included on the basis of assumptions they would become childed in future.

4.3. Strengths and Limitations

The study had a number of limitations. In relation to the qualitative component, neither iterative data collection and analysis nor participant validation was possible in the context of an anonymous questionnaire. In relation to the quantitative component, its cross-sectional design precluded an examination of causality. Selection bias may have been introduced by the fifty-five per cent completion rate, and non-probability sampling limited external validity. Although self-selection was unavoidable due to the absence of a sampling frame, it may have produced a sample that was more likely to experience pronatalism-driven stigmatisation and exclusion. While the sample was not comparable with Australian women, participants' high educational attainment, employment rates, personal incomes and proportion of voluntary childlessness were consistent with research on the characteristics of childless women (Abma & Martinez, 2006; Miranti et al., 2009; Waren & Pals, 2013). Finally, due to its exploratory nature, the study did not control for confounding factors.

Despite its limitations, this study was the first to investigate social exclusion in multiple domains of life of different types of childless women in their reproductive years. Furthermore, the mixed methods approach facilitated a deeper understanding of social exclusion, the large sample provided sufficient power and rich qualitative data, the use of existing and validated scales reduced the potential for measurement bias, and self-administration minimised socially desirable responses. In addition, data immersion, participant quotations, locating the findings within existing research, and researcher reflexivity enhanced the qualitative component's rigour.

5. Conclusions

This research suggests societal-level pronatalism manifests in a continuum of childless women's connection and inclusion within, exclusion within, and exclusion from domains of life in Australian society, with more exclusion in the social and civic domains than the service and economic domains. Future research using a more comprehensive suite of indicators will further elucidate the nature of social exclusion. The study further suggests circumstantially and involuntarily childless women, followed by voluntarily childless women, perceive more stigmatisation and exclusion due to being childless than undecided and future childed women. Such differences may be influenced by the nature of women's 'deviance' from pronatalism.

Given social exclusion is a firmly established social determinant of health, it is essential to work towards an Australian society in which women's motherhood status is irrelevant to judgements of their worth, such that none would feel excluded in connection with being childless. Inclusive research can contribute to this change by measuring and exploring motherhood status and types of childlessness in health and social research. In addition, practitioners and policy-makers can develop inclusive interventions and policies by ensuring childless women's needs are considered in interventions and policies for all women, directly targeting different types of childless women with support groups, activities and events, and constructing counter-discourses of being childless as a positive and valued attribute.

Acknowledgements

The authors thank the women who participated in this research.

Conflict of Interests

The authors declare no conflict of interests.

References

Abma, J. C., & Martinez, G. M. (2006). Childlessness among older women in the United States: Trends and profiles. *Journal of Marriage and Family, 68*(4), 1045-1056.

Australian Bureau of Statistics. (2007). *2006 Census community profile series: Basic community profile: Australia*. Canberra: ABS.

Australian Bureau of Statistics. (2008). *Australian social trends, 2008.* Canberra: ABS.

Australian Bureau of Statistics. (2010a). *Australian social trends, Dec 2010.* Canberra: ABS.

Australian Bureau of Statistics. (2010b). *General social survey*. Canberra: ABS.

Australian Bureau of Statistics. (2011). *Census household form*. Canberra: ABS.

Australian Bureau of Statistics. (2012a). *2011 Census of population and housing: Basic community profile: Australia*. Canberra: ABS.

Australian Bureau of Statistics. (2012b). *Australia 2011 Census of population and housing: Basic community profile*. Canberra: ABS.

Australian Bureau of Statistics. (2012c). Income data in the census. Retrieved from http://www.abs.gov.au/websitedbs/censushome.nsf/home/factsheetsuid?opendocument&navpos=450

Australian Bureau of Statistics. (2013). *Australian health survey: Users' guide, 2011-13*. Canberra: ABS.

Albertini, M., & Mencarini, L. (2014). Childlessness and support networks in later life new pressures on familistic welfare states? *Journal of Family Issues, 35*(3), 331-357.

Australian Institute of Health and Welfare. (2010). *Australia's mothers and babies 2008*. Canberra: AIHW.

Baker, M. (2003). *Infertility, social exclusion and social policy*. Paper presented at the Australian Social Policy Conference, Sydney.

Bell, K. (2013). Constructions of "infertility" and some lived experiences of involuntary childlessness. *Affilia, 28*(3), 284-295.

Bernstein, A. B. (2001). Motherhood, health status, and health care. *Women's Health Issues, 11*(3), 173-184.

Brown, B., Brauner, C., Chan, A., Gutierrez, D., Herson, J., Lovato, J., . . . Vienier, J. (2010). *STPLAN Version 4.5: February, 2010: Calculations for sample sizes and related problems*. Houston, Texas: University of Texas M.D. Anderson Cancer Center.

Butterfield, L, Borgen, W, Amundson, N., & Maglio, A. (2005). Fifty years of the critical incident technique: 1954-2004 and beyond. *Qualitative Research*, *5*(4), 475-497.

Cannold, L. (2005). *What, no baby? Why women are losing the freedom to mother, and how they can get it back*. Fremantle: Curtin University Books.

Çopur, Z., & Koropeckyj-Cox, T. (2010). University students' perceptions of childless couples and parents in Ankara, Turkey. *Journal of Family Issues, 31*(11), 1481-1506.

Daniluk, J. C. (2001). Reconstructing their lives: a longitudinal, qualitative analysis of the transition to biological childlessness for infertile couples. *Journal of Counseling & Development, 79*(4), 439-449.

Debest, C., & Mazuy, M. (2014). Childlessness: A life choice that goes against the norm. *Population & Societies, 508*, 1-4.

Dermott, E., Fahmy, E., Gordon, D., Heslop, P., Levitas, R., & Patsios, D. (2012). *Poverty and social exclusion in the UK: Living standards questionnaire 2012*. Bristol: PSE.

Doyle, J., Pooley, J. A., & Breen, L. (2013). A phenomenological exploration of the childfree choice in a sample of Australian women. *Journal of Health Psychology, 18*(3), 397-407.

Fieder, M., Huber, S., & Bookstein, F. L. (2011). Socioeconomic status, marital status and childlessness in men and women: An analysis of census data from six countries. *Journal of Biosocial Science, 43*(05), 619-635.

George, L., Blazer, D., Hughes, D., & Fowler, N. (1989). Social support and the outcome of major depression. *The British Journal of Psychiatry, 154*(4), 478-485.

Gillespie, R. (2000). When no means no: Disbelief, disregard and deviance as discourses of voluntary childlessness. *Women's Studies International Forum, 23*(2), 223-234.

Graham, M., & Rich, S. (2012a). Representations of childless women in the Australian print media. *Feminist media studies, 14*(3), 500-518.

Graham, M., & Rich, S. (2012b) What's 'childless' got to do with it? Geelong: Alfred Deakin Research Institute.

Hammarberg, K., Astbury, J., & Baker, H. (2001). Women's experience of IVF: A follow-up study. *Human Reproduction, 16*(2), 374-383.

Huber, S., Bookstein, F. L., & Fieder, M. (2010). Socioeconomic status, education, and reproduction in modern women: An evolutionary perspective. *American Journal of Human Biology, 22*(5), 578-587.

Hughes, D., Blazer, D., & Hybels, C. (1990). *Duke social support index (DSSI): A working paper (revised)*. Durham, NC: Duke University Medical Center.

Koropeckyj-Cox, T., & Pendell, G. (2007). Attitudes about childlessness in the United States: Correlates of positive, neutral, and negative responses. *Journal of Family Issues, 28*(8), 1054-1082.

LaMastro, V. (2001). Childless by choice? Attributions and attitudes concerning family size. *Social Behavior and Personality, 29*(3), 231-243.

Leech, N. L., & Onwuegbuzie, A. J. (2009). A typology of mixed methods research designs. *Quality & Quantity, 43*(2), 265-275.

Letherby, G. (1999). Other than mother and mothers as others: The experience of motherhood and non-motherhood in relation to "infertility" and "involuntary childlessness". *Women's Studies International Forum, 22*(3), 359-372.

Levitas, R., Pantazis, C., Fahmy, E., Gordon, D., Lloyd, E., & Patsios, D. (2007). *The multi-dimensional analysis of social exclusion*. London: Cabinet Office.

Loke, A. Y., Yu, P.-L., & Hayter, M. (2012). Experiences of sub-fertility among Chinese couples in Hong Kong: A qualitative study. *Journal of Clinical Nursing, 21*(3/4), 504-512.

Malik, S. H., & Coulson, N. S. (2013). Coming to terms with permanent involuntary childlessness: A phenomenological analysis of bulletin board postings. *Europe's Journal of Psychology, 9*(1), 77-92.

McCarthy, M. P. (2008). Women's lived experience of infertility after unsuccessful medical intervention. *Journal of Midwifery & Women's Health, 53*(4), 319-324.

McNamee, B. G., & James, G. D. (2012). The impact of child-rearing status on perceptual and behavioural predictors of ambulatory blood pressure variation among working women. *Annals of Human Biology, 39*(6), 490-498.

Melbourne Institute of Applied Economic and Social Research. (2012). *Household, income and labour dynamics in Australia (HILDA) survey: Wave 12M new person questionnaire*. Melbourne: Melbourne Institute of Applied Economic and Social Research.

Miall, C. E. (1994). Community constructs of involuntary

childlessness: Sympathy, stigma, and social support. *Canadian Review of Sociology, 31*(4), 392-421.

Miranti, R., McNamara, J., Tanton, R., & Yap, M. (2009). A narrowing gap? Trends in the childlessness of professional women in Australia 1986–2006. *Journal of Population Research, 26*(4), 359-379.

Mollen, D. (2006). Voluntarily childfree women: Experiences and counseling considerations. *Journal of Mental Health Counseling, 28*(3), 269-282.

Onat, G., & Beji, N. K. (2012). Marital relationship and quality of life among couples with infertility. *Sexuality and Disability, 30*(1), 39-52.

Park, K. (2002). Stigma management among the voluntarily childless. *Sociological Perspectives, 45*(1), 21-45.

Parry, D. (2004). Women's lived experiences of infertility. *Canadian Woman Studies, 24*(1), 81-86.

Pinel, E. C. (1999). Stigma consciousness: The psychological legacy of social stereotypes. *Journal of Personality and Social Psychology, 76*(1), 114-128.

Popay, J., Escorel, S., Hernández, M., Johnston, H., Mathieson, J., & Rispel, L. (2008). *Understanding and tackling social exclusion: Final report to the WHO Commission on Social Determinants of Health from the Social Exclusion Knowledge Network*. Lancaster, UK: WHO Social Exclusion Knowledge Network.

Rich, S., Taket, A., Graham, M., & Shelley, J. (2011). 'Unnatural', 'unwomanly', 'uncreditable' and 'undervalued': The significance of being a childless woman in Australian society. *Gender Issues, 28*(4), 226-247.

Sawer, M. (2013). Misogyny and misrepresentation women in Australian parliaments. *Political Science, 65*(1), 105-117.

Sherbourne, C. D., & Stewart, A. L. (1991). The MOS social support survey. *Social Science and Medicine, 32*(6), 705-714.

Smith, A., Rissel, C. E., Richters, J., Grulich, A. E., & Visser, R. O. (2003). Sex in Australia: Sexual identity, sexual attraction and sexual experience among a representative sample of adults. *Australian and New Zealand Journal of Public Health, 27*(2), 138-145.

Sternke, E. A., & Abrahamson, K. (2015). Perceptions of women with infertility on stigma and disability. *Sexuality and Disability, 33*(1), 3-17.

Veevers, J. E. (1979). Voluntary childlessness. *Marriage & Family Review, 2*(2), 1-26.

Waren, W., & Pals, H. (2013). Comparing characteristics of voluntarily childless men and women. *Journal of Population Research, 30*(2), 151-170.

About the Authors

Beth Turnbull

Beth Turnbull is a PhD candidate in the School of Health and Social Development, Deakin University. Her research seeks to understand the social connection and exclusion in different areas of life of women with no children, and how those experiences influence health and wellbeing.

Dr. Melissa Graham

Melissa Graham is a Senior Lecturer in the School of Health and Social Development, Deakin University. She is the Deputy Director of the Centre for Health through Action on Social Exclusion (CHASE). Dr Graham's research explores the lives of women without children with a particular focus on social exclusion, and health and wellbeing.

Ann Taket

Ann Taket holds the chair in Health and Social Exclusion within the School of Health and Social Development, and is Director of the Centre for Health through Action on Social Exclusion (CHASE) at Deakin University. Professor Taket has over thirty years' experience in public health related research, with particular interests in research directed at understanding the complex interactions between social exclusion and health, prevention and intervention in violence and abuse and the value of human rights based approaches in policy and practice.

Appendix: Open-ended questions used in the data collection instrument.

Topic/domain	Question
Stigmatisation	Can you think of a time when you felt you felt you were stereotyped or stigmatized because you have no children? If so, please describe the incident in the space provided.
Social domain	Thinking about your family and friends, can you think of a time when you had a positive or negative experience related to not having children? If so, please describe the incident in detail in the space provided.
	Thinking about your participation in social and leisure activities, can you think of a time when you had a positive or negative experience related to not having children? If so, please describe the incident in detail in the space provided.
Civic domain	Thinking about your participation in community life, can you think of a time when you had a positive or negative experience related to not having children? If so, please describe the incident in detail in the space provided.
Service domain	Thinking about your access to and use of services, can you think of a time when you had a positive or negative experience related to not having children? If so, please describe the incident in detail in the space provided.
Economic domain	Thinking about your working life (including paid work and unemployment), can you think of a time when you had a positive or negative experience related to not having children? If so, please describe the incident in detail in the space provided.
	Thinking about your material and financial resources, can you think of a time when you had a positive or negative experience related to not having children? If so, please describe the incident in detail in the space provided.
General	Is there anything else you would like to tell us about being a woman in Australian society who does not have children?

17

Social Capital and Citizens' Attitudes towards Migrant Workers

Abdoulaye Diop [1,*], Yaojun Li [2,3], Majed Mohammed H. A. Al-Ansari [1] and Kien T. Le [1]

[1] Social and Economic Survey Research Institute, Qatar University, Doha, Qatar; E-Mails: adiop@qu.edu.qa (A.D.), mansari@qu.edu.qa (M.M.H.A.A.-A.), kienle@qu.edu.qa (K.T.L.)
[2] Department of Sociology, University of Manchester, Manchester, M13 9PL, UK; E-Mail: yaojun.li@manchester.ac.uk
[3] Cathie Marsh Institute for Social Research, University of Manchester, Manchester, M13 9PL, UK

* Corresponding author

Abstract
This study examines Qatari citizens' attitudes toward migrant workers. While much research has been conducted on citizens' attitudes toward the abolition, tightening, or loosening of the Kafāla system in the Gulf Cooperation Council (GCC) countries with regard to migrant workers' residency rights, and on their contribution to the economic development of these countries, little is known about how citizens' religiosity and social engagement impact their acceptance of migrant workers. In the present study, we address this question by examining the effects of religious and social capital on Qatari citizens' preferences for having Arab and Western migrant workers as neighbours, drawing on data from two nationally representative surveys in Qatar. The results indicate that, even after controlling for a wide range of socio-demographic attributes, social capital in terms of trust and bridging social ties has a strong effect on the Qatari nationals' preferences.

Keywords
Gulf Cooperation Council countries; kafāla system; migrant workers; public attitudes, social capital

Issue
This article is part of the issue "International Migration and Ethnic Integration", edited by Yaojun Li (University of Manchester, UK) and Anthony Heath (University of Oxford, UK).

1. Introduction

The influence of migration on ethnic diversity and community cohesion has been extensively studied in the USA and Europe. Scholars have generally found that large inflows of migrants change the demographic composition of the receiving countries and have a strong and largely negative impact on community cohesion. Consequently, much of the discussion about migration is focused on the mainstream population's (or nationals') attitudes towards, and the socio-economic integration of, the migrant workers and their children. However, in the Gulf Cooperation Council (GCC) countries, surprisingly few studies have investigated these issues. In this context, the migration literature has mostly been centred around understanding the recruitment of migrant workers, their lives and working conditions in the host countries, their remittances to family members back home, the impact of remittances on the lives of their family members, and economic development in the sending countries. It was not until recently that the focus shifted slightly to an examination of the attitudes of nationals towards migrant workers and the kafāla system which regulates their employment and residential status in the GCC countries. In the GCC countries, 'foreigners' are guest workers who have little prospect of becoming naturalized citizens of the countries even though they may work and live alongside nationals.

More than anywhere else in the world, the countries of the Arabian Gulf are dependent on foreign labour to sustain their economic growth and development. Across the region, these workers play a vital role, carrying out jobs that are both mundane (e.g. janitorial services, domestic work) and critical to the national economy of these countries (e.g. construction, natural resource extraction). Unlike in Europe, in the GCC generally, and in Qatar and the UAE in particular, these 'foreigners' constitute the majority of the population at the present time. These workers also bring with them their various religious traditions and customs, introducing significant diversity to countries for which Islam has long been overwhelmingly dominant. The growing presence of these workers has led GCC nationals to re-examine their nationhood and their place within society. According to some critics, these demographic changes have led some nationals to look inward, becoming more insular and less engaged civically within their local communities and neighbourhoods. This may be more pronounced in Qatar with the commitment to the FIFA 2022 World Cup. Such commitment has maintained or increased the need for migrant workers in the country to complete the infrastructure development projects but nationals' attitudes towards 'foreigners' have so far remained under-researched.

In this context, we thought it high time that a systematic study be conducted which linked nationals' religious and social-civic engagement with their attitudes towards migrant workers. We use Qatar as a case study because it typifies Gulf countries, which have a very highly proportion of migrant workers in the population (Ministry of Developmental Planning and Statistics, 2016). The insight from the study of nationals' attitudes to and their preferences for migrant workers as neighbours, a fairly intimate form of personal interaction in the Qatari context, has important implications both for the on-going debate on immigration[1] and social cohesion, and for the socio-economic integration and well-being of immigrants. To carry out the research, we have used two national representative surveys that we conducted in Qatar. We find that religious affiliation, social trust, and bridging social ties play a significant role in citizens' attitudes towards migrant workers.

This paper is structured as follows. In the next section, we give a review of the literature on social capital, social cohesion, and social trust. Based on this literature, we introduce our hypotheses, to be followed by the presentation of our data and findings. We conclude the paper with some discussions and suggestions for future research.

2. Literature Review

Social capital is a complex and highly controversial concept; nonetheless, it is widely used by scholars in various social science disciplines as a measure of connectedness at the individual, community, and national levels. Social capital theorists use the term to refer to resources inherent in the social networks, whether such resources are informational, material or psychological (Bourdieu, 1986; Coleman, 1988; Lin, 2001; Putnam, 2000). Such resources could be beneficial to individuals in terms of children's education, job acquisition, career advancement, health enhancement, and a range of other outcomes. The benefits are not only for those in the networks, but extend to people who are onlookers or who are not directly involved in the networks. Thus, social capital is assumed to be helpful for community building too. Researchers tend to differentiate between two types of social capital: bonding and bridging (Putnam, 2000). Bonding refers to connections and networks within a homogeneous group, while bridging refers to social ties among people with dissimilar characteristics such as race, ethnicity, education or personal attributes. As such, bridging is more related to the concept of social cohesion (Cheong, Edwards, Goulbourne, & Solomos, 2007) and is a point of interest for this analysis. A more comprehensive definition of bridging social capital is offered by Putnam, who says that it 'concerns voluntary associations and horizontal ties based on common interests that transcend heterogeneous differences of ethnicity, religion and socio-economic status' (2000, p.22).

Scholars have different views on how to assess the relationship between social cohesion and social capital. Putnam (2000) suggested that bridging social ties are a means of 'getting ahead' in society, as opposed to bonding social ties, which he describes as helping people to 'get by'. The two forms of social capital tend to go hand in hand although they might serve different purposes: chicken soup for the sick and 'sleeve-rolling' for community building. He holds that, in order to maintain and enhance community cohesion, people need to acquire connections with members of other groups who may possess different types of social resources. However it is important to note, at this juncture, that as a political scientist, Putnam's main interest was in the effect of social capital on social-political governance. Much of his analysis tends to link the state of democracy to the stock of social capital in a society. For example, he attributes the successful functioning of socio-economic life in northern Italy to the high level of social capital in the region and the opposite in the south, and different crime rates in the different states of his own country to the different levels of social capital in those states. In this regard, it would be fair to say that he has paid insufficient attention to the sociological causes of what he saw as the declining stock of social capital, which has been examined by sociologists investigating the determinants of bonding and bridging social capital and concomitants such as trust in capitalist countries like the USA or Britain (e.g., Hall, 1999; Li, Savage, & Pickles, 2003; Li, 2015; Paxton, 1999).

Sociological critiques of the relationship between social cohesion and social capital offer considerable insights. Cheong et al. (2007), for example, argue that more social capital does not necessarily lead to better social cohesion, as more social capital within groups tends to erode connections with other groups. Thus, for these authors, the 'proposal to (re)create cohesive communities via social capital building may therefore be inter-

[1] In the Qatari context, the term "immigrants" is used to refer to guest workers as there is no formal path to citizenship.

preted as a diversion from the fundamental injustices' (Cheong et al., 2007, p. 36). Leonard thinks that even the transition from bonding to bridging social capital will reinforce existing inequalities through the affirmation of their existence and, therefore, 'in order to set in motion the framework for bridging social capital to emerge, the conditions that led to the development of bonding social capital need to be undermined' (2004, p. 927). This view is also echoed by Rajulton, Ravanera and Beaujot (2007), who show that a strong sense of belonging can be associated with low tolerance of diversity. But Rajulton et al. (2007) do not specify what kind of belonging leads to low tolerance. In this paper, we argue and demonstrate that personal belonging among family and kin is different from neighbourhood belonging: the former may be associated with low tolerance whereas the latter may foster tolerance in the Qatari context.

The socio-economic insecurity of individuals and communities has been found in numerous studies to be the main influence behind weak and falling levels of social capital and social cohesion (Fieldhouse & Johnson, 2008; Letki, 2008; Li et al., 2003). Viewed from this perspective, social cohesion is best achieved by battling poverty and correcting social injustice. A society that acknowledges diversity while ensuring justice and prosperity for all will more likely be a cohesive one. This, of course, does not mean that social connections, social belonging or civic engagement play no role in social cohesion. Beyond economic factors, we may find that bridging social ties and neighbourhood belonging have a positive effect on people's attitudes or behaviour, especially in societies such as Qatar where citizens account for only a small proportion of the population.

Social cohesion is not unidimensional but encompasses different components such as trust and civic participation. Trust between members of society is a precondition for social cohesion. It would be difficult to imagine a well-functioning society composed solely or even predominantly of mutually distrusting and unconnected individuals. Maintaining social cohesion for ethno-culturally diverse societies is even more challenging when waves upon waves of immigrants from various backgrounds, religious traditions, and group identities come to the country. In Qatar, the high level of segregation between Qataris and out-groups offers a good opportunity to study the relationship between social interaction and intergroup cooperation.

A major issue in the conceptualization and measurement of social cohesion concerns individual versus group levels of social interaction (Friedkin, 2004). Individual-level interaction refers to one's willingness to remain within one's own social group and strengthen ties with it. Group-level cohesion refers to the breadth and depth of ties with out-groups. This is similar to the 'bonding' versus 'bridging' classification made by Putnam, but we can make more refined distinctions. Individual-level cohesion can be further differentiated into personal bonding with family and kin, extended friendship ties with others with similar or dissimilar characteristics, and meso-level acquaintances with neighbours and others in the local community. The effects of these connections on people's attitudes and tolerance may be different: close bonding within family and kin may restrict people's outlook whereas friendship with others, particularly with people of different ethnic backgrounds, may broaden people's horizons, as will a sense of community belonging that bridges to out-groups. Almost all Qataris belong to the same group in terms of racial and religious affiliation; they are Arab Muslims. The traditional and conservative nature of Qatari society and the constant influx of immigrants from non-Arab and non-Muslim backgrounds may lead Qatari nationals to 'hunker down', or become apathetic or even antipathetic towards outsiders, but one might also expect those with bridging ties or a greater sense of neighbourhood belonging to be more open-minded. To understand how social cohesion operates in Qatar, we therefore need to understand how social Qataris are and how their identification with in- and out-groups might impact upon attitudes to out-groups.

The discussion of in-group versus out-group relations is related to the differentiation mentioned above between bonding and bridging forms of social capital. In our context, bonding ties can be seen to reflect interaction among Qataris or with the larger Arab groupings. Bridging concerns horizontal ties based on shared interests that go beyond differences of race, religion, and socio-economic characteristics. In a way, social cohesion can be reached by realising the benefit of cross-community relations: the more the different social groups in a society work together, the higher the likelihood that all groups will benefit. In Qatar, the realisation of national-level social cohesion needs more bridging connections across groups, namely, between Qataris and immigrants who are different from them culturally.

Building strong bridging social capital is a way to ensure that the benefits of bonding social capital become society-wide rather than group specific. As Pieterse (2003) says, for bonding social capital to yield positive outcomes, bridging social ties need to be strong. Some authors, such as Leonard (2004) and Rajulton et al. (2007), also point to the potentially negative effects of bonding ties on social cohesion through increased prejudice towards members of out-groups, which is likely to develop when there are strong ties within tightly knit communities (see also Portes & Landolt, 1996). In Qatari society, there are many commonalities between Qataris, as almost all of them are Muslims and Arabic speaking. Also, most Qataris are tribally affiliated and therefore strong group ties are apparent (Al-Kathim, 1991). Apart from ethno-religious differences, immigrants in Qatar, and especially non-Arabs, are also socially segregated from Qataris through economic status, living conditions, and cultural boundaries. This social setting encourages each group to remain in their own spheres of life, which is not conducive to inter-group interactions. Qataris share strong ties amongst themselves due to tribal affiliations and a specific image that includes traditions and religion as the core national identity. Yet, Qataris and immigrants also share workplaces, neighbourhoods and even the education system, making inter-group tensions and associated problems more likely to occur. Therefore, it is of considerable importance, in our context, to understand how the strong intragroup ties among Qataris affect their attitudes to immigrant groups.

One of the key indicators of social cohesion is social trust at the macro (generalized) and meso (situational) levels (Li, Pickles, & Savage, 2005). Defining trust in the Arab context is no easy task. As the Arabic proverb goes, 'the most complicated of tasks is explaining that which is in no need of explanation'. Trust is a word we frequently use in our parlance and, more importantly, a practice that we even take for granted in much of our social life, a situation which is made possible through *repeated* social interactions.

Deutsch (1958) suggests that due to the expectation of a positive outcome, the trusting party would be more affected by betrayal of trust than affirmation of it. If you trust someone, you have decided beforehand that the outcome will be positive. If you are in doubt about the positive outcome you don't have trust. Trust is therefore a relationship between two actors, the first extending trust and the second receiving it (Baier, 1986; Hardin, 1993; Luhmann, 1980). This relationship centres on the belief that the second party will react positively to trust by delivering on the subject of trust in a material or sentimental manner.

The concept of trust explains why one would take risks in dealing with others, participate in solving collective problems, or act in ways that seem to be in conflict with the definition of self-interest (Levi & Stoker, 2000). It has also been argued that it is sometimes in our own interest to trust, as this enables us to gain access to benefits that accrue when we deal with other people, lowers the cost of everyday business, and fosters reciprocation by others (Alesina & La Ferrara, 2002). Trust is mutually beneficial when it is reciprocal, when the trusting and the trusted parties act according to expectation. In highly diverse settings, the prospect of cross-group cooperation may be hampered by differences and tensions between groups. As earlier noted, the presence of trust presumes a predisposition to cooperation and a relative absence of tensions. For our study, this is the desired outcome, a state of mutual predisposition to cooperate and work together between Qatari citizens and non-citizen residents in Qatar.

It is therefore plausible to suggest that trust is a rational choice whereby both parties can expect to gain from the relationship. It is in the interest of the trusted party to maintain the trustworthy status through delivering on expectation (Guth, Levati, & Ploner, 2008). When the trust cycle is broken, both parties lose out. This is why social trust is seen by researchers as being sociological rather than psychological or purely economic (Lewis & Weigert, 1985). It is a result of social actions and repeated interactions. In order to get by and get ahead in our personal and social life, we need to work together and trust one another (Arrow, 1972).

However, just as with many other social factors, trust may have a downside. Bad, or so-called 'blind', trust is a situation where the trusting party extends trust without receiving the desired results from the trusted party because of the personal or ideological dispositions of the latter. This bad trust could lead to manipulative political and religious figures advancing their own agendas, which could do much damage to the social fabric. Arguably, voting for someone is partly a manifestation of trust that the candidate will deliver on his or her promises. Many Germans in the 1930s placed their trust in the Nazis and their leader to solve the country's economic, social and political problems, but that trust led to a disaster for the world.

Good trust is the focus of our study. By this, we mean the kind of trust that encourages cooperation between members of different groups in society regardless of race, religion or nationality. Understanding what trust exists between Qataris and migrant workers and what factors affect it is the first step in advancing social cohesion. Good trust reaps the benefits of a cooperative society and avoids the dangers of prejudice and non-cooperation.

Trust as a measure in survey research has taken many forms. With regard to trusted parties, researchers identify three domains: trust in those we know, trust in institutions, and trust in undefined others. The first kind of trust, sometimes called familial, particular or thick trust (Delhey, Newton, & Welzel, 2011; Field, 2008; Levi & Stoker, 2000; Li, Heath, & Devine, 2015), is direct: the trusted party is known and the relationship is easily explained. Repeated co-operation within the inner circle provides an abundance of the information necessary for people to decide whether or not to trust someone (Stolle, Soroka, & Johnston, 2008). The second kind of trust, referred to as trust in political institutions (legislative, executive, and administrative bodies), is also fairly stable as such institutions have evolved over dozens or hundreds of years. However, trust in the office-holders could vary (Paxton, 1999). The final domain is commonly known as generalised trust, namely, trust in others with whom one has had no prior interaction. This concept is widely used in social science literature. Stole defines it as 'the potential readiness of citizens to cooperate with each other and [the] abstract preparedness to engage in civic endeavours with each other' (Stolle et al., 2008, p. 4).

Whilst some scholars regard generalised trust as inherently good, it is not without its critics. Arneil (2006), for example, argues that while generalised trust might function well in homogeneous societies, it is not as effective in ethnically diverse settings. This may be especially true in Qatar where the population is clearly divided into Qataris, white-collar, and blue-collar migrant workers, with racial and religious divides. Results from the Social Capital survey in Qatar (2011) show that levels of generalised trust vary a great deal between the three groups. Qataris exhibited the highest levels of trust while blue-collar workers showed the least. This is intensified by the high levels of in-group trust and the extremely low levels of out-group trust.

The high level of trust shown by Qataris merits closer scrutiny. As Wilson (n.d.) says, a respondent may often be thinking of the intra-group relations when prompted to assess his or her trust in unspecified 'others' and therefore the answer may not accurately reflect the level of inter-group trust in society. This was confirmed by the fact that the level of generalised trust and of Qataris' trust in Qataris was similar but it dropped significantly when discussing out-groups (Al-Emadi, Diop, Le, Al-Ansari, Jardina, Tessler, & Wittrock, 2011; Diop, Jardina, Tessler, & Wittrock, 2016).

These considerations on personal trust focus on the radius of trust, whereas the level of trust in the civic sphere relates to the intensity of civic cooperation in a society, which may or may not depend on personal acquaintance between fellow members in civic organisations. By analysing indicators of in-group and out-group trust, Delhey et al. (2011) conclude that it is possible to control for radius of trust. Their results suggest that societies with more familial and tribal ties tend to have a narrow radius of trust while more advanced societies exhibit a wider radius.

As Qatari society is highly familial and tribal, the expectation is that the strong social divide between Qataris and immigrants will yield a narrow radius of generalised trust that focuses on Qataris as a community rather than extending trust to the overall, highly diverse society. Qataris view themselves as 'the' group in society as they are citizens of the country while all others are simply sojourners. Yet, as they live in proximity to these immigrants, their perception of the 'general' public is also hampered by the way society is structured. For Qataris, it is easier to view society in a segmented way: Qataris and highly integrated Arabs; white-collar non-Arabs, who mostly interact with Qataris in the workplace and in educational institutions; and blue-collar workers, who very rarely have personal contact with Qataris (Diop, Le, Johnston, & Ewers, 2016). Overlaid on this economic divide are cultural differences, with much greater preference shown for Arabs than for Westerners and Asians. Given this, invoking particularised trust by asking Qataris about their trust in specific out-groups, identified by their background, is better suited to our research questions.

Underlying particularised trust is the extent of contact which a member of mainstream society has with members of out-groups, as has been demonstrated by much of the previous research (Forbes, 1997; Putnam, 2007; Schmid, Al Ramiah, & Hewstone, 2014; Sigelman & Welch, 1993; Stein, Post, & Rinden, 2000). In Qatar, contact is of prime importance as different groups have different contact dynamics with Qataris. Arabs are more integrated, as they speak the same language as Qataris and share many social and cultural norms. Asians are usually found in low-skilled jobs which don't give them many opportunities to have contact with Qatari nationals. Westerners, on the other hand, share very little with Qataris as most of them do not speak Arabic, do not live in Qatari neighbourhoods, and their children do not attend public schools. However, they are more likely than Asians to interact with Qatari nationals in the workplace as they are usually engaged in white-collar work. This social setting requires a measurement of contact that acknowledges these different dynamics.

Another factor in the Qatari context is related to religious affiliation. Religiosity and religious practice have been found to have a significant impact on inter-group trust (Alesina & La Ferrara, 2002; Brambilla, Manzi, Regalia, & Verkuyten, 2013; Brenneman, 2008; Schmeets & Te Riele, 2014; Schoenfeld, 1978; Traunmuller, 2011). The religiously conservative nature of Qatari society encourages an exploration of the relationship between religion and trust as immigrant groups include both Muslims and non-Muslims. However, religion is not the only aspect of Qataris' conservatism: social norms are also highly important to Qataris.

Social conservatism and social attitudes in general affect social trust, especially towards immigrants. Low trust in members of other groups has been attributed to strong adherence to group-specific norms (Dawes, Van de Kragt, & Orbell, 1988; Uslaner & Conley, 2003). The strong tribal nature of Qatari society elevates the significance of social conservatism as social norms for gaining an understanding of trust between Qataris and immigrants. However, it is also important to note that the increased presence of civic organisations and charities may increase the likelihood of Qataris interacting with immigrants in a new setting where more or less equal status is apparent through volunteering and charitable work.

The ever-changing social (and political) milieu is also important for understanding social trust. Immigration is becoming an increasingly important political issue in many parts of the world but, in the Qatari context, political orientation is difficult to gauge, as no political parties exist in the country. Nevertheless, the Arab Spring and the resulting chaos in the region have had a notable impact on all Arab countries and Qatar is no exception. Pro-Islamist and anti-Islamist propaganda flooded Arab media and generated high levels of public interest in Qatar. This allows us to test for the effects of Islamism manifested as, for example, a desire for out-groups to adopt Qatari customs.

The above discussions offer various ways in which we could seek to understand social trust and social attitudes in Qatar. Many of the factors are, of course, intertwined in the Qatari context. Understanding how religious, social, and political attitudes impact one another is necessary in order to determine how significant these effects are and which of them holds greater importance in explaining trust in and attitudes to immigrants and social inclusion.

3. Hypotheses

Based on the literature review, we have developed a number of hypotheses in order to explain Qataris' preferences for having Arab and Western expatriate families as next-door neighbours and the impact of religiosity, social capital, and civic engagement on these preferences. For this purpose, we use separate models for each group (Arab and Western families) and estimate a series of logistic regression models. For each subgroup, the base model (*Model 1*) contains individual, household, and regional characteristics as control variables, including gender, marital status, education, age, employment, household income, region, and year of survey.

Model 2 introduces attitudinal and behavioural dimensions of religiosity. The former is self-reported religiosity. All respondents were asked to describe themselves as very religious, moderately religious, somewhat religious, or not religious at all. This variable is dichotomized with 1 indicating 'very religious' and 0 otherwise. For the behavioural dimension of religiosity, respondents were asked how often they go to a place of worship, with answers ranging from daily, more than once a week, once a week, once a month, more than once a month, a few times a year, to seldom or never. This variable is also dichotomized, with 1 for daily and more than once a week, and 0 for the other responses. Drawing on our discussions above, we can formulate our hypotheses as follows.

Hypothesis 1.1: Religiosity is positively related to preferences for having Arab families as next-door neighbours, with greater religiosity associated with stronger preferences.

Hypothesis 1.2: Religiosity is negatively related to preferences for having Western families as next-door neighbours, with higher religiosity associated with weaker preferences.

The multitude of items discussed above can, following Putnam (2000) and Li (2015), be grouped into what might be termed 'core' and 'derived' domains of social capital. The former includes items such as social ties and relationships constitutive of social networks per se and the latter includes outcomes of being embedded in such networks such as trust, preferences for assimilation and, for our present purposes, preferences for neighbours. Based on the two domains, we present the regression in the sequence which follows.[2]

The third model, *Model 3*, introduces elements of family and friendship networks into the model. The family network tests whether the family-inward orientation of Qataris has a negative impact on their preferences for next-door neighbours and the friendship network tests whether the diversity of close friends is associated with a positive impact on preferences for having Arab or Western families as next-door neighbours. With regards to family-inward orientation, respondents were asked how often they get together with family members including siblings or extended kin for a social event or family occasion. Responses with 'daily' and 'more than once a week' frequencies are coded as 1 and other responses as 0. As for friendship networks, the variable is coded as 1 if respondents have mixed friends, including Qataris, Arabs, Westerners or friends living in other countries, and 0 otherwise.

Hypothesis 2.1: Family-inward orientation is associated with weaker preferences for having Arab/ /Western families as next-door neighbours.

Hypothesis 2.2: Diversity of close personal friends is associated with stronger preferences for having Arab/Western families as next-door neighbours.

The fourth model, *Model 4*, introduces elements of civic engagement and tests whether volunteering for civic organizations or donating to charities has a positive impact on Qataris' preferences for having Arab and Western families as next-door neighbours. Respondents were asked whether they had volunteered to civic organizations and whether they had donated to charities. Both questions used the twelve-month period preceding data collection as a time reference for each wave. The two variables are also dichotomized with 1 indicating positive, and 0 negative, responses.

Hypothesis 3: A high degree of civic engagement is associated with stronger preferences for having Arab/Western families as next-door neighbours.

The fifth model, *Model 5*, tests whether generalised trust in Arabs/Westerners is associated with Qataris' preferences for having Arab or Western families as next-door neighbours. Trust in Arabs and Westerners was rated on a 0–10-point scale.

Hypothesis 4: Higher levels of trust in Arabs/Westerners are associated with preferences for having Arab/Western families as next-door neighbours, with higher trust associated with stronger preferences.

Model 6 tests whether a desire for out-groups to adopt Qatari customs has a strong impact on Qataris' preferences for having Arab families as neighbours and a weak impact on Qataris' preferences for having Western families as neighbours. All respondents were asked to rate the level of importance of out-groups adopting Qatari customs as part of the requirements for seeking citizenship of Qatar. Responses for this question are coded as 1 for very important and 0 for other responses.

Hypothesis 5.1: The importance Qataris attach to out-groups adopting Qatari customs is associated with

[2] We thank the anonymous reviewer who recommended this regression sequence.

stronger preferences for having Arab families as next-door neighbours.

Hypothesis 5.2: The importance Qataris attach to out-groups adopting Qatari customs is associated with weaker preferences for having Western families as next-door neighbours.

Model 7 adds the respondents' perception of neighbourhood belonging and Model 8 adds that of neighbourhood cohesion. The belonging question is worded *'I feel accepted as a member of this neighbourhood'* on a four-point agree/disagree scale. This variable is dichotomized as well, with 1 equalling 'agree' and 0 otherwise. The cohesion question in Model 8 asked respondents whether they agreed or disagreed with the statement: *'People here look out for the welfare of their own families and are not much concerned with neighbourhood welfare.'* We recoded the responses so that 1 means cohesive neighbourhood, namely, that people in the neighbourhood show concern for each other's welfare, and 0 otherwise.

Hypothesis 6: A positive sense of neighbourhood belonging is associated with stronger preferences for having Arab/Western families as next-door neighbours.

Hypothesis 7: A positive perception of neighbourhood cohesion is associated with stronger preferences for having Arab/Western families as next-door neighbours.

4. Data and Results

Our analysis draws on data from the first two waves of the survey *'From Fareej to Metropolis: A Social Capital Survey of Qatar'* conducted by the SESRI at Qatar University in 2011 and 2015 respectively. Both waves were funded by the Qatar Foundation for Education, Science and Community Development. The survey adopted multi-stage stratified probability sampling and collected information on representative samples of the Qatari population focussing on three groups: Qatari citizens, high-skilled migrant workers, and low-skilled migrant workers. Overall, 4,821 interviews were completed between the two waves (2,268 in the year 2011 and 2,553 in the year 2015) including a total of 1,631 Qatari nationals, 1,605 high-skilled workers, and 1,585 low-skilled migrant workers. To explore the effects of social capital, religiosity, and civic engagement on Qataris' preferences for having Arab or Western families as next-door neighbours, we restricted our analysis to data on the Qatari citizen sub-samples. The response rates were high (61% and 59% respectively). The data were weighted to account for probability selection and non-response. The analysis used in this paper is based on weighted data using STATA (version 14), which takes into account the survey design effect.

The survey asked a variety of questions on preferences from which we selected two as our outcome variables—preferences for having Arab and Western families as next-door neighbours. More specifically, respondents were asked whether they would have a *'strong preference, slight preference, neither a preference nor an objection, slight objection, or strong objection for having Arab families as their next-door neighbours.'* And they were asked the same question about Western families. The two variables are dichotomized—1 for strong preference, and 0 for the other response modes—and are used as our dependent variables in this analysis using logit models (further analysis using ordinal logit models yielded basically the same patterns). Our explanatory variables are summarized in Table 1.

Table 2 presents the descriptive statistics for the variables listed in Table 1. Results from the substantive analyses are presented in Tables 3 and 4 with regard to Qataris' preferences for having Arab and Western families as next-door neighbours respectively. Data in the last two tables pertain to average marginal effects (AMEs) derived from the logit models. While substantively the same, the AMEs show the effects in terms of percentage points rather than log odds as in logit models, offering easier exposition. Overall, only one in four Qataris (25%) wish to have Westerners as next-door neighbours, but over twice as many (55%) are happy to have Arabs as next-door neighbours.

Most empirical studies tend to explain findings in sequence. As our aim in this paper is to explain the socio-cultural determinants of Qataris' preferences for having Arab and Western expatriate families as next-door neighbours as a dual dimension, it makes more sense to make an exposition of the effects of our independent variables on the two groups simultaneously. We have also conducted prior analyses on bivariate associations and found that all our independent variables are significantly associated with both kinds of preference (with the sole exception of gender on preferences for Arabs). To save space, we thus move directly to multivariate analyses as shown in Tables 3 and 4 respectively.

With regard to individual and household characteristics in the two tables, we can see that, in terms of net effects, most variables in this domain (marital, employment and financial status, gender, age, education) do not have notable effects: none of the variables are significant with regard to preferences for Arabs in any of the eight models in Table 3 (with the sole exception of richer families unwilling to have Arab neighbours in Model 8); and most of them have non-significant effects with regard to preferences for Westerners (with the exception of older and employed Qataris being less welcoming but richer Qataris more receptive in the first four models). With regard to regional differences, Qataris residing in al Rayyan and other municipalities have stronger preferences for having Arab families as next-door neighbours as compared to those residing in Doha (Table 3). As for Western families, Qataris living in Al Rayyan are little dif-

Table 1. Dimensions and indicators.

Dimensions	Indicators
Demographic	• Individual characteristics • Household characteristics • Year of survey • Municipalities
Religiosity	• Self-reported religiosity • Frequency of going to places of worship
Trust	• Trust in Arabs • Trust in Westerners
Networks	• Frequency of getting together with family members • Diversity of close personal friends
Qatari Identity	• Preferences of "adopting the customs of Qatar" for somebody seeking citizenship of Qatar
Civism	• Volunteering for organizations over the past year • Donating to charitable organizations over the past year
Neighbourhood belonging	• Feeling of being accepted as a member of the neighbourhood
Neighbourhood cohesion (reverse-coding)	• People in the neighbourhood only look out for their own welfare and are not concerned with neighbours' welfare

Table 2. Descriptive statistics.

Variables	N	Percentage		
Male	1631	45%		
Married	1631	71%		
Employed	1630	49%		
Household income ≥ 50, 000 QAR	1516	48%		
Very religious	1629	18%		
Daily attendance of place of worship	1624	43%		
Getting together with family members on a daily basis	1619	74%		
Diversity of friends (yes)	1631	62%		
Qatari customs for immigrants (very important)	1603	61%		
Volunteering (yes)	1626	22%		
Charitable Donations (yes)	1601	76%		
Neighbourhood belonging (yes)	1605	81%		
Neighbourhood cohesion (yes)	1601	36%		
Education				
Vocational or less	461	30%		
Secondary & post-secondary	598	36%		
University degree, Masters, & Ph.D.	571	34%		
Age				
30 years or younger	452	28%		
31–44 years	548	31%		
45 years or older	585	41%		
Municipality				
Doha	540	34%		
Al Rayyan	708	42%		
Other municipalities	383	24%		
	N	Min	Max	Mean
Trust in Arabs	1597	0	10	6.448
Trust in Westerners	1470	0	10	4.132

Table 3. Average marginal effects (AME) of Qataris' preferences for having Arab families as next-door neighbours.

Variables	Model1	Model2	Model3	Model4	Model5	Model6	Model7	Model8
Male	0.5	3.2	2.5	2.8	2.7	1.6	2.1	1.1
Married	−4.7	−4.5	−4.3	−5.0	−4.0	−4.3	−3.0	−3.3
Secondary	1.0	0.8	0.4	−0.2	−1.6	−1.2	−2.5	−2.1
Tertiary	3.1	3.4	2.6	2.1	−0.2	0.1	−0.2	0.6
Aged 31–44	1.2	0.8	0.9	0.4	−0.5	−0.2	−1.0	−1.0
Aged 45+	0.8	1.5	1.2	0.9	0.1	−0.4	−1.3	−0.1
Employed	2.0	2.2	2.1	1.9	2.0	2.2	2.1	2.1
Household income ≥ 50,000QAR	−3.8	−3.9	−3.4	−3.9	−3	−3.2	−4.3	−5.4 [b]
Living in Al Rayyan	6.6 [c]	7.5 [b]	7.5 [b]	7.2 [b]	7.1 [b]	7.6 [b]	7.0 [b]	7.6 [b]
Living in other areas	7.1 [c]	8.1 [b]	7.3 [c]	7.0 [c]	7.5 [c]	7.2 [c]	7.0 [c]	6.0
Year of survey (2015)	10.3 [a]	9.6 [a]	9.3 [a]	8.8 [a]	7.3 [b]	8.4 [a]	8.9 [a]	8.9 [a]
Religiosity		−7.1 [c]	−6.9 [c]	−6.8 [c]	−6.9 [c]	−7.4 [c]	−8.4 [b]	−8.7 [b]
Religious attendance		−3.3	−3.7	−4.0	−4.0	−2.6	−3.9	−3.0
Getting together with family and kin			−2.5	−2.4	−2.8	−3.2	−4.6	−5.0
Diversity of friends			4.7	4.8	5.4 [c]	5.4 [c]	4.5	4.0
Volunteering				4.6	4.3	4.5	4.1	4.4
Donations				5.3	4.4	3.9	3.1	3.8
Trust in Arabs					3.1 [a]	2.9 [a]	2.8 [a]	2.8 [a]
Qatari customs for immigrants						8.3 [a]	7.7 [b]	7.6 [b]
Neighbourhood belonging							10.8 [a]	11.2 [a]
Neighbourhood cohesion								4.7
Wald χ^2	23.35	28.57	30.15	35.38	58.78	69.38	75.09	82.44
McFadden's Adj R^2	0.014	0.017	0.018	0.021	0.038	0.043	0.049	0.054
N	1479	1471	1462	1441	1420	1402	1382	1367

Notes: [a] $p < .01$, [b] $p < .05$, [c] $p < .10$; Reference categories are female, non-married, with primary education, age under 30, non-employed, household income ≤ 50,000 QAR, living in Doha, survey year 2011, less religious, with less bonding and bridging ties, less desirous of foreigners adopting Qatari customs, less volunteering and donating, and less attached to the neighbourhood; 1 QAR = 0.27 US Dollar.

ferent from those living in Doha and only those living in other municipalities show positive preferences for having Westerners as next-door neighbours (Table 4). These results suggest that Qataris residing in Doha are less keen to have them as next-door neighbours.

With reference to the waves, the results show a positive and significant (at 0.1 level) effect for the year (2015) variable in all models, indicating improved Qatari attitudes towards Arab and Western families between 2011 and 2015. This pattern is in line with two major changes that occurred during that period, namely, the awarding of the FIFA 2022 World Cup and a 60 percent salary increase for Qatari nationals. Though the announcement of Qatar hosting the 2022 FIFA World Cup was made in December 2010, it was around 2015 that outside scrutiny and criticism of Qatar's policies with respect to the treatment and welfare of its guest workers reached a critical point and required a response. This in turn increased awareness of migrant workers' issues among Qatari nationals. In addition, in 2011 the government increased the salary of Qatari nationals by 60 per cent. Taken together, these two events may have contributed to the change in nationals' attitudes towards both Arab and Western expatriate families. The national mood was happier and more welcoming of guest workers.

Turning to religiosity and religious attendance, we find a weak and negative association with preferences for having Arab or Western expatriate families as neighbours, with religiosity effects barely significant (at 0.1 level) for Arabs, indicating that Qatari nationals who consider themselves very religious are less likely to want Arab families living next-door. This is an unexpected result as Qataris and most Arabs share the same language and religion.

Family and friendship networks seem to play an important role. Family-inward orientation has no significant (albeit weakly negative) bearing on the Arab models but, as might be expected, a strong and significantly negative impact on Western expatriate families, indicating that strong bonds amongst family members tend to make Qatari nationals more disinclined to accept Western expatriate families as next-door neighbours. By contrast, we find in both tables that bridging social capital, as indicated by a diversity of friendship networks, tends to make Qataris more open and more willing to accept both groups as next-door neighbours, and indeed, more so for Westerners than for Arabs: around 10 percentage points for Westerners and 5 percentage points for Arabs. Whereas the impact is significant in early models (5 and 6) for Arabs, the effect becomes non-significant with models 7 and 8. On the other hand, the effect is fully significant for all models 4–8 with regard to Western families. Further analysis shows that the net effects of friendship diversity are significantly stronger for West-

Table 4. Average marginal effects (AME) of Qataris' preferences for having Western families as next-door neighbours.

Variables	Model1	Model2	Model3	Model4	Model5	Model6	Model7	Model8
Male	−0.4	−0.4	−0.5	−0.3	0.4	0.5	1.1	−0.6
Married	0.5	0.5	0.8	1.0	0.5	0.3	1.2	0.9
Secondary	4.1	4.1	3.4	2.7	1.4	2.6	1.7	2.0
Tertiary	4.0	4.0	2.5	2.1	0.2	1.5	1.2	1.2
Aged 31–44	−2.5	−2.5	−3.8	−3.6	−3.6	−3.5	−4.3	−3.3
Aged 45+	−6.5 [c]	−6.2	−7.4 [c]	−7.2 [c]	−8.0 [b]	−8.3 [b]	−8.6 [b]	−7.6 [c]
Employed	−3.5	−3.5	−4.1	−3.9	−5.2 [b]	−4.9	−4.4	−5.0
Household income ≥ 50,000QAR	4.8 [c]	5 c	5.7 [b]	5.8 [b]	4.1	3.9	3.7	3.0
Living in Al Rayyan	1.7	2.0	3.0	3.0	3.6	3.7	3.4	4.8
Living in other areas	11.5 [a]	11.9 [a]	10.5 [a]	10.0 [a]	11.7 [a]	11.4 [a]	11.6 [a]	10.1 [a]
Year of survey (2015)	11.4 [a]	11.1 [a]	10.8 [a]	10.6 [a]	8.8 [a]	9.9 [a]	10.1 [a]	9.6 [a]
Religiosity		−3.0	−2.3	−2.7	−2.1	−2.2	−2.3	−2.1
Religious attendance		0.3	−0.7	−1.4	−1.6	−1.7	−3.5	−1.8
Getting together with family and kin			−8.5 [a]	−8.4 [a]	−8.4 [a]	−8.2 [a]	−9.1 [a]	−9.2 [a]
Diversity of friends			10.5 [a]	11.1 [a]	9.5 [a]	10.0 [a]	9.1 [a]	8.9 [a]
Volunteering				2.4	1.7	2.0	1.3	1.6
Donations				1.9	1.8	1.5	0.7	1.5
Trust in Westerners					2.9 [a]	2.8 [a]	2.8 [a]	2.8 [a]
Qatari customs for immigrants						4.0	3.1	3.0
Neighbourhood belonging							10.1 [a]	10.3 [a]
Neighbourhood cohesion								10.9 [a]
Wald χ^2	37.92	38.02	59.72	62.02	93.49	95.56	101.76	112.58
McFadden's Adj R^2	0.031	0.032	0.050	0.051	0.087	0.091	0.097	0.110
N	1479	1471	1462	1441	1310	1295	1279	1267

Notes: [a] pv $< .01$, [b] $p < .05$, [c] $p < .10$; Reference categories are female, non-married, with primary education, age under 30, non-employed, household income ≤ 50,000 QAR, living in Doha, survey year 2011, less religious, with less bonding and bridging ties, less desirous of foreigners adopting Qatari customs, less volunteering and donating, and less attached to the neighbourhood; 1 QAR = 0.27 US Dollar.

erners than for Arabs across all models 3–8 (all significant at 0.1 level), which demonstrates the powerful effects of bridging social capital amongst Qatari nationals on acceptance of Western expatriates.

Existing studies of social capital highlight the role of a strong civil society through which individuals who actively participate in political and social life learn how to work with others to solve collective problems and, in the process, become more open-minded, tolerant, trusting and trustworthy, and more welcoming to fellow citizens and people from other countries (Diop, Jardina, et al., 2016; Jamal, 2006; Li & Marsh, 2008; Li, Savage, & Warde, 2008; Putnam, 2000). Given this, we might expect Qataris who volunteer and/or donate to charity and other organizations to exhibit stronger preferences for having Arab and Western families as next-door neighbours. However, as can be seen from the results (Model 4), volunteering and donations to charity play no significant role in this regard. This, of course, does not in itself constitute a simple rejection of the role of civic engagement in Qatari society. Our sample size is fairly small and we have included many variables, making it difficult for weak impacts to reach conventional levels of significance. There are signs of positive effects in both tables in this regard and further analysis shows, as noted above, that charitable giving does enhance the Qatari acceptance of Arabs (57% of givers compared to 50% of non-givers being happy to see Arabs as neighbours, p. 0.026).

As discussed above, trust is viewed in much of the social capital scholarship as a vital ingredient of social interaction that generates mutual benefits (Coleman, 1988; Field, 2008; Fukuyama, 1995; Putnam, 1993; Woolcock, 1998). With regards to attitudes towards immigrants, previous studies have shown that nationals with higher levels of trust—variously defined as generalized trust, social trust, or personal trust—tend to hold positive attitudes towards immigrants. These findings are supported by our results with both Arab and Western expatriate families. Trust in both groups has a strong predictive power. Overall, Qataris exhibit different levels of trust towards the different subgroups that comprise the expatriate population in Qatar. Though this level of trust has increased significantly between the two waves, it is much higher for Arabs than for Westerners although the rate of increase is higher for the latter. On the 0 to 10-point scale, Qataris' trust of Arabs increased from 6.18 in 2011 to 6.66 in 2015 while trust of Westerners increased from 3.57 in 2011 to 4.63 in 2015.

Regarding the importance Qataris attach to out-groups adopting Qatari customs as a requirement for obtaining citizenship, Qatari nationals seem to be more flexible with Western families. The variable is significant only for Arab families. Qataris who have a strong desire for people seeking citizenship of Qatar to adopt Qatari customs are here shown to favour Arab families as next-door neighbours but are rather neutral with regard to Westerners.

Neighbourhood belonging, as an indicator of local embeddedness or meso-level/situational social capital (Li et al., 2005) is also believed to foster feelings of tolerance and acceptance. Those who perceive their neighbourhoods as cohesive ones where people trust and help one another are also seen as being more open to Westerners. In our data, those with a strong sense of neighbourhood belonging show a strong preference for having Arabs and Westerners as next-door neighbours: around 10 percentage points more in both cases. In addition, those residing in cohesive neighbourhoods are, other things being equal, more willing by 11 percentage points to have Westerners as next-door neighbours.

5. Conclusion

While numerous studies have been conducted on the impacts of immigration upon local communities and social cohesion in receiving countries in western developed countries such as the USA and Europe, little research is available on the preferences of nationals in countries where immigrants outnumber the mainstream population. In this paper, we have carried out what we believe is the first systematic study on Qatari nationals' preferences for accepting Arab and Western expatriate families as their next-door neighbours. We use preferences for next-door neighbours as an indicator of tolerance and openness in a highly religious, conservative social context. Drawing on data from nationally representative samples and using a whole range of socio-demographic and cultural variables—including civic engagement, bridging and bonding social ties, as well as social trust—as explanatory variables, we have obtained some important findings. Our main results can be summarized as follows:

- Whilst at the bivariate level most socio-demographic attributes are significantly associated with Qataris' preferences for accepting Arabs and Westerners as next-door neighbours, net effects show that demographic-economic and educational differences do not have salient effects.
- Despite the fact that Qataris are predominantly Muslims, religiosity or practice per se do not have marked effects on Westerner acceptance, though it is weakly significant for accepting Arabs; rather, it is social trust that plays a significant role.
- Bonding social ties tend to be negative, but bridging social ties, in terms of diversity of friends, neighbourhood belonging, and perceived neighbourhood cohesion, are shown to engender greater tolerance and willingness to welcome out-groups.

Overall, while not negating the importance of socio-economic factors, we find that trust and socially engagement—in terms of diversity of friendship networks and active participation in neighbourhood affairs, which tend to result in a higher sense of belonging and cohesion—are seeds for tolerance, acceptance, and accommodation.

The implications of our research are manifold and we list three here. Firstly, as readers will know, social capital research reached its heights in the early 2000s, after Putnam's (2000) book on Bowling Alone (see Field, 2008, p. 3; Halpern, 2005, p. 9). Academic enthusiasm in this respect seems to have substantially waned in recent years. Scholars' interest may ebb and flow but the underlying social problems persist, as social capital in the form of trust and bridging ties show significant net effects even in a society where nationals comprise a relatively small proportion of the population such as Qatar. Seen from this perspective, we believe that our analysis has rendered a positive service, if not in reinstating the importance of social capital research, but at least in demonstrating the continued relevance of the concept of social capital in social life.

Secondly, as noted in earlier discussions, political scientists and sociologists seem to have travelled on separate tracks, with the former being more interested in documenting the rise and fall of the national stock of social capital and the relationship with democratic governance, and the latter keener to interrogate the socio-economic determinants of the differential possession of social capital. In the present study, we have managed to link both traditions in a simultaneous way in our comprehensive analysis of the socio-economic-cultural determinants of preferences for accepting out-groups in a fairly intimate way, as next-door neighbours. We have also conducted our analysis at both individual and meso-levels.

Thirdly, in terms of policy implications, we believe that our results on the positive effects of neighbourhood belonging and cohesion on Qatari nationals' acceptance of out-groups could be useful for authorities interested in making the country more welcoming and more inclusive. While it would be difficult to increase people's level of trust (Li et al., 2005; Uslaner, 2008), it might be more feasible to enhance community cohesion at the neighbourhood level.

Overall, while we have shown that social capital does have a significant role to play in enhancing social inclusion in a multi-ethnic and multi-cultural context, we wish to point out that there are many other aspects on which, due to limited space, we have not been able to report. These include findings related to policies on immigrants and their subsequent impact, such as immigrants' sojourner mentality and an associated (un)willingness to interact with nationals. These and other factors could impact on one another, making it more challenging for researchers and for policy-makers alike. We hope to report more findings in due course.

Acknowledgments

The authors wish to thank the Qatar National Research Fund (QNRF) for supporting the project titled *From Fareej to Metropolis: A Social Capital Survey of Qatar (II)* (NPRP7-186-5-021). This publication is one of the outputs from the project. The statements made herein are solely the responsibility of the authors. Any opinions, findings and conclusions or recommendations expressed in this paper are those of the authors and do not necessarily reflect the views of the QNRF.

Conflict of Interests

The authors declare no conflict of interests.

References

Alesina, A., & La Ferrara, E. (2002). Who trusts others? *Journal of Public Economics*, *85*, 207–234.

Al-Emadi, D., Diop, A., Le, K., Al-Ansari, M., Jardina, A., Tessler, M., & Wittrock, J. (2011). *From Fareej to metropolis: A social capital survey of Qatar executive summary report*. Doha, Qatar: Social & Economic Survey Research Institute (SESRI), Qatar University.

Al-Kathim, A. (1991). *Residents and immigrant workforce in Qatari society, interaction patterns and perceptions*. Cairo, Egypt: Hajar Publishing.

Arneil, B. (2006). *Diverse communities: The problem with social capital*. Cambridge, UK: Cambridge University Press.

Arrow, K. (1972). Gifts and exchanges. *Philosophy & Public Affairs*, *1*, 343–362.

Baier, A. (1986). Trust and antitrust. *Ethics*, *96*(2), 231–260.

Bourdieu, P. (1986). The forms of capital. In H. Lauder, P. Brown, J. Dillabough, & A. H. Halsey (Eds.), *Education, globalization and social change* (pp. 105–108). Oxford, UK: OUP.

Brambilla, M., Manzi, C., Regalia, C., & Verkuyten, M. (2013). Religiosity and prejudice: Different patterns for two types of religious internalization. *The Journal of Social Psychology*, *153*(4), 486–498.

Brenneman, R. (2008). *Faith and the foreigner: Exploring the impact of religion on immigration attitudes*. Saarland: VDM Verlag Dr. Muller.

Cheong, P., Edwards, R., Goulbourne, H., & Solomos, J. (2007). Immigration, social cohesion and social capital: A critical review. *Critical Social Policy*, *27*(1), 24–49.

Coleman, J. (1988). Social capital in the creation of human capital. *American Journal of Sociology*, *94*, S95–S120.

Dawes, R., Van de Kragt, A., & Orbell, J. (1988). Not me or thee but we. The importance of group identity in eliciting cooperation in dilemma situations: Experimental manipulations. *Acta Pyschologica*, *68*, 83–97.

Delhey, J., Newton, K., & Welzel, C. (2011). How general is trust in "most people"? Solving the radius of trust problem. *American Sociological Review*, *76*(5), 786–807.

Deutsch, M. (1958). Trust and suspicion. *Journal of Conflict Resolution*, *2*(4), 265–279.

Diop, A., Jardina, A., Tessler, M., & Wittrock, J. (2016). Antecedents of trust among citizens and non-citizens. *Journal of International Migration and Integration*. doi:10.1007/s12134-016-0474-0

Diop, A., Le, K., Johnston, T., & Ewers, M. (2016). Citizens' attitudes towards migrant workers in Qatar. *Migration and Development*, *6*(1), 144–160.

Field, J. (2008) *Social capital* (2nd ed.). Abingdon, UK: Routledge.

Fieldhouse, E., & Johnson, N. (2008). Social capital and ethnic diversity. In N. Johnson (Ed.), *Citizenship, cohesion & solidarity* (pp. 22–33). London, UK: Smith Institute.

Forbes, H. (1997). *Ethnic conflict: Commerce, culture, and the contact hypothesis*. New Haven, USA: Yale UP.

Friedkin, N. (2004). Social cohesion. *Annual Review of Sociology*, *30*(1), 409–425.

Fukuyama, F. (1995). *Trust: Social virtues and the creation of prosperity*. New York, USA: Free Press.

Guth, W., Levati, M., & Ploner, M. (2008). Social identity and trust: An experimental investigation. *The Journal of Socio-Economics*, *37*(4), 1293–1308.

Hall, P. (1999). Social capital in Britain. *British Journal of Political Science*, *29*, 417–461.

Halpern, D. (2005). *Social capital*. Cambridge, UK: Polity.

Hardin, R. (1993). The street-level epistemology of trust. *Politics & Society*, *21*(4), 505–529.

Jamal, A. (2006). Reassessing support for Islam and democracy in the Arab world? Evidence from Egypt and Jordan. *World Affairs*, *169*(2), 51–63.

Leonard, M. (2004). Bonding and bridging social capital: Reflections from Belfast. *Sociology*, *38*(5), 927–944.

Letki, N. (2008). Does diversity erode social cohesion? Social capital and race in British neighbourhoods. *Political Studies*, *56*(1), 99–126.

Levi, M., & Stoker, L. (2000). Political trust and trustworthiness. *Annual Review of Political Science*, *30*, 475–508.

Lewis, D., & Weigert, A. (1985). Trust as a social reality. *Social Forces*, *63*(4), 967–985.

Li, Y. (2015). Social capital in sociological research: Conceptual rigour and empirical application. In Y. Li (Ed.), *The handbook of research methods and applications on social capital* (pp. 1–20). Cheltenham, UK: Edward Elgar Publishing.

Li, Y., Heath, A., & Devine, F. (2015). Formal & informal social connections in the UK. In Y. Li (Ed.), *The handbook of research methods and applications on social capital* (pp. 187–203). Cheltenham: Edward Elgar Publishing.

Li, Y., & Marsh, D. (2008). New forms of political participation: Searching for expert citizens and everyday makers. *British Journal of Political Sciences*, *38*(2), 247–272.

Li, Y., Pickles, A., & Savage, M. (2005). Social capital and social trust in Britain. *European Sociological Review*, *21*(2), 109–123.

Li, Y., Savage, M., & Pickles, A. (2003). Social capital and social exclusion in England and Wales (1972–1999). *British Journal of Sociology*, *54*(4), 497–526.

Li, Y., Savage, M., & Warde, A. (2008). Social mobility and social capital in contemporary Britain. *British Journal of Sociology*, *59*(3), 391–411.

Lin, N. (2001). *Social capital*. Cambridge, UK: Cambridge University Press.

Luhmann, N. (1980). *Trust and power*. New York: Wiley.

Ministry of Developmental Planning and Statistics. (2016). *Qatar monthly statistics report*. Doha, Qatar: Ministry of Developmental Planning and Statistics (MDPS).

Paxton, P. (1999). Is social capital declining in the United States? A multiple indicator assessment. *American Journal of Sociology*, *105*, 88–127.

Pieterse, J. (2003). Social capital and migration: Beyond ethnic economies. *Ethnicities*, *3*(1), 29–58.

Portes, A., & Landolt, P. (1996). The downside of social capital. *The American Prospect*, *26*, 18–21.

Putnam, R. (1993). *Making democracy work: Civic tradition in modern Italy*. Princeton: Princeton University Press.

Putnam, R. (2000). Bowling alone: *The collapse and revival of American community*. New York: Simon & Schuster.

Putnam, R. (2007). E pluribus Unum: Diversity and community in the twenty-first century, the 2006 Johan Skytte Prize Lecture. *Scandinavian Political Studies*, *30*(2), 137–174.

Rajulton, F., Ravanera, Z., & Beaujot, R. (2007). Measuring social cohesion: An experiment using the Canadian national survey of giving, volunteering, and participating. *Social Indicators Research*, *80*(3), 461–492.

Schmeets, H., & Te Riele, S. (2014). Declining social cohesion in the Netherlands? *Social Indicators Research*, *115*(2), 791–12.

Schmid, K., Al Ramiah, A., & Hewstone, M. (2014). Neighborhood ethnic diversity and trust: The role of intergroup contact and perceived threat. *Psychological Science*, *25*(3), 665–674.

Schoenfeld, E. (1978). Image of man: The effect of religion on trust: A research note. *Review of Religious Research*, *20*(1), 61–67.

Sigelman, L., & Welch, S. (1993). The contact hypothesis revisited: Black–white interaction and positive racial Attitudes. *Social Forces*, *71*(3), 781–795.

Stein, R., Post, S., & Rinden, A. (2000). Reconciling context and contact effects on racial attitudes. *Political Research Quarterly*, *53*(2), 285.

Stolle, D., Soroka, S., & Johnston, R. (2008). When does diversity erode trust? Neighbourhood diversity, interpersonal trust and the mediating effect of social interactions. *Political Studies*, *56*(1), 57–75.

Traunmuller, R. (2011). Moral communities? Religion as a source of social trust in a multilevel analysis of 97 German regions. *European Sociological Review*, *27*(3), 346–363.

Uslaner, E. M., & Conley, R. S. (2003). Civic engagement and particularized trust: The ties that bind people to their ethnic Communities. *American Politics Research*, *31*(4), 331–360.

Uslaner, E. (2008). Where you stand depends upon where your grandparents sat: The inheritability of generalized trust. *Public Opinion Quarterly*, *72*(4), 725–740.

Wilson, J. (n.d.). Group identity and social trust in the American public. *Southern Methodist University*. Retrieved from http://faculty.smu.edu/jmwilson/Group%20ID%20&%20 Trust.doc.

Woolcock, M. (1998). Social capital and economic development: Toward a theoretical synthesis and policy framework. *Theory & Society*, *27*(2), 151–208.

About the Authors

Abdoulaye Diop (PhD) is Research Associate Professor and Head of the Research Department at the Qatar University Social and Economic Survey Research Institute (SESRI). His specific areas of interest include survey research methods, social capital, labor markets and migration and has authored and co-authored a number of publications in these areas. Prior to joining SESRI, Dr. Diop worked at the University of Virginia, the University of Connecticut, and the Advanced School of Applied Economics in Dakar, Senegal.

Yaojun Li is Professor of Sociology at the Department of Sociology and the Cathie Marsh Institute for Social Research, Manchester University, UK. His research interests are in social mobility and social stratification, social capital, and the socio-economic integration of ethnic minority groups. He has published widely in these areas, including papers in top sociology journals in Europe and the USA. He has also conducted numerous research projects funded by academic and government agencies in Britain, China, USA, Australia and Qatar.

Majed Al-Ansari is a senior researcher with the Social and Economic Research Institute (SESRI) at Qatar University. He received his Doctorate from the University of Manchester in 2017 where his thesis was titled "A Minority of Citizens: The effect of religious, social and political attitudes on trust in immigrants in Qatar". He also received his Master's degree in Social change from Manchester in 2010. Mr. Al-Ansari's research interests include Social capital, charitable donations, civil society and social change.

Kien Trung Le earned his PhD in Economics from the University of Virginia in 2008. His research areas are Survey Methodology and Applied Economics. He has publications in both economics and survey methodology journals. Before joining SESRI, Dr. Kien was a researcher at the Weldon Cooper Center for Public Service in the University of Virginia.

Permissions

All chapters in this book were first published in Social Inclusion, by Cogitatio Press; hereby published with permission under the Creative Commons Attribution License or equivalent. Every chapter published in this book has been scrutinized by our experts. Their significance has been extensively debated. The topics covered herein carry significant findings which will fuel the growth of the discipline. They may even be implemented as practical applications or may be referred to as a beginning point for another development.

The contributors of this book come from diverse backgrounds, making this book a truly international effort. This book will bring forth new frontiers with its revolutionizing research information and detailed analysis of the nascent developments around the world.

We would like to thank all the contributing authors for lending their expertise to make the book truly unique. They have played a crucial role in the development of this book. Without their invaluable contributions this book wouldn't have been possible. They have made vital efforts to compile up to date information on the varied aspects of this subject to make this book a valuable addition to the collection of many professionals and students.

This book was conceptualized with the vision of imparting up-to-date information and advanced data in this field. To ensure the same, a matchless editorial board was set up. Every individual on the board went through rigorous rounds of assessment to prove their worth. After which they invested a large part of their time researching and compiling the most relevant data for our readers.

The editorial board has been involved in producing this book since its inception. They have spent rigorous hours researching and exploring the diverse topics which have resulted in the successful publishing of this book. They have passed on their knowledge of decades through this book. To expedite this challenging task, the publisher supported the team at every step. A small team of assistant editors was also appointed to further simplify the editing procedure and attain best results for the readers.

Apart from the editorial board, the designing team has also invested a significant amount of their time in understanding the subject and creating the most relevant covers. They scrutinized every image to scout for the most suitable representation of the subject and create an appropriate cover for the book.

The publishing team has been an ardent support to the editorial, designing and production team. Their endless efforts to recruit the best for this project, has resulted in the accomplishment of this book. They are a veteran in the field of academics and their pool of knowledge is as vast as their experience in printing. Their expertise and guidance has proved useful at every step. Their uncompromising quality standards have made this book an exceptional effort. Their encouragement from time to time has been an inspiration for everyone.

The publisher and the editorial board hope that this book will prove to be a valuable piece of knowledge for researchers, students, practitioners and scholars across the globe.

List of Contributors

Kathleen E. Absolon
Faculty of Social Work, Wilfrid Laurier University, Waterloo, ON N2L 3C5, Canada

Juliet Pietsch
School of Politics and International Relations, Australian National University, Canberra, ACT 0200, Australia

Kateri Boucher and Jaime Kucinskas
Department of Sociology, Hamilton College, New York, NY 13323, USA

Walter Alando and Joachim Scheiner
Department of Transport Planning, Faculty of Spatial Planning, Technische Universität Dortmund University, 44227 Dortmund, Germany

Julie Christian , Daniella Nayyar and Joseph Cotler
School of Psychology, University of Birmingham, Birmingham, B15 2TT, UK

Dominic Abrams
School of Psychology, University of Kent, Canterbury, CT2 7NP, UK

David Clapham
Henley Business School, University of Reading, Reading, RG6 6UD, UK

Raquel Velho and Brian Balmer
Department of Science and Technology Studies, University College London, Gower Street, London, WC1E 6BT, UK

Catherine Holloway
Department of Computer Science, University College London, Gower Street, London, WC1E 6BT, UK

Andrew Symonds
Institute of Orthopaedic and Musculoskeletal Sciences, University College London, Stanmore, HA7 4LP, UK

Marjo Rouvoet and Halleh Ghorashi
Department of Sociology, Faculty of Social Sciences, Vrije Universiteit Amsterdam, 1081 HV Amsterdam, The Netherland

Melanie Eijberts
Amsterdam University College, 1098 XG Amsterdam, The Netherlands

Jeannette Waegemakers Schiff
Faculty of Social Work, University of Calgary, Calgary, T2N 1N4, Canada

Rebecca Schiff
Department of Health Sciences, Lakehead University, Thunder Bay, L3V 0B9, Canada

Alina Turner
Turner Research and Strategy Inc., Calgary, T2X 2P5, Canada

Ali Konyali and Maurice Crul
Department of Public Administration and Sociology, Erasmus University, 3000 DR Rotterdam, The Netherlands

Gökçe Yurdakul
Department of Diversity and Social Conflict, Humboldt University of Berlin, 10099 Berlin, Germany

Katrin Lättman, Margareta Friman and Lars E. Olsson
SAMOT/CTF—Service Research Center & Department of Social and Psychological Studies, Karlstad University, 65188 Karlstad, Sweden

Belén Fernández-Suárez
Department of Sociology, University of A Coruña, 15071 A Coruña, Spain

Russell Marshall, Steve Summerskill , Diane Gyi, Andrew Morris and Jo Barnes
Loughborough Design School, Loughborough University, Loughborough, LE11 3TU, UK

Keith Case
Mechanical and Manufacturing Engineering, Loughborough University, Loughborough, LE11 3TU, UK

Amjad Hussain
Department of Industrial and Manufacturing Engineering, University of Engineering and Technology, 54890 Lahore, Pakistan

Ruth Sims
Department of Psychology, University of Derby, Derby, DE22 1GB, UK

Joko Purwanto
Transport & Mobility Leuven, 3010 Leuven, Belgium

Lieke Kuiper
Health Sciences, VU University, 1081 HV Amsterdam, The Netherlands

Minne Bakker
Department of Medical Humanities, VU University Medical Center, 1081 HV Amsterdam, The Netherlands

Jac van der Klink
Tranzo Scientific Center for Care and Welfare, Department of Social and Behavioral Sciences, Tilburg University, The Netherlands

Beth Turnbull, Melissa L. Graham and Ann R. Taket
Centre for Health through Action on Social Exclusion (CHASE), School of Health and Social Development, Deakin University, Burwood, VIC 3125, Australia

Abdoulaye Diop and Majed Mohammed H. A. Al-Ansari
Social and Economic Survey Research Institute, Qatar University, Doha, Qatar

Yaojun Li and Kien T. Le
Department of Sociology, University of Manchester, Manchester, M13 9PL, UK
Cathie Marsh Institute for Social Research, University of Manchester, Manchester, M13 9PL, UK

Index

S

T

U

W